Treat Yourself!

HOW TO MAKE 93 RIDICULOUSLY FUN NO-BAKE CRISPY RICE TREATS

JESSICA SISKIN
@mister_krisp

WORKMAN PUBLISHING · NEW YORK

Library of Congress Cataloging-in-Publication Data is available.
ISBN: 978-0-7611-8980-0

Design by Becky Terhune
Cover and interior photography by Evi Abeler
Prop styling by Kristine Trevino

Workman books are available at special discounts when purchased in bulk for premiums and sales promotions as well as for fundraising or educational use. Special editions or book excerpts can also be created to specification. For details, contact the Special Sales Director at the address below, or send an email to specialmarkets@workman.com.

Workman Publishing Co., Inc.
225 Varick Street
New York, NY 10014-4381
workman.com

WORKMAN is a registered trademark of Workman Publishing Co., Inc.

Printed in China
First printing May 2017

10 9 8 7 6 5 4 3 2 1

Contents

Introduction

My name is Jessica Siskin, but people also call me "Misterkrisp" or "Krisp," or sometimes, if they know me well enough, "Krispie." When people find out that I'm a crispy rice treats artist or, more specifically, the woman behind @mister_krisp, I'm often confronted with a series of familiar questions. I've learned to fire off answers the way tollbooth operators fired off directions before everyone and their mother had GPS: *The idea came to me totally by accident. / Because I'm weird like that. / I add food coloring to the butter and marshmallow before the cereal goes in. / It's "mister" not "miss" because it's named after Mr. Crisp, the villain in the 1993 Whoopi Goldberg film* Sister Act 2—*yes, that movie does contain the greatest musical sequence of all time. / No, I haven't hired anyone. / I don't eat them in my kitchen, only when I'm at a celebration where I would be eating dessert anyway. / No, I'm not sick of crispy rice treats yet.*

In 2012, the idea to make a crispy rice treat cheeseburger came to me suddenly when I discovered that food coloring could be added to the traditional side-of-the-box recipe.

I didn't (and still don't) know how to cook, and a friend and I had been invited to bring dessert to a potluck birthday dinner in Brooklyn with the kind of cool, edgy people who probably hadn't eaten anything that came in store-bought packaging since beepers were the pinnacle of mobile communication. Crispy rice treats had been my specialty (aka the only thing I knew how to make) for years, and my friend had seen me mold them into simple hearts and stars. Since the birthday girl loved to surf, my friend suggested we make a crispy rice treat surfboard, so I did what any good millennial would do, and googled "crispy rice treats surfboard." The Internet, in its generous infinitude, somehow provided a recipe for exactly what I sought. The recipe called for food coloring, and later that night in my kitchen when I added color to the mixture I'd made so many times, I experienced what Oprah would call an "aha! moment." I was struck by the immediate and overwhelming impulse to make a crispy rice treat cheeseburger.

The following night, I returned to my kitchen to answer the call of my heart (or Oprah—still not sure). I carefully colored each batch with food coloring, from the yellow of the bun to the bright red tomatoes, orangey-yellow American cheese, and vibrant green lettuce before molding it into shape. I used Cocoa Krispies to make the burger patty, and ripped mini marshmallows into tiny pieces to stud the top of the bun with "sesame seeds." When I assembled all the pieces, I actually screamed out loud—this burger was the coolest thing I'd ever seen. (None of my neighbors came to check on me.)

I snapped a photo, filtered it in Lo-Fi, and posted it to Instagram, where I broke 100 "likes" on a post for the first time, which is like the social media equivalent of becoming a Bat Mitzvah. I brought it to work the next day at a trendy women's fashion brand, where everyone freaked out and devoured it. I knew I was onto something. So I continued to experiment with quirky and fun treats on special occasions, crafting crispy rice treat bagels, donuts, pizza slices, and ice cream cones for friends' birthdays and other celebrations, always posting them on Instagram, and always getting many more "likes" than when I posted selfies or photos of my dog.

After about a year of playing around in the kitchen, I decided to start a separate Instagram account for my treats. I called it "Misterkrisp," and posted a few images of my projects. I put my email address in the profile field of the account, and on the very first day the account went live, I received my first order. And orders have continued to pour in every day since. After two months of waking up at 5 a.m. to make treats before putting in a full day at work and returning home to make even more of them at night, I decided to leave my job to focus on Misterkrisp full time while finally pursuing my dream of getting a master's degree in creative writing.

I could not have imagined all of the opportunities Misterkrisp has brought me. My work has been featured on *Today*, in *People*, the *Wall Street Journal*, *O* magazine, *New York* magazine, and countless other outlets. I've collaborated with Kellogg's and so many other amazing brands. One time, a girl recognized me in Target in another state. The best part of Misterkrisp, though, has been the opportunity to make bespoke treats for customers to help them celebrate special occasions. It's an intrinsically happy job; people want dessert when life is good.

I love that I get to spend my days doing something so deliciously silly and that I get to share that with other people. We live in an unprecedentedly fast-paced, information-soaked world, filled with scores of obligations and serious matters to attend to, but how can you possibly be stressed out when you come across something as ridiculous as a giant taco made out of crispy rice cereal?

For a long time I thought I was weird because, as a kid, I spent a lot of the time I should've been working or studying making art projects instead. Even into my late twenties, I'd sometimes find myself at work drawing cupcakes and other elaborate doodles on sales reports when I should have been analyzing the data. Instead of following my creative impulses, I'd been suppressing them. Today, I feel so fortunate that I get to share my creative outlet with you in this book, and inspire you to exercise some of your creativity in a way that is so much better than an average art project because . . . *you get to eat it in the end.*

Even if you're not the stereotypically crafty type, you'll be surprised at how easy it is to make a really cool-looking and delicious-tasting dessert. When friends come over to help or watch me make treats, they're always shocked by how quickly it all comes together. Rice crispy treats are super fast to make; the ingredients are widely available and a lot cheaper (and some might say healthier) than the ingredients in so many other desserts. It's also a very forgiving medium—I've made thousands of treats and plenty of mistakes, but I've only had to start over completely three or four times (and those were on very advanced designs. . . . Okay, the truth is that I got distracted listening to the *Hamilton* soundtrack). Because I have no professional training, many of the techniques I use are common sense and don't involve a lot of finesse. I mold with my hands, spread icing with my fingers, wash my hands *a lot* throughout the process, and generally wing it with a lot of details. These are methods anyone can use at home, which is good news for you.

As with anything, practice makes perfect (although there's no such thing as perfect). Don't expect your treats to look exactly like the ones in the book—even mine look a little different every time I make them. The most important thing to take from this book is a spirit of irreverence. Improvise, have fun, and customize your treats to make the people you love smile. Go off script and use these techniques to manifest your wildest creative imagination; just don't forget to share them with me by using the hashtag #misterkrisp. And remember, no matter how it looks in the end, it's nearly impossible to screw up this amazing-tasting recipe—just eat the evidence, and no one will ever know.

How to Use This Book

Every project in *Treat Yourself!* begins with the same basic recipe (page 6), using the same basic ingredients: crispy rice cereal, mini marshmallows, butter, and food coloring. It all starts there, and the only limits are the boundaries of your imagination. And the laws of physics. Add candies and icing, start introducing molds and other shaping tools, and you've already taken your treat-making ability to the next level.

The basic treat recipe can be multiplied by any factor and, for convenience and quick reference, I've broken it down into common batch sizes (see Batch Guide, page 7). To gather the appropriate ingredient quantities in advance, use the note at the top of each project that indicates which batch size (or sizes) you need to make. I'm not a planner (except when it comes to what snack I am going to eat next), but since time is of the essence when it comes to treat-making, it's very important that you approach each project with a plan. Once the mixture hardens, you won't be able to continue to mold it, so make each batch right before you use it to complete a step.

Most projects include a template that you can download by visiting workman.com/misterkrisp. (Exceptions include the Apples, Hot Dogs, Ice Cream Cones, Watermelon, and other more dimensional projects.) Once printed and pieced together, the templates will act as a guide for making different shapes, almost paint-by-numbers style. Refer to the instructions on page 10 for how to use them with best results. In the meantime, read on to discover more tips, tricks, and techniques in my *treatise on treats*. Yeah, that just happened.

Apologies in advance for the abundance of puns in this book. I can't help who I am.

Basic Treat Recipe and How-to

People are shocked when I tell them that I don't know how to cook anything besides crispy rice treats (and scrambled eggs). When my best friend taught me how to make this simple recipe on a snowy day in 2011, I was surprised by how easy it was. So here it is, the *ur*-recipe. From here spring all the iterations of crispy treats you see in these pages. Regardless of what size batch you're mixing up (see Batch Guide, page 7), the ratios of crispy rice cereal to marshmallows to butter stay the same.

Essential Ingredients
- **Butter** (I recommend using salted butter.)
- **Crispy rice cereal** (I use Kellogg's Rice Krispies.)
- **Food coloring** (I use AmeriColor Soft Gel Paste or McCormick Food Color. See notes at right.)
- **Mini marshmallows** (I use Kraft Jet-Puffed.)

Essential Tools and Equipment
- **Soup pot** (nonstick)*
- **Silicone spatula**
- **Parchment paper**
- **Cooking spray** (I use PAM Original.)

* I use a 12-quart nonstick stock pot for every treat I make, regardless of its finished size. The larger the pot (and higher the sides), the less chance I have of little bits of cereal escaping when I stir. I don't recommend using smaller than a 6- or 8-quart pot.

Essential ingredients

BATCH GUIDE

Batch Code	Cereal (cups)	Marshmallows (cups)	Butter (tablespoons)	Food coloring (total drops)
A	12	8	6	14
B	10	7	5	12
C	8	6	4	10
D	6	4	3	8
E	4	3	2	6
F	3	2	1½	5
G	2	1½	1	4
H	1	¾	½	3

Some Notes on Food Coloring

While the other ingredients in the basic recipe are precisely measured, the food coloring required will vary slightly depending on the type of food coloring you use and how vivid you want the colors to be. I've specified a conservative number of drops, because you can always add more. (If you find just *after* you've added the cereal, that you want more saturated shades, you can troubleshoot by adding a few more drops of food coloring while you're stirring.)

If there are two shades of food coloring listed in a single step, split the amount indicated for the batch size 50-50 unless otherwise noted. (For example, batch C has 10 drops of food coloring, so if a recipe says "use white and 2 drops of green," you should use 8 drops of white to make the total 10.)

I primarily use AmeriColor Soft Gel food coloring, but any brand you can find at your local supermarket will work, too; you can mix your own colors by combining different shades.

Note: The time measurements in these instructions are based on the C batch (8-cup) treat recipe. The time will fluctuate slightly depending on batch size. In general, though, it's important to work quickly and keep your eye on what's happening in the pot. The marshmallows should never become liquid.

1. In a large stockpot, melt the butter over low heat until it's 80 percent melted (see photo), about 1 minute 20 seconds. *Note:* If the butter begins to sizzle, lower the heat. It should melt very slowly.

2. Add the mini marshmallows and stir gently, coating them with melted butter, about 30 seconds.

3. When the marshmallows are about 80 percent melted (when you can still see the individual marshmallow shapes but they are beginning to run together), add the food coloring. Stir for another 15 seconds and then turn off the heat.

4. Stir gently until the color is well distributed but the marshmallows are still only about 80 percent melted, about 35 seconds (you should still be able to identify individual pieces within the melted ones). *Note:* If the marshmallows melt too much, the mixture will be too hot to handle—wait 1–2 minutes and then mold quickly!

5. Add the cereal and mix well, until the marshmallows and cereal are fully combined, about 40 seconds. Do not overmix!

6. Once the mixture is combined, coat the palms of your hands with cooking spray before handling it. Pour the mixture onto your work surface and begin molding it with your hands. Spray your hands again throughout the process, as needed.

Using the Templates

I love coloring. When I go to restaurants with coloring-book-style menus meant for children under 10, I *always* ask for crayons and don't even bother pretending I'm accompanied by a child. These templates are to crispy treat making what coloring books are to coloring. Use them as a guide to make the base shapes before adding dimension and detail on top. The idea for these templates came from my sister, who made her own Halloween "sisterkrisp" by drawing the shape of a ghost in Sharpie on a piece of paper and covering it with parchment paper to help guide her as she molded. You can use her technique to make your own unique crispy treats, or download the templates in this book at workman.com/misterkrisp.

1. Download and print all four pieces of the template on standard 8½ × 11-inch paper (or A4 paper for non–U.S. regions) with scaling turned off, at 100%. Arrange the pieces on a flat surface, and tape them together. Most of the templates will be 17 × 22-inch (or 43 × 56 cm) dimensions when tiled together.

2. Place the template on a sturdy, flat surface such as a cake board (see Resources and FAQs, page 292), a cutting board, or a cookie sheet (flipped upside down), and cover it with parchment paper.

3. Pour the crisp mix onto the parchment paper and fill the template per the instructions.

4. Place the finished project in the freezer for at least 1 hour before moving it.

5. Squeeze a small amount of icing onto the surface of a serving platter or cardboard cake board. Gently lift the treat from the parchment paper and place it on the portable surface.

Note: If you plan to serve your treat directly on the parchment, slide out the template, and use a warm, damp paper towel to clean up any messy marshmallow or icing residue left over from the molding process.

Special Tools and Equipment

In addition to the essential tools and equipment, there are a few instances in which extra stuff is needed to properly construct the project. You probably already have most of these items in your kitchen, but make sure to read through the project recipe thoroughly beforehand to see if you might need to acquire something new for it. While I always encourage you to improvise and get creative during the process, using these items when they're called for will ensure that the projects turn out like they're pictured in this book.

- Aluminum foil (not pictured)
- Cake rings (8-inch and 10-inch diameters)
- Cardboard cake boards (not pictured)
- Cookie cutters (4-inch diameter round, flower, football)
- Icing tubes (small)
- Knives (4-inch paring knife and/or 8-inch chef's knife)
- Measuring tape
- Mini donut pan

- Mixing bowl (small, about 6-inch diameter)
- OodleTip piping bags
- Pie pan
- Plastic spoons (not pictured)
- Rolling pin (not pictured)
- Spatula (small and large, metal offset)
- Toothpicks
- Wilton icing tips (round, star, leaf, petal)
- Wooden skewers
- Zip-top bags

Special tools and equipment

Special Ingredients (for Decorating)

My kitchen looks pretty normal at first glance. But open my cabinets, and it begins to seem like a young Willy Wonka had a raging house party and had to clean up quickly before his parents got home. My shelves are overflowing with unique candies that I use to decorate my crispy treats in innovative ways. I love problems that end in candy solutions—I once made candy cold cuts for a "turkey sandwich" treat using white Airheads that I painted carefully with brown and gold icings. Yellow Starburst candies make great pats of butter for crispy treat pancakes, and black M&M's are perfect animal eyes.

Icing I use Wilton Decorating Icing and Wilton Sparkle Gel, which are sold in individual tubes. You can make your own icing, but I find that the Wilton brand products work really well with the texture of crispy treats. You can purchase icing tips (specially shaped nozzles that fit on the end of a tube of icing) for the decorating icings—I often have several sets on hand because I'm usually working with multiple colors at once, but you can rinse the tips with warm water and switch colors as often as you'd like.

For extra control when adding details, fill small squeeze bottles with icing using a tube of Wilton Decorating Icing with a round tip. Make sure to rinse them out before use! Alternatively, you can use the Wilton Writing Tip Set, stainless steel icing tips (sold with couplers to attach to a standard icing tube), to achieve a similar level of detail.

After adding icing detail, wait 10 to 30 minutes to let it set, then gently pat down any raised bits for a more uniform look.

Candy Melts Many recipes include candy melts, round discs of colored candy. In a lot of cases, these can be replaced with icing of the same color to reduce the number of supplies you need to purchase. For example, the centers of the flowers on the Flowerpot project (page 117) use candy melts, but you can easily substitute circles of yellow decorating icing.

Working with food dye If a recipe calls for making the treat mixture in multiple colors, you only need to rinse the pot out if the next color is a lighter shade (but feel free to rinse as often as you'd like). Make sure to wash your pot thoroughly between uses.

- Airheads (orange, white, red)
- Aluminum foil
- Buttercream icing
- Candy Melts (white, red, pink, yellow, purple, orange, green, blue)
- Celebration Candy Crumble (blue, purple)
- Chocolate chunks
- Chocolates, assorted
- Confetti sprinkles
- Cookies-and-cream sprinkles
- Decorating Icing, Wilton (all colors)
- Food color spray (gold, silver)
- Froot Loops
- Fruit Roll-Ups (blue/green)
- Gummi Watermelon Rings
- "Happy Birthday" candles
- Haribo Fruit Salad
- Haribo Red Licorice Wheels
- Jelly Belly Gummi Pet Tarantula
- Lollipop sticks
- M&M's (colors specified in the recipes)
- Marshmallows, regular and mini
- Oreo cookies, Original and Golden
- Pearl sugar
- Rainbow sprinkles (classic cylinder, round)
- Red, White, and Blue Sprinkles, Wilton
- Rice Krispies (or other crispy rice cereal)
- Sixlets (pink)
- Sparkle Gel (Wilton Sparkle Gel recommended)
- Sweetened coconut flakes
- Twizzlers (flavors specified in the recipes)
- Wafer ice cream cones

*Special ingredients and materials
for decorating*

Tricks, Techniques, and Troubleshooting

Despite the results being edible, I consider making these treats to be a lot more like arts and crafts than cooking or baking. My younger sister went to pastry school, and whenever she observes me making crispy rice treats, she reminds me I'm technically doing everything wrong. This is good news for you because it means anyone can replicate these methods—no experience or training required. As long as the final product looks (and tastes) good, the process should be all about having fun. I sculpt the mixture like it's Play-Doh and finger paint details just like I did in kindergarten. Follow your instincts and use your hands to craft these projects. Nonetheless, here are some tips and tricks.

Your new best friend: Cooking spray. You can never spray your hands too many times. Keeping your hands lubricated will make molding the sticky treats into shapes exponentially easier. If you find that the mixture is still too loose or sticky, wait a couple of minutes and try again.

Photo reference: When I make crispy rice treats at home, I usually look at a photo of what I'm replicating on my phone while I work (my phone is always coated with butter!). Because I consider referring to photos (on a phone or on paper) to be the best method for making and decorating creative treats, I've included step-by-step photos for you to use as a visual guide. Each photo corresponds to a step in the written instructions, but after a little practice, you may not even need to read the instructions anymore!

Like putty in your hands: When you begin to think of the crispy mixture as a kind of clay, you'll realize that you can use your hands for all kinds of molding techniques. Create cylinders by rolling it back and forth between your hands, or mold balls by pressing it in your palms. *Note:* Wash and dry your hands thoroughly before getting started. I find that I'm able to achieve fine detail with my fingers (rather than with gloves or shaping tools) and simply wash my hands frequently throughout the process.

Emergency stash: Even when the instructions tell you to use all of the mixture in a step, always reserve a small handful off to the side. If you mess up the icing (it happens!), just scrape it off (and eat it) and cover it with some of your emergency-stash crisp mixture.

For the kids: When working with kids, allow the mixture to cool a bit longer (about 2 to 5 minutes total). Even though it might be more challenging to make precise shapes once the mixture has cooled, it's easier and more fun for kids to work with—and hey, sometimes it's about the journey, not the destination.

What to do with scraps: In some cases, the recipe calls for more mixture than you will use. You can eat the extra right away, but you can also make what I call "scrapcakes": Spray a cupcake tin with cooking spray and fill the cups bit by bit with all of the different-colored scraps as you go. Sometimes the color combinations are pretty and sometimes they're hideous, but they're always delicious.

Serving and Storing

Once the last Twizzler piece has been placed and the last dot of icing has been blended, it's time to eat or . . . wait to eat! I highly doubt your treats will go very long without being devoured, but just in case you have self-control (what's that like?), here are a few things to consider . . .

Yields and recipe-doubling: Each recipe includes the number of servings or an approximate finished size. For individual treats (like the Ice Cream Cones, page 153, or the Smiley Emojis, page 229), multiply the recipe as desired to fit your crowd—one serving is one piece. The sheet cake–style treats, on the other hand, feed ten to twenty people depending on how you slice them. (Use a large chef's knife to cut your treat into servable pieces!) And, if you're looking to serve more than twenty, it's easier to make two treats (two Fire Engines, for example, page 111, two Avocados, page 23) than to double the recipe to make a single large treat. It's hard to find a serving surface that big, and the templates are sized to match the printed recipe.

Storage: Crispy treats are best served fresh, but if you're making treats in advance of an event (or somehow manage to have some left over), store the treat, covered with a sheet of parchment or in a closed container, in the freezer for up to three days. (*Note:* Do not substitute the refrigerator for the freezer. Storing in the refrigerator will leave the treats stale.) When you're ready to eat the treat, let it thaw for about 10 minutes before serving.

RECIPES

Apples

It may not be super original to begin an alphabetized book with apples, but aardvarks aren't that cute. These apples are a unique twist on the traditional teacher gift or a fun addition to a New York City–themed party. Slice them open to reveal their "flesh," just like real apples, and the chocolate-flavored stem is an added bonus!

MAKES 10 APPLES

TREAT RECIPES
(see page 6)
1 D batch, no food coloring
1 C batch, with 8 drops red and
    2 drops brown food coloring

SPECIAL INGREDIENTS
3 chocolate Twizzlers

EQUIPMENT
Parchment paper
Scissors
Cooking spray

1. Using scissors, cut each Twizzler in half. Set aside the 6 cut pieces for the apple stems. **2.** Mix the D batch recipe for the inside of the apples, and let sit, about 2 minutes. Generously coat your hands with cooking spray. Take one large handful of the mixture and place a Twizzler piece in the top center. **3.** Mold the handful into a ball around the Twizzler and place it on the parchment-covered work surface. **4.** Repeat Step 3 five times, then place the 6 treats in the freezer while you mix the next batch.

5. Mix the C batch recipe. Remove the 6 treats (the apple insides) from the freezer and cover each treat in the red mixture. **6.** Flatten the bottom of each apple and press down around the stem to create an apple shape. **7.** Using scissors, trim the Twizzler stems so they're proportionate to the finished apples (about 1½ inches from the tops of the apples).

Avocado

I don't know how avocados became associated with being "basic," but I know that basic things are basic because a lot of people like them, and a lot of people like them because they are good. And avocados are *the best*. Even if you're tired of seeing photos of avocado toast on social media, you'll never get tired of photographing this treat or eating it. After all, it's a super food incredibly high in nutrition and low in sugar . . . oh, wait, JK.

MAKES 1 AVOCADO, 11 INCHES TALL

TREAT RECIPES
(see page 6)
1 C batch, lime green food coloring
1 E batch, green food coloring
1 H batch, brown food coloring

SPARKLE GEL
Lime green

EQUIPMENT
Avocado template (see page 10)
Parchment paper
Cooking spray

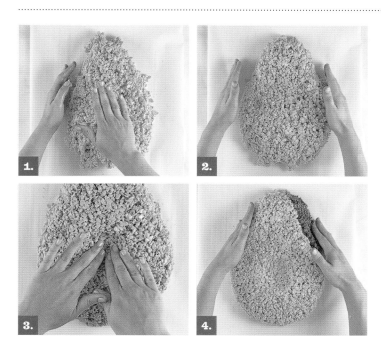

1. Mix the C batch recipe and pour the mixture onto the parchment-covered template on the work surface. Generously coat your hands with cooking spray. **2.** Use both hands to mold the mixture over the inner portion of the template, smoothing the edges until the mixture begins to firm. **3.** Press down with both hands to make a depression in the center. **4.** Mix the E batch recipe and, in small handfuls, press the dark green mixture over the outer section of the template.

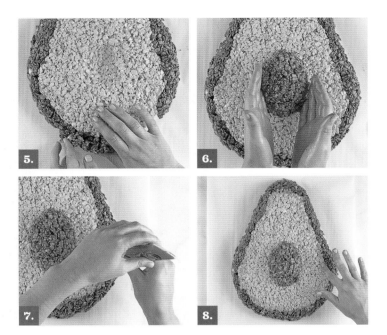

5. Continue applying handfuls and smoothing the mixture until you've created a border all the way around the treat. **6.** Mix the H batch recipe and shape it into an oval. Place it in the depression in the center of the treat. **7.** Using lime green sparkle gel, outline the border where the dark and light green mixtures meet. **8.** Use your finger to smudge and blend the outline.

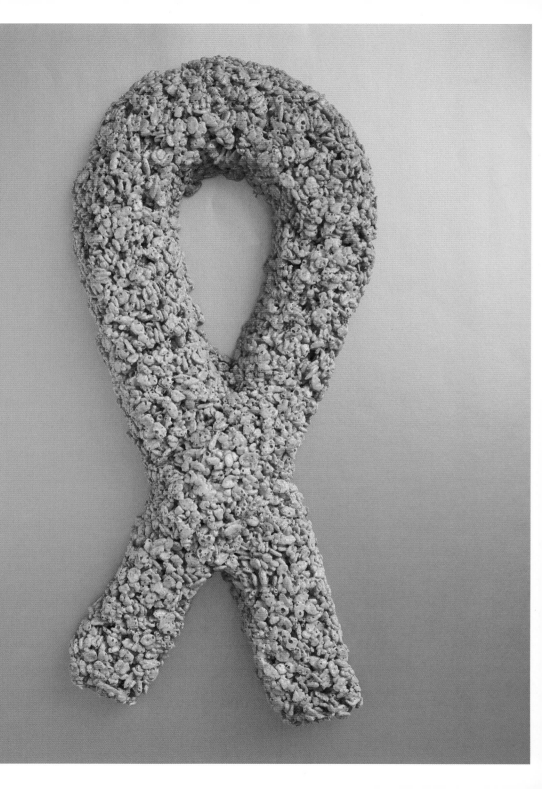

Awareness Ribbon

Chances are, if you care about something, there's a corresponding ribbon to wear. Seriously, there's a ribbon for everything, from free speech to love. With this treat, the cause closest to your heart can also be the cause closest to your stomach. Use food coloring to render this design in the shade corresponding to your favorite cause—this treat is guaranteed to brighten fundraisers, bake sales, silent auctions, and your stomach.

MAKES 1 RIBBON, 14 INCHES TALL

TREAT RECIPE
(see page 6)
1 C batch, pink food coloring
(or your favorite cause's
signature color)

EQUIPMENT
Awareness Ribbon template
(see page 10)
Parchment paper
Cooking spray

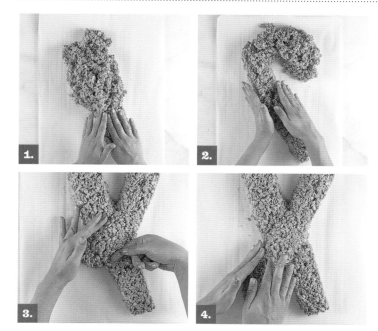

1. Mix the C batch recipe and pour two thirds of the mixture onto the parchment-covered template on the work surface. Generously coat your hands with cooking spray. **2.** Use both hands to mold the mixture over the template, smoothing the edges until the mixture begins to firm up. **3.** When you reach the ribbon crossing at the center, use your hands to place the remaining one third of the mixture across the existing treat. **4.** Mold the extra mixture over the template, maintaining slightly raised edges where one end of the ribbon crosses over the other.

Bagels and Lox

New York may have the best bagels, but thankfully you can make these yummy bagel treats *anywhere*. The orange-flavored "lox" and white frosting make these bagels taste like Creamsicles, and the "everything" sprinkles bring it all together with cuteness and crunch.

MAKES 6 BAGELS WITH LOX

TREAT RECIPE
(see page 6)
1 D batch, no food coloring

SPECIAL INGREDIENTS
Cookies-and-cream sprinkle mix
6 orange Airheads

DECORATING ICING
White

EQUIPMENT
Parchment paper
Two mini 6-donut baking pans
   (makes 2¾-inch donuts)
Cooking spray
Star icing tip

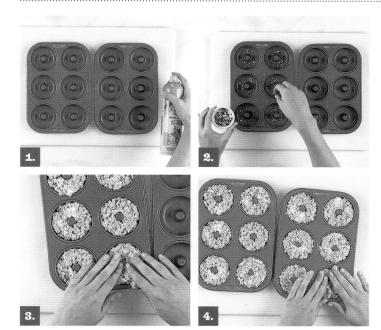

1. Generously coat both donut pans with cooking spray.
2. Sprinkle the cookies-and-cream sprinkles into one pan.
3. Mix the D batch recipe. Generously coat your hands with cooking spray and press the mixture flat into both pans, making sure not to fill the center of the donuts.
4. Once both pans are full (but not overfilled), place them in the freezer for 10 minutes. (*Note:* You'll have a large handful of crispy mixture left over, but a smaller batch won't be quite enough!)

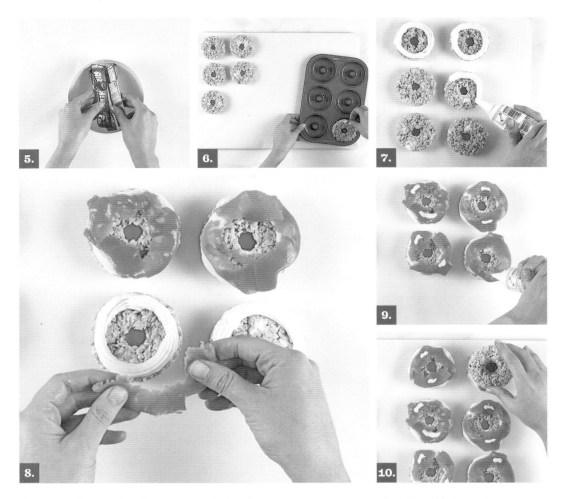

5. Meanwhile, fill a bowl or tray with hot water and place the wrapped Airheads in the water to soften. **6.** Remove the pans from the freezer. Wait 2 minutes, remove the treats from the molds, and place them on the parchment-covered work surface. (*Note:* If you have a hard time removing them, use the edge of a butter knife or small spatula.) **7.** Trace a circle of white icing along the edge of each of the 6 treats *without* the sprinkle mix. **8.** One at a time, remove the Airheads from the water and unwrap them. Rip the candy in half and press it between your thumbs and forefingers to make the edges irregular, rounded, and large enough to cover the bagels. Lay the "lox" on top of the iced bagels. **9.** Using white icing with a star tip, place small dots of the icing "cream cheese" on top of the Airhead lox. **10.** Place the 6 treats with the sprinkle mix on top of the 6 treats without (sprinkle side up!) and press gently to seal.

TREAT YOURSELF!

Balloons

It's wild how a little bit of inflated rubber on a string can really boost the mood. The minute someone shows up with balloons, a regular gathering becomes a P-A-R-T-Y. I'm not gonna lie—every time I see someone carrying a bundle of balloons on the street, I'm tempted to follow them. Whenever I'm a little bit stumped over what kind of treat to make for an occasion, these save the day. Use your choice of colors to represent your favorite team, school, holiday, or organization.

MAKES 1 BUNCH OF 3 BALLOONS, 8 BY 12 INCHES (NOT INCLUDING STRINGS)

TREAT RECIPES
(see page 6)
1 F batch, yellow food coloring
1 F batch, red food coloring
1 F batch, green food coloring
    (or whatever colors *you* like)

DECORATING ICING
White
Black

EQUIPMENT
Balloons template (see page 10)
Cooking spray
Parchment paper
Round icing tip
Cake board (or other serving surface)

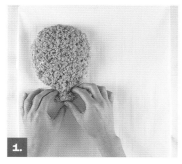  

1. Mix the yellow F batch recipe and pour it onto the parchment-covered template on the work surface. Generously coat your hands with cooking spray and mold the mixture into section 1 of the template, pressing and smoothing until the mixture begins to firm up. **2.** Mix the red F batch recipe and pour it onto the work surface. Mold it into section 2 of the template, pressing and smoothing until the mixture begins to firm up. **3.** Mix the green F batch recipe and pour it onto the work surface. Mold it into section 3 of the template, pressing until the mixture begins to firm up.

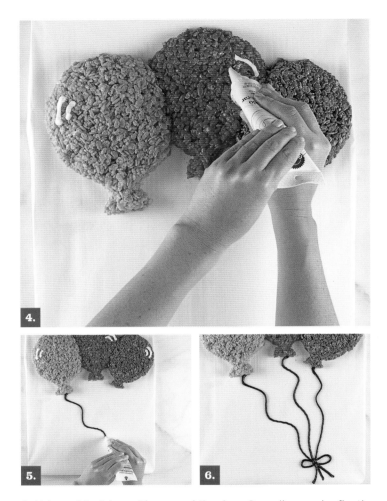

4. Using white icing with a round tip, draw 2 small curved reflection lines on each balloon. Then freeze the treat, flat, on the parchment paper for 1 hour. **5.** After 1 hour in the freezer, remove the treat from the parchment paper and place it on the serving surface. Using black icing with a round tip, draw a balloon string extending from each balloon. **6.** Finish the strings by connecting them in a bow.

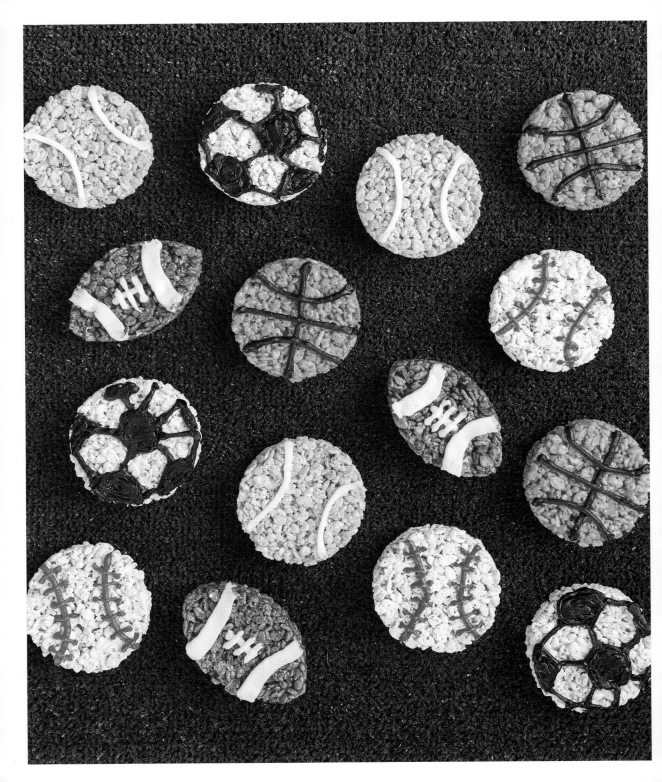

Balls

Go . . . sports! I'm definitely not an athlete and don't love watching games, but I really enjoy feeding my friends crispy treats while they watch. Bring these to bake sales, fundraisers, and team gatherings to add to the sweet, sweet victory of your favorite team. With these treats, everyone's a winner.

Note: Adjust the portions to make an entire batch of baseballs, footballs, and so on, to suit the circumstances!

MAKES 3 BASEBALLS, 3 SOCCER BALLS, 3 TENNIS BALLS, 3 BASKETBALLS, AND 3 FOOTBALLS

TREAT RECIPES
(see page 6)
1 E batch, white food coloring
1 G batch, yellow food coloring
1 G batch, orange food coloring
1 G batch, brown food coloring

DECORATING ICING
Black
Red
White

EQUIPMENT
Parchment paper
Cooking spray
Round cookie cutter
    (4-inch diameter)
Football-shaped cookie cutter
    (4 inches long)
Round icing tip
1 mini icing tube
Petal icing tip

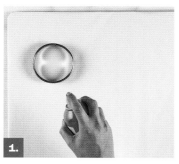  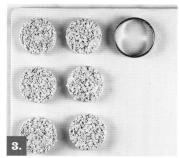

1. Coat the inside of the round cookie cutter with cooking spray and place it on the parchment-covered work surface. Mix the E batch recipe. Generously coat your hands with cooking spray. **2.** Press a medium-size handful of the white mixture into the cookie cutter to the edges, then gently slide the treat onto the work surface. **3.** Repeat Step 2 five times, spraying the cookie cutter between handfuls of mixture.

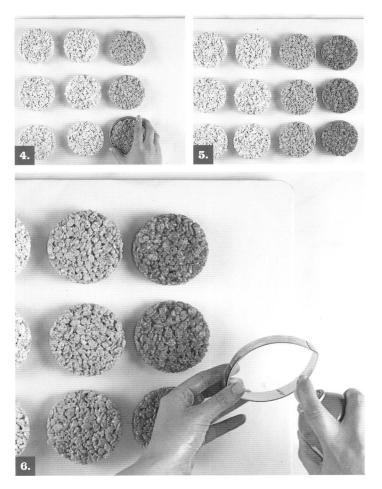

4. Mix the yellow G batch recipe, and follow Step 2, repeating until you have three yellow circles. **5.** Mix the orange G batch recipe, and follow Step 2, repeating until you have three orange circles. **6.** Coat the inside of the football cookie cutter with cooking spray. Mix the brown G batch recipe.

TREAT YOURSELF!

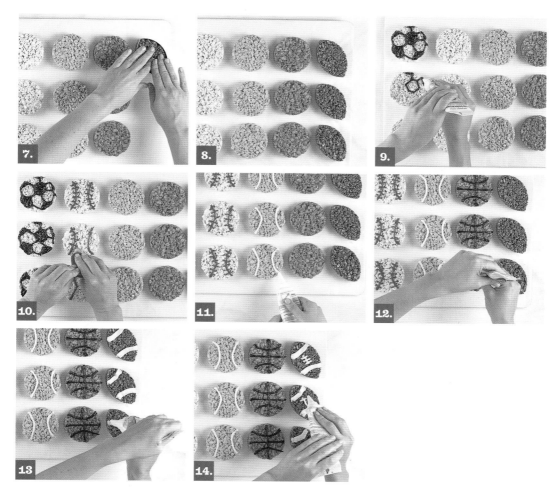

7. Press a medium-size handful of the brown mixture into the cookie cutter to the edges, then gently slide out the shape onto the work surface. **8.** Repeat Step 7 twice, spraying the cookie cutter between handfuls of mixture. **9.** Using black icing with a round tip, decorate three of the white circles as soccer balls, as shown, with intersecting hexagons and pentagons. **10.** Fill the mini icing tube with red icing, and decorate the remaining 3 white circles as baseballs, as shown, with two rows of red "stitching." **11.** Using white icing with a round tip, decorate the 3 yellow circles as tennis balls, as shown, with 2 white seams. **12.** Using black icing with a round tip, decorate the 3 orange circles as basketballs, as shown, with 4 black seams. **13.** Using white icing with a petal tip, draw 2 white seams on each football, as shown. **14.** Using white icing with a round tip, draw laces on each football, as shown.

Barbecue Grill

The ideal treat for backyard BBQs and family reunions is also an awesome idea for Father's Day. And, if your dad accidentally burns the meat on the grill, you can quickly whip up this treat so no one goes hungry.

**MAKES 1 GRILL,
11 INCHES IN DIAMETER**

TREAT RECIPES
(see page 6)
1 C batch, black food coloring
1 G batch, brown food coloring

SPECIAL INGREDIENTS
1 can white icing
Black food coloring
Haribo Fruit Salad

DECORATING ICING
Yellow

SPARKLE GEL
White
Black
Yellow

EQUIPMENT
Barbecue Grill template
   (see page 10)
Parchment paper
OodleTip piping bag (*Note:* If you do not have access to OodleTips, fill the corner of a zip-top bag and cut a small hole in one corner.)
Cooking spray
Wooden skewer
Round icing tip

1. In a bowl, measure 2 cups of white canned icing and add 1 or 2 drops of black food coloring. Mix the icing until the light gray color is evenly distributed. Fill the OodleTip bag and set it aside. Then mix the C batch recipe and pour the black mixture onto the parchment-covered template on the work surface. Generously coat your hands with cooking spray. **2.** Use both hands to mold the mixture into a flat circle over the template. **3.** Use your fingers to curve the edges up (like the crust of a pizza), smoothing the edges until the mixture begins to firm up.

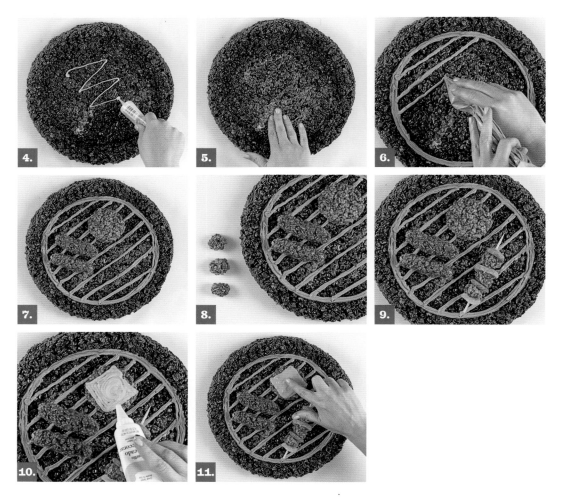

4. Zigzag white sparkle gel across the middle of the treat, as shown. 5. Use your fingers to smudge the sparkle gel over the surface. 6. Using the gray icing from Step 1, draw a circle just inside the raised edge of the treat and fill with straight, parallel lines, about 1 inch apart, to complete the grill surface. 7. Mix the G batch recipe and wait 2 minutes. Mold about two thirds of the mixture into three pieces as shown: a palm-size burger patty and two rolled "sausages." Place them on the grill. 8. Roll the remaining one-third of the mixture into three small balls. 9. Alternate four pieces of Haribo Fruit Salad candies with the small brown balls on the wooden skewer, and place on the grill. 10. Using black sparkle gel, draw grill marks on the sausages, as shown. Using yellow icing with a round tip, draw the outline of a square of cheese on the burger patty. Fill in the square completely with icing. 11. Using yellow sparkle gel, draw a zigzag on the yellow cheese square and use your finger to blend.

Bicycle

I learned how to ride a bike as a kid, but then I didn't ride for about twenty years. I thought I'd forgotten how, but it turns out that riding a bicycle is just like riding a bicycle, and that expression is trite because it's true. You can make this treat in any color to match your own two-wheeler; use icing to add details like streamers, bells, baskets, or flags.

Note: Because of the delicate nature of this design try to plan ahead and work directly on your serving surface.

MAKES 1 BICYCLE, 16 INCHES LONG

TREAT RECIPES
(see page 6)
1 E batch, red food coloring
(or a color of your choice)
1 G batch, black food coloring

SPECIAL INGREDIENTS
1 can white icing
Black food coloring

EQUIPMENT
Bicycle template (see page 10)
Parchment paper
OodleTip piping bag (*Note:* If you do not have access to OodleTips, fill the corner of a zip-top bag and cut a small hole in one corner.)
Cooking spray

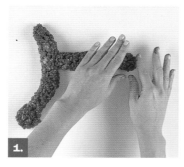

1. In a bowl, measure 2 cups of white canned icing and add 1 or 2 drops of black food coloring. Mix the icing until the light gray color is evenly distributed. Fill the OodleTip bag and set it aside. Then mix the E batch recipe. Generously coat your hands with cooking spray and, one large handful at a time, fill section 1 of the parchment-covered template on the work surface, using both hands to mold the edges. **2.** Work across the template, left to right, until the red mixture completely fills section 1 of the template. **3.** Mix the G batch recipe and, one handful at a time, fill section 2 of the template with the black mixture. Use both hands to smooth and mold the edges until the mixture begins to firm up.

4. Gently press together the "seams" where one color mixture meets the other. **5.** Using the gray icing from Step 1, draw a circle in the center of each wheel. **6.** Using the same gray icing, draw the spokes, straight lines that originate in the center of the wheel and extend out to the tires.

Bikini

Though one doesn't typically think of "crispy rice treats" and "bikini body" in the same sentence, this summery dessert recalls vacation days and sunbathing. The patriotic swimsuit adds a festive twist, and it's fun to pose with! Modify this design for a luau-themed celebration by using frosting to draw a coconut top, a colorful lei, and a grass skirt. Use food coloring (or none at all) to achieve any skin tone.

MAKES 1 BIKINI-CLAD TORSO, 18 INCHES TALL

TREAT RECIPE
(see page 6)
1 A batch, copper, brown, white, yellow, or no food coloring (depending on desired skin color)

DECORATING ICING
White
Blue
Red

EQUIPMENT
Bikini template (see page 10)
Parchment paper
Cooking spray
Round icing tip
Flat icing tip

1. Mix the A batch recipe and pour the mixture onto the parchment-covered template on the work surface. Generously coat your hands with cooking spray. Separate two handfuls of the mixture and place them back in the pot to reserve them. Use both hands to mold the mixture over the template, smoothing the edges until the mixture begins to firm up. **2.** Press your index finger into the center of the treat for the belly button. **3.** Remove the reserved handfuls of the mixture from the pot and place them, one handful at a time, on the upper half of the torso, forming raised areas for the bikini top.

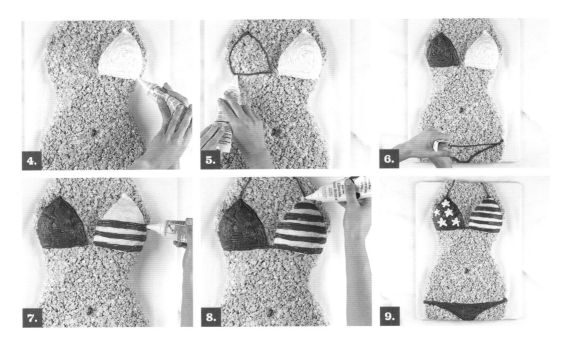

4. Using white icing with a round tip, outline and fill in the right side of the bikini top. **5.** Repeat Step 4, with blue icing and a round tip, on the left side. **6.** Still using blue icing with a round tip, outline and fill in the bikini bottom. **7.** Using red icing with a flat tip, add evenly spaced horizontal stripes to the white bikini top portion. **8.** Using blue icing with a round tip, draw halter strings, as shown. **9.** Using white icing with a round tip, draw stars on the blue bikini top portion, as shown.

TREAT YOURSELF!

Birthday Cake

Many of my customers reach out to order birthday treats for loved ones who just "don't like cake." Though I can't say I relate to these people personally (cake rules!), this treat provides a festive alternative to the traditional dessert. Customize for any celebratory occasion using your choice of colors or candles. Many party and stationery stores sell candles spelling out common names (which can be mixed and matched to spell more unusual ones), and numbered candles are available at most grocery stores.

MAKES 1 CAKE PROFILE, 12 INCHES TALL

TREAT RECIPE
(see page 6)
1 C batch, brown food coloring

SPECIAL INGREDIENTS
Pink Sixlets
Confetti sprinkles
"Happy Birthday" letter candles

DECORATING ICING
Yellow
Purple

EQUIPMENT
Birthday Cake template
  (see page 10)
Parchment paper
Cooking spray
Star icing tip

1. Mix the C batch recipe and pour it onto the parchment-covered template on the work surface. Generously coat your hands with cooking spray.
2. Use both hands to mold the mixture, smoothing the edges until the mixture begins to firm up. The bottom layer should be raised, about ½ inch thicker than the top layer.
3. Using yellow icing with a star tip, draw a scalloped line detail near the top edge of each of the layers. **4.** Press a pink Sixlet into each icing peak along the yellow scalloped line.

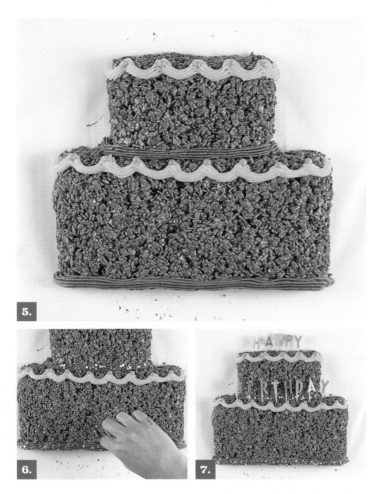

5. Using purple icing with a star tip, draw a straight line along the bottom of each layer. **6.** Use your fingers to sprinkle small amounts of confetti sprinkles along the purple icing lines. **7.** Insert candles into the top of each layer of the cake, parallel to the surface of the treat, as shown.

TREAT YOURSELF!

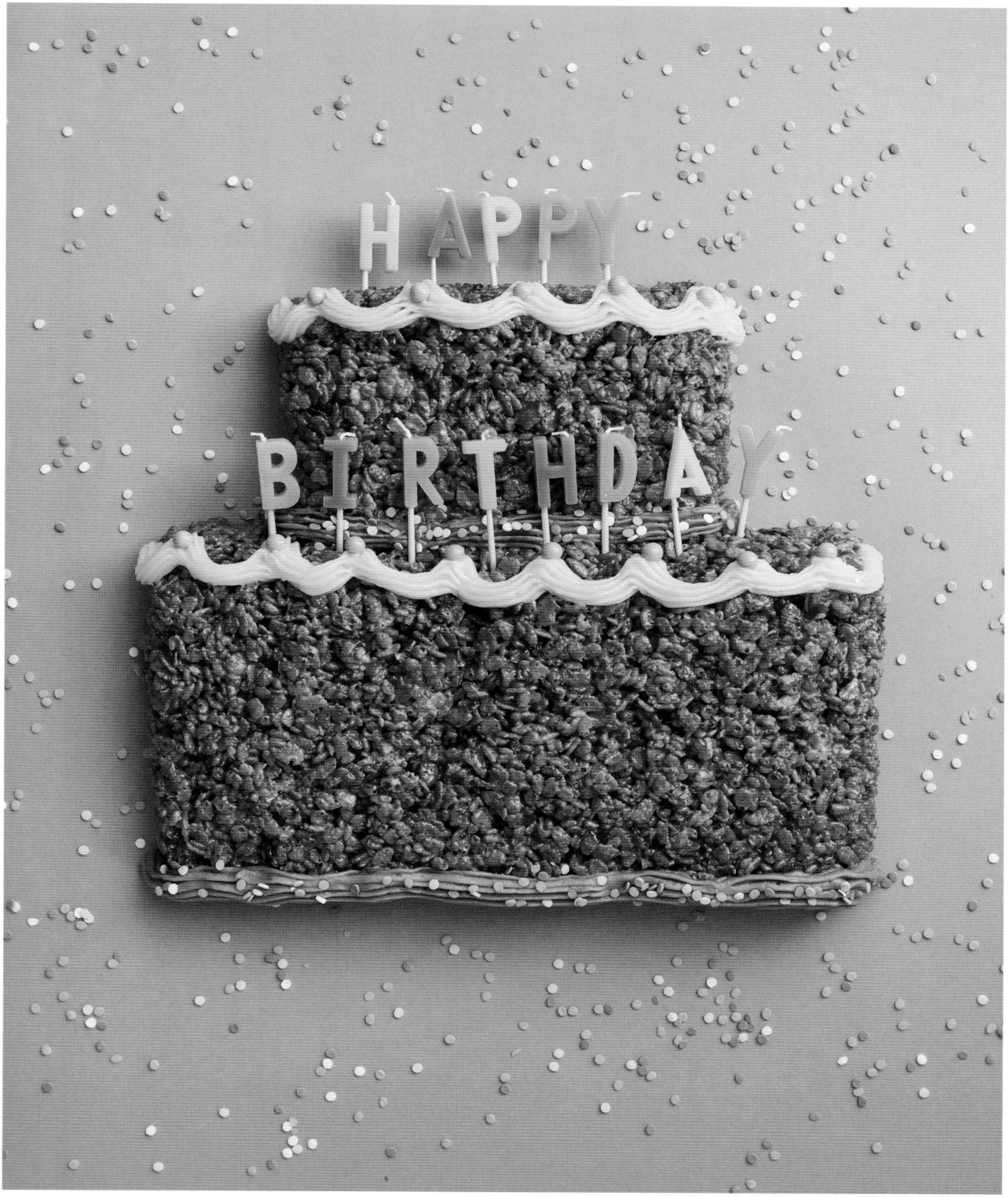
HAPPY
BIRTHDAY

Book

I asked if we could make the book you're holding in your hands out of crispy rice cereal too, but there were some production issues in bringing that vision to scale. It's probably for the best—I wouldn't want people eating it before reading it. For a book that feeds your stomach instead of your mind, customize the text on this literary treat to match your favorite book, or write your own story.

1 BOOK, 10 BY 14 INCHES

TREAT RECIPES
(see page 6)
1 C batch, 9 drops blue and
   1 drop black food coloring
1 D batch, white food coloring

DECORATING ICING
White
Black

EQUIPMENT
Book template (see page 10)
Parchment paper
Cooking spray
Large sharp knife
Round icing tip
1 mini icing tube (optional)

1. Mix the C batch recipe and pour the blue-black mixture onto the parchment-covered template on the work surface. Generously coat your hands with cooking spray. Use both hands to mold the mixture over the template, smoothing the edges until the mixture begins to firm up. **2.** Mix the D batch recipe and pour the white mixture onto the middle of the treat. Mold the white mixture into a rectangle that is one inch smaller on all sides than the layer below. **3.** Using a large knife, gently cut a line down the center of the white top layer, to create the "gutter" between the pages of the open book.

4. With the knife blade resting in the cut, press the flat side of the knife against the treat on both sides, molding the crevice into a small V. **5.** Using white icing with a round tip, draw an outline along the edge of the entire white rectangle. **6.** Using black icing with a round tip or a mini icing tube, write words or draw squiggles, as shown.

Bowling Ball and Pin

True story: I was kicked off the bowling team in high school for missing too many practices. (Oops.) For bowling leagues and birthday parties, this dessert will definitely be a *strike* and there won't be any left to *spare*!

**MAKES 1 BALL AND 1 PIN,
13 BY 8 INCHES OVERALL**

TREAT RECIPES
(see page 6)
1 D batch, 4 drops black food coloring
1 D batch, white food coloring

DECORATING ICING
Red
Black

SPARKLE GEL
White

EQUIPMENT
Bowling Ball and Pin template (see page 10)
Parchment paper
Cooking spray
Petal icing tip
Round icing tip

1. Mix the black D batch recipe and pour it onto the parchment-covered template on the work surface, filling section 1 of the template. Generously coat your hands with cooking spray. Use both hands to mold it into a rounded dome shape for the ball. **2.** Use your index finger to press three holes, arranged in a small triangle, into the surface. **3.** Mix the white D batch recipe and fill section 2 of the template. As you did with the bowling ball, use both hands to mold a rounded surface on the bowling pin.

4. Using red icing with a petal tip, draw 2 parallel lines across the "neck" of the bowling pin, as shown. **5.** Using white sparkle gel, draw a circle to line the inside edge of each of the three finger holes on the bowling ball (formed in Step 2). **6.** Using black icing with a round tip, line the outside edge of each of the three holes on the bowling ball.

Box of Chocolates

I love those boxes of chocolates that come with a map so you don't have to bite into each piece to find out what it is (though on second thought, maybe that method is more fun). Either way, this treat is two desserts in one: The crispy treat makes up the edible box and the real chocolates inside act as the irresistible filler. It's particularly on point for Valentine's Day, but I personally don't think we need a holiday to remind us to celebrate love (but mainly chocolate) all year round!

MAKES 1 HEART-SHAPED BOX

TREAT RECIPE
(see page 6)
1 C batch, red food coloring

SPECIAL INGREDIENTS
Box of at least 8 assorted
    chocolates
Gold food spray

DECORATING ICING
White
Red

EQUIPMENT
Box of Chocolates template
    (see page 10)
Parchment paper
Cooking spray
Round icing tip
Metal offset spatula

1.

2.

3.

1. Mix the C batch recipe and pour about 90 percent of the mixture onto the parchment-covered template on the work surface, reserving the rest in the pot. Generously coat your hands with cooking spray. Use both hands to mold the mixture over the template, smoothing the edges until the mixture begins to firm up. **2.** Working quickly so the remaining mixture doesn't harden too much, use white icing with a round tip to draw a line around the perimeter of the heart, about 1 inch from the edge. **3.** Draw squiggles inside the heart outline with the icing.

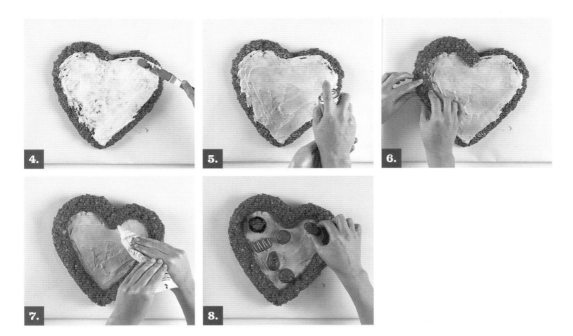

4. Use the spatula to spread the icing until it's smooth. **5.** Using the gold food spray, spray over the white icing. **6.** Remove the reserved mixture from the pot and place it on the treat, molding it to create a 1-inch-high raised border around the edges of the heart, covering the edge of the iced area. **7.** Using red icing with a round tip, line the seam where the bottom of the box and the border meet. **8.** Place the chocolates on the gold area, as shown.

TREAT YOURSELF!

Camera

This is a *camera*, which is a thing that people once used to take photographs before everyone had a smartphone. It's a great treat for your favorite shutterbug . . . but make sure nobody cuts into it before they have the chance to snap a bunch of pics! (Of it. Not with it. It doesn't work like that.)

**MAKES 1 CAMERA,
9 BY 12 INCHES**

TREAT RECIPE
(see page 6)
1 D batch, black food coloring
1 F batch, 5 drops white and
   1 drop black food coloring

DECORATING ICING
Black
White

SPARKLE GEL
Blue
White

EQUIPMENT
Camera template
   (see page 10)
Parchment paper
Cooking spray
Round icing tip

1. Mix the D batch recipe and pour it onto the parchment-covered template on the work surface. Generously coat your hands with cooking spray. Use both hands to mold it over section 1 of the template, smoothing the edges until the mixture begins to firm up. **2.** Mix the F batch recipe and, one handful at a time, fill section 2 of the template. You should have about two handfuls of this batch left over for Steps 3 and 4. **3.** Take one large handful and mold it into a circle for the camera lens. Place it right off center on the treat, as shown.

4. Take a second, slightly smaller handful and place it on top of the first circle, shaping it into another circle, about ½ inch smaller than the first. **5.** Gently press together all the "seams" where one color mixture or one piece of mixture meets the other. **6.** Using black icing with a round tip, line the seams where the gray mixture meets the black. **7.** Continuing with black icing and a round tip, draw and fill in a small rectangle at the top right of the camera for the viewfinder. Then draw a circle about ¼ inch from the edge of the circle in Step 4, and fill it in. **8.** Using blue sparkle gel, draw a circle on top of the black circle and use your fingers to blend. **9.** Repeat Step 8 with white sparkle gel. **10.** Using white icing with a small tip, draw an oval in the top left of section 1 and 2 dots below the lens on either side, as shown. **11.** Using white sparkle gel, draw a horizontal and reversed L shape along the top and right edge of the viewfinder, as shown.

Cereal Bowl

I used to eat cereal like it was my job. Now, cereal actually *is my job*. If you love cereal as much as I do, this is the treat for you. Go wild shopping in the cereal aisle and fill your cart with samplings from all of your childhood (or, um, current) favorites for fun flavor variety.

MAKES 1 BOWL, 8 INCHES IN DIAMETER

TREAT RECIPE
(see page 6)
1 C batch, blue and white food coloring
1 G batch, no food coloring, with Froot Loops (or similar)

SPECIAL INGREDIENTS
Froot Loops (or another cereal of your choice)

EQUIPMENT
Parchment paper
Cooking spray
Small mixing bowl, about 8 inches in diameter
Metal spoon
Large spatula

1. Spray the inside of the bowl with cooking spray until it's well coated. **2.** Mix the C batch recipe and pour about 90 percent of the mixture into the bowl. Generously coat your hands with cooking spray. Press the mixture to fill the bowl. **3.** Using the remaining 10 percent of the mixture, create a 1-inch-thick lip around the top of the bowl.

4. While the mixture is still soft, insert a metal spoon at the side of the bowl, then place the bowl in the freezer for 10 minutes.
5. Mix the G batch recipe using no food coloring, and replacing the crispy rice cereal with Froot Loops. Remove the bowl from the freezer and, using a large spatula, loosen the treat from the bowl and pop it out onto the parchment-covered work surface.
6. Pour the Froot Loops mixture into the center of the bowl-shaped treat. **7.** Press the mixture, with both hands, into a mound extending above the edges of the bowl.

TREAT YOURSELF!

Checkerboard

I know your parents probably told you not to play with your food, but as someone whose life revolves around doing just that, I ask you: What could feel more victorious than eating your opponent's pieces? Bring a batch to game night, where this treat does double duty as the entertainment *and* the snacks.

Note: In order to create a regulation board (64 squares), you'll need to double the recipe, and find a *very* large serving surface.

MAKES A 36-SQUARE CHECKERBOARD, PLUS OREO GAME PIECES

TREAT RECIPE
(see page 6)
1 C batch, no food coloring
1 C batch, black food coloring

SPECIAL INGREDIENTS
6 Oreo cookies, Original variety
6 Oreo cookies, Golden variety

DECORATING ICING
White (or any color available)

EQUIPMENT
Checkerboard template
  (see page 10)
Parchment paper
Cooking spray
Measuring tape
Large sharp knife
Cake board (or other serving
  surface)
Small round icing tip

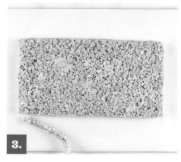

1. Mix the C batch recipe without food coloring and pour it onto the parchment-covered template on the work surface. Generously coat your hands with cooking spray. Use both hands to mold the mixture over the template, smoothing the edges until the mixture begins to firm up. **2.** Mix the C batch recipe with black food coloring and pour it onto another parchment-covered surface, reusing the template. Use both hands to mold the mixture over the template, smoothing the edges until the mixture begins to firm up. **3.** Using the measuring tape and a large knife, trim ¾ inch to 1 inch from each side of the light-colored rectangle, taking care to create straight lines. Discard (or eat!) the removed pieces.

4. Repeat Step 3 with the black-colored rectangle. **5.** Using the measuring tape as a guide, cut the light-colored rectangular treat into eighteen 2 by 2-inch squares. **6.** Repeat Step 5 with the black rectangle. **7.** Measure a 12 by 12-inch square on the cake board and, using white icing with a small tip, squiggle lines of icing to cover the area. **8.** Moving left to right, arrange the 36 pieces in a checkerboard pattern, alternating the colors as shown. **9.** When the grid is complete, line up the Golden and Original Oreo cookies and use them as pieces to play a modified game of checkers!

Cheeseburger

I've always loved doodling, painting, and sculpting (and eating) cheeseburgers. I covered sales reports with tiny ones rendered in blue ink at work, painted them in oils in a college painting course, and made a teeny-tiny Play-Doh version that I photographed on top of a credit card to demonstrate scale. Once, I even sculpted a mini burger out of colored Tootsie Rolls. I'm not sure why cheeseburgers have always been my muse, but they're colorful, delicious, and, when made of anything besides bread, cheese, and meat, they're pretty silly. It's no surprise that a cheeseburger was my first-ever creative crispy treat, and it's remained a fan favorite. Plus, it doesn't require any icing, so it's supremely easy to make and sure to impress. Pro tip: Substitute chocolate crispy rice cereal in the patty (E batch) for some flavor variety.

**MAKES 1 CHEESEBURGER,
8 INCHES IN DIAMETER AND 9 INCHES TALL**

TREAT RECIPE
(see page 6)
1 C batch, no food coloring
1 E batch, brown food coloring
**1 H batch, 1 drop orange and
    1 drop yellow food coloring**
1 H batch, green food coloring
1 H batch, red food coloring

SPECIAL INGREDIENTS
Pearl sugar

EQUIPMENT
**Cheeseburger template
    (see page 10)**
Parchment paper
Cooking spray

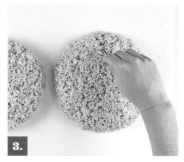

1. Mix the C batch recipe and pour the mixture onto the parchment-covered template on the work surface. Generously coat your hands with cooking spray. Split the mixture into two parts, in an approximately 3-to-5 ratio for the bottom and top of the bun. **2.** Mold the smaller portion into a flatter circle (the bottom of the bun), and the larger portion into a rounded dome shape (the top of the bun). **3.** Gently press pearl sugar into the top of the bun to look like sesame seeds.

4. Mix the E batch recipe and pour it onto the bottom of the bun. Mold the mixture into a patty shape that fits comfortably on the bun. **5.** Mix the orange-yellow H batch, then press a thin layer of the mixture into a rough square for the melted cheese, as shown. **6.** Mix the green H batch, then press a thin layer of the mixture over the cheese to make the lettuce, as shown.

7. Mix the red H batch, then press a thin layer of the mixture atop the lettuce to make the tomato, as shown. 8. Carefully lift the top of the bun with both hands to place it on top of the tomato. 9. Press down gently on the top bun to fuse the layers and complete the cheeseburger.

Christmas Tree

The perfect treat for Easter. Just kidding! Craft this Christmas *tree*t to make an already festive holiday even more festive. Change the colors of the ornaments to support your favorite sports team or showcase the colors you love. To add an extra dose of holiday flare, mix up one E batch in the color of your choice, press it into a pan, and cut it into standard square-shaped treats. Use decorating icing to draw ribbons and bows for gifts to put under the "tree."

MAKES 1 TREE, 14 INCHES TALL

TREAT RECIPE
(see page 6)
1 C batch, green food coloring

DECORATING ICING
Yellow
Red
Green
Blue
Brown

EQUIPMENT
**Christmas Tree template
  (see page 10)**
Parchment paper
Cooking spray
Round icing tip

1. Mix the C batch recipe and pour the mixture onto the parchment-covered template on the work surface. Generously coat your hands with cooking spray. **2.** Use both hands to mold the mixture over the template, smoothing the edges until the mixture begins to firm up. **3.** Using yellow icing with a round tip, draw a star topper and 2 or 3 circular ornaments. **4.** Using red icing with a round tip, draw 2 or 3 circular ornaments.

5. Repeat Step 4 using green and blue icings with round tips.
6. Using brown icing with a round tip, draw and color in the tree trunk. **7.** Once the tree is trimmed, let it sit for 10 minutes so the icing sets, then gently pat the ornaments and trunk to smooth their surfaces.

Cola Bottle

Everyone loves a classic, and like the beverage it's modeled after, this treat is both timeless and nostalgic. Replace the "cola" label with a friend's name for a bespoke twist—or modify the shape and color of the bottle a bit to craft a more adult beverage.

MAKES 1 BOTTLE, 13 INCHES TALL

TREAT RECIPE
(see page 6)
**1 C batch, 9 drops brown and
1 drop black food coloring**

DECORATING ICING
Red
White

EQUIPMENT
**Cola Bottle template
(see page 10)**
Parchment paper
Cooking spray
Round icing tip
Petal icing tip

1. Mix the C batch recipe and pour the mixture onto the parchment-covered template on the work surface. Generously coat your hands with cooking spray. Use both hands to mold the mixture over the template until the surface is slightly rounded and the mixture begins to firm up. **2.** When the shape of the bottle is formed, use the side of your hand to mold vertical grooves into the lower portion. **3.** Using red icing with a round tip, outline and then fill in the label. Use your fingers to smooth the icing.

4. Still using the red icing, draw a red cap at the mouth of the bottle. **5.** Using white icing with a petal tip, draw a line each along the top and bottom edge of the red label. **6.** Using white icing with a round tip, underline the bottle cap with a squiggly line. **7.** Still using the white icing with the round tip, write *Cola* across the label.

Cookies

Okay, so I know we all love cookies, but these not only taste better, they're also easier to make. And cookies are *already* pretty easy to make. They're sure to stand out at bake sales, but if you can't bear to part with them (completely understandable), they're a fun no-bake dessert for a girls-night-in, a slumber party, or a night alone on your couch (been there).

MAKES 15 COOKIES, EACH 4 INCHES IN DIAMETER

TREAT RECIPE
(see page 6)
1 C batch, 1 drop brown and
    3 drops white food coloring

SPECIAL INGREDIENTS
Chocolate chunks

EQUIPMENT
Parchment paper
Cooking spray

1. Mix the C batch recipe and, after stirring in the cereal, add 1 handful of chocolate chunks. Stir until they are distributed (they will start to melt). Generously coat your hands with cooking spray. Gather one handful of the mixture and place it on the parchment-covered work surface. **2.** Mold the mixture into a circular mound about 4 inches across, and continue, a handful at a time, until the "cookie sheet" is full. **3.** Press extra chocolate chunks into the top of each cookie, placing them in the crannies between cereal pieces.

Crown

Who says a crown has to be passed down by royalty? Coronate yourself with a few easy (and cheap) ingredients. This treat is simply regal for birthday parties, bachelorette parties, or any time you feel like being queen or king for a day (i.e., every single day). Add a name, age, or accomplishment to commemorate a special occasion.

MAKES 1 CROWN, 12 INCHES ACROSS

TREAT RECIPE
(see page 6)
1 C batch, 9 drops yellow and
   1 drop brown food coloring

SPECIAL INGREDIENTS
Gold food spray

DECORATING ICING
Yellow
Purple
Red

EQUIPMENT
Crown template (see page 10)
Parchment paper
Cooking spray
Round icing tip

 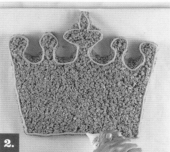 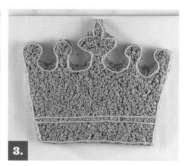

1. Mix the C batch recipe and pour the mixture onto the parchment-covered template on the work surface. Generously coat your hands with cooking spray. Use both hands to mold the mixture over the template, smoothing the edges until the mixture begins to firm up. **2.** Using yellow icing with a round tip, draw an outline along the outer edge of the crown shape. **3.** Draw two horizontal, parallel lines about 1½ inches from the crown base.

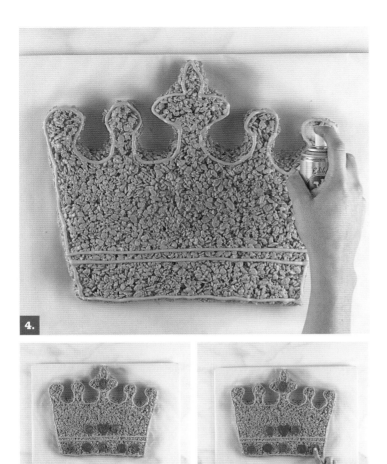

4. Use the gold food spray to coat the entire treat, including the icing lines. 5. Using purple and red icings with round tips, draw the remaining details—dots and hearts—as shown. 6. Wait 10 minutes, then use your fingers to pat the purple and red icing shapes to smooth them.

Dancing Lady Emoji

Emoji are an important area of study over at Misterkrisp University, and this sassy lady is one of my favorites—you can't *not* respect her dedication to dance. She livens up the party for any celebration, be it a birthday, dance recital, bachelorette party, or, you know, Friday. Use brown, white, pink, yellow, or copper food coloring to achieve any skin tone, and play with hair color, too!

MAKES 1 LADY, 16 INCHES TALL

TREAT RECIPE
(see page 6)
1 C batch, red food coloring
1 E batch, 3 drops brown and 3 drops white food coloring
1 G batch, brown food coloring

DECORATING ICING
Red

EQUIPMENT
Dancing Lady Emoji template (see page 10)
Parchment paper
Cooking spray
Round icing tip

1. Mix the C batch recipe, and pour the mixture onto the parchment-covered template on the work surface. Generously coat your hands with cooking spray. Use both hands to mold the mixture over section 1 of the template, smoothing the edges until the mixture begins to firm up. **2.** Mix the E batch recipe and, applying the mixture one handful at a time, fill section 2 of the template.

3. Continue filling section 2, gently pressing together the "seams" where one color mixture meets the other. **4.** Mix the G batch recipe and, applying the mixture one handful at a time, fill section 3 of the template, gently pressing together the seams. **5.** Using red icing with a round tip, draw her shoes, as shown.

Dinosaur

I'm deeply fascinated by the idea that our planet was once occupied by what were essentially colossal lizards. Sometimes I'll look at a Walmart or a middle school and think about how millions of years ago, a dinosaur was probably chilling right in that spot. Anyway, this dinosaur treat makes a terrific surprise for kids' birthday parties. You can easily make this dinosaur in any color, or transform him into a fossil with some well-placed icing (for the aspiring paleontologist). On the other hand, you can also bring this dino treat to an adult's birthday party to remind them how old they are.

MAKES 1 DINOSAUR, 15 INCHES HEAD TO TAIL

TREAT RECIPE
(see page 6)
1 C batch, green food coloring

DECORATING ICING
White
Blue

SPARKLE GEL
Black

EQUIPMENT
Dinosaur template (see page 10)
Parchment paper
Cooking spray
Round icing tip

1. Mix the C batch recipe, and pour 90 percent of the mixture onto the parchment-covered template on the work surface, reserving the rest of the mixture inside the pot. Generously coat your hands with cooking spray. **2.** Use both hands to mold the mixture over the template to form the body, neck, head, and tail, smoothing the edges until the mixture begins to firm up.

3. Using the reserved mixture from the pot, add pieces to the template one small handful at a time to complete the dinosaur's legs. Make sure that the front legs are slightly more elevated than the hind legs, and gently press together the pieces, attaching the legs of the dinosaur to the body. **4.** Using white icing with a round tip and black sparkle gel, draw a white dot for the eye, as shown; then add a dark pupil at its center. **5.** Using blue icing with a round tip, draw claws at the ends of the legs as shown.

Donuts

"Food made out of other food" is another required reading category at Misterkrisp U, and these donuts were among my first experiments. They're just as sweet as the original but chewier and more buttery. And like traditional donuts, the middle of these treats has zero calories! See, they're practically diet food. At least that's what I tell myself.

**MAKES 12 DONUTS,
EACH 2¾-INCH DIAMETER**

TREAT RECIPE
(see page 6)
1 D batch, no food coloring

SPECIAL INGREDIENTS
Rainbow sprinkles

DECORATING ICING
Pink
Brown
White

EQUIPMENT
Parchment paper
2 mini six-donut baking pans (*Note:* **If you don't have a donut pan, you can form these by hand. Make small, round handfuls and use your index finger to push a hole into the center.**)
Cooking spray
Round icing tip
Small icing tube

1. Generously coat both donut pans with cooking spray. **2.** Mix the D batch recipe. Generously coat your hands with cooking spray and, one handful at a time, press the mixture into the donut pans, making sure not to fill the center of the donuts. Once both pans are full (but not overfilled), place them in the freezer for 15 minutes. (*Note:* You'll have a large handful of crispy mixture left over, but a smaller batch won't be quite enough!) **3.** Remove the pans from the freezer. Wait 2 minutes; remove the treats from the molds, and place them on the parchment-covered work surface.

4. Using pink icing with a round tip, color in the rounded side of 6 of the treats, as shown. **5.** Using brown icing with a round tip, color in the rounded side of the remaining 6 treats. **6.** Using your fingers, drop small amounts of sprinkles onto the icing on the pink iced donuts. **7.** Fill the small icing tube with white icing and draw a zigzag pattern on each of the brown iced donuts, as shown (alternatively, you can use white sparkle gel).

Drumsticks

No surprise here, but I love food that you can eat with your hands. Drumsticks are a favorite in this category, so naturally I had to crispify them! (I know *crispify* is not a real word, but I'm going with it. Language is fluid.)

MAKES 9–12 DRUMSTICKS, EACH 5 INCHES LONG

TREAT RECIPE
(see page 6)
1 F batch, white food coloring
1 F batch, brown food coloring

EQUIPMENT
Parchment paper
Cooking spray
Dog bone cookie cutter

1. Coat the inside of the dog bone cookie cutter with cooking spray. Mix the white F batch recipe and let it sit about a minute. Generously coat your hands with cooking spray. Then, one small handful at a time, press the mixture into the dog bone cookie cutter, on a parchment-covered work surface, making sure that the entire shape is filled before lifting the cookie cutter. **2.** Continue making bones, spraying the cookie cutter in between bones as needed, until you have 9 to 12 total. Place the treats in the freezer for about 10 minutes. **3.** Mix the brown F batch recipe. Remove the bone treats from the freezer and, using one large handful at a time, cover three quarters of a bone shape with the brown mixture. Round the brown mixture into a drumstick shape using both hands. Repeat until all drumsticks are complete. **4.** Allow the drumsticks to set for at least 3 hours before serving.

Earth

Anyone else ever feel like a teeny-tiny insignificant speck in this infinite universe? (Asking for a friend.) Either way, this dessert is out of this world. Celebrate Earth Day or *any* day you're spending on this sweet planet—and don't forget to recycle your cereal boxes.

MAKES 1 EARTH, 10 INCHES IN DIAMETER

TREAT RECIPES
(see page 6)
1 C batch, blue food coloring
1 F batch, green food coloring

EQUIPMENT
Earth template (see page 10)
Parchment paper
Cooking spray
Reference map showing all the
    continents (optional)

1. Mix the C batch recipe and pour it onto the parchment-covered template on the work surface. Generously coat your hands with cooking spray. Use both hands to mold it into a dome shape. Shape it until the edges are smooth and the mixture begins to firm up, maintaining the rounded surface as you work. **2.** Mix the F batch recipe and, using small amounts of mixture at a time, press the green mixture onto the blue globe for the continents. (*Note:* You'll likely have a good portion of crispy mixture left over, but a smaller batch won't be quite enough!) **3.** Look at a map for reference, if needed, to complete the arrangement of the continents, as shown. (*Note:* The continents may be arranged differently depending on your location and preference.)

Easter Egg

In a sea of bunnies, be an egg. Okay, that isn't a real saying. But this quick and adorable Easter egg is a great last-minute and unexpected treat to take to an Easter celebration. And when everyone is out looking for hidden eggs, you can snack on this one.

MAKES 1 EGG, 11 INCHES TALL

TREAT RECIPE
(see page 6)
1 C batch, 5 drops turquoise and
    5 drops white food coloring

SPECIAL INGREDIENTS
Pink candy melts
Purple candy melts

DECORATING ICING
Yellow

EQUIPMENT
Easter Egg template (see page 10)
Parchment paper
Cooking spray
Round icing tip

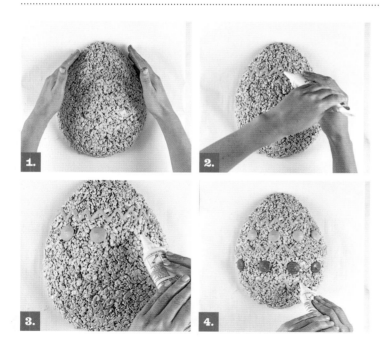

1. Mix the C batch recipe and pour it onto the parchment-covered template on the work surface. Generously coat your hands with cooking spray. Use both hands to mold it into a dome-shaped oval. Shape it until the edges are smooth and the mixture begins to firm up, maintaining the rounded surface as you work. 2. Using yellow icing with a round tip, draw a zigzag line across the egg, about one quarter down from the top, as shown. 3. Still using the yellow icing with a round tip, draw a row of dots below the zigzag line. Press a candy melt into each dot of icing to adhere it to the egg. 4. Continue to alternate rows of icing and candy melts, repeating Steps 2 and 3 as shown, until the egg is decorated.

Eggs and Bacon

I wonder who decided what kinds of foods are appropriate for consumption at breakfast. Why is it frowned upon to eat pizza in the morning, yet we regularly consume breakfast foods containing bread, cheese, and tomatoes, the very ingredients that compose a pizza? These snack-size breakfast-themed desserts are *eggs*-ellent (sorry) for bake sales or brunches, and most of their ingredients are technically found in breakfast foods, too.

MAKES 6 OR 7 FRIED EGGS, EACH 3½–4 INCHES IN DIAMETER, AND 6 TO 9 STRIPS OF BACON, EACH 6 INCHES LONG

TREAT RECIPES
(see page 6)
1 F batch, white food coloring
1 F batch, 4 drops brown and
  4 drops red food coloring

DECORATING ICING
Yellow

SPARKLE GEL
Yellow
White
Gold
Pink

EQUIPMENT
Parchment paper
Cooking spray
Round icing tip

1. Mix the white F batch recipe. Generously coat your hands with cooking spray and, one handful at a time, place the mixture on the parchment-covered work surface. Use both hands to mold each handful into a fried-egg shape, as shown. There should be enough mixture to make 6 or 7 egg whites. **2.** Mix the red-brown F batch recipe and, one handful at a time, place the mixture on the work surface. Use both hands to mold each handful into bacon strip shapes, as shown. There should be enough mixture to make 6 to 9 bacon strips. **3.** Using yellow icing with a round tip, draw yellow circles on the egg shapes for yolks.

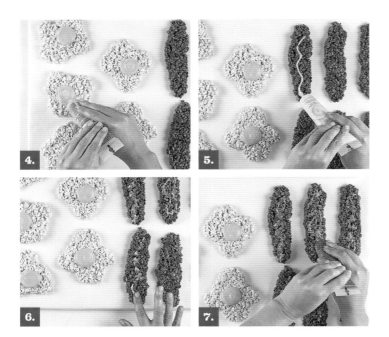

4. Using the yellow sparkle gel, cover each of the yellow yolks. **5.** Using the white sparkle gel, draw a squiggly line along each bacon strip. **6.** Use your finger to blend the white sparkle gel into the bacon treats. **7.** Repeat Steps 5 and 6 with the gold and then pink sparkle gel.

Eiffel Tower

You don't have to travel halfway around the world to visit the Eiffel Tower. Make this treat for a Parisian or a bon voyage celebration and hear the crowd say "ooh-la-la" (which, btw, is not a thing French people actually say, just American people who want to sound French).

MAKES 1 TOWER, 16 INCHES TALL

TREAT RECIPE
(see page 6)
1 C batch, 9 drops white and
    1 drop black food coloring

DECORATING ICING
Black, 2 tubes

EQUIPMENT
Eiffel Tower template
    (see page 10)
Parchment paper
Cooking spray
Round icing tip
Small icing tube

1. Mix the C batch recipe. Generously coat your hands with cooking spray and, one handful at a time, mold the mixture, with both hands, over the parchment-covered template on the work surface.
2. Fill the template, using both hands to smooth and mold the edges, working from top to bottom, reserving just a pinch of the gray mixture. **3.** After the tower has firmed up a bit, about 8 minutes, use the mixture you reserved in Step 2 and roll it between your fingers to make a thin needle.

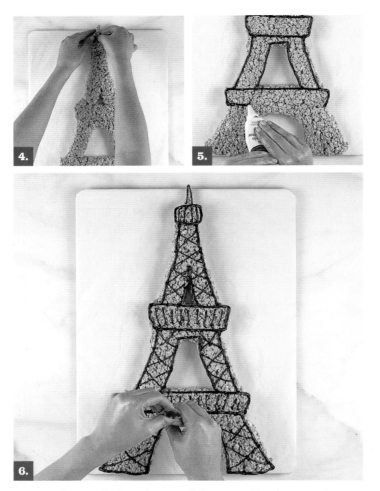

4. Press the needle into the top of the tower. Pat the rest of the treat to smooth the edges and finesse the shape. **5.** Using black icing with a round tip, outline the basic wrought-iron shape. **6.** To add finer detail, fill the small icing tube with black icing and draw a series of intersecting lines over the gray tower for the wrought-iron latticework, as shown.

Elephant

The only situation when having an "elephant in the room" is actually a good thing. Elephants are symbols of luck and wisdom and make great additions to baby showers, birthday parties, or animal-themed celebrations. I love making these—the adorable lil' marshmallow tusk gets me every time!

MAKES 1 ELEPHANT, 10 BY 13 INCHES

TREAT RECIPE
(see page 6)
1 C batch, pink food coloring

SPECIAL INGREDIENTS
Black M&M
Regular-size marshmallow

DECORATING ICING
Black

EQUIPMENT
Elephant template (see page 10)
Parchment paper
Cooking spray
Round icing tip
Scissors

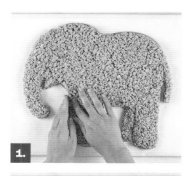

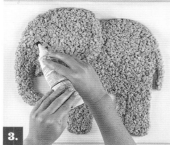

1. Mix the C batch recipe and pour about 90 percent of the mixture onto the parchment-covered template on the work surface. Reserve the rest. Generously coat your hands with cooking spray. Fill in the shape until the edges are smooth and the mixture begins to firm up, taking care to make the foreground legs slightly more elevated. **2.** Use the mixture you reserved in Step 1 to create the ear shape, as shown. **3.** Using black icing with a round tip, draw a black dot for the eye. Press a black M&M over the black dot, as shown, to complete the eye. **4.** Using scissors, slice the edge off of a marshmallow to make a tusk, as shown, and gently press it onto the treat near the trunk.

Empire State Building

For when you're so hungry you could eat a skyscraper! Make this treat to take any NYC-themed celebration to new heights, and watch out for giant gorillas (I heard they love crispy treats).

MAKES 1 BUILDING, 17 INCHES TALL

TREAT RECIPE (see page 6)
1 C batch, 9 drops white and 1 drop black food coloring

DECORATING ICING
Black, 2 tubes

EQUIPMENT
Empire State Building template (see page 10)
Parchment paper
Cooking spray
Round icing tip
Small icing tube

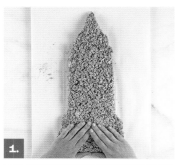

1. Mix the C batch recipe and pour the mixture onto the parchment-covered template on the work surface. Generously coat your hands with cooking spray. Reserve one small handful of mixture and place it back in the pot. Use both hands to mold the mixture over the template, smoothing the edges until the mixture begins to firm up. **2.** To make the top spire, roll a large pinch of the reserved mixture between your hands and press it firmly into the top of the treat. **3.** Using the black icing with a round tip, outline the basic shape of the building. **4.** To add finer detail, fill the small icing tube with black icing and draw a series of vertical lines, as shown.

Engagement Ring

She said yes, and now she's probably hungry. This celebratory treat brings bling to engagements, bachelorette parties, bridal showers, or any wedding-related celebration. (And hey, if she says no, that just means more treats for you—all for eating your feelings.)

**MAKES 1 RING,
11 INCHES IN DIAMETER**

TREAT RECIPE
(see page 6)
1 C batch, 8 drops white and
   2 drops black food coloring

SPECIAL INGREDIENTS
Silver food spray

DECORATING ICING
White

SPARKLE GEL
Light blue

EQUIPMENT
Engagement Ring
   template
   (see page 10)
Parchment paper
Cooking spray
Round icing tip

1. Mix the C batch recipe and pour the mixture onto the parchment-covered template on the work surface. Generously coat your hands with cooking spray. **2.** Use both hands to mold the mixture over the template, smoothing the edges until the mixture begins to firm up. **3.** Using silver food spray, coat the treat and use a warm, wet paper towel to wipe excess spray from the work surface.

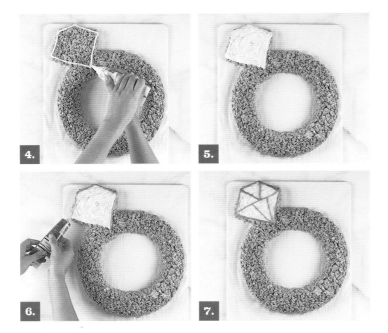

4. Using white icing with a round tip, draw the outline of a diamond shape. **5.** Still using white icing, fill in the diamond shape. Use your fingers to smooth and spread the icing.
6. Using light blue sparkle gel, outline the diamond design.
7. Still using the sparkle gel, draw more lines to reveal the facets, as shown.

Fire Engine

Ring the alarm, this treat is way too cute! But seriously, make sure to turn off your stove when you finish making this fire engine or else a real one might show up at your house. And the worst part of that would be feeling obligated to share your treats with hungry firefighters.

MAKES 1 FIRE ENGINE, 14 INCHES LONG

TREAT RECIPES
(see page 6)
1 C batch, red food coloring
1 F batch, 3 drops white and
    2 drops black food coloring

DECORATING ICING
White
Yellow
Orange
Black

SPARKLE GEL
Light blue

EQUIPMENT
Fire Engine template
    (see page 10)
Parchment paper
Cooking spray
Round icing tips

1. Mix the C batch recipe and pour the mixture onto the parchment-covered template on the work surface. Generously coat your hands with cooking spray. **2.** Mold the mixture over section 1 of the template and shape it until the edges are smooth and the mixture begins to firm up. **3.** Mix the F batch recipe and, in small handfuls, begin to fill in section 2 of the template to form the ladder, siren, and wheels. **4.** Continue filling section 2 of the template with the gray mixture to form the bumper. Extend the line of the bumper over section 1, curving around the wheels for the wheel wells. Form two thin rectangles on the side of the truck to make the grates, as shown.

5. Using white icing with a round tip, draw and fill in 3 windows on the front of the truck. **6.** Using light blue sparkle gel, draw one dot on each window and use your fingers to blend. **7.** Using yellow icing with a round tip, fill in the siren. **8.** Using orange icing with a round tip, add the headlight. **9.** Using white icing with a round tip, draw small circles at the center of the wheels and tiny rectangles on the ladder. **10.** Using black icing with a round tip, fill in the tires, and draw all of the additional details (grate texture, door handles, ladder rungs), and outline the windows, bumper, fenders, etc., as shown.

Flag

Let your freak flag (or whatever flag you want) fly, and then eat it. Show your patriotism with this American flag, the perfect potluck treat to bring to a July 4th celebration, or whip up a banner for the team you're rooting for in the next soccer matchup. *Note:* The American flag employs a cutting and piecing technique, but to make other flags, you can use the Golf Course template (just fill in the hole) to make a rectangle and then decorate with your choice of icings!

MAKES 1 FLAG, 14 BY 12 INCHES

TREAT RECIPES
(see page 6)
1 E batch, white food coloring
1 E batch, red food coloring
1 G batch, blue food coloring

DECORATING ICING
White

EQUIPMENT
2 flag templates (see page 10)
Parchment paper
Cooking spray
Large sharp knife
Round icing tip
Cake board (or other serving surface)

1. Mix the white E batch recipe and pour the mixture onto one of the parchment-covered templates on the work surface. Generously coat your hands with cooking spray. Mold the mixture over section 1 of the template and shape it until the edges are smooth and the mixture begins to firm up. **2.** Make the red E batch recipe and pour the mixture onto the other parchment-covered template. Mold the mixture over section 2 of the template and shape it until the edges are smooth and the mixture begins to firm up. **3.** Let the treats sit for one hour at room temperature. Then, using a sharp knife, cut the white treat horizontally into 2-inch-wide strips. **4.** Cut the red treat into 2-inch-wide strips to match the white strips.

5. Starting with the top strip of the red treat, on a fresh serving surface, alternate the placement of the red and white strips, as shown. Gently press each strip together at the "seams" where one color mixture meets the other. **6.** Mix the G batch recipe and pour the mixture onto the work surface and mold it with both hands so that it fits in the upper left corner of the striped treat, as shown. **7.** Using white icing with a round tip, draw rows of stars on the blue portion of the treat. Wait 10 minutes, then pat down the stars with your fingers to smooth.

Flowerpot

I love receiving flowers just as much as the next girl, but I prefer presents I can eat. This flowerpot treat is a two-in-one, combining beautiful blooms with delicious dessert. The sandwich cookie soil adds a crunchy twist, and the fruity stems make for a fun snack, too. Plant a little something for Mother's Day, a bridal shower, a thank-you or congratulations gift, or any springtime celebration.

MAKES 1 FLOWERPOT, 14 INCHES TALL (INCLUDING 6 FLOWERS)

TREAT RECIPES
(see page 6)
1 D batch, 4 drops brown and 4 drops orange food coloring
1 E batch, pink food coloring

SPECIAL INGREDIENTS
6 Oreo cookies
6 green Twizzlers
Yellow candy melts

DECORATING ICING
Brown
Light green

EQUIPMENT
Flowerpot template (see page 10)
Parchment paper
Cooking spray
Butter knife
Small zip-top bag
Rolling pin
Round icing tip
Cake board (or other serving surface)
Spoon
Flower cookie cutter
Scissors

1. Make the C batch recipe and pour the mixture onto the parchment-covered template on the work surface. Generously coat your hands with cooking spray. Use both hands to mold the mixture over the template, smoothing the edges until the mixture begins to firm up. **2.** Mold the top edge of the flowerpot so that it's slightly more raised than the rest. Set aside the flowerpot treat. **3.** Use a butter knife to remove the filling from inside the sandwich cookies.

4. Place the cookies in a zip-top bag, seal it, and use a rolling pin to crush the cookies into a fine crumble. **5.** Using brown icing with a round tip, draw a line along the top of the flowerpot treat, as shown. **6.** Following the instructions on page 10, remove the treat from the template and adhere to a cardboard cake board or serving surface. Using your fingers, gently press the cookie crumbs onto the strip of brown icing to form the dirt. Use a spoon to smooth it down and clear away the excess. **7.** Using light green icing with the round tip, draw 6 vertical lines coming up from the dirt. **8.** Press a Twizzler into each green icing line, making sure to bury the end of each stem in the "soil."

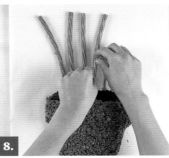

9. On a separate parchment-covered work surface, coat the inside of the flower cookie cutter with cooking spray. **10.** Mix the E batch recipe. Press a medium-size handful of the pink mixture into the cookie cutter to the edges, then gently slide out the shape onto the work surface. Repeat 5 times, spraying the cookie cutter between treats. **11.** Using light green icing with a round tip, draw one dot in the center of each flower. Press a yellow candy melt over each of the green dots. **12.** Eyeball how much room each flower will take up and trim the green Twizzler stems accordingly. **13.** Draw a dot of green icing on the serving surface at the top of a stem where you'd like to place a flower, and press one of the flower treats over it. Repeat with each flower.

Football Stadium

Forget showing up with a bucket of chicken on football Sunday (unless they're the drumsticks on page 93). Instead, show your team spirit with this super-size stadium treat filled with sprinkle spectators. Disagree with the ref's last call? Eat the end zone!

MAKES 1 STADIUM, 13 BY 9 BY 7 INCHES

TREAT RECIPES
(see page 6)
1 C batch, green food coloring
2 C batches, blue food coloring

SPECIAL INGREDIENTS
Red, white, and blue sprinkle mix

DECORATING ICING
Red
White

SPARKLE GEL
Light blue

EQUIPMENT
Football Stadium template
   (see page 10)
Parchment paper
Cooking spray
Cake board
   (or other serving surface)
Star icing tip
Round icing tip
Aluminum foil
Small icing tube

1. Mix the green C batch recipe and pour onto the parchment-covered template on the work surface. Generously coat your hands with cooking spray. Use both hands to mold the mixture, smoothing the edges until the mixture begins to firm up. **2.** Mix the first blue C batch recipe and, one large handful at a time, press the blue mixture into a wide cylinder shape around the perimeter of the green mixture to form the stadium walls, as shown. **3.** Continue building the shape upward until you've used all of the blue mixture. Press until firm and place the treat in the freezer for 10 to 20 minutes.

4. Mix the second blue C batch recipe. Remove the treat from the freezer and place it on the serving surface. Then, one handful at a time, continue to build the stadium walls, making sure to leave a green rectangle shape in the center. 5. Using red icing with a star tip, outline the border of the treat where it meets the surface. 6. Using red icing with a round tip, add the rim details, as shown. 7. Using white icing with a round tip, outline the rim, as shown. 8. Fold a piece of aluminum foil into a rectangle with raised edges to form a tray. 9. Place the foil tray inside the stadium, covering the football field. 10. Using light blue sparkle gel, draw squiggles on the inside walls of the stadium and use your fingers to blend the gel across the surface. 11. Use your fingers to adhere sprinkles to the gel on the inside walls of the stadium. 12. Carefully remove the foil and discard. Fill a small icing tube with white icing and draw the details of the football field, as shown.

Fruit

I love fruit, but sometimes I just wish it had more butter in it. These bananas, grapes, oranges, and strawberries are sure to please crowds at school fundraisers, classroom celebrations, and tropical-themed get-togethers.

MAKES 2 BANANAS, 2–3 ORANGES, 6–8 STRAWBERRIES, AND 1 BUNCH OF GRAPES

TREAT RECIPES
(see page 6)
1 F batch, yellow food coloring
1 F batch, orange food coloring
1 F batch, red food coloring
1 F batch, purple food coloring

SPECIAL INGREDIENTS
1 green Twizzler

DECORATING ICING
Dark green
Light green
Brown

SPARKLE GEL
Gold

EQUIPMENT
Fruit templates (see page 10)
Parchment paper
Cooking spray
Star icing tip
Round icing tip
Scissors

1. Mix the yellow F batch recipe and pour half of the mixture onto the parchment-covered template on the work surface. Generously coat your hands with cooking spray. Use both hands to form the mixture over template 1 (the banana), smoothing the edges until the mixture begins to firm up. Once finished, carefully slide the banana to the side and repeat the process with the remaining yellow mixture. **2.** Mix the orange F batch recipe and allow the mixture to cool, 1 to 2 minutes. Using half of the orange mixture, roll it between your hands to form a ball. Once finished, place the orange to the side and repeat the process with the remaining orange mixture. **3.** Mix the red F batch recipe and allow the mixture to cool, 1 to 2 minutes. Using a small handful at a time (about the size of a real strawberry), roll the mixture between your hands to form a ball. Pinch one side of the ball to taper it into a strawberry shape. Repeat with the rest of the red mixture to make a total of 6 strawberries.

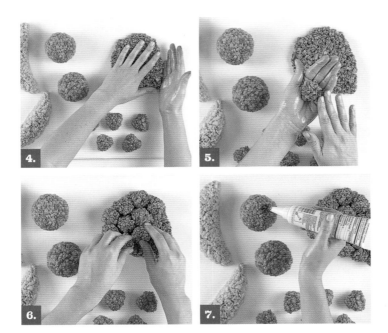

4. Mix the purple F batch recipe and pour half of the mixture onto the parchment-covered template on the work surface. Use both hands to spread the mixture over template 2 (grapes), smoothing until the mixture begins to firm and the top surface is flat. **5.** Using a small handful of the remaining mixture at a time, roll the mixture between your hands to form small balls. **6.** Press the small balls into the flat purple treat to form a bunch of grapes, as shown. **7.** Using dark green icing with a star tip, draw small stems on the oranges by squeezing a small amount of icing directly on top of the treats.

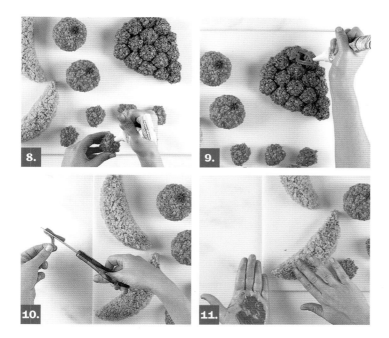

8. Using light green icing with a star tip, draw small stems on the strawberries using the same method as in Step 7. **9.** Using light green icing with a round tip, draw the leaf and vine design on the grapes, as shown. **10.** Use scissors to cut a quarter inch off the green Twizzler and then cut this piece lengthwise to form the stem of the grapes. Affix the stem to the grapes with additional light green icing. **11.** Squeeze a small amount of brown icing and a small amount of gold sparkle gel into your palm and mix them together using your finger. Use your fingers to add the mixed brown icing to the bananas, as shown.

Gift Box

You know how you buy a kid a gift and they only want to play with the box? This is kind of the same thing, only the gift *is* the box. This sweet treat can be modified using different food coloring and icing colors for any occasion.

MAKES 1 BOX, 9 BY 9 INCHES

TREAT RECIPE
(see page 6)
1 C batch, 5 drops turquoise and
5 drops white food coloring

DECORATING ICING
White

EQUIPMENT
Gift Box template (see page 10)
Parchment paper
Cooking spray
Round icing tip

1. Mix the C batch recipe and pour the mixture onto the parchment-covered template on the work surface. Generously coat your hands with cooking spray. Use both hands to form the mixture over the template, smoothing the edges until the mixture begins to firm up and the top surface is flat. **2.** Using white icing with a round tip, draw and fill in a slim rectangle across the height of the template to form the base of the ribbon. Next, draw and fill in a slim rectangle across the width of the template to complete the ribbon. **3.** Using white icing with a round tip, draw and fill in the bow on the center of the treat where the ribbon intersects. Lastly, draw and fill in the tails of the bow and add definition, as shown.

Gingerbread Man

Run, run, as fast as you—*UH-OH*. This little dude definitely didn't run fast enough! Decorate your gingerbread man (or woman!) in your favorite colors—no need to stick to traditional holiday shades (or gender roles).

MAKES 1 GINGERBREAD MAN, 12 INCHES TALL

TREAT RECIPE
(see page 6)
1 C batch, brown food coloring

SPECIAL INGREDIENTS
2 black M&M's
3 red M&M's

DECORATING ICING
Black
Red
Green
White

EQUIPMENT
Gingerbread Man template
   (see page 10)
Parchment paper
Cooking spray
Round icing tip

1. Mix the C batch recipe and pour the mixture onto the parchment-covered template on the work surface. Generously coat your hands with cooking spray. Use both hands to form the mixture over the template, smoothing the edges until the mixture begins to firm up. **2.** Using black icing with a round tip, draw two dots for the eyes of the gingerbread man. Press two black M&M's on the icing dots to form eyes. **3.** Using red icing with a round tip, draw a smile.

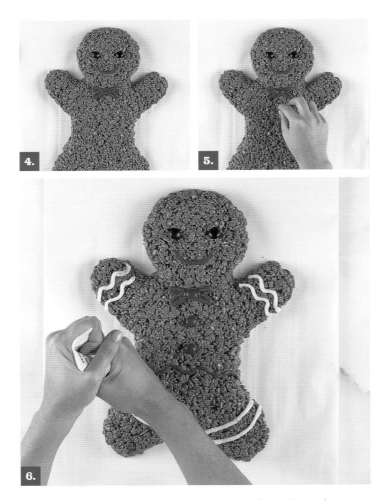

4. Using green icing with a round tip, draw a bow tie, as shown.
5. Using red icing with a round tip, draw one dot in the center of the bow tie and two dots below in a straight line. Press red M&M's on each icing dot to make the buttons. **6.** Using green and white icings with round tips, draw the additional decorative details (belt, sleeves, etc.), as shown.

Golden Retriever

Dogs are my favorite people. I say hello to every dog I see on the street and truly wish it wasn't frowned upon to enter dog parks without a canine companion. I'm not alone in loving dogs; the most popular order requests at Misterkrisp are edible dog portraits. I spend half of my time cooing over the inspiration photos of customers' dogs. This one is modeled after my family dog, Posey. I didn't think she could get any sweeter until I made her into a treat!

You can make a portrait of your own dog by customizing your food coloring and using a reference image while you mold. The steps are the same for every dog—mold the snout and eye depressions, then add the ears, brows, and details. For inspiration images for crispy treats of more breeds, go to misterkrisp.com/dogs.

MAKES 1 DOG PORTRAIT, 12 INCHES TALL

TREAT RECIPE
(see page 6)
1 C batch, no food coloring

SPECIAL INGREDIENTS
2 black M&M's

DECORATING ICING
Black
Pink

SPARKLE GEL
Black
Pink

EQUIPMENT
Reference photo of the dog subject
Golden Retriever template
  (see page 10)
Parchment paper
Cooking spray
Round icing tip

1. Place your reference photo next to your work surface. Mix the C batch recipe and pour 80 percent of the mixture onto the parchment-covered template on the work surface. Generously coat your hands with cooking spray. Fill section 1 of the template, using both hands to create a raised snout and depressed eye sockets, as shown. **2.** Take two large handfuls of the mixture and mold them into section 2 of the template to form the ears, making sure to press the mixture into section 1 to adhere the edges. **3.** Use a small amount of the mixture to form two slightly raised eyebrows, as shown.

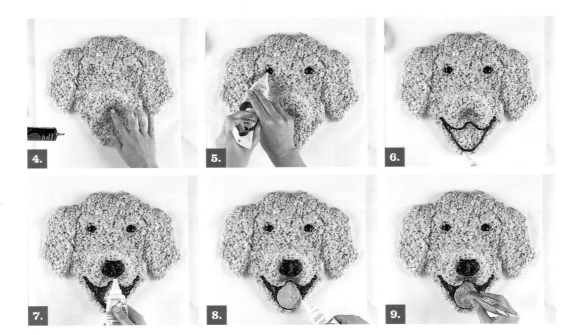

4. Using black sparkle gel, draw a small dot in the nose area and use your finger to spread the gel in the depression, as shown. **5.** Using black icing with a round tip, draw two dots in the eye sockets. Press black M&M's on the icing dots to form the eyes of the dog. **6.** Using black icing with a round tip, draw the outline of the mouth, as shown. **7.** Using black icing with a round tip, fill in the mouth (leaving space for the tongue, as shown) and nose. **8.** Using pink icing with a round tip, fill in the tongue. **9.** Using pink sparkle gel, draw a vertical line down the length of the tongue for definition.

Goldfish Bowl

This goldfish treat is even more low-maintenance than an actual goldfish, which is pretty low-maintenance. It's a fun way to enjoy pet ownership without the commitment of caring for a living thing.

MAKES 1 BOWL, 10 INCHES IN DIAMETER

TREAT RECIPE
(see page 6)
1 C batch, white food coloring

SPECIAL INGREDIENTS
Purple Celebration Candy Crumble
Blue Celebration Candy Crumble

DECORATING ICING
Purple
Green
Orange
White

SPARKLE GEL
Light green
Yellow
Black
Light blue

EQUIPMENT
Goldfish Bowl template
   (see page 10)
Parchment paper
Cooking spray
Round icing tip

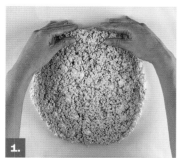  

1. In a small bowl, mix together 2 tablespoons of the purple candy crumble and 2 tablespoons of the blue candy crumble. Mix the C batch recipe, and pour the mixture onto the parchment-covered template on the work surface. Generously coat your hands with cooking spray. Use both hands to form the mixture over the template, rounding the surface and smoothing the edges until the mixture begins to firm up. **2.** Using purple icing with a round tip, draw the bottom of the fishbowl, as shown. **3.** Using your fingers, adhere the mixed candy bits to the purple icing.

4. Using green icing with a round tip, draw the plant, as shown. Add details to the plant with light green sparkle gel. **5.** Using orange icing with a round tip, draw the shape of the goldfish and fill in, as shown. Add fins and scales to the goldfish with yellow sparkle gel. **6.** Using white icing with a round tip, draw a dot to make the eye of the goldfish. Top the white dot of icing with a dot of black sparkle gel to complete the eye. **7.** Using white icing with a round tip, draw a series of dots coming out of the goldfish's mouth, as shown. **8.** Using light blue sparkle gel, outline the white dots of icing to form the bubbles.

Golf Hole

A lot of people love golf, but it's too slow for me. I don't have a lot of patience, which is why I make crispy treats instead of cakes (which require baking time *and* cooling time.) The incredible number of orders I get for this golf course treat, though, indicates there is signicant common ground to be found between golf enthusiasts and lovers of crispy rice treats. Tee up this dish for the golf fanatic in your life. For Father's Day, Mother's Day, or a birthday, it'll be a hole in one.

MAKES 1 PATCH OF GREEN, 14 BY 9 INCHES

TREAT RECIPES
(see page 6)
1 C batch, green food coloring
1 H batch, white food coloring

SPECIAL INGREDIENTS
Silver food spray

DECORATING ICING
Black

SPARKLE GEL
Black

EQUIPMENT
Golf Hole template
    (see page 10)
Parchment paper
Cooking spray
Star icing tip

1. Mix the C batch recipe and pour the mixture onto the parchment-covered template on the work surface. Generously coat your hands with cooking spray. Use both hands to form the mixture over the template, creating an empty circle for the golf hole and smoothing the edges until the mixture begins to firm up. **2.** Mix the H batch recipe and wait until the mixture firms up slightly, 1 to 2 minutes. Mold one handful of the mixture into a ball and place it next to the hole, as shown. (You can use a dot of icing to adhere it, if necessary.) **3.** On a separate parchment-covered surface, use another handful of the mixture to form the head of the golf club, as shown.

4. Using silver food spray, coat the head of the golf club. 5. Place the head of the golf club on top of the treat in the bottom left-hand corner, as shown. 6. Using black icing with a star tip, draw the shaft of the golf club, as shown. 7. Using black sparkle gel, draw horizontal lines on the head to form the face of the golf club, as shown.

Graduation Cap

They did it! What better way to sweeten the transition between the blissful life of a student and the crushing responsibility of the real world than to enjoy this yummy treat? Use food coloring to match the colors of your graduate's alma mater.

MAKES 1 GRADUATION CAP, 9 BY 9 INCHES

TREAT RECIPE
(see page 6)
1 C batch, black food coloring

DECORATING ICING
White
Yellow

EQUIPMENT
Graduation Cap template
    (see page 10)
Parchment paper
Cooking spray
Round icing tip
Cake board (or other
    serving surface)

1. Mix the C batch recipe and pour the mixture onto the parchment-covered template on the work surface. Generously coat your hands with cooking spray. Use both hands to form the mixture over the template, smoothing the edges until the mixture begins to firm up. **2.** Using white icing with a round tip, draw the outline detail, as shown. **3.** After 1 hour, carefully remove the treat from the parchment and place it on a cardboard serving platter. Using yellow icing with a round tip, draw the tassel detail, as shown.

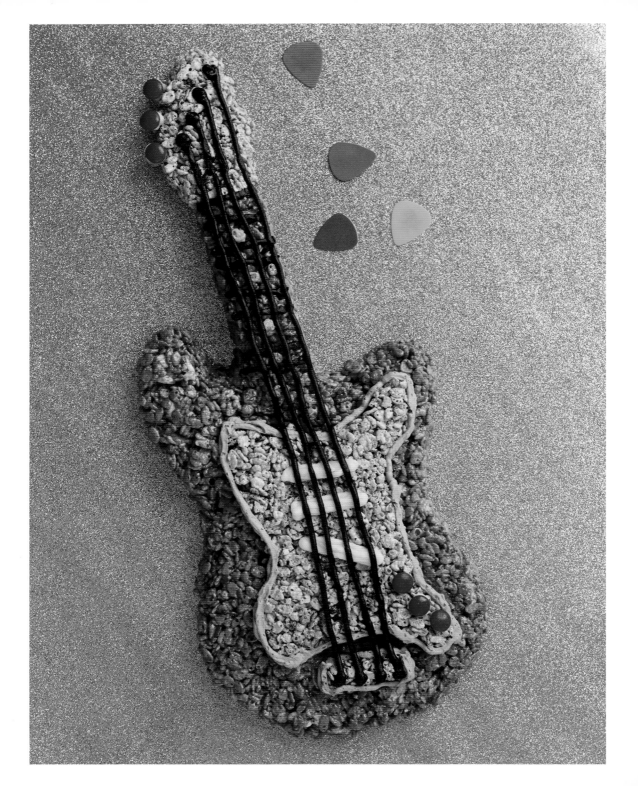

Guitar

Unlike what happens when you bring a regular guitar to a party, this crispy guitar will induce silence as everyone's mouths fill up with crunchy goodness. I make a lot of guitars for birthday parties celebrating music lovers and musicians alike. If you were wondering, which I already know you weren't, my favorite guitarist is Trey Anastasio. (And I'm thrilled that I was able to work a Phish reference into this book.)

MAKES 1 GUITAR, 13 INCHES LONG

TREAT RECIPES
(see page 6)
1 C batch, purple food coloring
1 E batch, 9 drops white and
    1 drop black food coloring

SPECIAL INGREDIENTS
1 can white icing
Black food coloring
6 red M&M's

DECORATING ICING
White
Black

EQUIPMENT
Guitar template
    (see page 10)
Parchment paper
OodleTip piping bag
    (*Note:* If you do not
    have access to OodleTips,
    fill the corner of a zip-top
    bag and cut a small hole
    in corner.)
Cooking spray
Round icing tips
    (small and medium)

1. Measure 2 cups of white canned icing and add 1 drop of black food coloring. Mix the icing until the gray color is evenly distributed. Fill the OodleTip bag and set it aside. Then mix the C batch recipe and pour the mixture onto the parchment-covered template on the work surface. Generously coat your hands with cooking spray. Fill section 1 of the template. Use both hands to shape the mixture until the top surface is flat and it begins to firm up. **2.** Mix the E batch recipe. Take one large handful and form the body detail of the guitar, as shown. **3.** Take a second large handful and form the handle of the guitar, as shown.

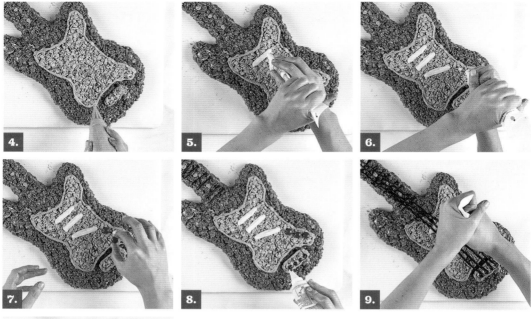

4. Using the gray icing from the OodleTip bag, draw dots down the handle and outline the gray body details of the guitar, as shown. **5.** Using white icing with a medium-size round tip, draw the pickups of the guitar. **6.** Still using white icing with a medium round tip, draw three dots on the lower right side of the pickups, as shown. **7.** Adhere three red M&M's to the dots of white icing. **8.** Using black icing with a small round tip, draw horizontal frets on the neck of the guitar and dots in the lower body detail, as shown. **9.** Using black icing with a small round tip, draw vertical strings along the neck of the guitar, connecting the head to the lower body detail, as shown. **10.** Using white decorating icing with a medium-size round tip, draw three dots on the left side of the head of the guitar. Adhere three red M&M's to the dots of white icing.

Gumball Machine

My dentist said I'm not allowed to chew gum anymore, but he didn't say anything about treats that look like gum. This colorful and nostalgic treat is as fun to make as it is to eat. I love placing the multicolored candy melt "gumballs" just as much as I love eating them shortly after!

MAKES 1 GUMBALL MACHINE, 15 INCHES TALL

TREAT RECIPES
(see page 6)
1 E batch, white food coloring
1 D batch, red food coloring

SPECIAL INGREDIENTS
1 can white icing
Black food coloring
Candy melts in yellow, pink, blue, purple, orange, white, and green

DECORATING ICING
White

EQUIPMENT:
Gumball Machine template (see page 10)
Parchment paper
OodleTip piping bag (*Note:* If you do not have access to OodleTips, fill the corner of a zip-top bag and cut a small hole in corner.)
Cooking spray
Round icing tip

1. Measure 2 cups of white canned icing into a small bowl and add 1 drop of black food coloring. Mix the icing until the gray color is evenly distributed. Fill the OodleTip bag and set aside. Mix the E batch recipe, and pour the mixture onto the parchment-covered template on the work surface. Generously coat your hands with cooking spray. Use both hands to mold it over section 1 of the template and form a dome shape, smoothing the edges until the mixture begins to firm up.
2. Mix the D batch and, one large handful at a time, fill section 2 of the template, making sure to press the mixture into section 1 to adhere the edges. **3.** Fill section 3 of the template with the remainder of the red mixture. Use both hands to form the shape, smoothing the edges until the mixture begins to firm up.

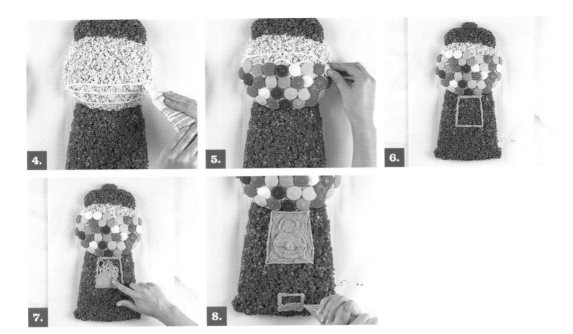

4. Using white icing with a round tip, draw horizontal lines across three-fourths of section 1 of the template, as shown. 5. Adhere the candy melts to the horizontal lines of icing, as shown. 6. Using gray icing, draw a rectangular box to form the coin slot and dial of the gumball machine, as shown. 7. Using gray icing, fill in the rectangular box and smooth it out with your fingers to make a flat surface. 8. Using gray icing, draw the coin slot, dial, and gumball slot, as shown.

TREAT YOURSELF!

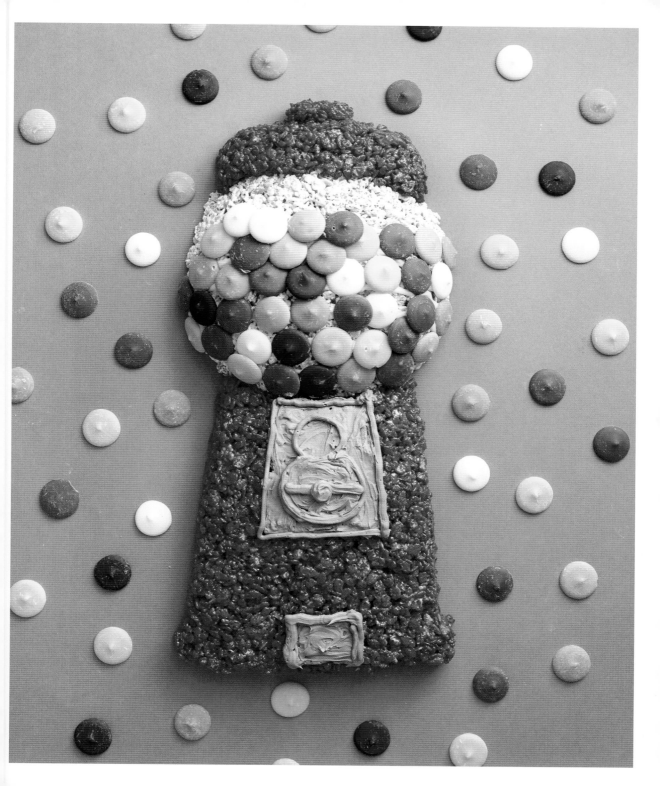

Hot Dogs

These mini hot dogs are always a hit at BBQs and other summer gatherings. They're snack-size and adorable, making for a fantastic single-serving treat. I also think they're hilarious and laugh every time I make them. (I'm easily amused.)

MAKES 12–14 MINI HOT DOGS WITH BUNS, EACH 4 INCHES LONG

TREAT RECIPES
(see page 6)
**1 E batch, 4 drops brown and
    4 drops red food coloring**
1 D batch, yellow food coloring

DECORATING ICING
Yellow
Red

EQUIPMENT
Parchment paper
Cooking spray
Round icing tip

1. Mix the E batch recipe and allow the mixture to cool for 2 minutes. Generously coat your hands with cooking spray. Then, one small handful at a time, use both hands to roll the mixture into a hot dog shape, about 4 inches long, and place it on the parchment-covered work surface. Repeat 11 times and place the hot dogs in the freezer for 10 minutes. **2.** Mix the D batch recipe and, taking one large handful, flatten it into a disk, about 3½ inches in diameter. **3.** Place one hot dog in the center of the disk.

4. Use both hands to curve the edges of the disk around the hot dog and press together to form the bun. **5.** Place the treat on its side and repeat Steps 2–4 with the remaining hot dogs. **6.** Using yellow and red icing with small round tips, draw the mustard and ketchup squiggles along the top of each hot dog, as shown. Return the treats to the work surface and allow to set for at least 1 hour before serving.

Ice Cream Cones

Okay, seriously. How cute are these? These handheld treats are dessert overload: Are they ice cream? Are they crispy treats? IDK, but I don't care as long as they taste good. Besides being incredibly easy to make, the store-bought cones make them easy to eat without getting your hands sticky. Customize these treats with colorful sprinkles, food coloring, or even flavored extracts—I love mixing mint extract, green food coloring, and chocolate sprinkles to make mint chip, or using chocolate rice cereal, crushed almonds, and a few extra mini marshmallows mixed in later to make Rocky Road!

MAKES 12 ICE CREAM CONES

TREAT RECIPE
(see page 6)
1 C batch, pink food coloring

SPECIAL INGREDIENTS
Cooking spray
**12 wafer ice cream cones
    (flat-bottomed)**
Round rainbow sprinkles

1. Mix the C batch recipe. Generously coat your hands with cooking spray and press a small amount of mixture into each of the cones, filling them to the top. **2.** Taking one small handful, mold one flat circular patty slightly larger than the tops of the cones. **3.** Press the patty on the top of one of the cones.

4. Take one handful of the mixture and mold it into a ball. **5.** Press the ball on top of the patty shape on top of the cone, and place the cone standing up on the work surface. **6.** Repeat Steps 2–5 for the remaining 11 cones. Pour a handful of sprinkles into a bowl and, one at a time, gently press each cone into the sprinkles until they stick.

Ice Pop

I invented an ice pop that doesn't melt so I'm probably going to be rich, right? No?! Okay. This pretty treat is a nice addition to any summer gathering, although you could also make it in the winter as a reminder of sunnier days without the risk of getting too cold while eating it.

MAKES 1 BAR, 14 INCHES TALL

TREAT RECIPES
(see page 6)
1 G batch, no food coloring
1 C batch, white food coloring
1 E batch, 3 drops white and
   3 drops orange food coloring

EQUIPMENT
Ice Pop template (see page 10)
Parchment paper
Cooking spray

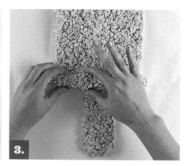

1. Mix the G batch recipe and pour the mixture onto the parchment-covered template on the work surface. Generously coat your hands with cooking spray. Use both hands to mold the mixture over section 1 of the template, smoothing the edges and flattening the surface until the mixture begins to firm up. **2.** Mix the C batch and pour the mixture over section 2 of the template. Use both hands to mold the mixture, smoothing the edges and flattening the surface until the mixture begins to firm up. **3.** Mold a slightly raised section along the bottom of section 2 to create a raised lip.

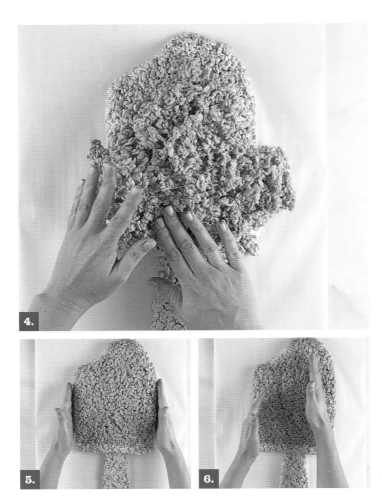

4. Mix the E batch recipe and pour the mixture onto section 2 of the template, pressing it gently to cover the white mixture.
5. Make sure this layer is flush with the raised lip in Step 3, leaving the lip exposed, and that the top left "bite" area is also exposed.
6. Use the side of your hand to create two parallel depression lines, as shown.

Laptop

When I'm not in my kitchen making treats, I'm at my computer writing essays. It only felt appropriate to include a delicious representation of what I'm looking at half the time—a blank computer screen (writer's block is real, people). This treat is a thoughtful gift for not only writers but pretty much any computer geek in your life (which nowadays means everyone).

MAKES 1 LAPTOP, 10 BY 14 INCHES

TREAT RECIPE
(see page 6)
1 C batch, 8 drops white and
    2 drops black food coloring

DECORATING ICING
White
Black

SPARKLE GEL
Light blue

EQUIPMENT
Laptop template (see page 10)
Parchment paper
Cooking spray
Round icing tip
Small icing tube
Silicone spatula (optional)

1. Mix the C batch recipe and pour the mixture onto the parchment-covered template on the work surface. Generously coat your hands with cooking spray. Use both hands to mold the mixture over the template, smoothing the edges until the mixture begins to firm up. **2.** Using white icing with a round tip, draw the outline of a rectangle on the top portion of the treat for the laptop screen. **3.** Fill in the rectangle with white icing and use your fingers or a spatula to spread it evenly.

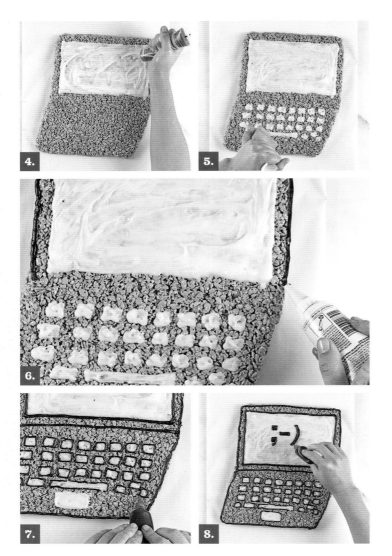

4. Squeeze a small amount of light blue sparkle gel onto the white icing and use your fingers to spread it over the white. **5.** Using white icing with a round tip, draw a series of squares and rectangles arranged so they look like a laptop keyboard. **6.** Using black icing with a round tip, draw an outline along the edge of the entire laptop and an outline around the screen, then draw a line separating the screen and the keyboard. **7.** Fill the small icing tube with black icing and draw an outline around each of the keyboard keys. **8.** To complete the treat, continue using the small icing tube with black icing to draw a semicolon, hyphen, and close parenthesis on the screen to form an emoticon.

Lemonade

There's an old proverb that goes "when life gives you crispies, make lemonade." Okay, maybe that's not *exactly* how it goes, but making lemonade is always a good idea. A lovely addition to any summer gathering, this treat will bring some extra sugar to bridal/baby showers or luncheons, and will raise the bar at your everyday neighborhood lemonade stand.

MAKES 1 GLASS OF LEMONADE, 12 INCHES TALL

TREAT RECIPE (see page 6)
1 C batch, white food coloring

DECORATING ICING
Yellow, 2 tubes
White
Pink
Black

SPARKLE GEL
Yellow

EQUIPMENT
Lemonade template (see page 10)
Parchment paper
Cooking spray
Round icing tips
Small spatula (optional for spreading icing)
Small icing tube

1. Mix the C batch recipe and pour the mixture onto the parchment-covered template on the work surface. Generously coat your hands with cooking spray. Reserve three handfuls of the mixture and place them back in the pot. Use both hands to mold the mixture over section 1 of the template, smoothing the edges until the mixture begins to firm up. **2.** Remove the reserved handfuls of the mixture from the pot and place them, one handful at a time, over sections 2 and 3 of the template. **3.** Using yellow icing with a round tip, outline the lemonade in the cup, as shown. Then fill in the outline by drawing one horizontal line at a time or, alternatively, drawing squiggles and using a spreading spatula or your fingers to spread the icing evenly.

4. Using white icing with a round tip, outline and fill in the lemon slice center. **5.** Squeeze a small amount of yellow sparkle gel, over the white area on the lemon and use your fingers to spread it evenly. **6.** Using yellow icing with a small round tip, outline the lemon rind.

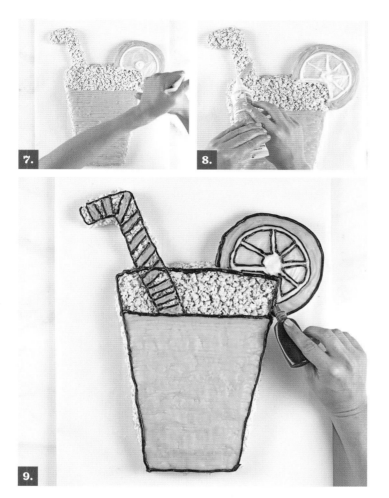

7. Using white icing with a round tip, draw lines extending out from the center of the lemon slice, for the segments. **8.** Using pink icing with a round tip, draw parallel diagonal stripes on the straw, making sure to extend the detail all the way down to the yellow section (the lemonade). **9.** Fill the small icing tube with black icing. Using black icing with both a round tip and the small icing tube where necessary, outline each element of the treat: glass, straw, stripes, lemon, and lemon segments.

Letters

By far the most versatile treat in this book, you can customize these irresistible letters to spell out a name, a catchphrase, or even the entire alphabet (although you'd be very full if you ate all that). I chose "OMG" because it's my go-to response when something leaves me speechless, as a book of artful and bizarre crispy rice treat recipes probably would if I hadn't written it.

**MAKES 3 LETTERS
(9 BY 17 INCHES OVERALL
WHEN SQUEEZED TOGETHER)**

TREAT RECIPES
(see page 6)
1 E batch, pink food coloring (or your choice of color)
1 E batch, orange food coloring (or your choice of color)
1 E batch, lime green food coloring (or your choice of color)
(*Note:* Use 1 C batch in a color of your choice for a single cake-size letter.)

EQUIPMENT
Letters templates (see page 10) (*Note:* Enlarge any template in order to make a single cake-size letter, 10 by 16 inches.)
Parchment paper
Cooking spray

1. Mix the pink E batch recipe and pour the mixture onto the parchment-covered template on the work surface. Generously coat your hands with cooking spray. Use both hands to mold the mixture over the template, smoothing the edges until the mixture begins to firm up. **2.** Mix the orange E batch recipe, and repeat Step 1, making sure that the letter template is arranged close to the one from Step 1. **3.** Mix the lime green E batch recipe, and repeat Step 1, making sure that the letter template is arranged close to the one from Step 2. **4.** Once your letter arrangement is complete, make small adjustments to ensure the letters work together as you intended (initials, name, words, etc.).

Lips

This incredibly easy design makes a sweet Valentine's Day gift or a thoughtful birthday treat for the beauty-obsessed person in your life.

MAKES 1 PAIR OF LIPS, 13 INCHES WIDE

TREAT RECIPE
(see page 6)
1 C batch, red food coloring

EQUIPMENT
Lips template (see page 10)
Parchment paper
Cooking spray
Knife

1. Mix the C batch recipe, and pour the mixture onto the parchment-covered template on the work surface. Generously coat your hands with cooking spray. **2.** Use both hands to mold the mixture over the template, smoothing the edges until the mixture begins to firm up. Sculpt the surface of the treat so that it's slightly rounded, and create a grooved depression horizontally across the center. **3.** Use a sharp knife to press down gently along the groove to further define the separation between the two lips without cutting through the treat.

Lobster

A muuuch cheaper alternative to real lobsters, this dessert brings whimsy to casual summer clambakes and fancy dinners alike. No need for melted butter on the side, though—this one has enough built in! And, you're not exactly lying when you invite a love interest to "come over. I'm making lobster. . . ."

MAKES 1 LOBSTER, 12 INCHES LONG

TREAT RECIPE
(see page 6)
1 C batch, red food coloring

SPECIAL INGREDIENTS
Red Twizzler

DECORATING ICING
Red
Black

EQUIPMENT
Lobster template (see page 10)
Parchment paper
Cooking spray
Scissors
Round icing tips

1. Mix the C batch recipe and pour about 70 percent of the mixture onto the parchment-covered template on the work surface, reserving the rest in the pot. Generously coat your hands with cooking spray. Use both hands to mold the mixture over section 1 of the template, smoothing the edges and rounding the surface until the mixture begins to firm up. **2.** Retrieve one handful from the reserved mixture to mold the lobster tail in section 2 of the template. **3.** Take another small handful of the mixture, and roll it between your hands to form 2 long thin pieces for the front claw shafts.

4. Press each front claw shaft to adhere it to the body (you can use icing if necessary). Divide another small handful of the mixture in half to form pincers. **5.** Press the pincers firmly onto the ends of the front claw shafts. **6.** Using one small handful of the mixture at a time, roll additional claw shafts as in Step 3. Make sure to press them onto the body before bending the ends. **7.** Continue rolling and attaching claw shafts until there are 10, including the ones with pincers.

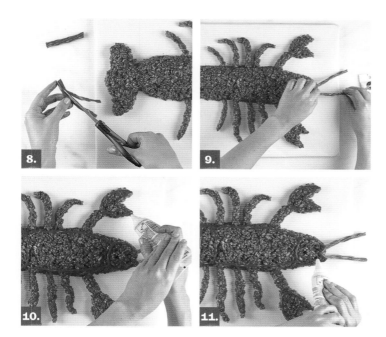

8. Use scissors to cut the Twizzler in half and then lengthwise to make 4 pieces. Use two pieces for the lobster antennae. **9.** Using red icing with a round tip, "glue" the antennae to the head of the lobster. **10.** Still using red icing with a round tip, outline the front claws, head, body, and tail. **11.** Use black icing with a round tip to draw 2 small dots for eyes.

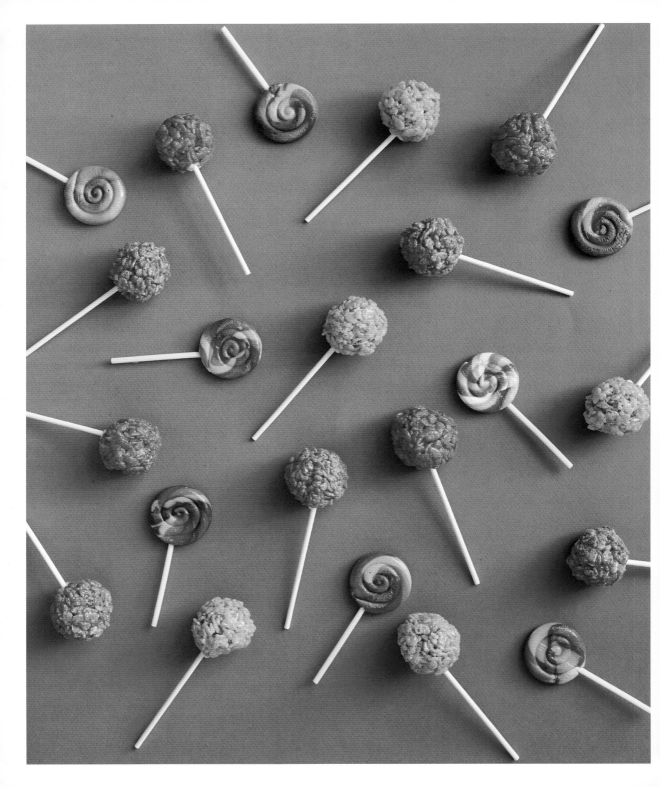

Lollipops

It is an (unproven) scientific fact that everything tastes better on a stick. These bite-size lollipops are no exception. I use melted chocolate only to adhere the sticks to the treats, but feel free to dip the entire pop (or just half) in chocolate!

MAKES 8 LOLLIPOPS

TREAT RECIPE
(see page 6)
1 E batch, your choice of food coloring (or, to make multiple colors, as shown, mix 3 E batches one at a time)*

SPECIAL INGREDIENTS
White (or your choice) candy melts or melting chocolate

EQUIPMENT
Parchment paper
Cooking spray
8 lollipop sticks

Note: **Although more than 8 lollipops are shown here, don't try to double or triple this recipe; the mixture will harden before you can form all of it into balls!**

1. Mix the E batch recipe. Coat your hands with cooking spray. Using one very small handful at a time, mold the mixture to form a ball about 1½ inches in diameter and place it on the parchment-covered work surface. **2.** Repeat until all of the mixture has been used. **3.** In a microwave-safe bowl, melt candy melts or chocolate per the instructions on the packaging. One at a time, push a lollipop stick into each ball and remove it to make a hole. **4.** Dip a lollipop stick into the candy melts, and insert it firmly into the hole in one of the balls. **5.** Repeat until all the sticks and balls have been paired.

Masterpiece

Do you like this piece of art I designed myself with absolutely no outside inspiration? Okay fine, I may have been a teensy bit inspired by that Van Gogh guy. *Starry Night* has always been one of my favorite paintings to visit at the MoMA in New York City, so I decided to make my own (edible) version. Though this design is definitely the most detailed in this book, most of the technique is actually just like finger painting, but with icing.

MAKES 1 PAINTING, 12 BY 18 INCHES

TREAT RECIPES
(see page 6)
1 B batch, blue food
   coloring
1 G batch, black food
   coloring

**DECORATING
ICING**
Blue
Yellow
White
Brown
Black

SPARKLE GEL
Yellow
Dark blue
Black
White
Light blue
Gold

EQUIPMENT
Parchment paper
Cooking spray
Round icing tips

1. Mix the B batch recipe and pour the mixture onto the parchment-covered work surface. Generously coat your hands with cooking spray. Use both hands to mold the mixture into a rectangle, approximately 12 by 18 inches, smoothing the edges until the mixture begins to firm up. **2.** Using blue icing with a round tip, draw the horizon line as shown. **3.** Using yellow icing with a round tip, draw the moon and stars, as shown. Smudge the icing at the edges of the shapes with your fingertips.

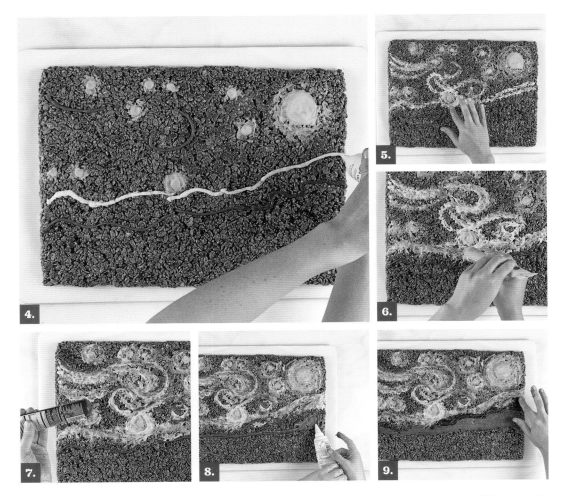

4. Using the blue icing with a round tip, draw the horizon line. Then, using white icing with a round tip, draw the cloud line. **5.** Still using the white icing, draw the swirls surrounding the stars. Use your fingertips to smudge the icing at the edges of the lines. **6.** Line the horizon line with yellow sparkle gel and blend using your fingertips. **7.** Using dark blue sparkle gel, line the white swirls. **8.** Using blue icing with a round tip, draw and fill in the mountain line above the horizon line and spread the color evenly with your fingertips. **9.** Using black sparkle gel, fill in the top portion of the mountain line.

TREAT YOURSELF!

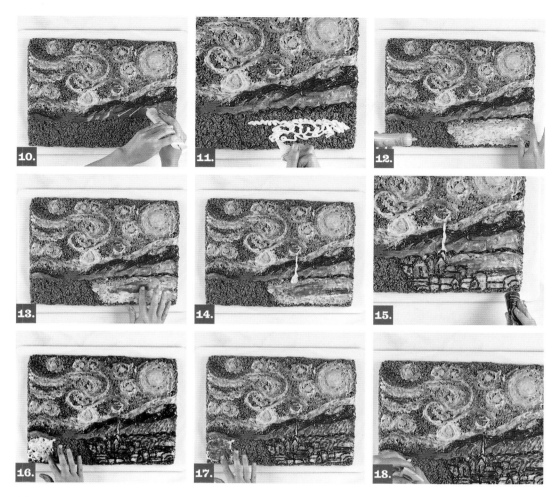

10. Using white sparkle gel, shade the blue portion of the mountain line and spread the color evenly with your fingertips. **11.** Using white icing with a round tip, fill in the city area and spread the color evenly with your fingertips. **12.** Using yellow sparkle gel, shade the city area and spread the colors evenly with your fingertips. **13.** Repeat Step 12 with the light blue and dark blue sparkle gels. **14.** Using the white icing with a round tip, draw the spire. **15.** Using black sparkle gel, draw the houses, as shown, and outline the spire. **16.** Using white icing with a round tip, fill in the lower left corner and spread the color evenly with your fingertips. **17.** Using dark blue sparkle gel, layer over the white in the lower left corner. **18.** Using yellow sparkle gel, add accents to the lower left corner.

19. Mix the G batch recipe and, one handful at a time, mold the tree shape in the foreground. **20.** Form the tree firmly over the icing on top of the treat. **21.** Using the gold and the dark blue sparkle gel, add dimension to the tree, spreading the color evenly with your fingertips. **22.** Squeeze just a dab of the brown icing onto your fingers and shade the tree further. **23.** Using the black icing with a round tip, draw an outline around the tree.

Menorah

Let's be real—it's hard to think of eight gifts for anyone; cross one off by making this sweet treat for one of the nights of the Festival of Lights. The licorice candles add festive color, and you can fill in the flames to indicate which night of Hanukkah you're celebrating.

**MAKES 1 MENORAH,
12 INCHES TALL**

TREAT RECIPE
(see page 6)
1 C batch, 8 drops white
    and 2 drops black food
    coloring

SPECIAL INGREDIENTS
Rainbow Twizzlers

DECORATING ICING
White

SPARKLE GEL
Yellow
Orange

EQUIPMENT
Menorah template
    (see page 10)
Parchment paper
Cooking spray
Cake board (or other
    serving surface)
Scissors
Round icing tips

1. Mix the C batch recipe. Generously coat your hands with cooking spray and, using one large handful at a time, mold the mixture over the parchment-covered template on the work surface, starting with the central shaft of the candleholder, and smoothing the edges until the mixture begins to firm up. **2.** Using another handful of the mixture, mold the base. **3.** Adding one handful of the mixture at a time, mold the remaining 8 candlesticks, working out from the center.

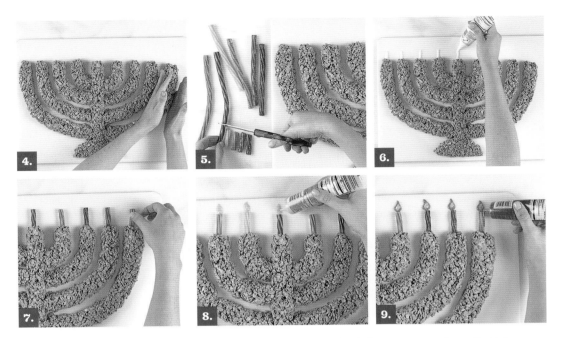

4. When all 9 candlesticks are complete, take a moment to check for evenness of candlestick thickness and adjust or smooth any edges. Using the instructions on page 10, remove the treat from the template and adhere it to a cardboard cake board or serving surface. **5.** Use scissors to cut the rainbow Twizzlers into 2-inch pieces. **6.** Using white icing with a round tip, draw 2-inch vertical lines at the top of each candlestick, where you will place the Twizzler candles. **7.** Place one Twizzler piece over each line of icing. **8.** Using yellow sparkle gel, draw flames above each candle (or fewer, depending on which night of Hanukkah you're celebrating). **9.** Outline each flame with orange sparkle gel.

Monkey

Confession: I didn't actually write this book. What I *did* do was make a hundred monkey crispy rice treats and left them in a room with a typewriter for a month. Not too shabby, right?

Pair this monkey treat with some banana-shaped treats (see page 125) for a fun jungle-themed celebration. *Note:* Double the undyed E batch recipe, mold little monkey hands over its eyes, and you've got a treat to celebrate one of everyone's favorite emojis.

For a variation, use cocoa-flavored cereal and leave out the food coloring!

MAKES 1 MONKEY FACE, 10 INCHES ACROSS

TREAT RECIPES
(see page 6)
1 C batch, brown food coloring
1 E batch, no food coloring

DECORATING ICING
Black

SPARKLE GEL
White

EQUIPMENT
Monkey template (see page 10)
Parchment paper
Cooking spray
Round icing tip

1. Mix the C batch recipe and pour the mixture onto the parchment-covered template on the work surface. Generously coat your hands with cooking spray and separate two small handfuls for the ears. **2.** Use both hands to mold the mixture over the template, smoothing the edges until the mixture begins to firm up. **3.** Mix the E batch recipe and pour the mixture over the face area of the brown mixture, reserving one large handful for the ears.

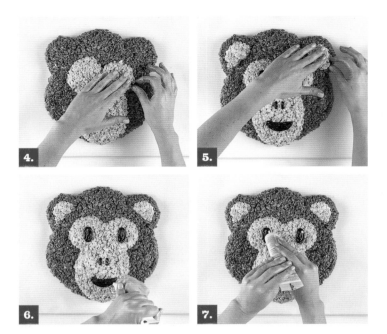

4. Mold the face in 3 parts, one handful at a time: the nose and mouth area, then each eye. 5. Using the remaining mixture, shape half-circles to fill the inside of both ears, as shown. 6. Using black icing with a round tip, draw the eyes, nose, and mouth, as shown. 7. Using white sparkle gel, draw a dot in the upper right of each eye, for highlights.

Movie Popcorn

I'm one of those people who head straight to the artificial butter machine the minute I have my popcorn at the movies. Then I pour Peanut M&M's into the bag and hope they melt a little for a salty and sweet surprise once the theater lights go out. *This* popcorn treat is a surprising addition to any movie night or Academy Awards party. The marshmallow "popcorn" is fun to munch on before moving on to the rest of the treat. Eat it alongside real popcorn for that perfect sweet/salty mix.

MAKES 1 TUB, 12 INCHES TALL

TREAT RECIPE
(see page 6)
1 C batch, white food coloring

SPECIAL INGREDIENTS
2 cups mini marshmallows

DECORATING ICING
White
Red

SPARKLE GEL
Gold

EQUIPMENT
Movie Popcorn template
    (see page 10)
Parchment paper
Cooking spray
Round icing tips
Petal icing tip
Star icing tip

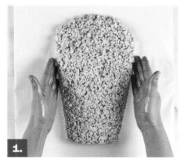  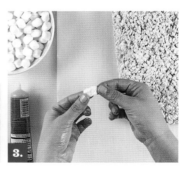

1. Mix the C batch recipe and pour the mixture onto the parchment-covered template on the work surface. Generously coat your hands with cooking spray. Use both hands to mold the mixture over the template, smoothing the edges and gently rounding the surface until the mixture begins to firm up. **2.** Using white icing with a round tip, outline and fill in the top portion of the treat (where the popcorn will be) with squiggles. **3.** Take one mini marshmallow at a time and gently tear it open, separating the edges to create "popcorn" pieces.

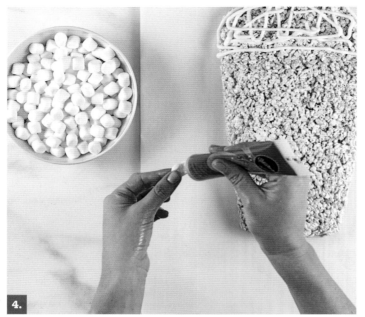

4. Using gold sparkle gel, squeeze a generous dot into the center of each popcorn piece, then place the pieces one at a time onto the iced section of the treat. Repeat until the top section is covered. **5.** Using red icing with a petal tip, draw vertical stripes on the lower section of the treat for the popcorn tub. **6.** Using white icing with a star tip, draw a horizontal line across the top of the tub to create the rim.

New Year's Hat

If you don't have a midnight kiss lined up, you'll definitely find one when you show up at a New Year's Eve party toting this celebratory treat. The countdown begins now! *Note:* A change of color makes for an easy transition to a leprechaun's hat for St. Paddy's day, Uncle Sam's red, white, and blue, or a magician's black top hat.

MAKES 1 HAT, 10 INCHES ACROSS

TREAT RECIPE
(see page 6)
1 C batch, 9 drops yellow and 1
   drop brown food coloring

SPECIAL INGREDIENTS
Gold food spray

DECORATING ICING
Black

EQUIPMENT
New Year's Hat
   template
   (see page 10)
Parchment paper
Cooking spray
Round icing tip

1. Mix the C batch recipe and pour the mixture onto the parchment-covered template on the work surface. Generously coat your hands with cooking spray. Use both hands to mold the mixture over the template, smoothing the edges until the mixture begins to firm up. **2.** Coat the treat with gold food spray. **3.** Using black icing with a round tip, draw the outline of the hat band and fill it in. **4.** Still using black icing with a round tip, write the *Happy New Year!* message.

Newspaper

EXTRA! EXTRA! Just kidding, there will be no extra; this treat will be gone faster than yesterday's news. Write your own headline to announce a special birthday, engagement, retirement, graduation, or any significant celebration.

MAKES 1 NEWSPAPER, 11 BY 9 INCHES

TREAT RECIPE
(see page 6)
1 C batch, white food coloring

SPECIAL INGREDIENTS
1 regular-size marshmallow

DECORATING ICING
Black

SPARKLE GEL
White

EQUIPMENT
Newspaper template
 (see page 10)
Parchment paper
Cooking spray
2 small icing tubes
Small round icing tips

1. Mix the C batch recipe and pour the mixture onto the parchment-covered template on the work surface. Generously coat your hands with cooking spray. Reserve one large handful and place it back in the pot. Use both hands to mold the mixture over section 1 of the template, smoothing the edges until the mixture begins to firm up. **2.** Remove the reserved handful of mixture from the pot and mold it over section 2 of the template, flattening it enough so that it remains at a lower elevation than the treat in section 1. **3.** Fill the small icing tube with black icing and write the name of the newspaper and draw a horizontal line separating it from the lower portion of the paper.

4. Write the main headline below the line, and draw additional text flourishes as desired. **5.** Use black icing with a round tip to outline and fill in a square picture box. **6.** Cut up a marshmallow to add details to the image—in this example, cut off one round end of the marshmallow, flatten it, and center it in the picture box for the moon. **7.** Fill a small icing tube with white sparkle gel and draw additional details on the front page image—in this example, add small stars around the moon. **8.** Fill a small icing tube with black icing and draw additional squiggles for the article text.

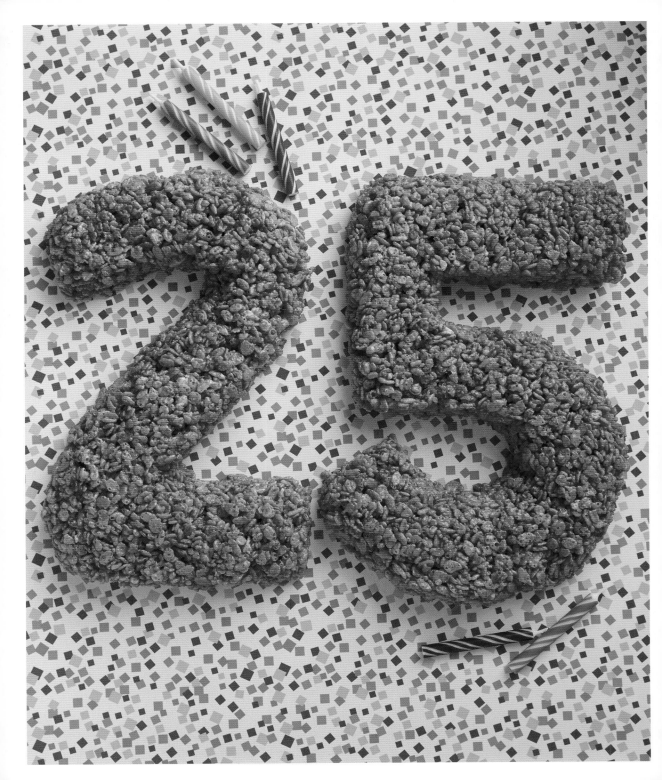

Numbers

Age is just a number, so why not snack on some digits to mark your next birthday celebration? Use these numbers to ring in the New Year, celebrate anniversaries or milestones, or guess the winning lotto numbers. Combine with the letters on page 167 and the opportunities to express yourself are endless!

MAKES 2 NUMERALS, EACH APPROXIMATELY 12 BY 8 INCHES

TREAT RECIPE
(see page 6)
1 C batch, your choice of food coloring

EQUIPMENT
Numbers template (see page 10)
Parchment paper
Cooking spray

1. Mix the C batch recipe and pour half the mixture onto the parchment-covered template on the work surface. Reserve the remaining mixture for the second numeral. Generously coat your hands with cooking spray. **2.** Use both hands to mold the mixture over the template, smoothing the edges until the mixture begins to firm up. **3.** Using the reserved mixture, repeat Step 2 for the second numeral. **4.** Once your number arrangement is complete, make small adjustments so that the numerals work together as you intended (age, date, anniversary number, etc.).

Paper Coffee Cup

Wake up and smell the crispies! Ideal when your team could use a caffeine-free (but sugar-filled) boost late in the day, this treat also pairs well with actual coffee.

MAKES 1 TAKEOUT CUP, 11 INCHES TALL

TREAT RECIPE
(see page 6)
1 C batch, blue food coloring

DECORATING ICING
White
Orange

EQUIPMENT
Paper Coffee Cup template (see page 10)
Parchment paper
Cooking spray
Round icing tip
Star icing tip
Small icing tube

1. Mix the C batch recipe and pour the mixture onto the parchment-covered template on the work surface. Generously coat your hands with cooking spray. Use both hands to mold the mixture over the template, smoothing the edges until the mixture begins to firm up. **2.** Using white icing with a round tip, draw a crest shape in the center of the cup, as shown. **3.** Fill in the outline with icing and use your fingers to spread it evenly. Then outline the shape again with white icing. **4.** Still using white icing with a round tip, create the geometric patterned border, as shown. **5.** Using white icing with a star tip, line the top and bottom of the cup. **6.** Fill the small icing tube with orange icing and draw coffee cup images with steam lines at the bottom of the white crest. Then write the words *We Are Happy To Serve You*, as shown.

Passover Seder Plate

Why is this treat different from all other treats? Though this sweet seder plate may not technically be kosher for Passover, it's the perfect dessert to enjoy when the holiday is over! Sidenote: My favorite Passover snacks are those toasted coconut-covered marshmallows. Shocking that I love marshmallows, right?

**MAKES 1 PLATE,
13 INCHES IN DIAMETER**

TREAT RECIPES
(see page 6)
1 C batch, white food coloring
1 H batch, brown food coloring

SPECIAL INGREDIENTS
1 green Airhead
(or 2 green mini Airheads)
Green Twizzlers
(or green Sour Punch Straws)
Gummi Watermelon Rings
Red M&M's

DECORATING ICING
Blue
White

SPARKLE GEL
Green
Red

EQUIPMENT
Passover Seder Plate template (see page 10)
Parchment paper
Cooking spray
Round icing tip
Scissors

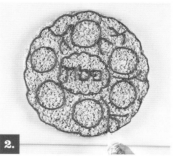

1. Mix the C batch recipe and pour the mixture onto the parchment-covered template on the work surface, reserving one handful in the pot. Generously coat your hands with cooking spray. Use both hands to mold the mixture over the template, smoothing the edges until the mixture begins to firm up. **2.** Using blue icing with a round tip, draw a slightly scalloped wavy line around the outside edge of the treat. Draw the additional plate details on the interior of the treat, as shown. Be sure to outline 7 sections, including the center. **3.** Remove the reserved handful of the mixture from the pot and mold it into a three-dimensional egg shape.

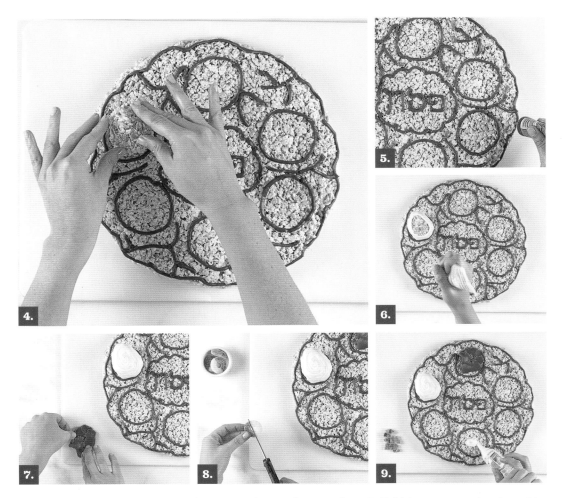

4. Place the egg on the plate as shown, gently pressing to adhere it. 5. Using green and red sparkle gels, draw additional plate details, as shown. 6. Using white icing with a round tip, outline and fill in the egg shape using a circular motion. 7. Tear the green Airheads into small pieces (about 3 inches wide). Arrange the pieces so they overlap, as shown, and place them inside the section adjacent to the egg on the plate. 8. Use scissors to separate the pink areas of the watermelon rings and cut them into ¼-inch pieces for the bitter herbs. 9. Using white icing with a round tip, draw a quarter-size dot in another section on the plate.

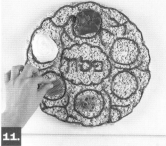

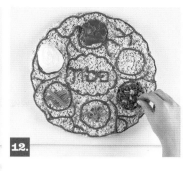

10. Arrange the watermelon ring pieces over the dot, "gluing" them in place. **11.** Use scissors to cut the green Twizzlers into 2 to 3-inch pieces for vegetables. Using white icing with a round tip, follow the instructions in Steps 9 and 10 to attach the vegetables, stacked in a pile, to another section of the plate. **12.** Mix the H batch recipe and place a small handful into another section of the plate, for the *charoset*. Add dry crispy rice cereal and the red M&M's for highlights. **13.** Mold another handful of the brown mixture into a shankbone shape, as shown, and place it on the last open section of the plate.

Pie

It's as easy as pie! I know that's a cliché, but in this case it's true. Despite it being a rather unconventionally shaped crispy rice treat, it's one of the easiest treats in the book to make. The overall design doesn't require much artistic finesse (it's just a bit of fitting shapes together), and the M&M "cherries" add a delightful splash of color to this crunchy twist on a classic dessert.

MAKES 1 PIE, 10 INCHES IN DIAMETER

TREAT RECIPE
(see page 6)
1 B batch, no food coloring

SPECIAL INGREDIENTS
1 bag red M&M's, 7 ounces

EQUIPMENT
Pie template (see page 10)
(Note: The Pie template has been created for a 10-inch pie pan. If your pie pan is larger, make sure that your template's width matches the pie pan's diameter.)
Parchment paper
Cooking spray
Pie pan
Sharp knife

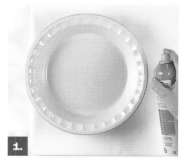

1. Coat the inside of the pie pan with cooking spray. **2.** Mix the B batch recipe and pour about half of the mixture into the pie pan, reserving the rest in the pot. Generously coat your hands with cooking spray. Press the mixture into the bottom of the pan and add more as needed to fill the pan nearly to the top, about 1 inch from the rim. **3.** Adding small amounts of the reserved mixture at a time, mold a 1½-inch raised border around the circumference of the pan. Set the pie pan aside.

4. One large handful at a time, mold the balance of the reserved mixture over the parchment-covered template on the work surface, smoothing the edges and flattening the rectangle to about ½-inch thick until the mixture begins to firm up. Then let the treat sit for about 30 minutes. **5.** Pour the red M&M's into the center of the pie until they completely cover the bottom. **6.** After the rectangle treat has rested for 30 minutes, use a sharp knife to cut it lengthwise into 1½-inch-wide strips. **7.** Place 2 or 3 strips horizontally across the pie, pressing them into the crust at the sides to attach them. **8.** Place 2 or 3 strips vertically across the pie, over the strips placed in Step 7, to complete the latticework. Press them into the crust at the sides to attach them. **9.** Use any remaining strips (and other excess mixture, if necessary) to form another layer of crust around the edges, pressing firmly to cover the ends of the crisscrossed pieces.

Piñata

I know, I know, normally the treats are *inside* the piñata, but in this clever break from tradition, the treat *is* the piñata. Add extra flair to the serving platter in the form of scattered wrapped candies adhered with icing.

**MAKES 1 PIÑATA,
13 INCHES LONG**

TREAT RECIPES
(see page 6)
**1 E batch, turquoise food
   coloring**
1 F batch, yellow food coloring
1 F batch, purple food coloring

SPECIAL INGREDIENTS
1 purple Twizzler

DECORATING ICING
White
Black

EQUIPMENT
Piñata template (see page 10)
Parchment paper
Cooking spray
Scissors
Round icing tips

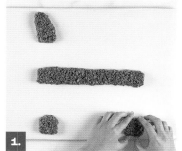

1. Mix the E batch recipe and pour the mixture onto the parchment-covered template on the work surface. Generously coat your hands with cooking spray. Use both hands to mold the mixture over section 1 of the template, smoothing the edges until the mixture begins to firm up. **2.** Mix the yellow F batch recipe and, one handful at a time, mold the mixture over section 2 of the template, making sure to press the mixture together at the "seams" where the colors adjoin. **3.** Mix the purple F batch recipe and, one handful at a time, mold the mixture over section 3 of the template, making sure to press the mixture together at the "seams" where the colors adjoin.

4. Using scissors, cut a 4-inch piece from the purple Twizzler. Then, without cutting all the way through it, cut three strips lengthwise into one end of the piece, stopping ½ inch from the opposite end, for the piñata's tail. **5.** Using white icing with a round tip, squeeze a dot of icing at the piñata's rear and attach the tail, as shown. **6.** Still using white icing, draw a circle for the eyeball. **7.** Using black icing with a round tip, draw a small dot for the nostril, outline the eye and fill in the pupil, and draw the hooves. Using white icing, make a highlight in the pupil.

Pizza

If I could eat only one food for the rest of my life, it would be a tough call between pizza and crispy treats. With this treat, I don't exactly have to choose. I love the shredded coconut "cheese," which adds some variation in flavor. You can experiment with different toppings: Beyond the licorice swirls making the perfect "pepperoni," black M&M's are delicious as "olives" and sliced-up green Sour Punch Straws pass for "peppers."

Note: Use the template and curved edges technique from the Barbecue Grill (page 39) and top with the same icing and coconut below for a round pizza pie that you can then cut into slices.

MAKES 1 SLICE, 14 INCHES LONG

TREAT RECIPE
(see page 6)
1 C batch, no food coloring

SPECIAL INGREDIENTS
Yellow food coloring
1 cup sweetened coconut flakes
½ package red licorice swirls

DECORATING ICING
Red, 2 tubes

EQUIPMENT
Pizza template (see page 10)
Parchment paper
Cooking spray
Round icing tip
Small metal spatula

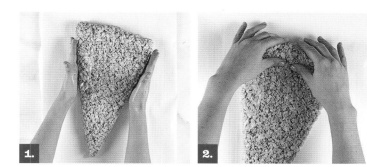

1. Mix the C batch recipe and pour the mixture onto the parchment-covered template on the work surface. Generously coat your hands with cooking spray. Use both hands to mold the mixture over the template, smoothing the edges until the mixture begins to firm up. **2.** Mold a slightly raised section along the curved edge for the pizza crust.

3. In a small bowl, add 2 drops of yellow food coloring to the shredded coconut. **4.** Mix the coconut lightly (do not cover all the coconut in yellow) for multicolored shredded cheese. **5.** Using red icing with a round tip, outline and begin to fill in the slice below the crust.

6. Use the spatula to smooth and spread the icing evenly. **7.** Sprinkle the coconut on top of the red icing. **8.** Place the licorice wheels on top of the coconut for pepperoni.

Pretzel

A fun *twist* on one of my favorite snacks, this pretzel treat makes up in sweetness what it lacks in saltiness. It has a classic NYC vibe, and I love the crunchy pearl sugar on top.

MAKES 1 PRETZEL, 13 INCHES ACROSS

TREAT RECIPE
(see page 6)
1 C batch, 8 drops brown and
   2 drops yellow food coloring

SPECIAL INGREDIENTS
Pearl sugar

EQUIPMENT
Pretzel template (see page 10)
Parchment paper
Cooking spray

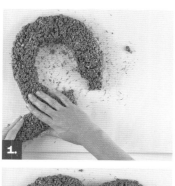

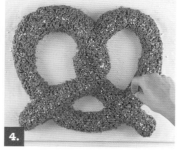

1. Mix the C batch recipe. Generously coat your hands with cooking spray and, one large handful at a time, place the mixture onto the parchment-covered template on the work surface. **2.** Use both hands to mold the mixture over the template, smoothing the edges and rounding the surface until the mixture begins to firm up. **3.** Once the basic shape is complete, mold the twist detail at the center by adding one handful of mixture at a time to create a raised surface, as shown. **4.** Using your fingers, carefully sprinkle pearl sugar over the surface to represent salt.

Purse

What do you do when someone you love wants an expensive handbag for their birthday? Make one on the cheap using this recipe! So what if it won't last long? It's timeless. This can be made in any color, though I'm partial to classic (and classy) black.

MAKES 1 HANDBAG, 10 BY 7 INCHES

TREAT RECIPE
(see page 6)
1 C batch, black food coloring

DECORATING ICING
Black
Yellow

SPARKLE GEL
Gold

EQUIPMENT
Purse template
   (see page 10)
Parchment paper
Cooking spray
Round icing tips
Star icing tip
Cake board (or other serving surface)

1. Mix the C batch recipe and pour the mixture onto the parchment-covered template on the work surface. Generously coat your hands with cooking spray. Use both hands to form the mixture over the template, smoothing the edges until the mixture begins to firm up. **2.** Create an elevated purse flap by pressing down the bottom half of the treat. **3.** Use both hands to make a square-shaped clasp in the center of the purse flap, which should also be slightly raised. **4.** Using black icing with a round tip, outline the flap and clasp area.

5. Using yellow icing with a round tip, draw the clasp design and re-outline the design with gold sparkle gel. Then follow the instructions on page 10 to remove the treat from the template and place it on a serving surface.
6. Using black icing with a star tip, draw the purse strap.
7. Using gold sparkle gel, draw a squiggle going in one direction on top of the strap.
8. Using gold sparkle gel, draw an overlapping squiggle to create an interlocking chain design.

Rainbow Cake

Everyone's dream birthday cake might not be a cake at all! This impressive-looking layer "cake" can be customized for any celebration by experimenting with different colors and decorations. I'm obsessed with the sprinkle mix on top, which I made by combining every variety of sprinkle I had in my pantry. Sometimes (always) more is more!

MAKES 1 CAKE, 8 INCHES IN DIAMETER AND 8 INCHES TALL

TREAT RECIPES
(see page 6)
1 F batch, yellow food coloring
1 F batch, green food coloring
1 F batch, turquoise food coloring
1 F batch, purple food coloring
1 F batch, pink food coloring
1 F batch, orange food coloring

SPECIAL INGREDIENTS
1 large tub (32 ounces) buttercream icing (or two 16-ounce tubs white icing)
Assorted sprinkles

EQUIPMENT
Parchment paper
Cooking spray
Cake ring, 8-inch diameter
Silicone spatula

1. Coat the inside of the cake ring with cooking spray and place it on the parchment-covered work surface. **2.** Mix the yellow F batch recipe and pour the mixture into the cake ring. Generously coat your hands with cooking spray. Press to flatten until the mixture begins to firm up. Place the treat with the cake ring in the freezer while you mix the green F batch recipe. (*Note:* Each layer should stay in the freezer for at least 10 minutes.) **3.** Remove the cake ring from the yellow treat (leave the treat itself in the freezer), and recoat it with cooking spray. Pour the green mixture into the cake ring and press to flatten until the mixture begins to firm up. Place the green treat with the cake ring in the freezer while you mix the turquoise F batch recipe.

4. Remove the cake ring from the green treat (leave the treat itself in the freezer), and recoat it with cooking spray. Pour the turquoise mixture into the cake ring and press to flatten until the mixture begins to firm up. Place the turquoise treat with the cake ring in the freezer while you mix the purple F batch recipe. 5. Repeat with the remaining purple, pink, and orange F batch recipes until you have six frozen layers. 6. Determine the order in which you'd like the six treats to be stacked. Using the spatula, spread buttercream frosting over the top of the bottom layer, making sure to reach the edges. 7. Carefully place a treat on top, for the second layer. 8. Spread buttercream frosting over the top of the second layer, and place another treat on top. 9. Continue in this manner until all of the layers have been frosted and placed. 10. Spread one last layer of frosting over the top layer, making sure to reach the edges. 11. In a bowl, use your hands to mix together the different varieties of sprinkles, then sprinkle them over the frosting.

Robot

Across the world, many of our generation's smartest people believe that the continued development of artificial intelligence could pose the greatest threat to humanity yet, but this cute lil' crispy guy won't hurt anybody. Or, maybe that's just what he wants us to think. And hey, if he *does* step out of line, you can eat him.

MAKES 1 ROBOT, 13 INCHES TALL

TREAT RECIPE
(see page 6)
1 C batch, 8 drops white and
   2 drops black food coloring

SPECIAL INGREDIENTS
3 yellow candy melts
2 red candy melts

DECORATING ICING
Black
Blue
Yellow
Red

EQUIPMENT
Robot template (see page 10)
Parchment paper
Cooking spray
Round icing tips

1. Mix the C batch recipe and pour half of the mixture onto the parchment-covered template on the work surface, reserving the rest of the mixture in the pot. Generously coat your hands with cooking spray. Use both hands to mold the mixture over section 1 of the template. One handful at a time, fill sections 2, 3, 4, and 5, smoothing the edges until the mixture begins to firm up. **2.** Roll a small amount of the reserved mixture between your hands to form a thin log for the top of the head. Add a very small amount of the mixture to the bottom of the log to make the end slightly bulbous and press it to the top of the head. **3.** Roll a small amount of the reserved mixture between your hands to form a thin log for part of the robot hand. Place it on the end of the right arm and repeat, placing another log on the same arm, as shown. Repeat for the left arm.

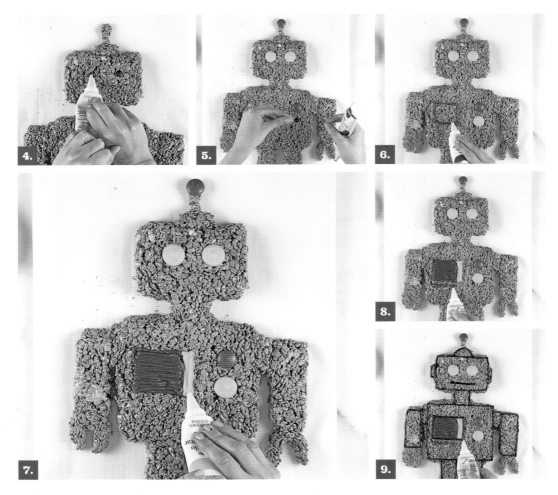

4. Using black icing with a round tip, draw two dots for the eyes, a vertical row of two dots on the right side of the robot body, and a dot at the end of head "receptor." **5.** Attach the yellow and red candy melts to the dots of icing. **6.** Using blue icing with a round tip, draw the processor box on the body, as shown. **7.** Still using blue icing with a round tip, fill in the blue box. Using yellow icing with a round tip, draw a yellow stripe on the right side of the blue box. **8.** Using red and blue icings with a round tip, draw two alternating dots underneath the blue box. **9.** Using black icing with a round tip, draw the mouth and outline the body details, as shown.

Smartphone

Phone-obsessed millennials love this design, which can display anything on the screen from a text conversation to the social media platform of the moment. I chose Instagram, which is where @mister_krisp started.

**MAKES 1 PHONE,
14 INCHES LONG**

TREAT RECIPE
(see page 6)
1 C batch, white food coloring

DECORATING ICING
Black
Blue
White
Yellow
Orange
Red
Pink

SPARKLE GEL
White
Gold

EQUIPMENT
**Smartphone template
   (see page 10)**
Parchment paper
Cooking spray
Round icing tips
2 small icing tubes

1. Mix the C batch recipe and pour the mixture onto the parchment-covered template on the work surface. Generously coat your hands with cooking spray. Use both hands to mold the mixture over the template, smoothing the edges until the mixture begins to firm up. **2.** Using black icing with a round tip, draw the speaker details. **3.** Still using black icing with a round tip, draw and fill in a circle for the front camera. Using blue icing with a round tip, draw the top of the screen, as shown.

4. Using white icing with a round tip, draw an empty circle for the home button of the phone.
5. Using black icing with a round tip, draw the bottom of the screen and outline the outside of the whole screen, as shown. **6.** Using white icing with a round tip, draw and fill in the white screen.
7. Using blue icing with a round tip, draw a box in the center of the black bar on the screen, as shown. Using gold sparkle gel, outline the white "home button" circle. **8.** Using blue icing with a round tip, fill in the blue box. Fill a small icing tube with white icing and draw the Instagram details, as shown. **9.** Using yellow icing with a round tip, draw a circle for an emoji in the center of the white part of the screen and fill it in.

10. Using red and black icings with round tips, draw a heart and comment bubble, respectively, as shown. **11.** Using orange icing with a round tip, draw a notification bubble, as shown. **12.** Fill a small decorating tube with blue icing and write the handle of the Instagram account. **13.** Using the small icing tube with white icing, draw and fill in a heart, along with a number for "likes" next to the heart, on the orange notification bubble, as shown. **14.** Using the black, white, and pink icings with round tips, complete the emoji design, as shown.

Smiley Emoji

In the same way that you text an emoji when you just don't know what else to say, these treats are a lifesaver when you don't know what to make for a celebration or gathering. These crowd-pleasers are fun, easy, snack-size, delicious, super-customizable, and work for every imaginable occasion.

MAKES 12 EMOJI

TREAT RECIPE
(see page 6)
1 C batch, yellow food coloring

DECORATING ICING
Black
Red
White
Pink

SPARKLE GEL
White
Red
Pink
Light blue
Dark blue

EQUIPMENT
Parchment paper
Cooking spray
Round cookie cutter, 4-inch diameter
Round icing tips

 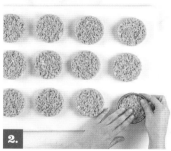 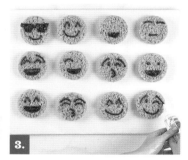

1. Coat the inside of the cookie cutter with cooking spray and place it on the parchment-covered work surface. Mix the C batch recipe. Generously coat your hands with cooking spray. **2.** Using one handful at a time, place the mixture in the center of the cookie cutter and press the mixture to the edges until it begins to firm up and the top surface is flat. Remove the disk from the cookie cutter and repeat 11 times. **3.** Using black icing with a round tip, draw the smiley details.

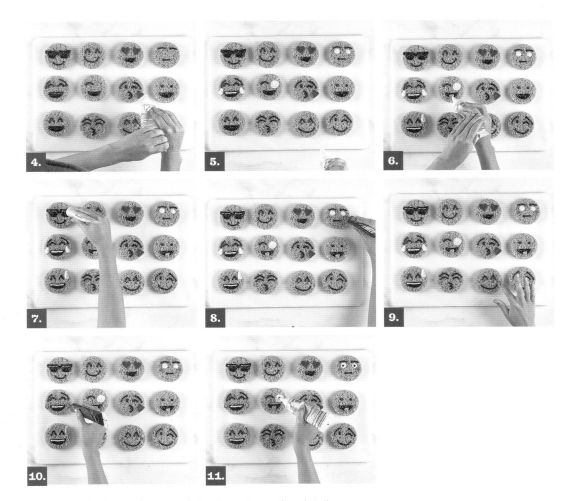

4. Using red icing with a round tip, draw the smiley details.

5. Using white icing with a round tip, draw the smiley details.

6. Using pink icing with a round tip, draw the smiley details.

7. Using white sparkle gel, draw details on the sunglasses emoji.

8. Using red sparkle gel, draw two small dots on the cheeks of the embarrassed emoji and blend them into the mixture with your fingers. **9.** Using pink sparkle gel, add cheek details to the kiss face and happy faces, as shown, and blend with your fingers.

10. Using light blue sparkle gel, draw tears on top of the white icing, as shown. Outline the tears with dark blue sparkle gel.

11. Using black icing with a round tip, draw black dots in the center of the white circles to finish the eyes.

Sneaker

The only kicks fresher than the ones you just bought are the ones you made in your own kitchen. Experiment with different designs, or stick to the classics, like I did here.

MAKES 1 SNEAKER, 13 INCHES LONG

TREAT RECIPE
(see page 6)
1 C batch, red food coloring

DECORATING ICING
White, 2 tubes
Black

SPARKLE GEL
Dark blue
Black
White

EQUIPMENT
Sneaker template
   (see page 10)
Parchment paper
Cooking spray
Round icing tips
1 small icing tube
Leaf icing tip
Toothpick

1. Mix the C batch recipe and pour the mixture onto the parchment-covered template on the work surface. Generously coat your hands with cooking spray. Use both hands to mold the mixture over the template, smoothing the edges until the mixture begins to firm up, and molding a slightly elevated tongue, as shown. **2.** Using white icing with a round tip, add the sole, toe, label, and eyelets of the shoe. **3.** Fill the small icing tube with white icing and draw the stitching detail. **4.** Using blue sparkle gel, draw the star logo.

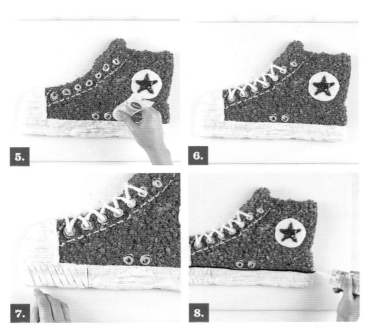

5. Using black sparkle gel, outline the eyelets. Repeat with white sparkle gel. **6.** Using white icing with a leaf tip, draw the laces. **7.** Using a toothpick, press a crisscross design into the front third of the sole, as shown. **8.** Using black icing with a round tip, draw the line details on the sole.

Snowman

Building a snowman sounds really fun until your boots fill with melted snow and your fingers have gone completely numb. Now, you can finally build a snowman without going outside in the freezing cold! A great activity for those days when you're snowed in—try experimenting with details using different candies to dress up your snowman (or snowwoman!).

MAKES 1 SNOWMAN, 14 INCHES TALL

TREAT RECIPE
(see page 6)
1 C batch, white food coloring

SPECIAL INGREDIENTS
3 black M&M's
1 orange Twizzler
2 chocolate Twizzlers

DECORATING ICING
Black
Orange
Brown

EQUIPMENT
Snowman template (see page 10)
Parchment paper
Cooking spray
Round icing tips
Scissors
Cardboard cake board
    (or other serving surface)

1. Mix the C batch recipe and pour the mixture onto the parchment-covered template on the work surface. Generously coat your hands with cooking spray. Use both hands to mold the mixture over the template, rounding the surface and using the side of your hand to make depressions between the three parts of the snowman. **2.** Using black icing with a round tip, draw dots for the eyes, smile, and buttons. Adhere three black M&M's to the dots of the icing on the body to form the buttons. **3.** Use scissors to cut the orange Twizzler into a carrot shape by making a diagonal cut about 1½ inches from one end.

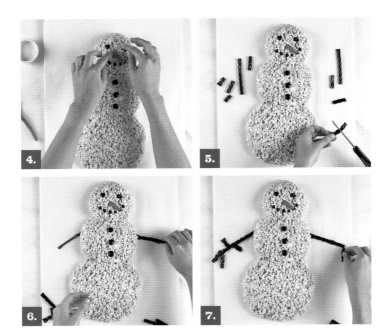

4. Using orange icing with a round tip, draw a dot for the nose. Adhere the orange Twizzler carrot to the dot of icing to form the nose of the snowman. 5. Use scissors to cut the chocolate Twizzlers into two 4-inch pieces and several 1-inch pieces. Following the instructions on page 10, remove the treat from the template and adhere it to a cardboard cake board or serving surface. 6. Using brown icing with a round tip, draw a line on both sides of the body for the arms. Adhere the 4-inch Twizzler pieces to the icing to form the arms. 7. Using brown icing with a round tip, draw lines for the twig hands. Adhere the 1-inch Twizzler pieces to the icing to form the twig hands.

TREAT YOURSELF!

Spiderweb

Spiders are scary, which is only a good thing on Halloween, when you can spook people and feed them a yummy treat at the same time. I found this gummy spider at an airport candy shop, but they're easy to track down online. In a pinch, you can draw your own eight-legged friend with black decorating icing.

MAKES 1 WEB, 11 INCHES ACROSS

TREAT RECIPE
(see page 6)
1 C batch, orange food coloring

SPECIAL INGREDIENTS
1 gummy tarantula

DECORATING ICING
Black

EQUIPMENT
Spiderweb template
  (see page 10)
Parchment paper
Cooking spray
Round icing tip

1. Mix the C batch recipe and pour the mixture onto the parchment-covered template on the work surface. Generously coat your hands with cooking spray. Use both hands to mold the mixture over the template, smoothing the edges until the mixture begins to firm up. **2.** Using black icing with a round tip, draw the spiderweb: Begin by drawing the straight lines that run through the center, as shown. **3.** Draw a circle shape near the center that connects all of the straight lines. Continue drawing the concentric shapes outward, then draw the final outline of the entire shape. **4.** Place the gummy tarantula on the web.

State Pride

Bringing new meaning to "home *sweet* home," these treats can be customized with your state's landmarks to show everyone why your home state is the best!

MAKES 1 STATE

TREAT RECIPE
(see page 6)
1 C batch, your choice of food coloring

DECORATING ICING
Your choice

SPARKLE GEL
Your choice

EQUIPMENT
State Pride template for your state (see page 10)
Parchment paper
Cooking spray
Round icing tips

1. Mix the C batch recipe and pour the mixture onto the parchment-covered template on the work surface. Generously coat your hands with cooking spray. Use both hands to mold the mixture over the template, smoothing the edges until the mixture begins to firm up. **2.** Using black icing with a round tip, draw the name of your state. **3.** Using icings with round tips and sparkle gels, draw 3 to 5 of your state's landmarks.

Statue of Liberty

Give me your tired, your poor, your crispy.... This patriotic dessert is a reminder that the United States is a country where we have the freedom, no matter where we start, to grow up to be anything we want ... even a crispy treats artist.

**MAKES 1 STATUE,
15 INCHES TALL**

TREAT RECIPE
(see page 6)
1 C batch, 3 drops turquoise
    and 3 drops white food
    coloring

DECORATING ICING
Black
Yellow

SPARKLE GEL
Gold

EQUIPMENT
Statue of Liberty template
    (see page 10)
Parchment paper
Cooking spray
Round icing tips

1. Mix the C batch recipe and pour the mixture onto the parchment-covered template on the work surface. Generously coat your hands with cooking spray. Grab 3 large handfuls of the mixture and place them back in the pot. Use both hands to mold the mixture over section 1 of the template, smoothing the edges and using your fingers to create diagonal ridges to form the gown, as shown. **2.** Using a small handful of the reserved mixture, fill section 2 of the template to make the head, pressing the edges of section 1 and 2 together. **3.** Using a small amount of the reserved mixture at a time, fill section 3 of the template, making sure that the sleeve is slightly raised.

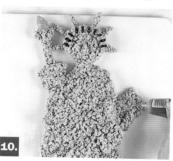

4. Roll a small amount of the reserved mixture between your hands to form a cylinder for the arm. Press the arm to the sleeve in section 3. **5.** Using a small amount of the reserved mixture at a time, fill section 4 of the template, making sure that the hand is slightly more raised than the tablet. Press the edges of sections 1 and 4 together. **6.** Using a very small amount of the reserved mixture at a time, roll the mixture between your hands to form 6 small cylinders. Press each cylinder to the top of the head. **7.** Using the same technique, create a longer cylinder for the base of the crown and place it on top of the head underneath the points of the crown. **8.** Using black icing with a round tip, draw the crown detailing. **9.** Using yellow icing with a round tip, draw fire for the torch and text on the tablet. **10.** Using gold sparkle gel, cover the yellow icing.

Suitcase

A rare situation where "having baggage" is actually a good thing. This is a thoughtful treat for a bon voyage celebration or for your favorite world traveler to ensure they won't forget you, no matter how far they go.

MAKES 1 SUITCASE, 11 BY 9 INCHES

TREAT RECIPES
(see page 6)
1 C batch, 4 drops brown, 3 drops white, and 1 drop yellow food coloring
1 F batch, brown food coloring

DECORATING ICING
Yellow
Light green
Dark green
White
Red
Black

SPARKLE GEL
Light blue
Gold

EQUIPMENT
Suitcase template (see page 10)
Parchment paper
Cooking spray
Round icing tips
Small icing tube

1. Mix the C batch recipe and pour the mixture onto the parchment-covered template on the work surface. Generously coat your hands with cooking spray. Use both hands to mold the mixture over the template, smoothing the edges until the mixture begins to firm up. **2.** Mix the F batch recipe and allow it to sit for 1 to 2 minutes. Using a small amount at a time, press the brown mixture between your hands to mold 2 rectangular flat strips and place them onto section 1. **3.** Press a small amount of the brown mixture onto all four corners of the suitcase.

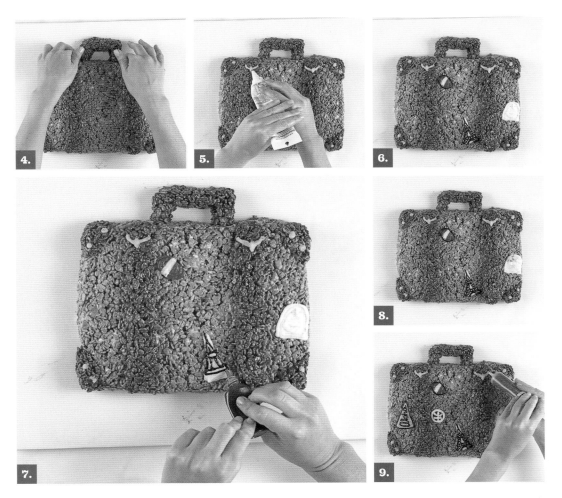

4. Using a small amount of the brown mixture, form the handle shape and press the edges to attach it. **5.** Using yellow icing with a round tip, draw the buckle and grommet details. **6.** Using light and dark green, white, and red icings with round tips, draw the luggage stickers. **7.** Fill the small icing tube with black icing and draw the details on the luggage stickers. **8.** Using white and yellow icings with round tips, black icing in the tube, and light blue sparkle gel, draw the additional luggage stickers and details. **9.** Using gold sparkle gel, cover the buckles and grommets.

Sun

This treat actually makes it possible to have sunshine on a cloudy day. Make this dessert to brighten dreary days or celebrate happy ones!

MAKES 1 SUN, 12 INCHES IN DIAMETER

TREAT RECIPES
(see page 6)
1 C batch, orange food coloring
1 D batch, yellow food coloring

DECORATING ICING
Black

SPARKLE GEL
White

EQUIPMENT
Sun template (see page 10)
Parchment paper
Cooking spray
Round icing tip

1. Mix the C batch recipe and pour the mixture onto the parchment-covered template on the work surface. Generously coat your hands with cooking spray. Use both hands to mold the mixture over the template, smoothing the edges until the mixture begins to firm up. **2.** Mix the D batch recipe and pour the mixture over the center of the treat. Use both hands to mold the yellow mixture into a circle on top of the orange mixture, smoothing the edges until the mixture begins to firm up. **3.** Using black icing with a round tip, draw the sunglasses and smile. **4.** Using white sparkle gel, draw detail on the sunglasses.

Sunglasses

Future's so bright you need shades! Customize these specs to match the latest eyewear trends: Use metallic food spray to create mirrored lenses, make a few smaller batches of varying shades of brown and alternate them to create tortoiseshell frames, or skip section 1 for classic eyeglasses.

MAKES 1 PAIR OF SUNGLASSES, 15 INCHES ACROSS

TREAT RECIPES
(see page 6)
1 C batch, black food coloring
1 C batch, purple food coloring

SPECIAL INGREDIENTS
1 can white icing
Black food coloring

DECORATING ICING
Black

EQUIPMENT
Sunglasses template
  (see page 10)
Parchment paper
Cooking spray
OodleTip piping bag
  (*Note:* If you do not have access to OodleTips, fill the corner of a zip-top bag and cut a small hole in one corner.)

Tip: You can substitute black decorating icing covered in white sparkle gel here for the gray icing, if you'd like.

1. Mix the black C batch recipe and pour half of the mixture onto each part of section 1 of the parchment-covered template on the work surface. Generously coat your hands with cooking spray. Use both hands to mold the mixture over the template, smoothing the edges until the mixture begins to firm up. **2.** Mix the purple C batch recipe and, using a small amount at a time, shape the mixture into a thin cylinder shape. Place the cylinder over section 2 of the template, continuing to shape the mixture and pressing the edges of sections 1 and 2 together. **3.** Using a small amount at a time, press the purple mixture between your hands to flatten and mold it over section 3 of the template, pressing the edges of sections 2 and 3 together.

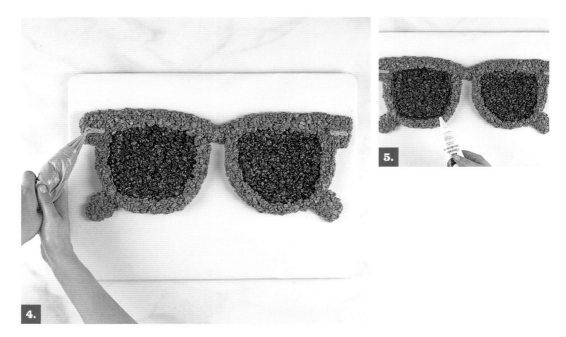

4. Place 3 tablespoons of white icing in a small bowl and add 1 drop of black food coloring. Mix the icing until the gray color is evenly distributed and then transfer it to the OodleTip bag. Using the gray icing, draw the details in the top corners of the sunglasses, as shown. (*Note:* Alternatively, use one line of black icing with a round tip and cover with 1 line of white sparkle gel.) **5.** Using black icing with a round tip, outline the lenses.

TREAT YOURSELF!

Sushi

This colorful spread brings new meaning to "sushi rice." This impressive-looking dessert uses Airheads candy to emulate fish and doesn't require the skill of a real-life sushi chef. Eat these treats with chopsticks for an extra-authentic (albeit somewhat absurd) experience.

MAKES APPROXIMATELY 23 PIECES

TREAT RECIPES
(see page 6)
1 D batch, white food coloring
1 E batch, black food coloring

SPECIAL INGREDIENTS
2 regular-size (or 4 mini) red Airheads
2 regular-size (or 4 mini) orange Airheads
1 regular-size (or 1 mini) white Airhead

DECORATING ICING
Black
White
Light green

SPARKLE GEL
White
Red
Pink
Yellow
Gold

EQUIPMENT
Parchment paper
Cooking spray
Round icing tips
Scissors
Large sharp knife

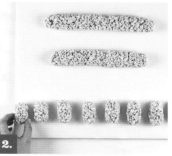

1. Mix the D batch recipe and allow it to sit for 2 to 3 minutes. Pour the mixture onto the parchment-covered work surface. Generously coat your hands with cooking spray and separate the mixture into 3 even parts. Roll the parts into cylinders about 2 to 3 inches in diameter, with the third cylinder approximately 3 inches longer than the other two. **2.** Separate the third cylinder by using your fingers to pinch off small amounts at a time and shape them into rounded rectangular pieces, each about 1 inch by 2½ inches by 1 inch (there should be 8 pieces total).

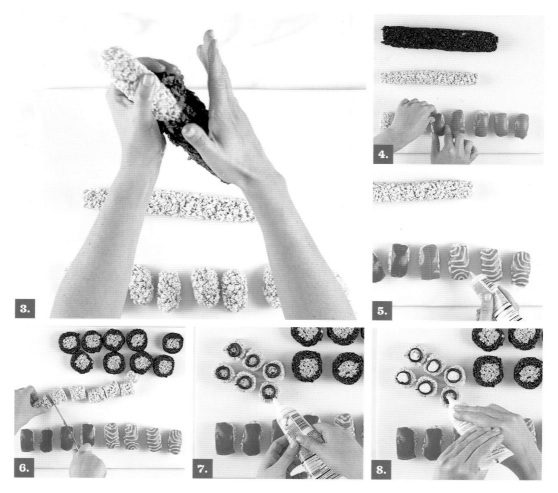

3. Place the cylindrical treats in the freezer for 20 minutes. After about 15 minutes, check that they haven't flattened out on one side. (*Note:* If they have, let them thaw for 5 to 10 minutes, and squeeze them into a rounded shape once again, using pressure as needed.) Then, mix the E batch recipe. Remove the treats from the freezer and, using one handful at a time, cover the first cylinder with a thin layer of the black mixture. **4.** If you're using regular-size Airheads, cut all of the red and orange ones in half with scissors and place each half on top of a small rectangular piece. Mini Airheads can be placed whole on each piece. **5.** Using the white sparkle gel, draw a series of curved lines on the orange Airheads to form the salmon. **6.** Let the treats sit for about 1 hour, then use cooking spray to coat a large sharp knife. Slice off the ends of the 2 cylinders and discard them. Continue cutting the cylinders into slices approximately 2 inches wide. **7.** Stand all of the pieces vertically on the work surface and use black icing with a round tip to draw circles on the white pieces. **8.** Using white icing with a round tip, fill in the center of the black circles.

9. Layer red sparkle gel over the white circles, then draw accents on top of the red sparkle gel with white sparkle gel. **10.** Using white icing with a round tip, draw and fill in small circles in the center of the black coated pieces. **11.** Using green icing with a round tip, draw dots for the avocado next to the small circles of white icing. **12.** Using pink, red, and yellow sparkle gels, draw the additional details on the sushi. **13.** Using green icing with a round tip, draw small dots of icing on the orange Airhead pieces for the wasabi, and add a swirl of wasabi to the serving surface, as shown. **14.** Cut 1 regular-size white Airhead in half with scissors (if you are using mini Airheads, omit this step) and draw a large dot of gold sparkle gel on 1 piece. Spread the sparkle gel with your fingers and crumple the Airhead. Place it next to the wasabi for the pickled ginger.

Taco

I love tacos. Nothing else to add there, just wanted you to know that. Everyone's favorite south-of-the-border treat becomes another kind of treat that's perfect for any fiesta, from Cinco de Mayo to any *cumpleaños.*

MAKES 1 TACO, 13 INCHES ACROSS

TREAT RECIPE
(see page 6)
1 C batch, yellow food coloring

DECORATING ICING
Brown
Light green
White
Red

SPARKLE GEL
Gold
Yellow

EQUIPMENT
Taco template (see page 10)
Parchment paper
Cooking spray
Round icing tips

1. Mix the C batch recipe and pour the mixture onto the parchment-covered template on the work surface. Generously coat your hands with cooking spray. Use both hands to mold the mixture over the template, smoothing the edges until the mixture begins to firm up. **2.** Use the side of your hand to create a long depression arching just below the top edge, to carve out the space for the "taco fillings." **3.** Using brown icing with a round tip, outline and fill in the bottom section of the fillings space to represent the protein.

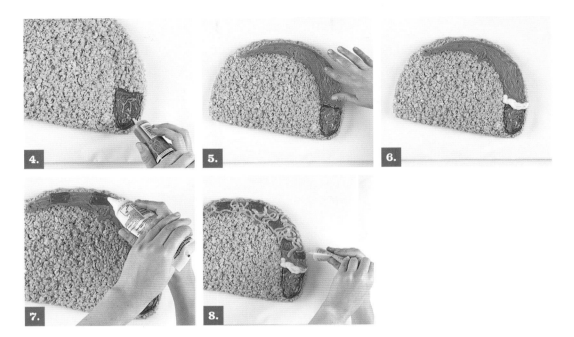

4. Using gold sparkle gel, draw a squiggle detail over the brown icing and use your fingers to blend it. 5. Using green icing with a round tip, outline and fill in the rest of the fillings space above the protein for the lettuce area. Use your fingers to spread and smooth the icing. 6. Using white icing with a round tip, add a line at the seam between the protein and the lettuce for the sour cream. 7. Using red icing with a round tip, draw and fill in small squares over the lettuce section for tomato chunks. 8. Using yellow sparkle gel, draw some squiggly lines over the lettuce section for shredded cheese.

Teddy Bear

This is not just any teddy bear; this is Fritz, my beloved teddy bear and most prized possession who still shares my bed each night even though I'm over 30. I get a lot of orders from customers asking me to replicate their loved ones' stuffed animals, and bears are definitely the most popular. Modify this design to match a bear you know and love, or go with Fritz for the best bear in the whole wide world.

MAKES 1 BEAR, 13 INCHES TALL

TREAT RECIPE
(see page 6)
1 C batch, brown food coloring

SPECIAL INGREDIENTS
2 black M&M's

DECORATING ICING
Black
Red

EQUIPMENT
Teddy Bear template
   (see page 10)
Parchment paper
Cooking spray
Round icing tips

1. Mix the C batch recipe and pour the mixture onto the parchment-covered template on the work surface. Generously coat your hands with cooking spray. Reserve one small handful and place it back in the pot. Use both hands to mold the mixture over the template, smoothing the edges and rounding the surface until the mixture begins to firm up. **2.** Take two pinches of the reserved brown mixture, and mold and attach the ears. **3.** Remove the rest of the reserved handful of mixture from the pot and mold it, as shown, into a small dome for the snout. Press it gently onto the center of the head.

4. Use your index finger to make indentations for the eyes and, using black icing with a round tip, squeeze a dot in each indentation. **5.** Press one of the black M&M's over each of the black dots for the eyes. **6.** Using black icing with a round tip, draw a small inverted triangle for the nose. **7.** Using red icing with a round tip, draw the outline of a bow tie and fill it in.

Tennis Racquet

I took tennis lessons every week for most of my teenage years, and yet I still can't play with any degree of skill. I may not be able to return your volley, but hey, at least I can *serve* you some tennis-themed crisps. It doesn't take a *pro* to make this racquet, but everyone will *love* it. See, at least I picked up some lingo!

MAKES 1 RACQUET, 14 INCHES LONG

TREAT RECIPES
(see page 6)
1 F batch, white food coloring
1 D batch, 4 drops blue and
　　4 drops white food coloring

DECORATING ICING
White
Black

EQUIPMENT
Tennis Racquet template
　　(see page 10)
Parchment paper
Cooking spray
Petal icing tip
Round icing tip

1. Mix the F batch recipe and pour the mixture onto the parchment-covered template on the work surface. Generously coat your hands with cooking spray. Use both hands to mold the mixture over section 1 of the template, smoothing the edges until the mixture begins to firm up. **2.** Mix the D batch recipe and, one handful at a time, mold it over section 2 of the template, pressing the mixtures together at the seams. **3.** Continue molding the light blue mixture from the frame all the way to the handle.

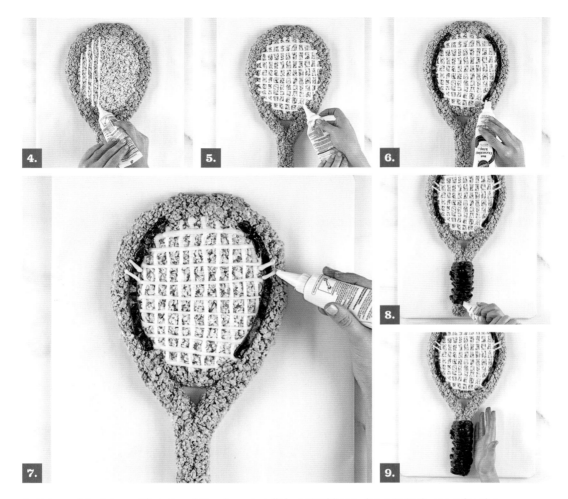

4. Using white icing with a round tip, draw parallel vertical lines about ½ inch apart for the strings. **5.** Still using white icing, draw horizontal lines that cross the lines made in Step 4, also ½ inch apart. **6.** Using black icing with a petal tip, draw two arcing lines on the inside edge of each side of the frame. **7.** Using white icing, draw two diagonal parallel lines across the frame on either side of it. **8.** Using black icing with a petal tip, color the handle. Start at the top, and employ a side-to-side motion as you work your way down the handle to create the grip. **9.** Let the treat sit for 20 to 30 minutes. Gently pat down on the grip to flatten the icing flush to the treat, especially at the sides.

Thanksgiving Turkey

Level: EASY

Isn't it wild how even after a Thanksgiving feast, there's always room for dessert? With this turkey on the table, there's one more thing to be thankful for! *Note:* To make the accompanying side dishes, mix 1 H batch (1 drop red, 1 drop brown food coloring) for the cranberry sauce, mix 1 H batch (2 drops white food coloring and gold sparkle gel) plus a yellow Starburst for the butter for the mashed potatoes, and mix 1 G batch (2 drops orange food coloring) plus extra mini marshmallows for the sweet potatoes.

MAKES 1 TURKEY, 10 INCHES LONG

TREAT RECIPE
(see page 6)
1 C batch, 9 drops brown and
   1 drop yellow food coloring

SPECIAL INGREDIENTS
5 blue/green Fruit Roll-Ups

EQUIPMENT
Thanksgiving Turkey template
   (see page 10)
Parchment paper
Cooking spray
Cake board (or other serving surface)
Scissors

1. Mix the C batch recipe and pour the mixture onto the parchment-covered template on the work surface. Generously coat your hands with cooking spray. Use both hands to mold the mixture over the template, smoothing the edges and rounding the surface until the mixture begins to firm up. Use your fingers to gently create divisions between the breast and the wings/legs. **2.** Place the treat in the freezer for 10 minutes and then carefully transfer it onto a serving surface. Use scissors to separate the green section from the blue and green Fruit Roll-Ups. Discard (or eat) the blue parts. **3.** Press the green pieces onto the serving surface around the turkey, folding them unevenly to resemble lettuce. **4.** Continue to press the green pieces around the turkey until the bed of greens is complete.

T-shirt

Okay, so I haven't figured out how to make wearable crispies *yet*, but this T-shirt treat can be used to show love for anything from your favorite city (I went iconic with this Milton Glaser design) to your preferred sports team, fraternity, sorority, or slogan. For a challenge, try a tie-dye shirt!

MAKES 1 SHIRT, 10 INCHES LONG

TREAT RECIPE
(see page 6)
1 C batch, white food coloring

DECORATING ICING
Red
Black

EQUIPMENT
T-shirt template (see page 10)
Parchment paper
Cooking spray
Round icing tips

1. Mix the C batch recipe and pour the mixture onto the parchment-covered template on the work surface. Generously coat your hands with cooking spray. Reserve one handful and place it back in the pot. Use both hands to mold the mixture over the template, smoothing the edges until the mixture begins to firm up. **2.** Remove the reserved mixture from the pot and place it on the treat, one small handful at a time, molding it to create a raised collar at the neckline. Gently press to adhere. **3.** Using red icing with a round tip, draw and fill in the heart. **4.** Using black icing with a round tip, add the letters around the heart.

Twins Emoji

This emoji has come to represent both friendship and sisterhood, which are two very important things in my life. Make it for your best gal pal so she'll love you even more! Best friends are forever, but this treat will be eaten in a moment. Use brown, white, pink, yellow, or copper food coloring to achieve any skin tone.

MAKES 1 EMOJI, 18 INCHES ACROSS

TREAT RECIPES
(see page 6)
1 C batch, no food coloring
1 F batch, yellow food coloring

DECORATING ICING
Black, 2 tubes

EQUIPMENT
Twins Emoji template
    (see page 10)
Parchment paper
Cooking spray
Round icing tip
Small icing tube

  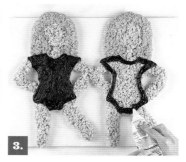

1. Mix the C batch recipe. Generously coat your hands with cooking spray and, one large handful at a time, fill section 1 of the parchment-covered template on the work surface, smoothing the edges until the mixture begins to firm up. **2.** Mix the F batch recipe and, one handful at a time, fill section 2 of the template. **3.** Using black icing with a round tip, draw the leotards, using your fingers to smooth and spread the icing.

4. Using black icing with a round tip, draw the shoes and hair bows.
5. Fill a small icing tube with black icing and draw the eyes, noses, and mouths, as shown.

Video Game Controller

This dessert is a definite *win* for any gamer. Present it before cutting into bite-size pieces so they can snack while keeping their eyes on the screen.

MAKES 1 CONTROLLER, 11 INCHES ACROSS

TREAT RECIPE
(see page 6)
1 C batch, 8 drops white and
    2 drops black food coloring

SPECIAL INGREDIENTS
1 regular-size marshmallow

DECORATING ICING
Yellow
Red
Light green
Blue
Black

EQUIPMENT
Video Game Controller template
    (see page 10)
Parchment paper
Cooking spray
Round icing tips
Scissors
Cake board (or other
    serving surface)

1. Mix the C batch recipe and pour the mixture onto the parchment-covered template on the work surface. Generously coat your hands with cooking spray. Use both hands to mold the mixture over the template, smoothing the edges until the mixture begins to firm up. **2.** Using yellow, red, green, and blue icings with round tips, draw a dot of each to make the controller buttons. **3.** Use scissors to cut the marshmallow in half. Using black icing with a round tip, draw a dot underneath the controller buttons. Press one marshmallow half onto the dot of icing.

4. Using black icing with a round tip, cover the marshmallow with icing in a circular motion. **5.** Still using black icing with a round tip, draw the additional buttons on the controller. **6.** After 1 hour, remove the treat from the parchment and place it on a cardboard cake board. Using black icing with a round tip, draw the cord on the serving board.

Watermelon

This watermelon with licorice "seeds" was among my early Misterkrisp experiments, but it's still one of my favorites. Show up at any BBQ or summer celebration with a green mound of crispy treat and make a performance of slicing it into wedges to show everyone what you're capable of in the kitchen.

MAKES 1 WATERMELON, 12 INCHES LONG

TREAT RECIPES
(see page 6)
1 C batch, pink food coloring
1 E batch, 3 drops green and
    3 drops white food coloring
1 D batch, green food coloring

SPECIAL INGREDIENTS
6 chocolate or black Twizzlers
    (or other dark licorice sticks)

EQUIPMENT
Parchment paper
Cooking spray
Large knife

1. Mix the C batch recipe and pour one-third of the mixture onto the parchment-covered work surface, reserving the rest of the mixture in the pot. Generously coat your hands with cooking spray. Use both hands to form the mixture into a mound, approximately 6″ x 10″, smoothing the edges until the mixture begins to firm up. **2.** Place 4 Twizzlers horizontally on top of the pink mixture. Using one large handful of the reserved mixture at a time, cover the Twizzlers completely. **3.** Place 2 more Twizzlers horizonally on top of the pink mixture. Using one large handful of the reserved mixture at a time, cover the Twizzlers completely, molding the mixture over the entire treat into an oval shape.

4. Mix the E batch recipe and, one handful at a time, cover the treat in a thin layer, making sure to maintain the oval shape and pressing gently to adhere the light green mixture to the pink mixture. **5.** Mix the green D batch recipe and, one handful at a time, cover the treat, making sure to maintain the oval shape and pressing gently to adhere the green mixture to the light green mixture. **6.** Let the treat sit for 30 minutes. Using a large sharp knife, cut into the watermelon about a quarter of the way in from the end. **7.** Once a slice is removed, cut it in half. Continue slicing through about half of the watermelon.

Wedding Cake

This wedding cake will be *dearly beloved* by anyone who tries it! Topped with fresh flowers or classic figurines, this tiered creation tastes as good as it looks. The "naked cake" design means you can use this cake for any celebration, and the simple stacking method means you can make it in any size.

MAKES 1 CAKE, 10 INCHES IN DIAMETER AND 15 INCHES TALL

TREAT RECIPES
(see page 6)

3 C batches, no food coloring
   (mixed one at a time)
1 C batch, no food coloring
1 G batch, no food coloring

SPECIAL INGREDIENTS
1 large tub white buttercream icing, 32 ounces

EQUIPMENT
Parchment paper
Cooking spray
Cake rings, 10-inch diameter and 8-inch diameter
Circle cookie cutter or cake ring, 4-inch diameter
Silicone spatula
Cake board (or other serving surface)

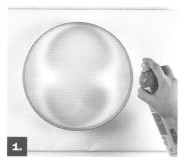

1. Coat the inside of the 10-inch cake ring with cooking spray and place it on the parchment-covered work surface. **2.** Mix one C batch recipe and pour the mixture into the cake ring. Generously coat your hands with cooking spray. Press to flatten until the mixture begins to firm up and the top surface is flat. Place the treat with the cake ring in the freezer while you mix the second C batch recipe.

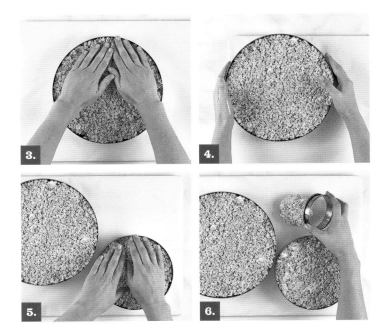

3. Remove the cake ring from the treat in the freezer (leave the treat itself in the freezer) and recoat it with cooking spray. Pour the second C mixture into the cake ring and press to flatten until the mixture begins to firm up. Place the treat with the cake ring in the freezer while you mix the third C batch recipe. **4.** Repeat Step 3, then place the treat with the cake ring in the freezer. **5.** Coat the inside of the 8-inch cake ring with cooking spray. Mix the F batch recipe and pour half of the mixture into the cake ring. Press to flatten until the mixture begins to firm up and the top surface is flat. Carefully remove the cake ring, recoat the ring, and repeat with the other half of the F mixture. When finished, place both treats in the freezer. **6.** Coat the inside of the 4-inch cookie cutter with cooking spray. Mix the G batch recipe and, one handful at a time, press the mixture into the cookie cutter. Once the shape is formed, lift the treat out of the cookie cutter and set aside. Recoat the cookie cutter and repeat this technique, so you have two 4-inch disks.

7. Using the silicone spatula, place a small amount of the icing on the serving surface. Remove one 10-inch layer from the freezer and place the treat on the icing to keep the treat in place while you work. **8.** Using the spatula, cover just the top of the treat with buttercream icing, making sure to reach the edges. **9.** Remove the second 10-inch layer from the freezer and place the treat on top of the buttercream icing. **10.** Using the spatula, cover just the top of the treat with buttercream icing. Repeat the process in Step 9 with the third 10-inch layer.

11. Remove one 8-inch layer from the freezer and place it in the center of the top 10-inch layer. (The layers will stick together naturally as they thaw.) **12.** Using the spatula, cover just the top of the treat with buttercream icing. Repeat the process in Step 11, placing the second 8-inch layer on top of the first. **13.** Repeat the process in Steps 11 and 12 with the two 4-inch layers until all of the layers have been frosted and placed. **14.** Use the spatula to smooth out any icing that is emerging from between the layers.

Wizard Hat

No magic is required to make this totally bewitching treat! Make this tasty topper for a Halloween celebration, or use brown food coloring and forget the stars to make a sorting hat for a Harry Potter–themed party.

P.S. An online quiz has confirmed my long-held instinct that I am a Ravenclaw.

MAKES 1 HAT, 12 INCHES FROM TIP TO BRIM

TREAT RECIPE
(see page 6)
1 C batch, 3 drops blue food coloring

DECORATING ICING
Black
Yellow

EQUIPMENT
Wizard Hat template (see page 10)
Parchment paper
Cooking spray
Round icing tips

1. Mix the C batch recipe and pour the mixture onto the parchment-covered template on the work surface. Generously coat your hands with cooking spray. Use both hands to mold the mixture over the template, smoothing the edges until the mixture begins to firm up. **2.** Using black icing with a round tip, draw a horizontal line to define the hat brim. **3.** Using yellow icing with a round tip, draw and fill in stars in different sizes across the top portion of the hat.

Yourself

You've heard of "taking a selfie," but what about *making* a selfie? When I say "Treat Yourself" on the cover of this book, I actually mean it literally in this case—make yourself into a treat! Portraits are definitely among the most difficult designs I'm asked to make, but follow these steps to craft a dessert in your likeness (or use a photo of a friend or celebrity!).

MAKES 1 SELFIE, 9 BY 12 INCHES

TREAT RECIPES
(see page 6)
1 C batch, copper, brown, white, or yellow food coloring (depending on skin tone)
1 E (long hair), 1 F (medium-long hair), 1 G (medium-length hair), or 1 H (short hair) batch with brown, black, white, red, yellow, gold, or orange food coloring (depending on hair color)
(*Note:* Skip this batch for no hair! Use appropriate other colors for dyed hair—pink, blue, purple, etc.)

DECORATING ICING
Black
White
Pink
Additional colors of your choice based on the subject's features (hair and eye colors, jewelry, clothing, etc.)

SPARKLE GEL
A variety of colors based on subject's hair color

EQUIPMENT
Tracing paper
Printed photographic portrait
Pencil
Permanent black marker
Parchment paper
Cooking spray
Small icing tube

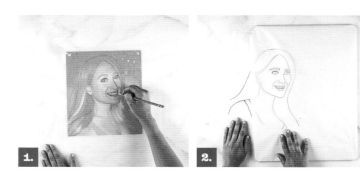

1. Place the tracing paper over the printed portrait and use the pencil to outline the head, face, and any prominent features, including eyes, nose, mouth, and any other visible lines you want to include, making sure to delineate the separation between the face and hair. This is the template. **2.** Place the tracing paper under parchment paper on the work surface and mix the C batch recipe using food coloring (or none) to achieve the desired flesh tone. Generously coat your hands with cooking spray.

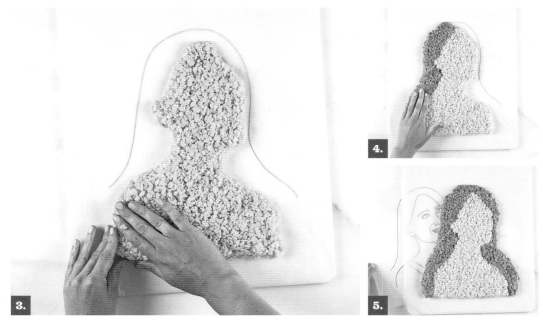

3. Pour the mixture over the face and neck sections of the template, smoothing the mixture until it begins to firm up. **4.** Mix one E, F, G, or H batch recipe (depending on hair length) and, using one handful at a time, fill in the hair section of the template, shaping and smoothing it until the mixture begins to firm up. **5.** Carefully slide the tracing paper out from underneath the parchment paper. **6.** With the tracing paper template as a guide, use icings and sparkle gels to add personalized features, clothing, and accents.

Zebra

Okay, so I needed a treat that started with the letter Z to finish this book, and who wants a dessert that looks like a zipper? Zebras don't change their stripes, but you can eliminate them altogether to make a horse, or add a little horn (using a small spiral lollipop) and a mane of colorful icing to make a magical unicorn.

MAKES 1 ZEBRA, 14 INCHES FROM NOSE TO TAIL

TREAT RECIPE
(see page 6)
1 C batch, white food coloring

DECORATING ICING
Black

EQUIPMENT
Zebra template (see page 10)
Parchment paper
Cooking spray
Round icing tips

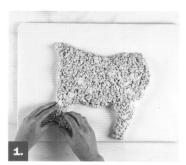  

1. Mix the C batch recipe and pour two thirds of the mixture onto the parchment-covered template on the work surface. Generously coat your hands with cooking spray. Use both hands to mold the mixture over section 1 of the template, smoothing the edges until the mixture begins to firm up. **2.** Using one handful at a time, flatten a small amount of the remaining mixture in your hands and fill section 2 of the template to make the back legs, which should be slightly less elevated than those in section 1. **3.** Using a large handful of the remaining mixture, fill section 3 of the template to form the head, which should be the same elevation as section 1.

4. Roll a small amount of the remaining mixture between your hands to form a cylinder. Place it over section 4 of the template to make the tail. Roll another small amount of the mixture into a bulb shape and place it on the end of the tail. **5.** Using a small amount at a time, flatten pieces of the mixture between your hands and place them over section 5 of the template to make the mane, which should be slightly less elevated than section 1. Press the edges of sections 1 and 5 together to adhere. **6.** Using black icing with a round tip, draw the snout and stripes, then outline the entire shape.

Resources

The ingredients for making a crispy rice treat, as we know, are pretty basic and easily available, but it helps to know where to shop. Here are some of the places I frequent most regularly.

Amazon.com The online megastore is my go-to place for cookie cutters, OodleTips, gel food coloring, and other hard-to-find supplies.

Michaels The icing and frostings (Wilton brand) and other baking materials (including 6-packs of Wilton cake boards, which are key to my crisp-making) are well-stocked at this craft store. Note: The cake boards should be coated.

Party City A great source for the icing and frostings (Wilton brand), as well as 6-packs of Wilton cake boards.

Local baking supply stores Though standard McCormick food coloring from your grocery store can work, I get more color variety using AmeriColor Soft Gel Paste food coloring from N.Y. Cake.

FAQs

Because the crispy rice treat recipe is so simple—and it's no-bake so it can replace a cake in many dessert scenarios—I get a lot of questions about dietary restrictions and substitutions. Here are some frequently asked questions—and answers!

Are crispy rice treats gluten free?
It depends. Some brands of crispy rice cereal are actually gluten free—others, because of the factories they're processed in, aren't completely. (Kellogg's, for instance, includes a malt food coloring that contains gluten.) While some people who have gluten sensitivities choose to consume products processed alongside gluten-rich ones, people who have serious gluten allergies steer clear. Always check the ingredients on the box, know your restrictions, and proceed accordingly.

Can I substitute vegan marshmallows? I've experimented with vegan marshmallows a bit, and though Dandies brand is the closest I've come to success, there are some caveats. Though their marshmallow

consistency is good, these vegan mallows don't melt at the same speed as a standard mallow, so you have to keep the stove on while mixing in the cereal, making the mixture extremely hot to the touch when molding. I know there'll be some diehards out there, but please proceed with caution!

Can I substitute for the butter? Yes, for a dairy-free option, coconut oil can replace butter in a straight 1:1 ratio—and it delivers a subtle coconutty flavor, too. Margarine also works, in the same ratio.

Can I make treats with other kinds of dry puffed cereal? Crisp rice cereal is the best medium for treat-making by far, but feel free to experiment as you see fit.

Please note that all conversions are approximate but close enough to be useful when converting from one system to another.

LIQUID CONVERSIONS

US	Imperial	Metric
2 tbs	1 fl oz	30 ml
3 tbs	1½ fl oz	45 ml
¼ cup	2 fl oz	60 ml
⅓ cup	2½ fl oz	75 ml
⅓ cup + 1 tbs.	3 fl oz	90 ml
⅓ cup + 2 tbs	3½ fl oz	100 ml
½ cup	4 fl oz	125 ml
⅔ cup	5 fl oz	150 ml
¾ cup	6 fl oz	175 ml
¾ cup + 2 tbs	7 fl oz	200 ml
1 cup	8 fl oz	250 ml
1 cup + 2 tbs	9 fl oz	275 ml
1¼ cups	10 fl oz	300 ml
1⅓ cups	11 fl oz	325 ml
1½ cups	12 fl oz	350 ml
1⅔ cups	13 fl oz	375 ml
1¾ cups	14 fl oz	400 ml
1¾ cups + 2 tbs	15 fl oz	450 ml
2 cups (1 pint)	16 fl oz	500 ml
2½ cups	20 fl oz (1 pint)	600 ml
3¾ cups	1½ pints	900 ml
4 cups	1¾ pints	1 liter

APPROXIMATE EQUIVALENTS

1 stick butter = 8 tbs = 4 oz = ½ cup = 115 g

WEIGHT CONVERSIONS

US/UK	Metric	US/UK	Metric
½ oz	15 g	7 oz	200 g
1 oz	30 g	8 oz	250 g
1½ oz	45 g	9 oz	275 g
2 oz	60 g	10 oz	300 g
2½ oz	75 g	11 oz	325 g
3 oz	90 g	12 oz	350 g
3½ oz	100 g	13 oz	375 g
4 oz	125 g	14 oz	400 g
5 oz	150 g	15 oz	450 g
6 oz	175 g	1 lb	500 g

INCHES TO CENTIMETERS

½	=	1.3	9	= 22.9
1	=	2.5	9½	= 24.1
1½	=	3.8	10	= 25.4
2	=	5.1	11	= 27.9
2½	=	6.4	12	= 30.5
3	=	7.6	13	= 33.0
3½	=	8.9	14	= 35.6
4	=	10.2	15	= 38.1
4½	=	11.4	16	= 40.6
5	=	12.7	17	= 43.2
5½	=	14.0	18	= 45.7
6	=	15.2	19	= 48.3
6½	=	16.5	20	= 50.8
7	=	17.8	21	= 53.3
7½	=	19.1	22	= 55.9
8	=	20.3	23	= 58.4
8½	=	21.6	24	= 61.0

Index

Acknowledgments

Thank you times a million with marshmallows on top to everyone at Workman, especially Suzie Bolotin, Megan Nicolay, Rachael Mt. Pleasant, Anne Kerman, Becky Terhune, Barbara Peragine, Steven Bucsok, Kate Karol, and Kim Daly for believing in this project from the beginning; for devising ways around every problem and eating the evidence; and for literally MAKING IT RAIN CEREAL. For making me feel at home the minute I first walked in and for making work feel as much like play as possible.

To Megan, for always getting it, for your calming presence, your creative energy, for reliably picking up where my brain leaves off, and for patiently guiding me the whole way.

I'm grateful to Evi Abeler for endless patience and warmth, for capturing the weirdness that is Misterkrisp, for my favorite socks, and for letting all of us essentially move in with you for two weeks. I loved living at your house. Let me know if a room opens up.

Thank you Sarah Choi for your cheerful, thoughtful, experienced help and company, for keeping all of it moving, for teaching me what all the tools I'd been using for over three years were actually called. "Long Bendy Metal Spreader Thingy" = Offset Spatula, who knew?

This book never. would. have. happened if not for my tenacious and brilliant rockstar agent (I've always wanted one of those), Sarah Passick, who straight-up cyberstalked me until I finally gave in and put together a proposal, who has been there for me every single step of the way and never misses a social media post or fails to respond to a text at any hour of the night, who I occasionally have work-related conversations with on Snapchat. Sarah—thank you for being the most on-it person I know, for believing in this book and for being not just my agent, but also my friend throughout this entire process and beyond.

Thank you to my Instagram followers and my customers, who are the only reason Misterkrisp exists, for legitimizing my weird hobby with your interest and showing me how kind and supportive total-strangers-who-definitely-don't-feel-like-strangers can be. For always suggesting creative ideas and for building a community around such an irreverent idea. I feel so lucky to be internet-surrounded by all of you!

To the staff at the building I live in which I don't want to name here because safety first (and also I don't want to start receiving more catalogs, they're bad for the environment)—I couldn't do any of this without you. Thank you for always keeping my treats safe and having my back and recycling a tremendous amount of cereal boxes. Even though I call Misterkrisp a one-woman business, it isn't—your companionship and support mean everything.

To the people who read this book in its early stages, who laughed with me about some of the ridiculous early words and really embarrassing jokes and who suggested better ones: Adam Greenberg, Esther Levy-Chehebar, Sarah Madges, Rebecca Merrill, and Danielle Sinay. You are my favorite!

Special thanks to the Grad Girls Club and Girl Gang: May this be the first of many published acknowledgments between us. I love you all. To the New School MFA program, especially Zia Jaffrey, Susan Cheever, and Brenda Wineapple, thank you.

Thanks to all of my best friends who had my back when I took a risk and I started this journey and who take Misterkrisp seriously, as silly as it is sometimes. There is not enough ink to give you the words you all deserve. If I listed all of your names, this book would look like a seventh grade AOL profile, so I won't, but you know who you are. If not, text me and I'll be honest.

All of the thank yous are not enough thank yous for Seth Horwitz but THANKYOU THANKYOUTHANKYOUTHANKYOUTHANKYOU and THANKYOU. Also, THANKYOU.

To my best friend Stephanie Leff for teaching me how to make crispy rice treats and for maintaining my sanity not just throughout the writing of this book but for the past twenty years. I couldn't live without you.

To Amanda Schabes for suggesting we make that first crispy surfboard, for always encouraging my creativity and for blowing krisp up on the 'gram, for being a best friend and always teaching me new things.

To Emily for always being my best everything. I will sign this book for you and then I will stop talking about the other thing!

To Debbie—I could not have done this (or, like, anything) without your patience, kindness, sense of humor, and insight.

To my sister, Jamie, who may or may not have noticed that she is a full-time unpaid consultant for Misterkrisp. If she has noticed, she hasn't said anything, so thanks for not asking for money. I cannot and will not make an important decision without your blessing—your opinion is the last word (most of the time). Thank you for helping brainstorm ideas for the projects in this book and beyond and for always being there to respond to frequent "what can I make that's blue?" requests. I feel so lucky to have you by my side.

To Andrew for always coming through with the last-minute puns and for being the chillest bro-in-law there ever was.

To my mom, the coolest person I know, whose creativity, business savvy, ambition, work ethic, generosity, love, and tremendous presence are the only reason any of this was ever possible. Thank you for setting the best example and supporting me in following this creative path and in every single thing I've ever done.

And to my dad for being Misterkrisp's #1 fan and hype man, for always facilitating my "projects" and most important, teaching me that "cleaning up is half the fun."

To all of my family for always being there for me, for supporting and encouraging me, for being the best. I couldn't do any of this without you.

I love you all!

About the Author

Jessica Siskin is the food artist behind Misterkrisp (Instagram: @mister_krisp), a business that specializes in customizable crispy rice treats. She left her job in the fashion industry to pursue Misterkrisp full-time after discovering her creative calling by accident. Jessica holds an MFA in creative nonfiction from The New School. She lives in New York City.

Bret Stephens, winner of the 2013 Pulitzer Prize for commentary, is the foreign affairs columnist and deputy editorial page editor of *The Wall Street Journal*. He was previously the editor in chief of the *Jerusalem Post*. He was raised in Mexico City, educated at the University of Chicago and the London School of Economics, and lives with his family in New York City.

*   *   *

Praise for
America in Retreat

"At a time when the president of the United States explicitly renounces the role of 'global policeman' and a remarkable proportion of Americans—conservatives and liberals alike—seem irresistibly drawn to isolationism in all but name, Bret Stephens has written a shrewd, sharp, and shamelessly unfashionable defense of American power as a force for good in the world. He makes it clear why now, even more than in the past, the supposed benefits of Uncle Sam's retreat will swiftly be eclipsed by the very real costs of advancing terrorism and authoritarianism."
—Niall Ferguson, Laurence A. Tisch Professor, Harvard University; author of *The Great Degeneration* and *Civilization*

"An important book for your well-being."　　　　—Bill O'Reilly, *The O'Reilly Factor*

"A powerful polemic, eminently quotable . . . [that] tackles the lingering confusion about Iraq and Afghanistan . . . [and] supplies the intellectual case for confident, world-spanning leadership by the United States."　　　—Mona Charen, *National Review*

"The best riposte yet to advocates of American retrenchment."
—James Kirchick, *The Daily Beast*

"Spellbinding . . . brilliantly executed . . . Bret Stephens has written a remarkable book that confirms him in the top rank of strategic thinkers and contributors to political thought in America."　　　　—Robert McFarlane, *The Washington Times*

"With a command of American history, a mastery of big foreign policy ideas, and a supple grasp of the conundrums of current events, Stephens shows that the dichotomy between domestic and international responsibilities is facile. For the world's sole superpower, international affairs inevitably impinge on our economy and our security. Defending our principles abroad advances our interests at home."
—Peter Berkowitz, *RealClearPolitics*

"Incisive . . . A provocative and original prescription for American renewal that would at least correct many of the flaws of Obama's foreign policy and provide a meaningful starting point for his successor."　　　—Tzvi Kahn, *The American Interest*

"Through the use of historical facts and analyses, the inclusion of compelling statistical realities, and the embrace of practical analogies, Stephens makes the case that the coming global disorder is inevitable if the country continues on a path of retreat. But he also gives readers like me, who feared prior to reading his book that America's decline was irreversible, a rational basis for hope that our preeminent place in history and the world can in fact be restored under the right leadership. It is not too late for America— especially if everyone reads *America in Retreat*." —*American Thinker*

"Bret Stephens has produced a powerful and exceptionally literate rebuttal of America's neoisolationists and a practical prescription for America's reemergence as the world's essential good cop, maintaining global order without seeking to remake the world in our own image. Americans ignore his message at their own peril."

—Karen Elliott House, Pulitzer Prize–winning reporter,
editor, and publisher; author of *On Saudi Arabia*

"Bret Stephens has the guts to make the case—and make it brilliantly—for why Americans need America to be the world's policeman (or at least the world's police chief when we can get allies to join our force). This book is worth buying even if you read only chapter nine in which Stephens foresees the chilling disorder in the world if America does not reassert its global leadership. That should be effective shock treatment for the isolationists in both parties as we think about the world we want to leave our children and grandchildren."

—Joseph I. Lieberman, U.S. senator from Connecticut, 1989–2013

"Given the U.S.'s recently renewed commitments in the Middle East, Stephens's clear, convincing apologia for American power will make especially timely reading for American foreign policy's skeptics and opponents."

—*Publishers Weekly*, starred review

"A provocative, carefully reasoned argument, anathema to politicians as disparate as Barack Obama and Rand Paul." —*Kirkus Reviews*

AMERICA
IN RETREAT

* * * *

THE NEW ISOLATIONISM AND
THE COMING GLOBAL DISORDER

BRET STEPHENS

Sentinel

SENTINEL
An imprint of Penguin Random House LLC
375 Hudson Street
New York, New York 10014
penguin.com

First published in the United States of America by Sentinel 2014
This paperback edition with a new preface published 2015

ISBN 978-1-59184-662-8 (hc.)
ISBN 978-1-59523-121-5 (pbk.)

Printed in the United States of America
1 3 5 7 9 10 8 6 4 2

Set in Adobe Garamond Pro
Designed by Spring Hoteling

For Charles J. Stephens
1937–2011
In Cherished Memory

The price of greatness is responsibility. If the people of the United States had continued in a mediocre station, struggling with the wilderness, absorbed in their own affairs, and a factor of no consequence in the movement of the world, they might have remained forgotten and undisturbed beyond their protecting oceans: but one cannot rise to be in many ways the leading community in the civilized world without being involved in its problems, without being convulsed by its agonies and inspired by its causes.

Winston Churchill

CONTENTS

Current event books have a way of getting old fast.

When I began writing *America in Retreat*, in the fall of 2012, the notion that we were on the cusp of a violently disordered world seemed far-fetched to many knowledgeable observers. "The world is a relatively forgiving place now and for the foreseeable future," wrote Richard Haass, president of the Council on Foreign Relations. President Obama picked up the theme, insisting in his second inaugural address that "a decade of war is now ending." Relations with Russia had been reset, Osama bin Laden was dead, a pivot to Asia was underway, Iraq was at peace, Europe had put the worst of the euro crisis behind it, the core of Al Qaeda was on a path to defeat, and the rest of Al Qaeda was "the JV team." The post-9/11, post–financial crisis world seemed finally to be coming around.

Today, in 2015, predictions that once seemed alarmist are now facts of international life. The coming global disorder has become the current one.

As I write, chemical weapons continue to be used in Syria. Russia continues to wage war in Ukraine. An Islamic caliphate, drawing recruits from

Manchester to Minneapolis, continues to wage a jihad that is increasingly global in scope. Four Arab states are in various stages of disintegration. Iran is on the verge of becoming a nuclear threshold state. China lays claim to nearly the whole of the South China Sea and routinely picks quarrels with Japan, Vietnam, the Philippines, and Indonesia. North Korea's arsenal of nuclear weapons may double within a year. Chronic youth unemployment in Europe, topping 50 percent in some countries, drives politics to the extremes. Liberal democracy, which twenty years ago was the undisputed political model for much of the world, no longer represents the "end of history," assuming it ever did.

It says something about the pace of the unfolding disorder that the name Islamic State did not make it into the book—the capture of Mosul by ISIS in June 2014 was the last major event I managed to squeeze into the manuscript before delivering it to my publisher, but I was still referring to it as "Al Qaeda in Iraq." (I have updated the reference for this edition.) If that was a mark of the book's datedness, I would like to think it's also a sign of its prescience. What matters for a book like this isn't whether it is making reference to the latest news. It's whether it is making sense of it.

A central contention of this book is that the cause of the new disorder is the retreat of American power, creating power vacuums that have been filled by willful and violent interlopers. This retreat has been partly physical: the retreats from Iraq and Afghanistan; our shrinking overseas military footprint (smaller than at any time in our post–World War II history); the hollowing out of the military itself. But mainly the retreat has been a matter of credibility and expectations. The president's red lines aren't real. America isn't coming to anyone else's rescue. Our enemies know this, as do our friends. The result is a world where the rogues do as they please while our friends do as they must.

Since the book's publication, my critics have argued that I misrepresented Obama's foreign policy, or misinterpreted the cause of the disorder, or exaggerated the ability of any president to influence the course of events. The book addresses these and other criticisms far more extensively than I can in this short preface, so I won't repeat myself here.

I would, however, like to address three particular criticisms. One is that the case I make in favor of America being the world's policeman neglects the fact that cops cannot be a law unto themselves. Police must obey certain rules and answer to higher authorities—the courts, the law, the citizenry the law is intended to serve. According to some critics, the only higher authority that conceivably fits that description is the United Nations, and surely I'm not arguing that U.S. foreign policy should be made subservient to it.

But it's worth repeating that the policing I'm calling for is based on the broken-windows model that worked so effectively in putting an end to the crime waves of the 1970s and 80s. Broken-windows policing is chiefly concerned not with reacting to instances of disorder, but with establishing a sense of *orderliness*, a palpable feeling that someone is in charge, someone is keeping an eye out, someone is on the side of the law-abiding—and that someone has a gun. The essential ingredient is *presence*. In foreign policy, this means keeping troops, planes, and ships stationed overseas, where they can serve as visible evidence of America's commitment to regional security. Legitimacy is satisfied by the consent of the host country, not the blessings of the UN.

A second criticism is that America cannot meet the requirements of global policing unless it is prepared to undertake lengthy occupations of broken nations such as Iraq, Yemen, or Syria—an undertaking few Americans are eager to embark upon and one I generally reject in the book. But the occupations I reject are *political* occupations, typified by Jerry Bremer's regency in Iraq, which seek to take charge of the entire life of a nation by writing constitutions, setting up elections, organizing economies, and so on. Maintaining military garrisons in foreign countries—as we do in Britain, South Korea, Japan, Germany, Spain, Italy, Turkey, and Afghanistan, to name the principal examples—is not occupation.

As it is, most of the policing actions I advocate are short and mission-specific, not broad and open-ended. There may be extraordinary times when the United States must respond to a threat in some very large way. That was the case after 9/11. But Washington cannot hope to eliminate every terrorist safe haven in the world by way of seizing, holding, and clearing territory.

What the United States can do is put our enemies on the run and, where necessary, support friendly proxies who can help us finish the job. In Syria, this would have meant carrying out punitive air strikes on the Assad regime (particularly its air force) for its use of chemical weapons; training, equipping, and sustaining the Free Syrian Army; establishing no-fly zones; encouraging the Saudis, Turks, and Jordanians to intercede if possible—all steps the administration conspicuously failed to take, with consequences obvious to all. Just because we don't want to be on the hook for the fate of other nations doesn't mean we have to embrace what my friend Michael Doran calls "The Sarah Palin, 'Let Allah Sort It Out' Doctrine of Foreign Policy." And just because we can't do everything doesn't mean our only option is to do nothing.

Then there's the argument that the world's disorders have little if anything to do with U.S. policy, and so therefore shouldn't involve us. But saying "we aren't to blame" is very different from saying "it's not our problem." Foreign policy, after all, is sometimes the business of cleaning up other people's messes before they become our own. It is also not enough to say that, just because there is a certain trend, there has to be a definite, inevitable result. No law of nature required Syria's uprising to descend into a state of nature. Nor is there anything inevitable about an Iranian nuclear bomb, or Chinese hegemony in East Asia, or Russian dominance of its "near-abroad." It remains in our hands to shape, and sometimes reverse, the trend.

One final point: My ninth chapter, written in the early months of 2014, offers a scenario for the years 2015–2019. So far, I've been proved right about the strengthening of the dollar, the sharp drop in the price of oil, the implosion of the Russian economy, and Saudi Arabia's geopolitical jitters. I chose not to update the chapter for this edition so the reader can judge for himself how well the scenario holds up over time. As it is, what matters is not the accuracy of the prediction but the need for showing some imagination in thinking through the potential consequences of decisions being made today.

It's normal for any author to find lines he would rephrase, arguments he would flesh out, phrases or sentences he might delete. So it is for me. But I also believe that the passage of time continues to vindicate my thesis. What's needed now is political leadership that can draw the right lessons and act on them.

May 15, 2015

INTRODUCTION

* * *

The World's Policeman

In the nearly nine years that I have been the foreign affairs columnist for *The Wall Street Journal*, I have received tens of thousands of letters from readers, many of them warm, a few of them rude, others critical or constructive. I publish my e-mail address, bstephens@wsj.com, at the foot of my column, read every note, and try to answer as many of my readers as I can. But there are times when a letter deserves a more extended reply than I have time for in the course of an ordinary workday. One reader, responding to a March 2014 column advocating a muscular U.S. stance against Russia's seizure of the Crimean peninsula, wrote me just such a letter.

> In response to your editorial today, please repeat after me: "We should not be the world's policeman." Repeat again. And again. Apparently, you just do not get it that an overwhelming majority of Americans would agree with this declaration. Unfortunately, you do not. So, given that, I encourage you to form your own

volunteer army to police the hotspots around the globe. Please do not remit any bills to the U.S. government.

Barack Obama agrees with my reader. "We should not be the world's policeman," he told Americans in September 2013. So does Rand Paul: "America's mission should always be to keep the peace, not police the world," the Kentucky Republican told an audience of veterans earlier that year.

This book is my answer to that argument.

In formulating the answer, it's important to acknowledge that the wish not to be the world's policeman runs deep in the American psyche. "For wee must Consider that wee shall be as a Citty upon a Hill, the eies of all people are uppon us," John Winthrop warned his fellow Massachusetts Bay colonists in 1630 as they were aboard the *Arbella* on their way to the New World,

> soe that if wee shall deale falsely with our god in this worke wee have undertaken and soe cause him to withdrawe his present help from us, wee shall be made a story and a byword through the world, wee shall open the mouthes of enemies to speake evill of the wayes of god and all professours for Gods sake; wee shall shame the faces of many of gods worthy servants, and cause theire prayers to be turned into Cursses upon us till wee be consumed out of the good land whether wee are going. . . .

Though the phrase "city upon a hill" is taken from Jesus's Sermon on the Mount ("A city that is set on a hill cannot be hid"), Winthrop's admonition is pure Old Testament. The Lord's blessing depends not on our worldly striving but on our moral performance. The fate of the enterprise rests on the virtue of its people. A bad reputation in the opinion of mankind can be fatal. The great task for Americans is to be supremely mindful of *our* business, not of someone else's. Our security as well as our salvation lie in the proper care of our souls, not the acquisition or exercise of power.

To study American history is to understand that Winthrop's admonition has been honored mainly in the breach. The citizens of a city upon a hill may be in "the eies of all people." But those citizens, in turn, will be able to see far over the surrounding lowlands. At a glance, they will see rich plains stretching in every direction. They will seek dominion over those plains and their scattered inhabitants, whether through purchase and treaties or confiscation and war. Beyond the plain they will find oceans to harvest and traverse. They will meet enemies on the seas, and to defeat those enemies they will build a navy. In faraway ports they will find wealth and wonders but also double-dealing and cruelty, arousing their appetite and greed—but also their conscience and charity.

And in mixing with the world they will become part of the world. Yet they shall still think of themselves as a city upon a hill.

So it is that America's encounter with the world has always been stamped with ambivalence about the nature, and even the necessity, of that encounter. It is an ambivalence that has often been overcome—because the temptation was too great, as it was with the war with Mexico, or because the danger was too great, as it was during the Cold War. But the ambivalence has never been erased. Nearly 240 years after our birth, we Americans haven't quite made up our minds about what we think of the rest of the world. Every now and then, we're tempted to return to our imaginary city, raise the gate, and leave others to their devices.

It says something about the politics of our time that I have no idea whether the reader who wrote me that letter is a Republican or a Democrat, a Tea Party activist or a lifelong subscriber to *Mother Jones*. This is new. Until recently, the view that "we should not be the world's policeman" was held mainly on the political left. Yes, the view also found a home on the fringes of the right, particularly among small-government libertarians and latter-day Father Coughlins such as Pat Buchanan. But it was typically the left that wanted America out: out of Southeast Asia, Central America, the Middle East, even Europe. And it was usually the left that made the case for a reduced role for the United States in global politics and for a radical rebalancing of spending priorities from guns to butter.

The case for "America Out" is still common on the left. But now it's being made from within the mainstream of the conservative movement. Many things account for this change, including the deep mistrust, sometimes slipping to paranoia, of the Obama administration's foreign policy aims. Many conservatives have also conceded the argument that the wars they once ardently supported in Iraq and Afghanistan were historic mistakes, and that imbroglios in Central Asia, Eastern Europe, or the South China Sea are other people's problems, best kept at arm's length.

The upshot is that there is a new foreign policy divide in the United States cutting across traditional partisan and ideological divides. It's no longer a story of (mostly) Republican hawks versus (mostly) Democratic doves. Now it's an argument between neoisolationists and internationalists: between those who think the United States is badly overextended in the world and needs to be doing a lot less of everything—both for its own and the rest of the world's good—and those who believe in Pax Americana, a world in which the economic, diplomatic, and military might of the United States provides the global buffer between civilization and barbarism.

Some readers of this book will reject these categories. They will note that there are vast differences between liberal and conservative internationalists; between, say, Samantha Power, President Obama's ambassador to the United Nations, and John Bolton, her predecessor in that job under George W. Bush. Or they will claim that the term "neoisolationist" is a slur on people who really should be thought of as "noninterventionists" or simply "Realists." They will point out that labels often do more to cloud thinking than to clarify it. They're right, up to a point. But labels also capture emotional reflexes, ideological leanings, and tendencies of thought that in turn help predict policy preferences and political behavior.

Where do you fall on the spectrum between internationalists and neoisolationists? Ask yourself the following questions:

- Does the United States have a vital interest in the outcome of the civil war in Syria, or in Israel's relationship with the Palestinians, or in Saudi Arabia's contest with Iran?

- Should Americans take sides between China and Japan over which of them exercises sovereignty over the uninhabited Senkaku Islands? Similarly, should we care whether Ukraine or Russia controls Crimea?
- Is America more secure or less secure for deploying military forces in hot spots such as the Persian Gulf and the South China Sea?

How you answer any one of these questions will likely suggest how you answer most if not all of the others. And how you answer all of the questions will be an excellent indicator of how you are likely to think about other foreign policy crises, now or in the future.

This book takes a side in this debate. No great power can treat foreign policy as a spectator sport and hope to remain a great power. A world in which the leading liberal-democratic nation does not assume its role as world policeman will become a world in which dictatorships contend, or unite, to fill the breach. Americans seeking a return to an isolationist garden of Eden—alone and undisturbed in the world, knowing neither good nor evil—will soon find themselves living within shooting range of global pandemonium. It would be a world very much like the 1930s, another decade in which economic turmoil, war weariness, Western self-doubt, American self-involvement, and the rise of ambitious dictatorships combined to produce the catastrophe of World War II. When Franklin Roosevelt asked Winston Churchill what that war should be called, the prime minister replied "the unnecessary war." Why? Because, Churchill said, "never was a war more easy to stop than that which has just wrecked what was left of the world from the previous struggle." That's an error we should not wish to repeat.

A final preliminary: To say America needs to be the world's policeman is not to say we need to be its priest, preaching the gospel of the American way. Priests are in the business of changing hearts and saving souls. Cops merely walk the beat, reassuring the good, deterring the tempted, punishing the wicked. Nor is it to say we should be the world's martyr. Police work isn't altruism. It is done from necessity and self-interest. It is done because it has to be and there's no one else to do it, and because the benefits of doing it accrue not only to those we protect but also, indeed mainly, to ourselves.

Not everyone grows up wanting to be a cop. But who wants to live in a neighborhood, or a world, where there is no cop? Would you? Should the president?

★   ★   ★   ★

Sangin Valley, Afghanistan—The fighting season will begin in a few days, just as soon as the poppy harvest has been brought in. But the Marines are already gone. They left FOB Nolay, the last of what were once thirty forward operating bases in the valley, late at night on May 4. I watched them gather in the yard to stow away the trash, turn over the garbage bins, and have one final smoke before getting into their heavily armored mine rollers and MRAPs for the slow drive toward Camp Leatherneck, sixty miles away in the desert of Helmand province. They arrived seven hours later without casualty or serious incident.

Their war was over. The withdrawal—code-named Operation Palang-Lee—was described as a "retrograde" by the colonels and generals who orchestrated it. Why use the word "retrograde," I asked one Marine major. "I guess they didn't want to call it a retreat," he answered.

I embedded with the Marines for their last days in Sangin. The generators at Nolay were gone by the time I arrived, and we had to make do with MREs for food and WAG bags for toilets. On all sides of the tiny base we were defended, and surrounded, by the Afghan National Army, which for the previous eleven months had been conducting combat operations in the valley on its own while Americans stayed behind in an advisory role. It was a source of pride to the Marines that the Afghans were taking the fight to the Taliban with native courage and increasing skill. But the Marines remained at risk. In November a gunnery sergeant at the perimeter of the camp was shot in the shoulder by a Taliban sniper. In April, an Afghan within the camp tried to kill Marine advisers at the camp's shooting range; he was wrestled to the ground by his fellow Afghan soldiers before he could get off a shot. Early one morning I heard an IED explosion, followed by a burst of gunfire, a mile or two outside the base. It was a common enough occurrence as to barely elicit a comment from anyone at Nolay.

By the standards of the valley, this is peace. For years Sangin was a Taliban stronghold, the bloody crossroads where fanatical convictions, tribal identities, and heroin profits met. The British lost more than one hundred men in the early years of the war trying to bring the place they called Sangingrad under control. They failed, and in 2010 they handed the effort to the Marines as part of Obama's surge. More than twenty thousand U.S. troops deployed in Helmand on more than two hundred bases. On a visit to the valley in March 2011, Defense Secretary Robert Gates called Sangin not just the most dangerous place in Afghanistan "but maybe in the whole world."

The Marines who fought here suffered heavier losses trying to take the valley than any other unit in the war. Fifty were killed, though the number doesn't capture the scale of sacrifice in terms of lost limbs, traumatic brain injuries, and third-degree burns. Patrolling the garbage-strewn lanes of the valley—a narrow green belt running alongside the Helmand River—the Marines were hit again and again by IEDs. As recently as February, the Afghan army found 178 of them along a two-mile stretch of road.

Still the Marines crushed the Taliban. They proved they had the will and the wherewithal to destroy the enemy. They were the strongest tribe. The people of Sangin gave them their trust and shared what they knew about the Taliban's movements. The poppies are still harvested; eradication and crop-substitution efforts are mostly a sham. But government authority—and legitimacy—has been established. In national elections in 2009, just 179 people from the Sangin district turned out to vote. In April 2014, more than 5,000 did—58 percent of eligible voters. Two years ago the Marines began training the Afghans to take control of their own security, first on patrols with Americans in the lead, then with Afghans in the lead, then without any Americans at all.

It was as it should be, following the parable of teaching a man to fish so he can feed himself for a lifetime. Afghans knew how to fight—nobody had ever doubted it. What impressed their American trainers was that they knew how to be soldiers, too, disciplined, professional, resourceful. And committed: This was not an army of soldiers of fortune, or soldiers for hire, or soldiers of one ethnic group out to get the better of ancient rivals. It was an army of Afghans trying at last to take charge of their national destiny. "At a time when nobody is talking about winning," said one Marine adviser at Nolay, "they are talking about winning." Thousands of Afghan troops have died in the effort; in Sangin alone, one Afghan battalion alone lost more than six hundred men over the course of eight years.

But that's where Afghanistan's predicament lies. Just when Afghans are beginning to find faith in their cause, Americans have lost faith in theirs.

It's a thought that weighs on Brig. Gen. Daniel Yoo, the Marine in charge of the Regional Command that oversees Helmand. On September 10, 2001, Yoo had just returned from a tour in the Mediterranean to be reunited with his wife and their one-year-old son. Within a day he knew he'd be going to war. He arrived in Afghanistan in mid-November, just as the Taliban were fleeing Kabul and being bombed out of Kandahar. He's one of thousands of Marines for whom the war in Afghanistan has defined their professional, personal, and family lives.

"I don't want people to think it wasn't worth it," he tells me the evening the Marines returned to Leatherneck. "I'm an optimist. I have to be an optimist. I've seen too many Marines die here. I have to think it is worth it."

There's no mistaking the conviction in Yoo's voice. If the Taliban return to power after we leave, how can we be sure we won't have to go in again? Is there no advantage to having U.S. forces stationed in a country that has Pakistan on one side and Iran on the other? Would Osama bin Laden and other senior Al Qaeda leaders be dead today had we not been able to go after them from bases in Afghanistan?

"We've spent a lot of blood and treasure in this country," Yoo says. "At the end of the day, whose credibility is at stake?"[1]

Yet as Yoo speaks, it occurs to me that he's trying to make himself believe that he will be believed. Most Americans couldn't care less whether or not the Marines have successfully pacified Sangin. They aren't interested in learning that we're winning, or that Afghans are making progress. They just want out. A CNN poll from December 2013 found that a mere 17 percent of the U.S. public supported the effort in Afghanistan, down from 52 percent in December 2008.

Americans didn't turn against the war in Afghanistan in the same way they turned on the war in Iraq—as in a failing marriage, it was more a case of gradual disenchantment than of scandalous revelation. But turn they did.

There is no shortage of reasons for that. Thirteen years is a long time to be at war. There's a depressing sameness to the conflict: the Taliban get pushed back; they creep forward; they get pushed back again. The Afghan government seems to repay generosity with corruption, honest dealing with shenanigans. Every instance of "insider attacks"— Afghan police or soldiers turning their guns on Westerners— tells Americans that no Afghan can ever fully be trusted.

None of this is untrue, but it's also a caricature of reality. Aside from special operations, American soldiers no longer do much actual fighting in Afghanistan. What they provide is training, logistics—and confidence. The Taliban have been defeated in the most important battlefield of all: public opinion. The Afghan government is undoubtedly corrupt, like governments in all developing countries, but at least the country is developing. Afghanistan now has nearly eight million children in school, up tenfold since 2001. More than 80 percent of people have access to health care, up from 8 percent under the Taliban. Westerners and their families continue to make their homes in Kabul.

A president who believed in his own war might say such things to the public. But Obama almost never speaks of Afghanistan. Long before the Marines withdrew from the battle, he withdrew from the politics of the battle. Why should Americans be expected to support a struggle that the commander in chief is so plainly not committed to winning? Why not join him in beating the global retreat that is the motivating impulse of his presidency?

Much of my time in Sangin was spent in the company of Afghans. Their attitudes combined bravado with apprehension. Again and again they told me they were ready to fight for themselves—but they still were counting on U.S. help. Who was I to tell them that Americans had grown frustrated and bored with them; that we weren't interested anymore in hearing about their progress or their sacrifice? A "transition" was taking place in Afghanistan, as well it should, but it was a transition being dictated by an overwhelming desire not to succeed but to depart.

We lifted off from FOB Nolay on a CH-53 Super Stallion at around 10:30 at night, maybe the last U.S. helicopter to leave the place. It was too dark to see anything; the roar of the rotors made it impossible to hear anything. I wondered what the Afghans were thinking, looking up at us for perhaps the last time. Mainly, though, I wondered: what are we thinking?

CHAPTER I

* * *

Come Home, America

America is in retreat.

Let's be clear about what retreat is *not*. Retreat is not decline—though it can be a symptom of decline, or a cause of it. Retreat is not surrender—though, as Napoleon is reputed to have said, "the logical outcome of retreat *is* surrender." Retreat is not cowardice; it can also be an act of prudence, even salvation, as Churchill knew from the deliverance at Dunkirk. Yet Churchill also knew, and warned, that "wars are not won by evacuations."

Nevertheless, America's retreat—or what the Obama administration prefers to call "retrenchment"[1]—is the central fact of this decade, just as the war on terror was the central fact of the last decade. We got out of Iraq—at least until we had to go back in. We are getting out of Afghanistan. We want no part of what's happening in Syria no matter how many civilians are brutalized or red lines crossed. We are dramatically curtailing our use of drones in Pakistan. We pretend to "pivot" to Asia, but so far the pivot has mostly been a feint. We are quietly backing away from our security guarantees to Taiwan. We denounce Russia's seizure of Crimea, accusing Moscow of being hopelessly out of touch with the accepted norms of the twenty-first century. But we refuse requests by the Ukrainian government to provide their diminished military with arms. In November 2013 Secretary of State John Kerry went so far as to renounce the mainstay of U.S. foreign policy in the Western Hemisphere for 190 years. "The era of the Monroe Doctrine is over," the secretary told the Organization of American States. "That's worth applauding, that's not a bad thing."

We're also in retreat at home. In the name of civil liberties we are taking apart the post-9/11 domestic security architecture—warrantless wiretaps, telephony metadata collection, police surveillance programs—brick by brick. In the name of budgetary savings the Army is returning to its June 1940 size, the month Nazi Germany conquered France. In 2013 the Navy put fewer ships to sea than at any time since 1916, before our entry into World War I,[2] and ship numbers keep falling. In the spring of 2014 the Pentagon announced it would cut U.S. nuclear forces, four years ahead of schedule, to comply with the terms of the 2010 New START treaty. Within days of the announcement Moscow test-fired its latest multiple-warhead ICBM. The size of Russia's nuclear arsenal has *grown* since it signed New START.[3] As for NATO, total military spending as a percentage of aggregate GDP is at the lowest point in the alliance's sixty-five-year history.

Not long ago, these trends would have prompted anxious and extensive public debate. These days, not so much. A growing number of Americans no longer want the United States to shape the world according to its interests and values, or out of a sense of global stewardship, or even from a concept of enlightened self-interest. Nowadays, Americans mainly want to be left alone.

Sounding this American retreat is Barack Obama with his signature foreign policy theme: "nation building at home." It's a revealing phrase. Every president since World War II has worked to strengthen the economy, reduce unemployment, build or repair infrastructure, mend the frayed edges of society, and launch major domestic initiatives—from the interstate highways to the Great Society to welfare reform. Never before have domestic ambitions prevented any president from championing America's forward strategic momentum in the world. That is, until Obama came to office and began treating foreign and domestic policies as if they were an either-or proposition. In academic parlance, "nation building" is an exercise reserved for failed states: Somalia, Bosnia, Afghanistan. It takes a remarkably dim view of the United States to suggest we fall into that category.

For Obama, an activist foreign policy isn't a complement to a strong domestic agenda. It's a distraction from it. His ideal foreign policy is to have *less* foreign policy, on the view that there's a sharp limit on what the United States can hope to achieve. The president insists he isn't a declinist. But as he told one interviewer in 2013, "I am more mindful probably than most of not only our incredible strengths and capabilities, but also our limitations."[4]

PRESIDENT CANUTE

Happily for the president, he believes nation building at home is possible because global trends are benign and don't demand our attention elsewhere. Hence the other line of which he is so fond: "The tide of war is receding."

In nature, tides wax and wane according to forces beyond the will, vanity, or wishes of men: the legendary King Canute, standing on the seashore ordering the tides to recede as the water laps his feet, is a parable for this reason. If war is indeed a tide then a president can *observe* it receding. But he cannot *make* it recede with a speech, an executive order, or even the removal of troops from a foreign country.

Since becoming president Obama has been engaged in a kind of conjurer's trick, pretending to make the tide recede when he's merely backing away from the waterline. "Core Al Qaeda," he likes to say, is "on a path to defeat." What remains of the group, he adds, poses mostly a nuisance threat. This being so, President Canute concludes, "we must define the nature and scope of this struggle, or else it will define us." War is what we choose it to be. It is in our hands to engage, or desist from engaging, just as we please.

This is a comforting thought. But it knows no precedent in the annals of human conflict. "You may not be interested in war, but war is interested in you," Leon Trotsky is said to have observed. War *is*; how we choose to speak or think of it doesn't change it. Wars end because they have been won, or lost, or brought to some kind of mutually agreed truce. Only in the age of Obama do wars end by means of attitude and expectation adjustment, of learning to "move on," in the parlance of left-wing politics and popular psychotherapy.

"I think of the New Yorkers who filled Times Square the day after an attempted car bomb as if nothing had happened," the president told Americans in May 2013, referring to the May 2010 terrorist attempt by Pakistani-American Faisal Shahzad. But New Yorkers only acted that way because, in fact, nothing happened. A different president might have urged people to remain calm while recognizing that only a bomber's incompetence spared the city from an atrocity at a crowded intersection. Obama's message about terrorism, like Jimmy Carter's message about communism, is that it's time Americans got over their "inordinate" fear of it.

In the year the president made this pronouncement, Al Qaeda in Iraq—a spent and discredited force when Obama took office—murdered 8,000 civilians in a country where 4,400 Americans had recently given their lives. A year later, as this book was going to press, Islamic State seized Mosul, Iraq's second city, and began marching on Baghdad. An Al Qaeda offshoot in North Africa nearly overran the nation of Mali and was only stopped by emergency French military intervention, an intervention Obama initially refused to support. That summer the United States closed more than twenty of its embassies and consulates after intelligence emerged of a terrorist plot "very reminiscent of what we saw pre-9/11," as one member of the Senate Intelligence Committee put it. "Regrouped Al Qaeda Poses Global Threat," *The Wall Street Journal* reported in a front-page headline. The National Security Agency even succeeded in listening in on a conference call of Al Qaeda leaders. "The intercept provided the U.S. intelligence community with a rare glimpse into how Al Qaeda's leader, Ayman al-Zawahiri, manages a global organization that includes affiliates in Africa, the Middle East, and southwest and southeast Asia," *The Daily Beast* reported.[5] A 2014 report by Seth Jones of the RAND Corporation found that between 2010 and 2013 the number of jihadist groups rose by 58 percent, the number of jihadist fighters doubled to 100,000, and the number of Al Qaeda attacks jumped from 392 to 1,000.[6] If Al Qaeda is on the path to defeat, as Obama often says, it remains a very long path.

The return of the jihadists arrives in tandem with the return of rogue states, another political category from the Bush years that Obama's presidency was supposed to have redefined out of existence or engaged into cooperation. As I write, North Korea appears to be close to conducting its fourth nuclear test. China is making legally risible but militarily serious territorial claims from India to Indonesia. The Assad regime continues to defy Obama's once-confident predictions of its imminent demise. Russia is orchestrating a covert takeover of eastern Ukraine and Vladimir Putin is speaking openly about a "new Russia" with new, bigger borders. Iran has successfully defended its client in Damascus and appears to be on the cusp of achieving its twin strategic objectives: the easing of international sanctions without the abandonment of core nuclear capabilities.

But the president does not seem overly perturbed: "There's a suggestion somehow that the Russian actions have been clever, strategically," he said about Moscow's Crimean caper. "I actually think that this is [*sic*] not been a sign of strength." Happy is the statesman who convinces himself that his adversaries' triumphs are not triumphs at all; that the cold water rising above his knees is something other than a waxing tide.

Obama's failings as a world leader—his habits of indifference, illusion, and self-regard—have not gone unnoticed among our allies. "In Europe, doubts about America's wisdom, strength and resolve are increasingly focused on the person of the president," notes John Vinocur, the former editor of *The International Herald Tribune*.[7] Former French president Nicolas Sarkozy is reported to have told an aide that Obama "is not a leader but a follower."[8] U.S. policy in Syria, says Saudi Arabia's Prince Turki al-Faisal, "would be funny if it were not so blatantly perfidious, and designed not only to give Mr. Obama an opportunity to back down, but also to help Assad butcher his people."⁹ "We can't continue in this state of limbo," complains Canada's foreign minister about the administration's endless postponement of a decision on the Keystone XL pipeline. "If your image is feebleness, it doesn't pay in the world," says Israeli defense minister Moshe Ya'alon. "We thought it would be the United States that would lead the campaign against Iran." Instead, Washington was "showing weakness. Therefore, on this matter [Iran's nuclear programs], we have to behave as though we have nobody to look out for us but ourselves."¹⁰

U.S. adversaries have noticed, too. Masoud Jazayeri, an Iranian general, calls Obama a "low-IQ president." Obama, he says, "speaks of the effectiveness of 'the U.S. options on the table' on Iran while this phrase is mocked at and has become a joke among the Iranian nation, especially the children."¹¹ A top adviser to the prime minister of Turkey calls Obama "a half-leader."¹² After Russia's formal annexation of Crimea, the United States sanctioned a handful of Russian individuals. "It seems to me that some kind of joker wrote the U.S. president's order :-)" tweeted Russian deputy prime minister Dmitry Rogozin, one of the sanctioned individuals.

These aren't mere words. Perceptions shape actions. Allies who doubt the credibility of American security guarantees, of its strength of will, will pursue their interests irrespective of Washington's wishes or commands. Enemies who think they have nothing to fear from the United States will do as they please. Should Americans care that Israel might strike Iran's nuclear facilities because Jerusalem has lost confidence in Obama's promises to prevent Iran from getting a bomb? Perhaps we should, because such a strike could draw the United States into a conflict in a time and manner not of our choosing. And should we mind that leaders in Beijing, Moscow, or Tehran think the president of the United States is a self-infatuated weakling? The answer is yes, assuming we don't want to see Taiwan, Estonia, or Bahrain become the next Crimea.

To all this criticism, defenders of the administration insist that the United States is not retreating under Obama. Instead, they say, it is merely reducing its exposure to the Middle East by backing away from unwinnable and fruitless wars, seeking acceptable strategic accommodations with adversaries such as Iran, "taking the long view" of sweeping historical currents such as the Arab Spring (to avoid getting swept into them), keeping the pressure on Al Qaeda while making fine-grained distinctions between truly dangerous enemies and mere local nuisances. They also say the administration is husbanding American energies by refusing to impose military solutions upon the world's every tragic situation, while attending to more important corners of the globe. "We have to be able to distinguish between these problems analytically," Obama told *New Yorker* editor David Remnick, "so that we're not using pliers where we need a hammer, or we're not using a battalion when what we should be doing is partnering with the local government to train their police force more effectively, improve their intelligence capacities."

Yet even the most ardent supporters of the president are hard-pressed to argue that a signature foreign policy initiative such as the Russian Reset has been a rousing triumph of American diplomacy. "The days when empires could treat sovereign states as pieces on a chessboard are over," Obama declared in Moscow in 2009, at the start of his presidency. Now the remark seems almost amusing. Russia has spent the Obama presidency pocketing one American concession after another: the abrupt cancellation of U.S. ballistic missile defense sites in central Europe in 2009; nuclear superiority over the United States via the New START treaty in 2010; vastly enhanced diplomatic leverage in Syria and Egypt following the Arab Spring; America's de facto acquiescence in the seizure of Crimea in 2014.

As for another signature administration move, the so-called pivot to Asia, a news story in Reuters took brutal stock of it in October 2013, three years after it was first announced: "When then U.S. Secretary of State Hillary Clinton declared two years ago 'we are back to stay' as a power in Asia, the most dramatic symbol of the policy shift was the planned deployment of 2,500 U.S. Marines in northern Australia, primed to respond to any regional conflict. At this point in time, however, there is not a single U.S. Marine in the tropical northern city of Darwin, according to the Australian defense ministry."[13] Several months later,

Assistant Secretary of Defense Katrina McFarland let slip that "right now, the pivot is being looked at again, because candidly it can't happen."[14] Next it emerged that the Navy was meeting the pivot's goal of deploying 60 percent of its ships to the Pacific through the simple expedient of decommissioning ships based in the Atlantic.[15] Even the semantics are telling: "The U.S. has significantly contributed to the confusion" about the meaning of the term "pivot," notes Trefor Moss in *The Diplomat*, "by repeatedly reframing the strategy, which was originally a 'pivot' and then evolved into a 'rebalancing,' a 'shift,' and now also a 'Pacific dream.'"[16] This is an administration for which no problem is beyond the reach of a semantic fix.

One looks in vain for other administration foreign policy successes. Obama's brief surge in Afghanistan to "disrupt" the Taliban, rather than defeat it, resulted in one thousand American deaths, proving that wars inevitably become expensive when their goals are made cheap. The killing of Osama bin Laden was a great operational achievement and a cathartic American moment, and Obama deserves full marks for ordering the mission. But a tactical success is not a strategic victory, and bin Laden's death has mainly served the administration's political objective of declaring victory in the war on terror and going home.

John Kerry's marathon efforts to broker Israeli-Palestinian peace ended in failure, all the more complete for being so completely predictable. Administration supporters will sometimes argue that it is better to try and fail than not to try at all. Yet diplomatic capital, like money itself, cannot be made limitless without also becoming cheap. Even if Kerry *had* succeeded—achieving the goal that eluded every former secretary of state from Dean Acheson to Hillary Clinton—what would it have accomplished for the United States? The symbolism might have been good, but the notion that resolving the Arab-Israeli conflict would ease other frictions in the Middle East, from Sunni-Shia tensions to the lack of opportunity for Arab youth to the theological attractions of militant Islam, does not withstand basic scrutiny.

At this writing it is too soon to say what will become of efforts to negotiate a nuclear deal with Tehran. What is clear is that any negotiated settlement will require the United States to abandon its long-held insistence, backed by multiple UN Security Council resolutions, that Iran give up its uranium-enrichment capability, which is the core of a nuclear-weapons program, in exchange for diplomatic concessions from the West. The best plausible deal will leave Iran six months away from being able to produce enough highly enriched uranium to produce a bomb, as opposed to two months away with its current capabilities. But that would require a degree of faith in Tehran's honesty that nothing in the Islamic Republic's history can justify. And why should Americans be confident that the same intelligence agencies that got the story of Iraq's WMD completely wrong would nonetheless be able to catch and prevent the Iranians from cheating?

Obama has even failed to restore a measure of international affection for the United States. In Egypt and Turkey—both places Obama went out of his way to woo early in his presidency—public perceptions of the United States plumb deeper lows than they did under George W. Bush. In Europe, the days when Obama could bring out crowds by the tens of thousands to listen to him speak are a distant memory. Instead, he has become the president who listens in on Angela Merkel's phone calls. Or so Europeans think. The truth is worse: "President Barack Obama went nearly five years without knowing his own spies were bugging the phones of world leaders," *The Wall Street Journal* reported in October 2013. It's hard to accuse the president of being malevolent when he's merely inattentive.

A CHANGE OF HEART

And yet the cascade of foreign policy failures and reversals seems not to make much of a dent on America's consciousness. It's all taking place far from our shores. And all of it, we seem to imagine, will remain beyond our shores so long as we don't overly concern ourselves about it. An era of American internationalism is giving way, with amazing swiftness, to a period of American indifference.

In the fall of 2013, the Pew Research Center found that for the first time since it began polling the question in 1964, a majority of Americans—52 percent—agree with the view that the United States "should mind its own business internationally." That's up from 20 percent in 1964 and 30 percent in 2002. The feeling is broadly bipartisan. Another Pew survey noted that in 2011 just 39 percent of conservative Republicans agreed that it is "best to remain active in world affairs," down from 58 percent in 2004. Across the political spectrum, 58 percent favor paying "less attention to problems overseas," with 65 percent saying they want to "reduce overseas military commitments." That includes a majority of self-identified Republicans. Several months later, after Russia's conquest of Crimea, another Pew poll found that 56 percent of Americans—including 50 percent of Republicans—thought the right policy was to "not get too involved in the situation." Only 29 percent of Americans favored taking a "firm stand against the Russians."[17]

To what degree Obama's approach to foreign policy has shaped these attitudes—and to what degree the attitudes have shaped the approach—is difficult to say. "The president had a truly disturbing habit of funneling major foreign-policy decisions through a small cabal of relatively inexperienced White House advisors whose turf was strictly politics," complained Vali Nasr, a State Department aide in the administration's early days. "Their primary concern was how any action in Afghanistan or the Middle East would play on the nightly news, or which talking point it would give Republicans."[18]

Then again, what message were Americans sending the administration when it came to foreign policy? Mainly, that they would rather neither hear nor know much about it. This, too, found a reflection in the White House. "Even as the debate about arming the [Syrian] rebels took on a new urgency," reported *The New York Times*, "Mr. Obama rarely voiced strong opinions during senior staff meetings. But current and former officials said his body language was telling: he often appeared impatient and disengaged while listening to the debate, sometimes scrolling through messages on his BlackBerry or slouching and chewing gum."[19] A former State Department aide noted bitterly that, even as it was becoming clear that Assad was crossing Obama's red line on chemical weapons, "there was no plan in place to respond to a major chemical attack by a regime that had already demonstrated its deep and abiding contempt for the president and his red lines."[20] The aide shouldn't have been surprised. Why should the administration draw up contingency plans for something neither the president nor the American people wanted to do?

The causes of this indifference can be summed up in two words: Iraq and recession. In the crude version of conventional wisdom, the United States embarked on a ruinous misadventure in Mesopotamia that wound up bankrupting the national coffers and led directly to the economic travails that followed. "For over the last decade," Obama said in May 2013, "our nation has spent well over a trillion dollars on war, exploding our deficits and constraining our ability to nation build here at home." Yet Obama spent more money in a single day—February 18, 2009—with the signing of the $787 billion stimulus package than the Defense Department spent in Iraq in an entire decade: $770 billion.[21] Many things are responsible for our "exploding deficits," involving more than $33 trillion in federal expenditures since 2001. The approximately $1.5 trillion spent in Iraq and Afghanistan is not the major part of it.

A smarter explanation for the new American indifference is that the hard experience of Iraq, followed by the long twilight of Afghanistan, shows that sometimes the game is not worth the candle. "Nation building" might have been worth American treasure and energy when the nations being built were postwar Japan and Germany, or post–Cold War Poland. But what serious hopes could there have been for nation building in Baghdad or Kabul? Were these going to be turned into democratic showcases for the rest of the Muslim world? It's a reasonable question. If Americans are now resistant to the idea of intervening abroad, so the argument goes, it's because they are drawing a firm line between core and peripheral U.S. interests, and don't want to squander their energies on the latter.

As for the U.S. economy, now in its sixth year of anemic growth, it's also not a shock that Americans should worry more about their next paycheck or their next job than about the outcome of a civil war in Syria or an island dispute near the Philippines. One might also fairly make the argument that our indifference to the rest of the world is a rational response to an international environment that does not really threaten us all that much. During the Cold War, the reality that thousands of Soviet ICBMs were a half hour's flight time away from every American city gave everyone a personal stake in the conduct of foreign policy. But the Cold War is over. There are other things to worry about, starting with ourselves.

No wonder, then, that we have entered a period in which Americans are generally turning their back on the rest of the world. It has a compelling superficial logic, and a potent political appeal. It's why Obama polled well in his handling of foreign policy, at least in his first term, and why an increasing number of Tea Party and libertarian-leaning Republicans like Sen. Rand Paul are espousing their own version of George McGovern's "Come Home, America" speech. If Barack Obama wants to retreat from America's global commitments in order to build bigger government, many Republicans want to reduce those commitments for the sake of smaller government. The ends differ, but the means are the same.

WHAT IS ISOLATIONISM?

The word for this point of view is *isolationism*. It's a worldview that deserves a measure of intellectual respect and a certain amount of moral rehabilitation. It is a principled approach to foreign policy that expresses a profound *Americanism*—a belief that the United States really is a nation apart, an exceptional nation. "The great rule of conduct for us, in regard to foreign nations, is in extending our commercial relations, to have with them as little political connection as possible," wrote George Washington in his Farewell Address. Jefferson's first inaugural expresses essentially the same idea in less dour terms: "Peace, commerce, and honest friendship with all nations, entangling alliances with none." The word *isolationism* itself derives from the proud phrase "splendid isolation," a late-nineteenth-century description of British policy toward Europe under the prime ministerships of Benjamin Disraeli and Lord Salisbury. When the America First Committee was formed in 1940 to urge America to keep out of the war, its membership was a who's who of the twentieth century's great and good: poet E. E. Cummings, Wisconsin senator Robert La Follette, future Supreme Court justice Potter Stewart, future president Gerald Ford, and future Peace Corps founder Sargent Shriver, to name a few.

These are not disreputable precedents. Nor is it right to suggest that "isolationism" is ipso facto an expression of parochialism or xenophobia, or a yearning for total economic self-reliance or minimal diplomatic contact with outsiders, or a word intended to denote a narrowly defined set of beliefs. Isolationism isn't even an ideology. It is a tendency, a frame of mind, an attitude. "Neo-isolationism signifies doubt about American omnipotence and omniscience and desire to confine intervention to areas of indisputable American interest," noted the historian Arthur Schlesinger, Jr., in 1983. "It does not signify economic, commercial, or cultural isolationism; but then neither did historic isolationism (which is why those historians altogether miss the point who think they have exposed isolationism as a 'legend' by demonstrating that 'isolationist' United States in the 1920s had financial relations with other countries)."[22]

More recently, *New York Times* columnist Bill Keller offered another useful working definition. "Isolationism," he wrote,

> is not just an aversion to war, which is an altogether healthy instinct. It is a broader reluctance to engage, to assert responsibility, to commit. Isolationism tends to be pessimistic (we will get it wrong, we will make it worse) and amoral (it is none of our business unless it threatens us directly) and inward-looking (foreign aid is a waste of money better spent at home).[23]

This is an excellent description, except in one respect: isolationists do not think of themselves as amoral. On the contrary, they are the ultimate moralists, and they are prepared to put their brand of morality ahead of most considerations of necessity and pragmatism. On the left, isolationism is the logical policy prescription for people whose instincts lean toward pacifism (war never solves anything), cultural relativism (who are we to judge?), and original American sin (it's all the fault of our own past misbehavior). On the right, isolationism suits people who believe that culture determines everything (we can't save others from themselves), and the law of unintended consequences (whatever we do will backfire). Left or right, isolationism has never made its case in the Machiavellian language of power, necessity, and fortune. On the contrary, it typically expresses itself in the Kantian terms of right and peace, categorical and perpetual.

For the purposes of this book, an isolationist is someone who:

1. Consistently views an activist foreign policy as a net drain on more important domestic considerations.

2. Believes that the United States enjoys little benefit from, and has no business, being the "world's policeman" or "leader of the free world."

3. Thinks that the United States should drastically curtail its overseas military presence.

4. Opposes nearly any military action that is not in direct response to an attack on U.S. soil.

5. Tends to view U.S. allies such as Israel and South Korea as freeloaders who should look after their own defense and not be given the "welfare check" of an American security umbrella.

6. Is convinced that even the best-intended U.S. foreign policy action will fall victim to unintended consequences, bureaucratic incompetence, and democratic fecklessness, and is therefore inadvisable to undertake in the first place.

7. Suspects either that America is in decline already, and therefore cannot shoulder its traditional global commitments, or that shouldering those burdens is an obstacle to economic renewal.

Why, then, should America *not* follow this route and tend to the disrepair in our own house?

The answer lies with the experience of America's last dalliance with isolationism, in the 1920s and '30s. Then, as now, the West had been burned by the experience of a war that did not seem to justify the reasons for which it was fought, much less the sacrifice it had exacted. Then, as now, presidents who took their nations to war in crusades for democracy left office politically discredited, to be succeeded by presidents from the other party who wanted to shift the nation's gaze back to domestic priorities, to give the country its "normalcy" back. Then, as now, peripheral conflicts— Spain in the 1930s, Syria in this decade—burned and bled unendingly, becoming proxy wars for ambitious outside powers as the West mostly looked away.

The similarities do not end there. Then, as now, prolonged global economic downturns in Europe and America profoundly weakened the democratic powers and made them reluctant stewards of global order. Then, as now, the international organizations supposedly responsible for upholding collective security and international law were utterly unequal to the task. Then, as now, the West was gripped by a mood of profound civilizational pessimism, a Spenglerian conviction of decline. Then, as now, economic anxiety provided fruitful political openings for political quacks and extremists. Then, as now, the reputation of liberal democracy as the best system of government suffered in the face of the apparent success of efficient autocracies that knew how to make the trains run on time.

And then, as now, the "revisionist powers" that wanted to rewrite a postwar settlement they considered outrageous realized that it was open season. In 1922, German and Soviet delegates to an international economics conference in Genoa quietly slipped away to the nearby town of Rapallo and signed a pact that settled claims, normalized relations, and paved the way to secret military ties. "If Russia and Germany could not be restrained separately, there was no chance of restraining them if they chose to work together," wrote the historian Norman Davies, observing the helplessness of the war's ostensible victors to impose their will on the losers.[24] After that, increasingly confident dictatorships crossed one Western "red line" after another without paying any price from the ostensible keepers of global order.

The satirical magazine *Punch* captured the foreign policy fecklessness of the era, so similar to our own, when it mocked the West's reaction to Mussolini's 1935 invasion of Abyssinia:

We don't want you to fight
but by jingo if you do
We will probably issue a joint memorandum
Suggesting a mild disapproval of you.

Analogies to the 1930s, or any other period in history, have their limitations and need to be made with humility and care. No two eras are exactly alike, and no law of history dictates that America's current retreat will have the same results as the last one.

Then again, no law dictates that it will not. Challenges to global order are multiplying with little evidence that the United States intends to do more than acquiesce in whatever comes next. Will Bashar al-Assad survive in Syria, and if so, what knock-on effects will there be for Lebanon, Iraq, Jordan, and Israel? Will Beijing seek to turn the South China Sea—over which one third of the world's maritime traffic crosses, and under which lie some of the world's largest energy reserves—into a Chinese lake? Will Iran obtain a nuclear weapon, or at least get close enough to persuade Saudi Arabia that it had better acquire a bomb of its own rather than rely on dubious U.S. security guarantees? Will Vladimir Putin take advantage of NATO's weakness to further consolidate Moscow's influence in the former Soviet republics? Will the American economy be able to power global economic growth in the event that the China bubble bursts, or the Eurozone sinks into another deep recession, or Abenomics founders on political resistance to serious structural reforms? These are the sorts of nightmare scenarios that become increasingly plausible as the United States chooses to recuse itself from its global responsibilities.

This book is not a lament for the United States. America is *not* in decline. It is in *retreat*. Nations in retreat, as the United States was after World War I, can still be on the rise. Nations in decline, as Russia is today, can still be on the march. Decline is the product of broad civilizational forces—demography, culture, ideologies, attitudes toward authority, attitudes about work—that are often beyond the grasp of ordinary political action. Retreat, by contrast, is often nothing more than a political choice. One president can make it; another president could reverse it. It is still within America's reach to make different choices. It has done it before.

WINTER 1947:
THE BIRTH OF PAX AMERICANA

* * * *

The United States was hand-delivered the job of world policeman on a cold and gray Friday in Washington, D.C. The date was February 21, 1947.

The previous evening, Dean Acheson, George C. Marshall's top deputy at the State Department, had received an urgent message from the private secretary to Archibald Clark Kerr, the United Kingdom's ambassador to the United States. It was essential, the private secretary told Acheson, that the ambassador personally deliver "a blue piece of paper" to Marshall—the color of the paper signifying the importance of the message. But Marshall was out of town for the weekend, so Acheson proposed that he obtain a copy of the message in the general's stead. The ambassador agreed.

The next day, the British presented not one but two papers. "They were shockers," Acheson would recall in his memoirs. The first summarized the disastrous financial condition of the Greek government, which the British were propping up in the face of a Communist insurgency. It needed an immediate bailout to the tune of about a quarter billion dollars,* with further large sums to follow. The second detailed the severe difficulties Turkey was facing as it sought to modernize and maintain its army in the face of Soviet pressure.

Then came the kicker: "The British could no longer be of substantial help," and they would terminate their support in just six weeks' time. "His Majesty's Government," wrote

---

* $2.5 billion in 2012 dollars. From the perspective of 2014, it is astounding that such a fundamental shift in U.S. foreign policy could have occurred over such a relatively trivial sum of money.

Acheson, summarizing the British message, "devoutly hoped we could assume the burden in both Greece and Turkey."[1]

Marshall, Acheson, and their staff were already acutely aware of conditions in both countries. They knew, also, that the British government had reached the limit of its capacity. The United Kingdom had already spent a quarter of its national wealth in the Second World War. It was $12 billion in debt and was quickly burning through an American loan. The coldest winter in a century had literally frozen the country's stocks of coal, causing electricity shortages that put two million Britons out of work. Yet it continued to spend a staggering 19 percent of its gross national product on military spending—nearly twice the American figure—in an effort to preserve its status as a global power, an empire in both name and fact. It was spending additional hundreds of millions feeding hungry people in Germany and policing restive Arabs and Jews in Palestine.[2]

It was Hugh Dalton, the chancellor of the exchequer in Clement Attlee's Labour government, who most aggressively pressed the case for immediately winding down most of Britain's foreign commitments. He had two arguments. First, economic: "We are, I am afraid, drifting in a state of semi-animation, towards the rapids." He insisted the government "put an end to our endless dribble of British taxpayers' money to the Greeks."

The second argument was geopolitical—and political: "I am very doubtful indeed about this policy of propping up, even with American aid, weak states in the Eastern Mediterranean against Russia," Dalton wrote Attlee in November 1946. "I am sure we should run into a tremendous political storm if we ever avowed such a policy in public."[3] In Dalton's view, exercises in nation building were prohibitively costly, probably futile, and a distraction from more important tasks at home. Among those tasks was funding the huge expansion of the postwar British state, including the nationalization of key industries, a 50 percent increase over prewar levels of welfare spending,[4] and the realization of a comprehensive state-run health care system known as the National Health Service.

For all this, the speed and completeness with which the British proposed to move stunned the Americans. The United Kingdom had been a leading global power since the defeat of the Spanish Armada in 1588. Now it wanted out, and the United States had just days to consider whether it would fill the vacuum.

That it would do so was no sure thing. In 1920 the U.S. Senate had rejected U.S. membership in the League of Nations, refusing to play any role in policing the postwar order, much less keeping the world "safe for democracy," the goal for which 117,000 American doughboys had paid with their lives. American foreign policy in the years between the First and Second World Wars consisted (on a fully bipartisan basis) of slashing defense budgets, passing Neutrality Acts, and calling for global disarmament—while offering no security guarantees to those countries that heeded the call and later found themselves defenseless in the face of aggression.

Yet in 1947 isolationism was becoming a discredited view. Millions of Americans had drawn from the war the lesson that the United States could not simply hold itself aloof from the rest of the world. Modern technology would not allow it. Germany, at least the part of it under Western control, had to be rebuilt as a responsible democratic power, as did occupied Japan. The march of the Red Army had to be stopped, as did the spread of Communist ideology. In March 1946, in Fulton, Missouri, Winston Churchill had warned Americans that an "Iron Curtain" had descended upon Europe from Stettin in the Baltic to Trieste in the

Adriatic. Also in 1946, Americans had stared down a Soviet attempt to seize one of Iran's northern provinces. To have allowed Greece or Turkey to descend into chaos or succumb to a Soviet-backed insurgency would have given Moscow the access it had coveted for a century (and which Britain had prevented for a century) to the Mediterranean, and from there to southern Europe, northern Africa, and the Levant.

Acheson and Marshall understood this—as did President Truman, who had matured from a foreign policy novice to a sure-footed statesman in just two years in office. Which meant that the British blue papers, while electric, were also energizing. "The Americans were primed for crisis," wrote historian Daniel Yergin in his account of the origins of the Cold War. "The mood in Loy Henderson's Office of Near Eastern Affairs was one of elation." As Marshall delivered a speech at Princeton, Acheson, his deputies, and representatives from the Army and Navy worked feverishly throughout the weekend, putting together estimates and plans for what would be needed to sustain the Greek and Turkish governments and assume the responsibilities Britain meant to forsake.

On Wednesday morning, February 26, just five days after the receipt of the British blue papers, Truman assembled congressional leaders, including Arthur Vandenberg, the Republican chairman of the Senate Foreign Relations Committee, so they could hear General Marshall make the case for aid to Greece and Turkey. Here is Acheson's description of the decisive meeting:

> When we convened the next morning in the White House to open the subject with our congressional masters, I knew we were met at Armageddon. We faced the "leaders of Congress"—all the majority and

minority potentates except Senator [Robert] Taft, an accidental omission to which Senator Vandenberg swiftly drew the President's attention.

My distinguished chief, most unusually and unhappily, flubbed his opening statement. In desperation I whispered to him a request to speak. This was my crisis. For a week I had nurtured it. These congressmen had no conception of what challenged them; it was my task to bring it home. Both my superiors, equally perturbed, gave me the floor. Never have I spoken under such a pressing sense that the issue was up to me alone. No time was left for measured appraisal. In the past eighteen months, I said, Soviet pressure on the Straits, on Iran, and on northern Greece had brought the Balkans to the point where a highly possible Soviet breakthrough might open three continents to Soviet penetration. Like apples in a barrel infected by one rotten one, the corruption of Greece would infect Iran and all to the east. It would also carry infection to Africa through Asia Minor and Egypt, and to Europe through Italy and France, already threatened by the strongest domestic Communist parties in Western Europe. The Soviet Union was playing one of the greatest gambles in history at minimal cost. It did not need to win all the possibilities. Even one or two offered immense gains. We and we alone were in a position to break up the play. These were the stakes that British withdrawal from the eastern Mediterranean offered to an eager and ruthless opponent.

A long silence followed. Then Arthur Vandenberg said solemnly, "Mr. President, if you will say that to the Congress and the country, I will support you and I believe that most of its members will do the same."

What would come to be called the Truman Doctrine—"to support free people who are resisting attempted subjugation by armed minorities or by outside pressures"—became formal American policy with the president's historic message to Congress on March 12. The handover from the United Kingdom to the United States was complete. The United States had accepted its responsibility to defend—at great cost in lives and treasure, but also for the greater benefits of prosperity, freedom, and relative peace—a world order reflecting its national interests and modeled, however imperfectly, on its own values.

CHAPTER 2

★ ★ ★

Pax Americana and Its Critics

What would postwar history have been like if a president with Barack Obama's worldview had been in Harry Truman's shoes at that fateful February 26 conference? And what would have happened if, instead of Vandenberg, someone in the ideological mold of Sen. Rand Paul had led the Republican Party?

Constructing counterfactual history is often fun but always moot, so the answer to both questions is that we will never know. But we can have an approximate idea of what might have happened if the leading progressive politician of his day had been in the Oval Office in 1947, and if the leading isolationist (or noninterventionist) had been chairman of the Senate Foreign Relations Committee.

THE PROGRESSIVE HOPE

It was only because of the vagaries of politics and an accident of history that Henry Agard Wallace missed his chance to become the thirty-third president of the United States.

He had served with distinction as secretary of agriculture in Franklin D. Roosevelt's first two terms in office, at a time when one in four Americans was a farmer. He was vice president in Roosevelt's third term, throughout most of World War II. A native Iowan, Wallace was a man of impressive scientific accomplishments and high social ideals. As an agronomist he made a fortune developing high-yield hybrid seed corn. At the Agriculture Department he was the father of the food-stamp program. As vice president he prominently denounced racial injustice in the United States, advocated national health insurance, and embraced the cause of Soviet-American friendship, at one point embarking on a (carefully sanitized) tour of a Russian gulag camp, where Wallace seemed to find nothing amiss. He rejected Henry Luce's famous 1941 call for an "American Century," contrasting it with his own vision of a "Century of the Common Man." In a 1942 speech to the Congress of American-Soviet Friendship, at New York's Madison Square Garden, Wallace called for a more even balance in the United States between "political or bill-of-rights democracy," which he feared could lead to an excess of "rugged individualism, exploitation," and Soviet-style "economic democracy."

At the 1944 Democratic National Convention in Chicago he beat Harry Truman by 110 votes for the vice presidential nomination on the first ballot. But Wallace had personal enemies among conservative southern Democrats such as former South Carolina senator James F. Byrnes, and among machine politicians such as Chicago mayor Edward Joseph Kelly. The tide turned on the second ballot, where Truman won 1,031 delegates to Wallace's 105.

Had Franklin Roosevelt died in April 1944 rather than a year later, Wallace would not only have filled out the remainder of FDR's third term. He might also have been elected president in his own right that fall. Harry Truman would have remained the "Senator from Pendergast," as he was known after the Kansas City political boss who had helped send him to Congress. It's a scenario American progressives have often imagined as one of the great what-ifs of U.S. history—a missed opportunity, in their view, to avoid needlessly antagonizing the Soviet Union and starting the Cold War.

The notion that a more enlightened American policy might have conciliated Joseph Stalin and muted Moscow's ambitions is pure fantasy. But Wallace, who had remained in the Truman administration as commerce secretary, thought otherwise. He reacted bitterly to Churchill's Iron Curtain speech, telling a dinner party at Acheson's home that "instead of talking about military alliances it was high time to talk about an effective method of disarmament," and that "the American people were not willing to send American boys to fight anybody now."[1] (*The Wall Street Journal*'s editorial page agreed.) His views became more pronounced after Truman fired him from his cabinet post in September 1946. His March 27, 1947, answer to the declaration of the Truman Doctrine crystallized his worldview:

> March 12, 1947, marked a turning point in American history. It is not a Greek crisis that we face, it is an American crisis. It is a crisis in the American spirit. . . . Only the American people fully aroused and promptly acting can prevent disaster.

Wallace then went on to attack the aid to Greece and Turkey as a "down payment on an unlimited expenditure" to stop communism, no matter whom the United States allied itself with to do it. "There is no regime too reactionary," no "country too remote," he said, that the United States would not support it so long as it stood in Russia's way. The result would be the opposite of what Truman intended. Billions would be spent arming foreign governments while their people went hungry—and became easy prey to Soviet propaganda. The United States would be seen as a reactionary power and quickly become "the most-hated nation in the world." The policy would prove "utterly futile." If the United States wanted to contain Communist expansion, the only way to do it would be to "give the common man something better than communism." Worse, he warned, the Truman Doctrine would put America's own liberties at risk:

> In proposing this reckless adventure, Truman is betraying the great tradition of America and the leadership of the great American

who preceded him. . . . Certainly it will not be freedom that will be victorious in this struggle. Psychological and spiritual preparation for war will follow financial preparation; civil liberties will be restricted; standards of living will be forced downward; families will be divided against each other; none of the values that we hold worth fighting for will be secure.

After the speech, and particularly after the American Communist Party endorsed Wallace's 1948 presidential bid at the head of the Progressive Party, he was widely accused of being a Soviet fellow traveler. In Churchill's estimation, Wallace was a "crypto-Communist," which he defined as "one who has not the moral courage to explain the destination for which he is making." The accusations were unfair. Wallace was not a Communist—he described himself as a "progressive capitalist who happened to believe in God"—and his critique of the Truman Doctrine was based on arguments that were in an old-school American tradition. Many Americans seemed to agree: "The size of the audiences [at Wallace's speeches] has amazed many commentators," noted an in-house, confidential State Department report from 1947.[2]

Yet there was truth to the charge that Wallace was willfully blind to the reality of Stalinist Russia. In March 1948, Communists in Czechoslovakia seized control of the government, outlawed opposition parties, and in all probability murdered foreign minister Jan Masaryk by throwing him from the third-story window of Prague's Czernin Palace. Wallace could only say that "the Czech crisis is evidence that a 'get tough' policy only provokes a 'get tougher policy'" by the Russians. Shortly afterward, Stalin imposed his brutal blockade on Berlin. Wallace blamed America. "Berlin did not happen," he told his fellow progressives. "Berlin was caused. When we were set on the road of the 'get tough' policy, I warned that its end was inevitable. Berlin is becoming that end. . . . In all earnestness, I assure you that if I were president, there would be no crisis in Berlin today."

In November, Wallace and his running mate, Idaho senator Glen Taylor, would win just 2.4 percent of the popular vote. Wallace would fade from public life until his death in 1965. Yet the views he articulated became the standard leftist critique of U.S. foreign policy throughout the Cold War to the present: that the United States wasn't so much sinned against in the world as it was the sinner; that America could do more to prevent Communist aggression by turning the other cheek than by confronting it head-on; that Americans had more to fear from what their own government might do in the name of security than from any foreign threat. Progressives have not had a single original foreign policy idea since then.

Wallace himself would prove to be a model of the globally minded progressive politician: the cosmopolitan rube, dallying with political ideas whose consequences he doesn't quite grasp; the Puritan sophisticate, cautious to a fault in his moral judgments of Stalin but thundering in his denunciations of Truman. Here again was the echo of John Winthrop's admonition to be as a city upon a hill, with the eyes of the world upon you. When conservatives today talk about "American exceptionalism," they forget the radical conclusions to which a belief in exceptionalism can easily lead. Exceptionalism is a call for introspection, not action; for *apartness*, not engagement: it offers at least as strong a case for isolationism as it does for internationalism or interventionism. Wallace's foreign policy can be accused of being short-sighted and naïve. Un-American it was not.

Mr. Republican

Wallace was not, however, the only major statesman of his day to make the case against a Pax Americana. Robert Alphonso Taft, eldest son of former president and chief justice William Howard Taft, was, like Wallace, a man of formidable intellectual gifts: first in his class at the Taft School, at Yale College, and at Harvard Law. Like Wallace, too, he was a fighter for civil rights, outspoken in his opposition to the Ku Klux Klan in Ohio and of the internment of Japanese-Americans in World War II, a champion of Zionism but also a principled critic of the Nuremberg Tribunals (a stand that earned him an admiring chapter in John F. Kennedy's *Profiles in Courage*). Like Wallace, he rejected visions of an American century, insisting there "isn't the slightest evidence we could make a success of our American raj."[3] And, like Wallace, he was ambitious to be president.

Though Taft is now remembered as "Mr. Republican" for his ferocious opposition to the New Deal in the 1930s and for the 1947 Taft-Hartley Act circumscribing the power of labor unions, he also supported Social Security and public housing projects for the poor. And he was more of an internationalist than his critics give him credit for, having been a member of the U.S. delegation to the 1919 Versailles conference, an advocate of U.S. membership in the League of Nations, and a believer in the need for military preparedness in the run-up to World War II.

Yet Taft fully earned his reputation as an isolationist, both before the war and after it. Like Wallace, Taft feared the enemy within: as he said in 1938, there was "a good deal more danger of the infiltration of totalitarian ideas from the New Deal circle in Washington than there will ever be from any activities of the communists or the Nazi bunds." (For the remark, Roosevelt dismissed Taft as "a horse's aft.")[4]

As the war approached, Taft's opposition to any involvement in European affairs intensified. In April 1939, just weeks after the Nazi occupation of Czechoslovakia, he jeered the Roosevelt administration for "stirring up prejudices" against Adolf Hitler. He voted against the 1940 Selective Service Act, the draft, which passed in August 1940 by a single vote in the House just weeks after the fall of France. He opposed the Lend-Lease agreement through which the United States shipped billions of dollars' worth of wartime supplies to its soon-to-be wartime allies, convinced that Lend-Lease conferred "unnecessary and dangerous additional powers" on the American president, and that it would inevitably provoke Hitler to declare war on the United States. In a May 1941 radio address titled "Shall the United States Enter the European War?" he insisted, "I detest every utterance of Mr. Hitler and every action of the German government." But that was not reason enough to fight: "We have a duty," he said, to consider the interests of the American people "before we consider the interests of millions of foreign people in other parts of the world."

Taft then gave his summary view of the American foreign policy tradition—at least as he saw it. "For many years the leaders in this country of every party have asserted that America should never go to war unless an attack is made on this continent." It was a remarkable claim for a politician whose father had once served as governor-general of the Philippines. But Taft pressed on, this time suggesting a certain kind of equivalency between the rhetoric of the Nazis and that of the Roosevelt administration: "Shall we now depart from that established policy by going to war with a country which has made no attack on us, and whose violent language only matches our own?"

Then Taft pressed his main, and best, point. A war would be brutally hard. "It is said that Hitler must be crushed and fascism eliminated from this world," he noted. "Can this be done?"

> How can we crush Hitler except by landing an armed force on the Continent of Europe? That may be easy for columnists to do in the newspaper, but it would take many years to build up an army that could do the real job. It would take class after class of American boys still in their teens. War is costing England 25 billion a year; it would cost this country 50 billion a year. What would be left of our economy or our prosperity when we had spent ourselves into bankruptcy? And then we could not be sure that we would finally be able to crush Germany.

And that would just be the beginning of America's problems. Even if victory was achieved, the United States would have no choice but to remain in Europe for decades to come. It would be the end of the American republic and the beginning of an American imperium:

> Suppose, however, that we were able to do it. What are we going to do after that? There are eighty million German people. Our most vociferous warriors do not propose to wipe out that people. They will remain the strongest people on the continent, and the most numerous except the Russians. If we wish to protect the small democracies, we will have to maintain a police force perpetually

in Germany and throughout Europe. Secretary [of War Henry] Stimson, [columnist] Dorothy Thompson and [publisher] Henry Luce seem to contemplate an Anglo-American alliance perpetually ruling the world. Frankly, the American people don't want to rule the world, and we are not equipped to do it. Such imperialism is wholly foreign to our ideals of democracy and freedom. It is not our manifest destiny or our natural destiny. We may think we are better than other peoples, but will they think so? Will they welcome an Anglo-American benevolent despotism any more eagerly than a German despotism?[5]

Taft's speech is remarkable in many ways for its clarity and moral force. If nothing else, it demonstrates that prewar isolationists were often serious people with serious ideas, drawn from every political quarter. "There were Democrats, Republicans, socialists, communists, anticommunists, radicals, pacifists and simple FDR-haters," writes historian Susan Dunn of the broad church of isolationism.[6] One can hear echoes of Taft's views across the decades on both the left and the right, from opposition to the Vietnam War in the 1960s to the interventions in the Balkans in the 1990s and in Iraq in the next decade.

What distinguished Taft, however, was his refusal to budge from his convictions once the war was over. Other prominent prewar isolationists such as Arthur Vandenberg famously declared their conversion "from isolationism to internationalism." Not Mr. Republican. He opposed the 1946 loan to Britain as an extension of "Rooseveltian give-away policies."[7] The Marshall Plan was equally suspect: "I am prepared to support some additional lending" to Europe, he wrote to his mentor Herbert Hoover, "but I think it ought to be held down to cover food stuffs shipped to prevent starvation levels of diet."[8] Speaking at Kenyon College, he warned that "we have drifted into the acceptance of the idea that the world is to be ruled by the power of the great nations and a police force established by them rather than by international law."[9]

As for the Truman Doctrine, he was deeply skeptical. "The proposed loans to Greece and Turkey represent a complete departure from previous American policy," he warned in a statement that echoed Wallace's critique from the left. "If we assume this special position in Greece and Turkey, we can hardly longer reasonably object to the Russians continuing their domination in Poland, Yugoslavia, Rumania and Bulgaria. The Loans, therefore, accept the policy of dividing the world into zones of political influence, communist and anti-communist."[10]

But Taft's strongest objections were to the creation of the North Atlantic Treaty Organization in the summer of 1949. The Atlantic Pact, he warned, "was more likely to produce war than peace." It would impose an almost unlimited obligation on the United States to spring to the defense of twelve other nations, regardless of circumstances. It was certain to spark an arms race: "We cannot build up the armaments of Western Europe without stimulating the Russians to increase still further their development of war forces." It would punch a hole in the deficit and divert funds from more urgent domestic needs: "This new project would cost more each year than the housing, education and limited health plans combined." And it risked putting American liberty at risk: "I am as much against Communist aggression as anyone," he said. "But we can't let them scare us into bankruptcy and the surrender of all liberty."

In the remaining four years of his life Taft would find himself reconsidering his anti-interventionist views, particularly after Mao's victory in China and the Soviet test of an atomic bomb in 1949. And, like Wallace, he would soon be a fading force in his own party—marginalized after Eisenhower's 1952 victory and the Republican acceptance of both the broad contours of the Rooseveltian welfare state and Truman's activist foreign policies. Nonetheless, between 1938 and 1949 he articulated, as few others did, a distinctive vision for the proper conduct of U.S. foreign policy.

Readers will note the resemblances between the foreign policy precepts of the era's leading progressive and its leading conservative. *Les extrêmes se touchent*. Wallace and Taft, the Iowa New Dealer and the conservative Ohio patrician, were faithful to an American creed that brought them together in ways they scarcely recognized themselves. America's providential role in the world was to serve not as a proselytizer for self-government, but as an inspiration for it. Among its core convictions:

- The goals and ideals of our allies are not our goals and ideals; we support theirs at the expense of our own.
- Policies and measures we perceive as defensive are likely to be perceived by our adversaries as threatening. We provoke the very behavior we had hoped to prevent.
- Client governments are, too frequently, morally unworthy of our support, and our alliance with them can only earn us international hostility.
- The financial and military resources we provide for other countries are resources denied to Americans.
- America cannot afford to be the world's policeman, nor does the world want us to be one.
- The principal danger to American liberty comes from the enemies within, not without.
- Power politics cannot be the basis for lasting international peace. Only international law and exemplary behavior can achieve that.
- Peace is in the hands of American policy makers, not America's adversaries, to give, if only American statesmen will follow the preceding precepts.

The similarities should not obscure their differences. Wallace and Taft took opposite views on what defined the proper role and reach of government. Wallace was a born idealist; Taft, a skeptic. Yet both believed that excessive U.S. engagement with the rest of the world would taint America morally, drain its resources financially, diminish the freedom of its people, generate foreign enmities where none need have existed, and, as in ancient Rome, trade republican virtue for martial glory and tempt a democracy into becoming an empire.

PAX AMERICANA

As prophecy, all this seemed both highly plausible and morally compelling. But now it's history. We know how things turned out. We know—or should know—how wrong Wallace and Taft were.

Europeans did, in fact, vastly prefer the "benevolent Anglo-American despotism" that Taft derided over German (or later Soviet) despotism; Pax Americana is not totalitarianism, and it is not imperialism, either. The "get tough" policy that Wallace decried worked: Berlin survived first as a besieged enclave of freedom, then as a highly visible rebuke to Communist propaganda. The "police force" that Taft warned would remain "perpetually" in Germany and the rest of Europe has been there exactly as he foresaw—with the blessing of three generations of voters on both sides of the Atlantic. Civil liberties were not, as Wallace predicted, "restricted" by the Cold War, notwithstanding a demagogic senator from Wisconsin and a snooping, malicious director of the FBI. On the contrary: from the end of racial segregation to the empowerment of women to the birth of the gay rights movement, civil rights flourished throughout the Cold War and possibly even *because* of it: Cold Warriors like Eisenhower and Johnson did not want to lose the ideological battle with the Soviet Union by allowing Jim Crow to persist. Readers may object that Pax Americana wasn't such smooth going, that it also involved support for pro-American dictators like Indonesia's Suharto and Chile's Pinochet, tense nuclear confrontations, ugly wars in Korea and Vietnam, the pervasive dread of mutually assured destruction. All true. But what, realistically, was the alternative? What might have been if, in a postwar Wallace administration, the United States had surrendered the freedom of Berlin, or if a Taft administration had rejected the Atlantic Alliance, shortchanged the Marshall Plan, and demanded prompt repayment from Britain of our wartime loans?

So much should have been obvious the moment the hammer and sickle was lowered for the last time over the Kremlin on December 26, 1991. Containment had worked. The Soviet Union stood revealed not as a misunderstood giant but as a malevolent ogre. The "military-industrial" complex that was supposed to eat the heart out of American democracy wound up becoming just another industry with a lobby, and not the most powerful one at that. Our long commitment to Western security paid fruitful dividends in the globalization of democracy and prosperity, from South Korea and Taiwan to Poland and the Baltic states. American military power and financial largesse underwrote peace between Egypt and Israel and helped midwife European integration. Germany and Japan were converted from militarism to pacifism. The world economy flourished. Global GDP, just $11 trillion in 1980, doubled by the time the Cold War ended a decade later. By 2012 it reached $72 trillion.[11] Americans were not shortchanged by the spread of wealth: U.S. per capita GDP, about $12,000 in 1980, rose to $46,000 by 2012.

Pax Americana is a world in which English is the default language of business, diplomacy, tourism, and technology; in which markets are global, capital is mobile, trade is increasingly free, and networks increasingly global; in which values of openness and tolerance are, when not the norm, often the aspiration. It is a world in which the possibility of another country imposing its will upon us remains, for the time being, remote. The wars we now fight may be long wars, but they are small: they do not require conscription or rationing. They don't even require a tax increase.

The debate over the inherent benefits of Pax Americana should have been settled long ago. But history only settles great debates for as long as people can remember the history. College seniors graduating next spring will have all been born after the USSR was buried. Their early memories about U.S. foreign policy likely begin with 9/11 and are dominated by images from the wars in Iraq and Afghanistan. So it's worth reexamining the course of U.S. foreign policy since the fall of the Soviet Union. It was the era when the sober reckonings of Pax Americana gave way to foreign policy as a field of dreams.

★   ★   ★   ★

In late 2005 I stood at the outermost edge of Pax Americana. It was a MASH unit in the devastated northern Pakistani city of Muzaffarabad, where the U.S. Army had encamped itself on a mission of human mercy and soft power. Just as the Roman Empire had once touched the shores of the Persian Gulf at the height of Trajan's reign, so too did this ruin of a city mark the very outer periphery of American power and influence, at least in recent history.

It was intended to be a temporary outpost. On October 8 of that year a massive earthquake ripped through northern Pakistan, killing more than 70,000 people, displacing three million, and destroying 400,000 homes. In the crucial hours immediately after the quake, the only country with the aerial capabilities to help was the United States, deployed right next door in Afghanistan. Tandem-rotor Chinook helicopters immediately began moving supplies to remote mountain villages, while airlifting the sick and injured to safety. Within days, the United States had deployed 1,000 soldiers for what would be a $200 million humanitarian operation. A mobile MASH unit offered the only real intensive care in northern Pakistan. Navy Seabees went to work rebuilding damaged infrastructure. U.S. helicopters operating from the airbase in Rawalpindi spent months moving men and supplies to and from the quake zone.

Thousands of Pakistani lives were saved by American efforts. It was—or so it seemed to me at the time—a textbook demonstration of how the combination of American power and American goodness could yield tangible results when it came to those all-important Muslim hearts and minds. In Muzaffarabad, I listened to a three-star Army general named

Steven Whitcomb give voice to that idea in a pep talk to his soldiers. "We're fighting two wars," he said, referring to Iraq and Afghanistan.

> *We're still doing recovery operations from our own natural disaster [Hurricane Katrina]. We still have soldiers manning the DMZ on the Korean peninsula. We still have sailors manning the flight decks of aircraft carriers at two in the morning. And we can still do this kind of thing.... You are all here for no other reason than that the United States asked you to be here. You've come to a place you can't find on a map. But you are making a difference.*[1]

I was moved by the general's words, and quoted them in an article I wrote for *The Wall Street Journal*. I called it "Chinook Diplomacy."

There were reasons to share the general's sense of optimism and possibility. In Iraq, the darkening gloom of insurgency suddenly seemed to break as millions of Iraqis participated in their first real parliamentary elections, triumphantly holding up their ink-stained fingers in defiance of their terrorist tormentors. In Kiev, defiant protesters, dressed in orange, took to Independence Square and successfully turned back efforts by Moscow's preferred candidate to steal an election. In Ramallah and Bethlehem I covered the first true Palestinian presidential contest, where Western-style elections had given Mahmoud Abbas what seemed like a decisive mandate to bring the second intifada to an end and replace Yasser Arafat's cult of personality with the genuine rule of law.

Not long afterward I was in Lebanon, reporting on the country's mood of optimism and sense of freedom after Syria ended its twenty-nine-year occupation under intense

Western pressure. A few months later, Ariel Sharon removed Israeli settlements from the Gaza Strip, and suddenly the possibility of a sustainable two-state settlement seemed tantalizingly close. In Afghanistan, U.S. combat fatalities were under one hundred a year, or a fifth of what they would be five years later, Hamid Karzai was cooperative, and the Taliban appeared to be on a path toward defeat.

In Europe, German chancellor Gerhard Schröder, the most vocal European critic of the Iraq war, was voted out of office in an election that turned partly on the frayed state of U.S.-German relations. In Britain, by contrast, Tony Blair— "Bush's poodle," according to caricature, for his vigorous support for the invasion of Iraq—handily won a third term. As for the United States, George W. Bush entered his second term promising to work for a world free of tyranny, and the goal didn't seem entirely far-fetched. In the midst of war, the U.S. economy hummed along at a healthy 3 percent clip, unemployment was 5 percent and falling, and there was talk of serious entitlements reform.

How distant that seems now. Few of the democratic hopes kindled in 2005 survived the next few years. Like the Arab Spring of 2011, the Beirut spring of 2005 would prove very brief, as Syria assassinated one pro-democracy leader after another and Hezbollah provoked Israel into a mutually disastrous war the following summer. The Orange Revolution in Ukraine quickly turned to disappointment; within four years, Viktor Yanukovych, who sought to steal the election in 2004, would take the presidency fairly, and then set out to undermine democracy from the top down. Democracy for Palestinians led within a year to the election of Hamas, then to civil war in Gaza, then to war with Israel. Iraq's democracy survived, more or less, but it isn't clear the country will. Afghanistan's liberation from the Taliban proved to be a momentary respite.

As for Pakistan, I look back at my own reporting and read it as the high point in my own naïve assumption that America's beneficence might be repaid by gratitude. In 2006 the Pew Global Attitudes Survey found that 27 percent of Pakistanis had a positive view of the United States, a post-9/11 high. The figure has dropped every year since, to 11 percent in 2013. Just 8 percent of Pakistanis see the United States as a partner, against 64 percent who see America as their enemy. And only 8 percent of Pakistanis think the impact of U.S. economic aid is "mostly positive."[2] When Pakistan was struck by another humanitarian disaster in 2010—this time in the form of floods—a conspiracy theory that made the rounds in the Pakistani media held that it was the doing of a weather-controlling device based in Alaska.

"Benefactors seem to love their beneficiaries more than the beneficiaries love those who have benefited them," noted Aristotle in the *Nicomachean Ethics*. "As this seems unreasonable, it should be investigated."

CHAPTER 3

* * *

The Overdose of Ideals

Americans expected too much from winning the Cold War. We expected a modicum of admiration and gratitude from a world saturated with envy and resentment. We imagined our supremacy was mostly uncontroversial and anticipated a world of friendly imitators, not ambitious challengers. We believed that the collapse of the Soviet Union put to rest the only serious ideological challenge to liberal democracy and permanently settled all the core questions of political philosophy. "The day of the dictator is over," George H. W. Bush proclaimed in his 1989 inaugural address. "We know what works: Freedom works. We know what's right: Freedom is right."

And so we conflated the West with the world, human ideals with human nature, a respite from history with a victory over it.

We also neglected Aristotle's insights into the nature of the relationship between benefactors and beneficiaries. It isn't (or isn't merely) that the beneficiary feels toward his benefactor the way a debtor feels toward his creditor—encumbered rather than grateful. It's that the benefactor tends to see the objects of his beneficence the way a poet would see his poems—as his own special creation, a source of pride and self-infatuation. But that's a feeling that's rarely if ever reciprocated.

Not that winning the Cold War was anything less than a wonderful event. The number of democracies grew by thirty-one countries between 1988 and 1998.[1] Millions were lifted out of poverty as countries abandoned socialism for free enterprise. Per capita income in Poland rose by 37 percent; in India by 41 percent; in China by 130 percent.[2] Americans enjoyed one of the most prosperous decades in history.

Yet victory in the Cold War was an incomplete event. Communism collapsed, but authoritarianism persisted. From their victory in Afghanistan, Islamic fundamentalists drew the lesson that if they could bring down one superpower through a holy war, perhaps they could bring down the other. The Western model of democratic capitalism gained new members, but not necessarily new converts: many of those who had hated it before the Berlin Wall fell continued to hate it afterward. When the West stumbled, as it did over Bosnia and Rwanda, it appeared ineffectual or hypocritical. When economic crises hit developing economies, the West and its "neoliberal" prescriptions made for a perfect scapegoat. Suddenly, dull meetings of the IMF, the World Bank, and the G8 became targets of violent demonstrations. When the United States went to war in the Middle East after 9/11 in the name of universal democratic ideals, it provoked cries that Washington was "imposing" democracy on people who didn't want it.

From the perspective of a quarter century, it becomes easier to see how the West traced a path from the triumphalism of 1989 to the retreat of the present decade. Actually, it traced two paths. One was a parabolic arc in which the West went from strength to strength all the way until September 11, 2001, when we abruptly entered a dark new world. The other is a straight-line story of storing and suppressing trouble until it finally exploded into plain sight.

Compare two time lines. The first is the one we typically associate with the last decade of the twentieth century: a second Belle Époque, much like the century's first decade.

November 9, 1989: Berlin Wall falls. The Dow closes at 2,603.

February 28, 1991: Victory in the Gulf War.

December 26, 1991: Dissolution of the Soviet Union.

February 7, 1992: Maastricht Treaty lays the legal groundwork for the euro.

March 24, 1993: F. W. de Klerk announces South Africa will dismantle its nuclear arsenal. Ukraine, Belarus, and Kazakhstan follow suit.

September 13, 1993: Israeli prime minister Yitzhak Rabin and Palestinian leader Yasser Arafat sign the Oslo Accords in a triumphant White House ceremony.

January 1, 1994: Establishment of NAFTA.

October 13, 1994: Introduction of Mosaic Netscape 0.9, the world's first commercial Web browser.

January 1, 1995: Establishment of the World Trade Organization.

August 22, 1996: Clinton signs welfare reform.

1998: First U.S. federal budget surplus in thirty years.

December 1998: Price of oil falls to $9.80 a barrel.

March 29, 1999: Dow closes above 10,000 after eight consecutive years of economic growth.

June 11, 1999: Victory in the Kosovo War, the first war in which not a single American dies in combat.

So much seemed possible. If the value of the Dow had more than tripled in a decade, why couldn't it triple again? If democracy could thrive in Estonia, the Czech Republic, or even Mongolia, why couldn't it flourish everywhere else? If Europe could have a single market and a single currency, why shouldn't it have a full political union? If American diplomacy could help bridge political divides in Northern Ireland, why not in the Holy Land, or on the Korean peninsula? And if the free market and democracy were indeed taking root across much of the globe—the one promoting the other—weren't we on the cusp of the peaceful, prosperous, and liberal international order dreamed of in the eighteenth century by the likes of Kant and Montesquieu?

Now consider a second time line:

1989: Pakistani nuclear scientist A. Q. Khan begins shipping centrifuges to Iran.

April 5, 1992: Four-year siege of Sarajevo begins.

October 1992: Boston Federal Reserve publishes a study inferring racial bias in mortgage lending. Mortgage lenders respond by dramatically relaxing lending standards.

February 26, 1993: First World Trade Center bombing.

December 1993: International Atomic Energy Agency says it can no longer offer "any meaningful assurances" that North Korea isn't making nuclear weapons.

August 23, 1996: Osama bin Laden declares war on the United States.

September 27, 1996: Establishment of Islamic Emirate of Afghanistan following Taliban capture of Kabul.

July 1997: "Asian (currency) flu" devastates economies of Thailand, Malaysia, South Korea, and Indonesia.

May 1998: India carries out five nuclear tests. Pakistan responds with five tests of its own.

August 7, 1998: U.S. embassies in Tanzania and Kenya are bombed.

August 17, 1998: Russian government defaults on its debt. Ruble loses two thirds of its value in two weeks.

December 6, 1998: Hugo Chávez elected president of Venezuela.

November 30, 1999: "Battle of Seattle": antiglobalization protests during ministerial conference of the World Trade Organization.

These events were not seen as insignificant in the 1990s. But they were mostly thought of as outliers: echoes from a fading past rather than harbingers of the looming future. What did it matter that the obscure scion of a wealthy Saudi family had declared his one-man "war" on the United States in the pages of an Arabic paper published in London? Or that a backwater state like Afghanistan had been taken over by a collection of backward religious students called "the Taliban"? Or that globalization aroused the ideological opposition of young activists who hadn't yet heard the news that Karl Marx's *Das Kapital* was smoldering on the ash heap of history?

It was an optimism that was exhilarating in its prospects and comforting in its conceits. But it failed to appreciate the fragility of the foundations on which a New World Order was being built. Globalization could speed the process of development, but it also accelerated the dislocations—not just economic or even physical, but also moral and spiritual. The goodness of liberal democracy was not universally self-evident. Advanced countries had not perfected methods of successful economic management. The spread of prosperity had not erased feelings of envy. Religious fanaticism, misguided idealism, and plain old foolishness all remained colors on the palette of political motivation.

Every illusion comes to an end, but every illusion also shapes thinking—and policy—for as long as it lasts. When the Cold War ended, American policy makers persuaded themselves that they could do more than merely help improve the world. They could redeem it. In so doing, they neglected a more prosaic responsibility: to police it.

CLOTHED IN A HUGE ILLUSION

In November 1937 Lord Halifax, Britain's soon-to-be foreign secretary, paid a visit to Nazi Germany and recorded his impressions of Adolf Hitler in his diary:

> He gave the impression of feeling that, whilst he had attained power only after a hard struggle with present day realities, the British Government was still living comfortably in a world of its own making, a make-believe land of strange, if respectable, illusions. It had lost touch with realities and clung to shibboleths—"collective security," "general settlement," "disarmament," "non-aggression pacts"—which offered no practical prospect of a solution of Europe's difficulties.[3]

Halifax perceived Hitler rightly. And Hitler perceived Britain rightly, too: as a status quo power that wanted to maintain its place in the world at the lowest possible price in terms of expenditure and risk. It saw diplomacy not as a penumbra of its military power but as a substitute for it.

The 1990s were also a period when a status quo power, this time the United States, sought to maintain its global preeminence, minimize the military expense, and replace hard power with strange, if respectable, illusions. In the name of a post–Cold War peace dividend, the military was cut to 3 percent of GDP in 2000 from 6 percent a decade earlier. The core concept of U.S. foreign policy became the peace process. With the exception of Northern Ireland, all of these processes failed. The Israeli-Palestinian talks disintegrated in slow motion over seven years, then erupted in the suicide bombings of the second intifada. Others quickly collapsed into orgies of bloodletting. For war-torn Sierra Leone, Susan Rice initiated a process that invited the Revolutionary United Front, a rebel group that specialized in chopping off people's limbs and gouging out their eyes, to take ministerial posts in the country's government. Rice, then the assistant secretary of state for Africa, justified the decision by noting that "there are many instances where peace agreements around the world have contemplated rebel movements converting themselves to political parties."⁴ Such was her faith in peace processes that she believed they could turn psychopaths into statesmen.

But the real-world results didn't matter, because the process was almost an end unto itself. As former diplomat and scholar Aaron David Miller has noted, the peace process is a "false religion," whose "truth" rests more on a concept of virtue than any empirical test of effectiveness.

"Rodney King–like, we believe that if people would only sit down and discuss their differences rationally and compromise, a way might be found to accommodate conflicting views," he writes. "After all, America is the big tent under which so many religious, political, and ethnic groups have managed to coexist, remarkably amicably."⁵ In reality, parties engaged in sectarian and ethnic conflicts usually follow a zero-sum logic: we win; you die.

The combination of naïveté, blind faith, and moral self-regard that came to typify U.S. foreign policy in the 1990s did not escape the notice of our enemies. Nor did the habit of the United States of retreating in the face of minor military reversals. Osama bin Laden's 1996 declaration of war on the United States captures his contempt for what he saw as a combination of American grandiosity and cowardice:

> [A] few days ago the news agencies had reported that the Defense Secretary of the Crusading Americans had said that "the explosion at Riyadh and Al-Khobar had taught him one lesson: that is not to withdraw when attacked by coward terrorists."
>
> We say to the Defense Secretary that his talk can induce a grieving mother to laughter! And shows the fears that had enshrined you all. Where was this false courage of yours when the explosion in Beirut took place on 1983 AD (1403 A.H). You were turned into scattered pits and pieces at that time; 241 mainly marine soldiers were killed. And where was this courage of yours when two explosions made you to leave Aden in less than twenty four hours!
>
> But your most disgraceful case was in Somalia; where—after vigorous propaganda about the power of the USA and its post

cold war leadership of the new world order—you moved tens of thousands of international force, including twenty eight thousand American soldiers into Somalia. However, when tens of your solders were killed in minor battles and one American Pilot was dragged in the streets of Mogadishu you left the area carrying disappointment, humiliation, defeat and your dead with you.

Note that bin Laden wasn't denouncing the *excesses* of U.S. power. He was mocking its *timidity*. In the years leading up to 9/11, the United States would give him few reasons to change that view.

In August 1998, Al Qaeda blew up two U.S. embassies in Africa. Clinton responded with an ineffectual cruise missile strike on sites in Sudan and Afghanistan three days after admitting a "not appropriate" relationship with Monica Lewinsky. In December 1998 Clinton ordered four days of bombing against Iraq on the eve of his impeachment in the House of Representatives. In October 2000 Al Qaeda attacked the destroyer USS *Cole* as it was being refueled in the port of Aden, Yemen, killing seventeen U.S. sailors. Clinton vowed that "we will find out who was accountable and hold them responsible." Once again the threat was empty. "There was not much White House interest in conducting further military operations against Afghanistan in the administration's last week," noted *The 9/11 Commission Report*. Instead, "President Clinton, [National Security Adviser Sandy] Berger and [Secretary of State Madeleine] Albright were concentrating on a last minute push for a peace agreement between the Palestinians and the Israelis."[6] The Bush administration, taking office the following January, was no better: Donald Rumsfeld felt that "too much time had passed" since the attack to merit a response.[7]

Al Qaeda took a different view. As the commission noted, "the attacks on the USS *Cole* galvanized al Qaeda's recruitment efforts. Following the attack, bin Laden instructed the media committee, then headed by Khalid Sheikh Mohammed, to produce a propaganda video that included a reenactment of the attack." Bin Laden also wrote a poem extolling the attack, read at the wedding of one of his sons in Kandahar in 2001:

A destroyer: even the brave fear its might.
It inspires horror in the harbor and in the open sea.
She goes into the waves flanked by arrogance, haughtiness and fake
    might.
To her doom she progresses slowly, clothed in a huge illusion.[8]

If ever a phrase captured the foreign policy of the United States in the years leading to 9/11, *clothed in a huge illusion* was it.

TAKE THE FORK

When Sarah Palin was famously asked by ABC's Charlie Gibson in September 2008 to give her opinion of the Bush Doctrine, she replied: "In what respect?" It was a more insightful remark than perhaps she knew. Was the Bush Doctrine the determination to prevent, if necessarily preemptively, the world's worst regimes from gaining the world's most destructive weapons? That would be the way in which Dick Cheney would define it. Or was the Bush Doctrine the promise to work toward the elimination of dictatorships the world over? This was the vision Bush laid out in his second inaugural address: "America's vital interests and our deepest beliefs are now one," he said. "It is the policy of the United States to seek and support the growth of democratic movements and institutions in every nation and culture, with the ultimate goal of ending tyranny in our world."

Every nation. *Every* culture.

Many charges are laid at the feet of the Bush administration and its foreign policy, not always coherently: that it was scheming *and* simplistic, self-dealing *and* overly idealistic, the stooge of Saudi Arabia *and* of Israel, too trusting of Putin *and* too hostile to Russia. But the administration's real problem was that it never really resolved the tension between the first and second versions of the Bush Doctrine. To adapt Yogi Berra's famous advice: when it got to the fork in the road, it took it.

The first version of the Bush Doctrine aims to uphold global order and punish its violators: terrorists, terror-sponsoring states, aspiring nuclear powers, revanchist or revisionist regimes. This is foreign policy with a view toward keeping nightmares at bay. That's not to say that it is hostile to liberal values: it values democratic allies and welcomes democratic aspirations—provided they do not threaten to become inimical to U.S. interests (as they were when the Muslim Brotherhood came to power in Egypt). But its central goal is to uphold, defend, and improve world order, not transform and improve human society.

The second version of the Bush Doctrine, the "freedom agenda" version, is very different. It's about making dreams come true. It holds that America's ultimate security lies in a world of democracies. It views a status quo of ostensibly "stable" autocracies such as Saudi Arabia as inherently unstable, a breeding ground for the toxic resentments and ideological disaffections that led to 9/11. It sees democracy not as a mechanism that will empower radical Islamists, but as one that will, over time, tame and defang them. It argues that, just as liberal values will ultimately generate democratic institutions, democratic institutions can help instill liberal values; that is, that the very act of political participation fosters a common interest among all political factions in free speech, pluralism, and tolerance for dissent. Its goal isn't just to keep the streets clear of thieves, bullies, and drunks. It's to put them through reform schools and twelve-step programs.

There is an intellectually coherent case to be made for the first version of the Bush Doctrine, and there is a coherent case to be made for the second. It is well illustrated by the dilemma Obama confronted in Egypt after the July 2013 military overthrow of Mohamed Morsi, a Muslim Brother and Egypt's first democratically elected president. Obama could have acknowledged that Morsi's disastrous tenure could not go on for another three years without causing irreparable harm to the Egyptian economy, regional security, and U.S. interests, and that Egypt's new rulers, however autocratic, were not religious fanatics. *Or* he could have credibly opposed the coup on the grounds that America's best interests—and Egypt's—were to allow Morsi's term to run its rocky course and establish a precedent that presidents come *and* go by means of the voting booth.

It was one or the other, not both. But Obama could never quite choose. His Egypt policy split the difference, a classic combination of mumble and muddle.

As for Bush, he didn't split the differences: he married them. The Big Stick foreign policy of Teddy Roosevelt was put in bed with the high idealism of Woodrow Wilson. It was a hybrid concept that was the foreign policy equivalent of Bush's "compassionate conservatism," his idea of putting big government in the service of traditional conservative ideals. "Our first priority must always be the security of our nation," the president said in his 2002 State of the Union. But he also declared:

America will take the side of brave men and women who advocate these values around the world, including the Islamic world, because we have a greater objective than eliminating threats and containing resentment. We seek a just and peaceful world beyond the war on terror.

This was well and good as long as the freedom agenda remained a matter of funding worthy civil-society efforts, championing the cause of individual dissidents, and finding productive opportunities to prod nondemocratic allies toward greater openness. These were moral investments, symbolic gestures, and long-term goals.

But then weapons of mass destruction were not found in Iraq. The freedom agenda, hitherto a secondary justification for war, became a primary one. The specific and essential goal of deposing a dangerous tyrant and keeping WMD out of the hands of a rogue state was now to be complemented, if not superseded, by an open-ended, long-term, costly, and uncertain goal of bringing democracy to the Muslim world. Bush would not be satisfied merely with making *examples* of global outlaws like Saddam Hussein and the Taliban. Instead, he was determined to make Iraq and Afghanistan *exemplary*. In this sense, Bush's foreign policy was of a piece with Clinton's: both believed in humanity's basic goodness, and in America's capacity to clear a path for that goodness. This was not a Hobbesian or even Madisonian view of the world, holding that the great task of government is to tame man's wickedness and channel his passions. It was, instead, closer to Rousseau: man was born good, and, with the right institutions, could be restored to goodness. Or, to put it another way, Bush did not see his foreign policy as being the business of disease management. It was, to borrow a phrase, a race for the cure.

IRAQ AND THE "MOTHER OF ALL SINS"

It took just twenty-one days for the United States to conquer Baghdad, at a cost of 139 American lives. It was a military, moral, and strategic triumph. Americans were justified in celebrating it, not just for the sake of the euphoric Iraqis who brought down Saddam's statue in Baghdad's Firdos Square, but for our own sake. We could finally wake up from one of the longest-running nightmares in U.S. foreign policy.

This was widely agreed by nearly all corners of the American political establishment. Though it goes too easily down the memory hole, Saddam's Iraq was a nonstop security crisis for the world from the time he came to power in the 1970s. Among the highlights of that career: starting the Iran-Iraq war; attempting to build a nuclear reactor at Osirak (destroyed by Israel in 1981); the "Anfal" campaign against Kurds using chemical weapons; his highly successful—and undisputed—efforts to reconstitute a nuclear program in the 1980s (destroyed by UN weapons inspectors after the Gulf War in 1991); his invasion of Kuwait; the bloody suppression of the 1991 Shiite uprisings and the Kurdish refugee crisis; the twelve-year no-fly-zone regime; the cat-and-mouse games with UN inspectors; the corruption of the oil-for-food program; the monetary support for Palestinian terrorists.

Given the record, it's worth recording what leading Democratic Party figures had to say about Saddam. "If we fail to respond today," said President Clinton in February 1998, "Saddam and all those who would follow in his footsteps will be emboldened tomorrow." His secretary of state, Madeleine Albright, warned that Saddam's goal "is achieving the lifting of U.N. sanctions while retaining and enhancing Iraq's weapons of mass destruction program." National Security Adviser Sandy Berger was no less admonitory: Saddam, he said, "will rebuild his arsenal of weapons of mass destruction and some day, some way, I am certain he will use that arsenal again, as he has 10 times since 1983."

And then there was Hillary Clinton, justifying her 2002 vote in favor of the authorization to use military force in Iraq:

> I believe the facts that have brought us to this fateful vote are not in doubt. Saddam Hussein is a tyrant who has tortured and killed his own people, even his own family members, to maintain his iron grip on power. He used chemical weapons on Iraqi Kurds and on Iranians, killing over 20,000 people. . . . It is clear, however, that if left unchecked, Saddam Hussein will continue to increase his capability to wage biological and chemical warfare and will keep trying to develop nuclear weapons. Should he succeed in that endeavor, he could alter the political and security landscape of the Middle East, which, as we know all too well, affects American security. This much is undisputed.

That is why we went into Iraq.

We went in, also, to put on notice other would-be Saddams that, after 9/11, we had a low tolerance for flagrant challenges to global order. Libya's Muammar Gaddafi got the point and abandoned his nuclear program a week after Saddam's arrest. The Iranians seemed to get the point, too: they temporarily halted their nuclear program in 2003. In 2005, Syria ended its twenty-nine-year occupation of Lebanon after its assassination of former Lebanese prime minister Rafik Hariri prompted a fierce response from Washington and Paris.

The real question, then, isn't why we went into Iraq. The justifications for it were, and remain, abundant. The question is how we went from a decisive victory in twenty-one days to a seven-year occupation in which some four thousand Americans perished.

One answer is that, even after taking Baghdad, we still hadn't captured Saddam. But that job was done by the end of the year, after Saddam's sons had been killed in a gunfight and Saddam himself was taken alive. We also needed to get to the bottom of the missing WMD story. But that job, too, was accomplished by early 2004 with the publication of the report by the Iraq Survey Group. Then there was Colin Powell's famous "Pottery Barn Rule," that we had to own the things we break. But we hadn't "broken" Iraq. Saddam had. And we didn't "own" Iraq. Iraqis did. We just decided they weren't quite ready for it. "The biggest mistake, honestly, if you go back, was not entrusting the Iraqis as partners, to empower them, to see them do their part, to fill the vacuum, to have a national unity government," Hoshyar Zebari, Iraq's talented foreign minister, told *The Wall Street Journal* in 2006. "I think the biggest sin was to change the mission from liberation to occupation. That was the mother of all sins, honestly."[9]

So it was that we set out to remake Iraq from the ground up. With America's benevolent help, Iraq would write a new constitution, vindicate the ideals of democracy, create the institutions necessary for a free-market economy, improve women's rights, serve as a role model for other Arab states, tame Shiite and Sunni extremism, bridge sectarian and ethnic differences, and share its oil wealth in an equitable sectarian ratio. Iraq was to become another Japan, transformed from dictatorship to democracy under the firm but wise tutelage of a new Douglas MacArthur named Paul Bremer.

Bremer, a former ambassador to the Netherlands, brought with him a Year Zero approach to the task: everything that had come before had to go, and go at once. He immediately ordered the army disbanded and dismissed tens of thousands of civil servants, many of them technocrats, who had been members of the Baath Party. The commendable intention (and intentions are invariably commendable) was to reassure ordinary Iraqis that their old bosses would not be coming back. The predictable result was that the Iraqi government was deprived of some of its more competent people, many of whom had joined the Baath out of fear or for ordinary personal advancement, when it needed them most. The police force was crippled. The disbanding of the army created a reservoir of recruits for the insurgency. Unemployment rose. Sunnis were politically alienated. Critical time was wasted as Bremer insisted that Iraq draft a constitution before he left the country, as if the country's fate depended on establishing not the state's monopoly on force but its legitimacy on paper. He transformed the perception of the United States among Iraqis from Mr. Big—the power not to be messed with—to Mr. Busybody—the nuisance not to be borne. It was a fatal turn. Like Henry Cabot Lodge, the U.S. ambassador in Saigon who helped mastermind the catastrophic 1963 coup against South Vietnam's Ngo Dinh Diem, Bremer is proof that few things in this world are as disastrous as the wrong man, with the wrong ideas, in the wrong job, at the wrong time.

By the time Bremer left Iraq the insurgency was in full fury. The city of Fallujah fell into terrorist hands. It needed to be dealt with swiftly and decisively. Instead, Bush called off the attack at the last minute, citing the fragile state of Iraqi politics, and prompting one Marine general to recall Napoleon's advice to a general: "When you start to take Vienna—take Vienna!" When Fallujah *was* finally taken several months later, the United States had to pay triple damages in higher casualties, diminished credibility, and a harder fight against a more confident enemy.

It would take another two years before Bush finally alighted on the right strategy for Iraq: the surge. The counterinsurgency concept is often maligned as a soft-headed hearts-and-minds effort that is hesitant about using force. It's the opposite: a deliberate, and emphatically visible, *show* of force; a way of reassuring civilians that American power was nearby—that the cop was on his beat and ready to act, not in the precinct house filling out paperwork. We only won the war when Bush realized that America's task in Iraq was not to lecture Iraqi leaders about how they should conduct their democracy. It was to use overwhelming power to reassure friends and crush enemies.

We would think of the Iraq war very differently now if Bush had stuck with the first version of the Bush Doctrine—if the surge had come at the beginning of the war, not the end of it.

THE IRAQ SYNDROME

For all the blunders, we owe it to Iraq veterans to acknowledge what they achieved. American soldiers won the war on the ground through a combination of courage, adaptability, perseverance, and ingenuity. American commanders won the trust of moderate Sunni and Shiite Iraqi leaders, shattered the insurgency, prevented the breakup of the country, and found myriad ways to make life for ordinary people better. When the last American troops left in 2011 the country was entirely at peace with its neighbors and mostly at peace with itself. The tragedies of Iraq that came later were the result of failures of leadership in Baghdad, and of an administration that wanted nothing more than never to have to do anything about Iraq again, except to trumpet our exit from it.

In short, it wasn't the war itself that was the mistake; it was the confusion of its aims. It wasn't the "hyping" of intelligence,[10] or the abuses of Abu Ghraib, or other American crimes and misdemeanors, real or alleged, that nearly shipwrecked the enterprise; it was the excess of good intentions, the intoxication of ideals. And it wasn't the overreliance on force that led to near fiasco; it was the timid application of force in the face of an enemy that knew only the logic of force.

But that was a hard case to make by the time Obama began his presidential bid. Though Obama's campaign slogan was "Hope and Change," when it came to foreign policy the theme song could just as easily have been The Who's "Won't Get Fooled Again." The United States had marched into Iraq in order to make the world a safer place. It ended up mainly feeling suckered and fleeced, like a tourist in a Mideast bazaar, promising himself "never again." So it has been with Americans and the idea of doing anything that conjures the ghost of Iraq. This is the Iraq Syndrome, a political reflex so automatic, uncontrollable, and twitchy as to more closely resemble an allergy than a point of view. Americans have made up their minds about Iraq; they want neither to hear of it nor to think of it; they want, like *Seinfeld*'s George Costanza, to "do the opposite"—whatever the opposite is.

They're getting what they want from Obama.

FALL 2009:
AFGHANISTAN AGONISTES

$\star$ $\star$ $\star$ $\star$

Public support in the United States for the war in Afghanistan dipped below the 50 percent mark for the first time in the late summer of 2009.[1] Coincidentally or not, it was then that Barack Obama stopped talking about Afghanistan as "the war that has to be won" and began treating it as the war from which the United States needed to extricate itself—win, lose, or draw.

Though it is mostly forgotten today, Afghanistan was once the liberals' war. Not that conservatives didn't also support it—George W. Bush had started it, after all, and polls consistently showed broad Republican support for the effort. But for liberals it had additional moral and political merits. It was a just war, a response to an unprovoked act of terrorist aggression. It had international legitimacy on its side, and broad international support. It was a war of freedom for Afghans, especially for the women who had been veiled and brutalized through the Taliban's five-year reign of terror in Kabul.

And it was the anti-Iraq: a liberation, not an occupation; a war of necessity against the people who attacked us, not a "war of choice" against a dictator toward whom the president and his advisers had nurtured a grudge ever since the first Gulf War. It was a way of showing that liberals in America were no woolly-headed dreamers but tough-minded realists who knew the difference between dumb and smart wars.

This was the banner Barack Obama would carry with him on his road to the White House.

"It is time to write a new chapter in our response to 9/11," then-Senator Obama urged in a speech to the Woodrow Wilson Center in Washington, D.C., in August 2007. "The first step must be getting off the wrong battlefield in Iraq, and taking the fight to the terrorists in Afghanistan and Pakistan. . . . We will not repeat the mistake of the past, when we turned our back on Afghanistan following Soviet withdrawal. As 9/11 showed us, the security of Afghanistan and America is shared."[2]

Obama was hardly alone in his views. "If Afghanistan fails," Joe Biden warned darkly in early 2008, "America will suffer a terrible setback." *The New York Times* was even more emphatic. "The battle against Al Qaeda and its Taliban allies is still winnable, and it is vital to American security," the paper opined in an August 2007 editorial. "But victory will require a smarter strategy and a lot more attention and resources."[3]

It was, in some ways, an overblown argument. Afghanistan was not on the verge of being lost in 2007, a year in which the United States lost a total of 111 troops in combat. It's true that there had been an uptick in Taliban attacks, but they were minor next to the insurgency that was then in the process of being routed in Iraq. Violence was largely confined to five of the country's thirty-four provinces. And while corruption and mismanagement were rife, there was no doubting that most Afghans were better off than they had been in 1997, when the Taliban ruled, or 1987, when the Soviets did.

Still, Obama, Biden, the *Times*, and everyone else urging greater effort were right to stress how much Afghanistan mattered to the overall effort against Al Qaeda and its allies. More was at stake there than the fate of a benighted country that had once given sanctuary to Osama bin Laden, and where the attacks of 9/11 had been planned.

Afghanistan was also the place where 9/11 had been *imagined*. Victory by the mujahideen against the Soviets in the 1980s, soon followed by the collapse of the Soviet

Union itself, had taught jihadists the lesson that superpowers could be beaten, even destroyed. The United States had gone into Afghanistan to teach jihadists the opposite lesson: that attacking America would bring about their certain destruction. To lose in Afghanistan would teach jihadis and other enemies of the West something else entirely: that NATO was a fragile shell and that the United States could be defeated; that it had no stomach for the long fight; that Washington was an unreliable ally, ultimately more dangerous to its friends than to its enemies. To leave Afghanistan without winning would compound the disaster of 9/11 with another humiliating, Vietnam-style defeat. It would demoralize the West. It would furnish the jihadists with another mythic triumph against a superpower adversary, a narrative of struggle with which to inspire the next generation of the fanatically faithful.

"If we don't win here, you'll have a staging base for global terrorism all over the world," James Jones, Obama's first national security adviser, told Bob Woodward on a trip to Afghanistan in June 2009. "People will say the terrorists won. And you'll see expressions of these kinds of things in Africa, South America, you name it. Any developing country is going to say, this is the way we beat [the United States], and we're going to have a bigger problem."[4]

All this made for a powerful case for staying, fighting, and winning. And that's just what the president was promising: "Despite the costs," Obama said of Afghanistan in his Cairo speech in June 2009, "America's commitment will not weaken."

Yet no sooner had liberals gotten what they claimed to want—a president committed to getting out of Iraq so as to fight better in Afghanistan—than they began to turn against the war. A 2009 *Washington Post* poll found that 70 percent of Democrats believed "the war had not been worth its costs."⁵ The fear was building among liberals that Afghanistan would do to Obama's domestic legacy what Vietnam had done to Lyndon Johnson's. The feeling only grew stronger as time went by—culminating in one of the more remarkable editorial about-faces in recent years.

"It is time for United States forces to leave Afghanistan on a schedule dictated only by the security of the troops," *The New York Times* editorialized in 2012.

> *We are not arguing that everything will work out well after the United States leaves Afghanistan. It will not. The Taliban will take over parts of the Pashtun south, where they will brutalize women and trample their rights. Warlords will go on stealing. Afghanistan will still be the world's second-poorest country. Al Qaeda may make inroads, but since 9/11 it has established itself in Yemen and many other countries.*
>
> *America's global interests suffer when it is mired in unwinnable wars in distant regions. Dwight Eisenhower helped the country's position in the world by leaving Korea;* Richard Nixon by leaving Vietnam; President Obama by leaving Iraq.*
>
> *None of these places became Jeffersonian democracies. But the United States was better off for leaving.*⁶

What happened? How was it that in the space of a few years, under a Democratic president, liberals went from demanding victory in Afghanistan to insisting on immediate retreat? And how did a newspaper with progressive political sympathies become so openly cavalier about the

---

*   South Koreans might be astonished to learn that the United States ever "left" their country, or that they didn't become a democracy.

prospect of women being brutalized and having their rights trampled on in the wake of an American exit?

It is tempting to suspect that there had been no liberal reversal at all, that their support for the war had never been more than a cudgel of political convenience to be used against the Bush administration—and dispensed with when Bush went away. There's probably something to that. But there is more. Things changed. A financial panic and a steep recession refocused American priorities. A tainted election in Afghanistan called into question the morality of a war being fought partly for the benefit of corrupt politicians in Kabul and Kandahar. One by one our allies in Afghanistan removed their forces. Bin Laden was killed in his Abbottabad compound by Navy SEALs. And Barack Obama offered a blueprint for a new foreign policy, demanding a smaller U.S. footprint in the world.

The Retreat Doctrine was born—or born again. Taft and Wallace had returned.

CHAPTER 4

* * *

The Retreat Doctrine

The Retreat Doctrine rests on several assumptions. First among them is the idea that, in modern warfare, victory is rarely a realistic option. In fact, it's not necessarily a desirable one. It rests, furthermore, on the idea that the containment most needed in the twenty-first century is not of authoritarian adversaries such as China, Russia, or Iran. It's containment of the United States itself—of its military power and its democratic zeal; of its presence and commitments abroad; of its global preeminence. "Reduce, reuse, recycle" is the mantra of the modern environmental movement. "Rebalance, resize, and retreat" could be the mantra of the president's foreign policy.

It's an idea that seems to have captured Obama as he undertook his strategic review of the situation in Afghanistan leading to his December 2009 decision, announced in a speech at West Point, to order thirty thousand additional troops to the country for a limited surge. The review turned out to be a massive bureaucratic undertaking, as Obama quickly realized that getting a handle on the "good war" was not a simple matter of shifting troops and attention away from Iraq. Afghanistan was its own problem: larger and more geographically remote than Iraq, more primitive, harder to stand up on its own human and economic resources.

In the midst of the review, a critical difference emerged over the choice of a single verb. Was it America's goal to *defeat* the Taliban in Afghanistan? Or was it, merely, to *disrupt* it? Defense Secretary Robert Gates insisted that the goal had to be defeat; so did Gen. David Petraeus, who was then in charge of Central Command; so did Sen. John McCain. "There's only one option the president should consider," the senator told Gen. Stanley McChrystal, "and that's the winning option."[1]

Why put so much emphasis on defeating the Taliban when it had been Al Qaeda that had attacked the United States on 9/11? One reason, the advocates of a defeat strategy insisted, was the symbiotic relationship between the Afghan Taliban, Al Qaeda, the Haqqani network, the Pakistani Taliban, and other terrorist groups operating in the hinterlands between Afghanistan and Pakistan; they were different heads of the same monster. A second reason was that a Taliban victory in Afghanistan would mean the large-scale return of Al Qaeda to the country. A third was that a Taliban victory would also turn Afghanistan into a base from which the Pakistani Taliban could seek to topple the government in Islamabad and gain possession of its large nuclear arsenal.

Then there was the example of Iraq. Contrary to the (pre-surge) conventional wisdom in Washington, Iraq showed that the intelligent application of military force in a counterinsurgency operation could succeed. An estimated 30,000 Iraqis were killed in 2006; by 2009, the number had fallen to below 5,000—a decline of more than 80 percent.[2] American casualties also plummeted over the same period, from 823 to 149.[3] Shiite and Sunni insurgents (including Al Qaeda in Iraq) were routed by a combination of American and Iraqi arms. The United States emerged, in author Bing West's useful phrase, as "the strongest tribe"—respected by its allies, feared by its enemies. By the time Obama took office, Iraq was able to conduct peaceful elections as the shattered neighborhoods of Baghdad came back to life.

Yet not everyone within the Obama administration believed in the goal of defeating the Taliban. Joe Biden was of the view that, if the United States could not beat the Taliban after eight years of effort, it never would beat it. Surging more troops, he thought, would merely guarantee more casualties, further eroding political support for the war. The better alternative, in the vice president's view, was to go for a narrow "counterterrorism" strategy that provided just enough forces for the United States to continue targeting Al Qaeda while preventing an outright Taliban victory. For Richard Holbrooke, the veteran diplomat nominally entrusted by Obama with the "Af-Pak" portfolio, military victory was also not an option: the Taliban sprang from the country's ethnic and religious soil in a way the United States could never hope to change. The best America could do was create the diplomatic conditions for a political reconciliation between Afghanistan's warring factions. According to John Brennan, the president's top counterterrorism adviser and future CIA director, Afghanistan was a country that was simply beyond the capacity of anyone to fix. "If you're talking about a completely uncorrupt government that delivers services to all of its people, that end state won't be achieved in my lifetime," he said. "That's why using terminology like 'success,' like 'victory,' and 'win,' complicates our task."[4]

There was also a matter of resources; of the balance the United States needed to strike between achieving an acceptable outcome in Afghanistan and pursuing American objectives elsewhere in the world, and at home. With the exception of iconoclastic military figures such as Petraeus, most of the senior brass hated long-term commitments that strained the fabric of military life. Lt. Gen. Douglas Lute, a White House holdover from the Bush administration who was helping to oversee the Af-Pak review, worried that a fully resourced "defeat" strategy would require an additional 85,000 troops to deploy to Afghanistan—more than the United States, with its globe-spanning security commitments, could really afford to give. "Disrupt," in this view, was strategically—and politically—realistic. "Defeat" was not.

And yet if the goal was merely to disrupt the Taliban, why throw in any additional resources or risk any additional lives at all? Who wants to die merely to disrupt?

Only President Obama could settle this debate. In an October 30 meeting with his Joint Chiefs, he did. "The goal," he stressed to them, "is to defeat and dismantle al Qaeda." When it came to Afghanistan, however, the mission was to "disrupt the Taliban, weaken them so that the Afghans can handle it."

In May 2013 the president would retreat even from his narrowed aims. "Neither I, nor any president, can promise the total defeat of terror," he conceded to an audience at the National Defense University in Washington, D.C.

Policy making is done in real time, not retrospect, and in October 2009 there was a superficially compelling logic to the president's approach. Focus first on the primary enemy, the terrorists who threaten ordinary Americans, not those who threaten ordinary Afghans. Don't dissipate U.S. energies in an impossible quest to turn Afghanistan into another Switzerland. Help Afghanistan stand up on its own feet, and don't make open-ended commitments to do for them what they ought to learn to do for themselves. Remain mindful that overinvesting in Afghanistan means underinvesting in other places where important U.S. interests are at stake. Don't make a totem of a word, "victory," if it's unlikely to be achieved.

Yet the logic has equally obvious defects. More than one thousand U.S. troops have been killed in action since Obama took office, double the number during the preceding seven years. What would induce the Taliban to negotiate in good faith if they knew that the United States was not determined to defeat them? On what basis was it reasonable to assume that Al Qaeda—a furtive transnational organization held together not by territory or ethnicity but by its ideology and methods—could be defeated, while the Taliban—narrowly based in the Pashtun belt straddling Afghanistan and Pakistan, and offering a more conventional military challenge—could not be? And what were the consequences to U.S. interests worldwide if America was seen to abandon the "good war" it had waged directly in response to 9/11? Didn't the United States have much to gain by demonstrating the will and the capability to win the wars it was in, and which the president had said must be won? And didn't America and its new president have much to lose by demonstrating the opposite?

A final consideration: if victory is rarely an option for the United States when it goes overseas to fight wars, why ever start them in the first place? The Retreat Doctrine begins as a form of prophylactic defense against supposedly inevitable failure, then proceeds as an acquiescence to a world hostile to American interests, values, and long-term security.

All of this was widely discussed by pundits and policy experts as Obama put the final touches on the speech he would deliver at West Point. But the president had additional considerations in mind.

LIGHT FOOTPRINT

"This needs to be a plan about how we're going to hand it off and get out of Afghanistan," Obama told his national security team shortly before he went to West Point. "Everything that we're doing has to be focused on how we're going to get to the point where we can reduce our footprint. It is in our national security interest. There can be no wiggle room."[5]

Reduce our footprint. Though the president was making a point about Afghanistan, "Light Footprint" is another core idea in the Retreat Doctrine: the United States has a way of treading a little too heavily in the world; staying out of other people's business is generally the best policy, even when their business infringes on our strategic interests; the United States should use minimalist means to achieve limited goals. "When I think back on . . . all the times when a key player in the Middle East actually did something that put a smile on my face," Thomas Friedman wrote in a 2009 column, "all of them have one thing in common: America had nothing to do with it."[6] Light footprint is an approach politically well suited to a country wearied by, and wary of, lengthy nation-building exercises, and fiscally well suited to a period of growing deficits and shrinking military budgets. But whether the light-footprint approach works is another question—as is the question of whether it is just a station on the road to a zero-footprint result.

Most discussions of light footprint revolve around military tactics, technologies, and strategy. "Whenever possible, we will develop innovative, low-cost, and small-footprint approaches to achieve our security objectives," stresses the Defense Department's 2012 Strategic Defense Guidance document.[7] In practice that has meant the use of drones and special forces to carry out strikes against terrorists, training and "partnering" missions with friendly countries, and the "leading from behind" method the administration employed in 2011 in Libya, where the United States provided just enough air support and assistance to NATO to tilt the military balance against Muammar Gaddafi's regime, without putting boots on the ground.

"In the past, the United States often assumed the primary role of defending others," Leon Panetta, then the secretary of defense, said in a June 2012 speech. "We built permanent bases. We deployed large forces across the globe to fixed positions. We often assumed that others were not willing or capable of defending themselves. Our new strategy recognizes that this is not the world we live in anymore."

On its face, it's hard not to be attracted to a light-footprint approach: Why *not* do more with less? Why do for others what they should do for themselves (and, when properly trained and equipped, can do better)? Why maintain a Cold War–style military to fight post–Cold War wars? These are legitimate questions. And there is a fair amount of evidence that a light-footprint approach often can reap larger strategic dividends for the United States at much lower cost. Starting in the late 1990s, the United States invested about $1 billion over a decade to train and equip the Colombian military in order to defeat a narco-terrorist insurgency nearly as brutal and determined as the Taliban. U.S. troops were never (visibly) on the ground, and the plan worked: Colombia has largely vanquished the insurgency while becoming a prosperous democracy and a safe tourist destination. Could the same be said about U.S. efforts in Afghanistan?

Yet even within the Obama administration there have been misgivings about light footprint. "There are two big ways we can make mistakes," an unnamed senior intelligence official told *The New York Times*' David Sanger in 2012. "One is to forget that sometimes light footprint can cost you more in the long run than going into a place with a much more decisive force—that was the lesson of Afghanistan. And the second is to fall in love with whiz-bang new technology, because it's easy to justify relying on it more and more. And that's when a tactical weapon can begin defining your strategy."[8]

The official might have added that "light footprint" was also the approach then–defense secretary Donald Rumsfeld and CENTCOM commander Gen. John Abizaid relied on for occupying Iraq following the fall of Baghdad, on the theory that it was both cheaper for the United States, safer for our troops, and less obnoxious to Iraqis to avoid being a constant, visible, heavyweight presence on Iraqi streets. But the result helped accelerate the country's descent into chaos. The subsequent surge was the opposite of light footprint.

Put simply, light footprint works in some places and not in others. It is, or should be, a military tactic. Under Obama, however, it has become a military *necessity*. "We are going to be smaller and leaner—that's a reality," Panetta said in the same June 2012 speech, adding that "we must remain agile, flexible, quickly deployable, and on the cutting edge of technology." His successor, Chuck Hagel, put the truth in starker terms: "We are entering an era," he said in February 2014 as he announced a new round of budget cuts, "where American dominance on the seas, in the skies and in space can no longer be taken for granted."[9] In 2013, the Army announced that it would be cutting 12 of its 45 brigades—a drop in 80,000 active-duty troops by 2017. A few months later the Pentagon announced it would accelerate that process, reaching that target by 2015, and cutting an additional 40,000 to 50,000 troops by 2019. The Navy may keep its 11 aircraft carriers, but it will temporarily retire 11 of its 22 cruisers. The Air Force will retire 25,000 airmen and 550 planes. The entire fleet of A-10 ground attack planes will be retired almost immediately in favor of the F-35, which is still in testing.[10]

"Risk to the Air Force means we may not get there in time; it may take the joint team longer to win; and more Americans may die," Air Force chief of staff Mark Welsh warned Congress in September 2013. "Speed is an inherent advantage of airpower. However, if our squadrons are grounded, if it takes weeks or months to generate global combat power, then we negate the responsiveness that is one of airpower's natural advantages."[11] In the era of light footprint, it is the budget that dictates strategy, not the other way around. The more the budget shrinks, the sharper the strategic constraints.

Nor is light footprint merely a military concept. It is also, for Obama, a diplomatic approach, a strategic posture, perhaps even a national ideal. "It is not productive, given the history of U.S.-Iranian relations, to be seen as meddling—the U.S. president, meddling in Iranian elections," he said in June 2009 after Mahmoud Ahmadinejad was fraudulently reelected and millions of Iranians took to the streets to denounce the result, in English as well as Farsi. In Syria, the administration waited six months after the beginning of the uprising to call for the removal of Bashar al-Assad. "It's not going to be any news if the United States says, 'Assad needs to go,'" Hillary Clinton said in August 2011.

Obama was less reticent when it came to demanding the immediate ouster of Egypt's Hosni Mubarak, a U.S. ally of thirty years. But Egypt—along, perhaps, with Israel—was an exception to the general Obama rule: *The more America removes itself from the domestic controversies and travails of other countries, the less they can hurt us, cost us, embroil us, and be blamed on us.* Light footprint means, or is supposed to mean, light responsibility. It is the hope that America won't always be on the hook.

In practice, the concept hasn't worked out as planned. When U.S. ambassador Chris Stevens and three members of his security detail were murdered in Benghazi, Libya, on September 11, 2012, many Americans wondered why U.S. forces couldn't be mustered in time to carry out some kind of rescue or intervention. "Obama's reluctance to put American forces on the ground during the fight [in Libya], and his decision to keep America's diplomatic and CIA presence minimal in post-Qaddafi Libya, may have helped lead the United States to miss signals and get caught unaware in the attack on the American mission in Benghazi," noted David Sanger in the *Times*. "Military forces were too far from Libya's shores during the Sept. 11 [2012] attack to intervene."[12]

The crisis in Syria proved to be another case study in the perils of light footprint. Obama did get around to calling for Assad's ouster, only to stay as far away as possible. The theory was that putting greater distance between the United States and Syria would contain the crisis and lessen Washington's exposure. The opposite happened. What began as an internal Syrian drama quickly became a regional one, as hundreds of thousands, then millions, of Syrians fled to Turkey, Lebanon, and Jordan, straining economic resources and political stability in each of the neighbor states. What began with peaceful demonstrations calling for Assad to step down descended into a terrorist free-for-all, as Hezbollah and Al Qaeda sought advantage in the appalling anarchy. What began as a potentially heavy blow to the interests of Russia and Iran became instead a strategic victory for both states. And what started as a crisis in Syria was transformed into a crisis of U.S. credibility, as Assad defied Obama's chemical red line. That, in turn, created a crisis in relations between the United States and Saudi Arabia, and a crisis in confidence between the United States and Israel.

In short, it is an open question whether a policy of attempting to remain aloof from the travails of other countries serves U.S. interests in the near term or enhances U.S. security in the long term. "Who *wouldn't* want a light footprint strategy?" General Petraeus asked in 2011, with more than a touch of irony. Light footprint is a convenient and appealing approach to a world as we'd like it to be. But we live in the world as it is.

JUDGE NOT . . .

When Obama speaks about foreign policy, he tends to do so in strikingly moral terms. So much so that it sometimes sounds as if he's running not a superpower but a social movement.

Ordering the closure of the prison at Guantánamo on his second day as president, he insisted that America should be "willing to observe core standards of conduct, not just when it's easy, but also when it's hard." During his first foreign trip as president in 2009, he made the case for nuclear arms reductions in example-setting terms: "As the only nuclear power to have used a nuclear weapon, the United States has a moral responsibility to act." At a summit of the G20 countries in London in 2009, Obama opened by telling his fellow leaders that he "took responsibility" for the financial crisis, "even if I wasn't president at the time." (The German newsweekly *Der Spiegel* enthused that the comment would "go down in history as one of the greatest statements ever made. . . . He has admitted that one of the excesses of the American way of life—the craving for huge profits—has brought the world to the brink of disaster.")[13] Explaining his decision to impose restrictions on the National Security Agency's collection of metadata in January 2014, he insisted that "as the nation that developed the Internet, the world expects us to ensure that the digital revolution works as a tool for individual empowerment, not government control."

Given Obama's emphasis on the need for the United States to live up to its values (as he sees them), one might expect a values-focused foreign policy as well. Yet the paradox of Obama's presidency is how skeptical the administration has been of traditional U.S. efforts to promote those values abroad. In a classic case of overcompensation for the overambitiousness of his predecessor's freedom agenda, Obama has largely given up on *any* efforts to foster democracy and liberalism abroad. Light footprint, it turns out, isn't just a military concept. It's also a retreat from ordinary moral judgment.

Thus, no sooner did Obama come to office in 2009 than he cut funding for democracy programs in Egypt to $20 million from the $50 million that had been allocated under Bush.[14] Hillary Clinton downplayed a harsh State Department report on human rights in Egypt and told reporters, "I really consider President and Mrs. Mubarak to be friends of my family."[15] Later that year, the State Department denied a funding request for the New Haven–based Iran Human Rights Documentation Center, which documented cases of human rights abuses in the Islamic Republic. "Many see the sudden, unexplained cutoff of funding as a shift by the Obama administration away from high-profile democracy promotion in Iran, which had become a signature issue for President Bush," reported *The Boston Globe*.[16] In February 2009, Hillary Clinton insisted that, in the U.S. relationship with China, human rights "can't interfere with the global economic crisis, the global climate change crisis and the security crisis." Later that year Obama refused to meet with the Dalai Lama when the Tibetan leader was in Washington. In 2011, the United

States cut all Voice of America radio and TV broadcasts in Mandarin and Cantonese, purportedly as part of a cost-cutting measure.[17]

As for Russia, *Time* magazine described a June 2010 meeting on the subject of human rights between Michael McFaul, one of Obama's advisers on Russia, and a Kremlin official named Vladimir Lukin. "In fact he didn't really make any criticism at all," Lukin said of his meeting with McFaul. "What's the point of criticizing us when we criticize ourselves? We criticized ourselves a little about corruption. They criticized themselves a little about Guantánamo. It was all very friendly.'"[18] Only a few months earlier, a Russian lawyer named Sergei Magnitsky had been beaten to death in prison for blowing the whistle on corrupt Interior Ministry officials who had defrauded the Russian state of more than $200 million. Sen. Ben Cardin, a Democrat, called for the administration to sanction sixty Russians complicit in the scheme. After dragging its heels for years, the administration wound up sanctioning about twenty people.

Then there was the drama following Iran's 2009 presidential election. After remaining mostly silent about the vote for days, Obama allowed that he was "deeply troubled by the violence." But what he mainly stressed was that he wanted the United States to play no part in the unfolding drama: "I want to start off by being very clear that it is up to Iranians to make decisions about who Iran's leaders will be; that we respect Iranian sovereignty and want to avoid the United States being an issue inside Iran, which sometimes the United States can be a handy political football." As for what, in fact, had happened in Iran, Obama was circumspect: "My understanding is, is that the Iranian government says that they are going to look into the irregularities that have taken place. We weren't on the ground, we did not have observers there, we did not have international observers on hand, so I can't state definitively one way or another what happened with respect to the election."

How did Obama's sensitivity to not being seen as a meddler play out in practice? "We are surprised at Mr. Obama," Ahmadinejad lectured. "Didn't he say he wanted change? Why did he interfere? They have revealed their intentions before the Iranian nation, before the world. Their mask has been removed."[19] Supreme Leader Ali Khamenei was more blunt: "The American president," he said, "introduced the street rioters as a civil movement."[20]

In 2011, in the aftermath of the Arab Spring, Obama appeared to reconsider his approach. "It will be the policy of the United States," he said in a State Department speech in May 2011, "to promote reform across the region, and to support transitions to democracy." But the policy was abandoned nearly as soon as it was announced as the hopes of the Arab Spring were disappointed in one state after another. Perhaps it was just as well: the United States did not need to twist itself into moral knots over questions of democratic legitimacy in places such as Egypt or Bahrain. Then again, it wasn't clear what interest was being served, morally or strategically, when the United States demurred from rendering judgment on its enemies, or from lending moral comfort to Iranians, Chinese, or Russians prepared to struggle for their own freedom. Learning from the excesses of the freedom agenda is one thing; substituting for it a policy of studious nonjudgmentalism in a world that still looks to America as a beacon of freedom is another.

"NATION BUILDING AT HOME"

The Retreat Doctrine is not an end in itself, however. Its higher purpose is to build America anew. It's a point Obama made explicitly in his West Point speech.

> As we end the war in Iraq and transition to Afghan responsibility, we must rebuild our strength here at home. Our prosperity provides a foundation for our power. It pays for our military. It underwrites our diplomacy. It taps the potential of our people, and allows investment in new industry. And it will allow us to compete in this century as successfully as we did in the last. That's why our troop commitment in Afghanistan cannot be open-ended—because the nation that I'm most interested in building is our own.

What were the cadets in the audience to make of what their commander in chief was saying? It was at once unobjectionable and astonishing. Balancing priorities, living within means, accounting for costs, husbanding resources, focusing on the home front, bringing long wars to an end: here was an attractively old-fashioned way of thinking of the world. And yet the Retreat Doctrine was being proposed as a measure of frugality by the president with the most ambitious social agenda since Lyndon Johnson was in the White House.

Since the 1960s, the federal government's spending has averaged out to 20.5 percent of gross domestic product. A 2013 study from the nonpartisan Congressional Budget Office warns that the figure will rise to 26 percent by 2038. The percentage change may seem small, but it is a difference worth trillions of dollars. Major entitlement programs will double as a share of the economy, to 14 percent of GDP in 2038 from a 7 percent average over the last forty years. To compensate for the increases in mandated spending, discretionary government spending—including defense—will fall from its forty-year average of 11 percent to 7 percent, "a smaller share of the economy," reports the CBO, than it has been "at any time since the late 1930s."[21]

And what was all this for? In the summer of 2012, the Obama campaign offered an idea of the kind of society it wanted to build with a cartoon slide show called "The Life of Julia." It tracks the life of a woman from infancy to old age. Young Julia begins her life's journey as a little girl in a Head Start program, attends college on a Pell Grant, and undergoes surgery while she's still covered under her parents' plan thanks to Obamacare. Later, her son goes to a school with "better facilities and great teachers because of President Obama's investments in education." When Julia decides to start her own Web business, she qualifies for a low-interest loan from the Small Business Administration. As she reaches retirement, she enrolls in Medicare and "retires comfortably" on Social Security. Every milestone is defined by her relationship with the government. Does government bureaucracy ever get in Julia's way? Apparently never. Does the government ever provide services that are anything less than smooth, efficient, and well designed? Apparently not. Not since the days of the

Kennedy administration has a president invested such unalloyed faith in the ability of government to function intelligently.

The utopia described in "The Life of Julia" isn't socialism, much less Marxism: Obama is not interested in nationalizing the means of production. It is social democracy—a belief in the redemptive power of what Obama would call, in his second inaugural, "collective action," mainly through the agency of government. Social democracy believes in social leveling. It is not illiberal, but it expresses a consistent preference for equality at the expense of liberty, particularly economic liberty. It is not against markets, but it sees them as innately unfair and unstable. It is not antibusiness, but the businesses it likes best are those that are joined to the state via regulation, mandates, and subsidies. Social democracy believes in "solidarity" between the employer and the labor union, the wage earner and the retiree, the middle and the working class.

In the real world, social democracy produces chronically low rates of growth, and persistently high levels of unemployment. But it also commands profound ideological and political identification. And, once entrenched, it is politically nearly impossible to abandon.

Nowhere has social democracy been practiced longer than in modern Europe. And nowhere are the effects of social democracy on foreign policy better seen than in Europe. By its nature, entitlement spending crowds out defense spending: faced with the choice of arming soldiers or funding pensions, voters will invariably go for the latter. In 1988, Britain spent 4 percent of its GDP on defense. By 2012 spending was down to 2.5 percent and falling. France's military spending fell from 3.6 percent to 2.5 percent, Germany's from 2.9 percent to 1.4 percent, Italy's from 2.3 percent to 1.7 percent.[22] What's more, social democracy turns the military itself into an extension of the welfare state. The Pentagon spends roughly one third of its budget on personnel costs: salaries, health care, and pensions. By contrast, France spends a remarkable 50 percent of its budget on personnel; one in five French defense euros go to pensioners. "On paper France has 230,000 men and women in uniform," noted *The Wall Street Journal* in 2013. "But only 30,000 are estimated to be deployable on six-months' notice."[23]

When you don't have a hammer, no problem ever looks like a nail. Europe expresses a consistent preference for diplomatic, "soft power" approaches to foreign policy in part out of sincere conviction, but also because those are the only options available to policy makers. On the few recent occasions European countries have pursued military options—the NATO action in Libya in 2011 and France's intervention in Mali in 2013—they've found themselves rapidly running out of munitions or short of critical logistics and intelligence support. And yet there has been no political appetite for increasing military spending. Even Russia's invasion of Ukraine had no effect on the trajectory of military spending. "Even with officials acknowledging the danger," *The Washington Post* reported in March 2014, Europeans "are reluctant to respond by reversing planned cuts in military spending that were enacted when Europe was more stable."[24] What *would* prompt a reversal in the trend is an open question: a Russian takeover of the rest of Ukraine? An invasion of a NATO member state?

Since World War II Europeans have relied on U.S. security guarantees to make up for the inadequacies in their own defenses; they have been able, as Robert Kagan suggested a decade ago, to live in a Kantian world of "perpetual peace" because the United States was rooted in a Hobbesian world of power. But U.S. security guarantees are no longer what they once were. If the result of the Retreat Doctrine is an America with entitlement programs that resemble Europe's, it will eventually have a military that resembles Europe's too. And it will have the same reluctance to pursue military options to deal with geopolitical crises. European policy makers need to begin thinking about their long-term security outlook in a world in which Uncle Sam has decided to take a European-style vacation from history.

In the meantime, Americans may consider that the reason Europe was able to afford that long holiday from history is because a friendly power across the sea was prepared to devote immense resources to its defense. When Americans go on that holiday, who will be minding the store for *us*?

SUMMER 2013:
"LET ALLAH SORT IT OUT"

★ ★ ★ ★

The temperature was approaching 100 degrees by the time the rally had assembled on the south steps of the Oklahoma State Capitol. There weren't that many people—two hundred or so—but what made this event noteworthy was its political composition and its cause. There were Republicans and Democrats, old-school hawks and peace activists, social conservatives and libertarians. But they were united on one thing: "We have spilled enough American blood in the desert sand," said Paul Wesselhoft, a retired military chaplain, Republican state representative, and one of the event's organizers. "This civil war is not our business."

The civil war to which Wesselhoft was referring was the uprising in Syria against Bashar al-Assad, a close ally of Iran, a patron of Hezbollah, a Baathist who had spent the better part of the previous decade allowing Al Qaeda–linked jihadists to infiltrate Iraq. Then, too, at the time of the July 12 rally, the prospect of an American intervention in Syria was not yet on the horizon. President Obama had made it clear he had no appetite for one. U.S. intelligence had gone out of its way to downplay evidence of Assad's chemical weapons use. U.S. assistance to the rebels was minimal. But even the possibility of another Mideast conflict was enough to motivate Wesselhoft and other Oklahomans.

"Our troops are exhausted, and I want to see it stopped now," he said. "I know it's a little arrogant to think we can start a movement here, but why not? Just because we're a fly-over state? No, I think we can start a movement here. That's what I hope the rally will do." Not far off, protesters sang refrains from Vietnam-era antiwar songs.

The event was covered in the local press as a curiosity. Yet it proved prescient—and potent. Five weeks later, the Syrian government used sarin gas to murder more than one thousand Syrian civilians in a rebel-held neighborhood of Damascus, unequivocally crossing the red line against chemical weapons the president had set a year earlier. Secretary of State John Kerry, in a conference call with congressional lawmakers, warned that the West faced a "Munich moment" if it failed to punish Assad with air strikes. Democratic and Republican leaders in the House and Senate offered their public support.

But the rank and file did not. They had gone the way of Wesselhoft.

"I will vote and work against President Obama's request for open-ended authority to launch military strikes against the Syrian army," Rick Nolan, a Democratic congressman from Minnesota, warned Kerry—a rare instance of a Democrat openly challenging Obama on foreign policy.[1] But that was as nothing compared with opposition in Republican ranks. "I literally cannot walk across the parking lot without being stopped to talk about this issue," admitted Oklahoma congressman Tom Cole. "I haven't seen anything quite like this." No more than a dozen House Republicans came out openly in support of air strikes; some who did raced to reverse themselves.[2] Most vocal in opposition were hard-core Tea Party activists—the people who, as caricature would have it, viewed Obama as a crypto-Muslim and were reflexively hawkish. A CBS poll found that, while 61 percent of Americans opposed military action in Syria, the intensity of opposition was far greater among Republicans than Democrats.[3]

Why the depth and fervor of opposition? CBS found that Americans were concerned that any U.S. involvement would prove "long and costly" for the United States, that it would lead to a wider war, and that it would harm innocent civilians. Yet that seemed disconnected from the "unbelievably small" strikes that the White House was, in fact, threatening. Typically, the Republican critique of such strikes was that they would not go far enough to take out an anti-American, terror-sponsoring tyrant like Assad. Now Republicans were joining antiwar Democrats in saying even too little force was going too far; that Syria was a civil war pitting one bad side against the other; that we should let "Allah sort it out" as Sarah Palin put it, and that the outcome was of no consequence to U.S. national security.

The argument easily won the day, at least politically. Obama agreed to give Congress an up-or-down vote on any military strike. Days later, he seized an offer from Russia to broker an agreement whereby Damascus would relinquish its abundant stocks of chemical weapons. Hardly anyone seemed to care whether Assad was giving up all of his weapons, or just a fraction of his arsenal. Hardly anyone seemed to care, either, that the deal gave the United States a stake in Assad's survival in power, even as he continued to rain terror on his own people, causing the very humanitarian tragedy opponents of intervention claimed to want to avoid. All that mattered, it seemed, was to keep Syria off America's mental map.

But Syria is not off the map, geographically or strategically. Hezbollah and Al Qaeda will not oblige Western fantasies of annihilating each other, just as Iran and Iraq did not do so in their long war in the 1980s. On the contrary, Iraq invaded Kuwait just two years after its war with Iran ended, while Iran embarked on its nuclear program and extended the reach of its terror network from Berlin to Buenos Aires. So, too, the protracted war in Syria is doing more to incubate terrorism than to weaken it. Meanwhile, it is exporting instability throughout the region. Should Assad win outright, it will also be an outright victory for Russia, Hezbollah, and Iran—the latter at the very moment it's bidding to become a threshold nuclear state.

Is it in America's interests to accept an Iranian crescent, stretching from Afghanistan in the east to Lebanon and Gaza on the Mediterranean? Or is that just all "over there"—a problem that isn't America's to solve; a problem that probably has no solution anyway? That is the conclusion to which more conservatives are increasingly drawn, almost without being conscious of where their thoughts are tending, or of the consequences that flow from the conclusions.

CHAPTER 5

★ ★ ★

Republicans in Retreat

On September 14, 2001, Barbara Lee, a Democratic congresswoman from the Bay Area of California and a onetime member of the Black Panther Party, cast the sole vote in Congress against the Authorization for Use of Military Force (AUMF), Congress's declaration of war against Al Qaeda and its affiliates. Lee was following in the footsteps of Montana Republican Jeannette Rankin, who in 1941 cast the only "nay" vote against the 1941 declaration of war on Japan. She followed Rankin also into immediate political obloquy. One conservative pundit dismissed her as a card-carrying member of the "blame America first" crowd.[1] Among Democrats, she was seen as an embarrassing footnote to their otherwise lockstep support for the Bush administration's war on terror. Even the far-left Democratic congressman Dennis Kucinich had voted for the AUMF.

Not long after her vote, Lee made her case in an op-ed in the *San Francisco Chronicle*.

Some believe this resolution was only symbolic, designed to show national resolve. But I could not ignore that it provided explicit authority, under the War Powers Resolution and the Constitution, to go to war.

It was a blank check to the president to attack anyone involved in the Sept. 11 events—anywhere, in any country, without regard to our nation's long-term foreign policy, economic and national security interests, and without time limit. In granting these overly broad powers, the Congress failed its responsibility to understand the dimensions of its declaration. I could not support such a grant of war-making authority to the president; I believe it would put more innocent lives at risk.[2]

A decade later, Lee's views hadn't simply become mainstream. They had become *conservative* mainstream. Republicans are busy writing their own retreat doctrine in the name of small government, civil liberties, fiscal restraint, "realism," a creeping sense of Obama-induced national decline, and a deep pessimism about America's ability to make itself, much less the rest of the world, better.

SAN ANDREAS FAULT

A major foreign policy shakeout within the conservative movement was probably inevitable. The ideological fault line separating small-government conservatives from big-military conservatives has been visible, if mostly dormant, for a long time. In 2013, however, three earthquakes hit the Republican Party, one right after the other.

First there was the debate over budget sequestration, which promised to enforce federal spending discipline by imposing draconian cuts on the Defense Department. Then came Edward Snowden's disclosures about the reach of the National Security Agency's data-mining operations, raising familiar questions about the balance between security and civil liberties. And there was the crisis over the use of chemical weapons in Syria. That, in turn, also raised questions about the appropriate reach of executive

authority and the price of preserving—or squandering—American credibility.

Just a few years earlier, it would not have been hard to guess where
most Republicans would come down on these matters. Sequestration
would have been out of the question for a country fighting a global war
on terror and ground wars in Iraq and Afghanistan, while facing looming
challenges from a rising China and a revanchist Russia. Snowden would
have been universally denounced as a spy and perhaps even a traitor. And
the GOP would have been happy to see Assad and his chemical weapons
stocks bombed to smithereens. After all, if Republicans could support the
war in Iraq *after* weapons of mass destruction were not found, how could
they oppose air strikes to destroy weapons whose existence was demonstrated by their use?

By 2013, however, times had changed, and so had minds: "Fiscal
questions trump defense in a way they never would have after 9/11," said
Oklahoma Republican congressman Tom Cole about sequestration. "But
the war in Iraq is over. Troops are coming home from Afghanistan, and
we want to secure the cuts." No longer would the conservative foreign
policy debate revolve mainly around questions of political tactics, nuances
of policy, or, at most, differences between realists in the Nixon mold and
idealists in the Reagan mold. It was about choosing between radically different conservative visions for America's proper role in the world.

Here, then, was a conversation begging for some intellectual depth.
Did being the land of liberty require America, also, to be the land of *lib-
erators*? Was freedom the best cure for whatever, politically, was the
disease? Or was culture destiny, and if so did that mean the wars in Iraq
and Afghanistan had been misbegotten from the start? Did conservatives
agree with the famous British statesman who said he had made "a conscious choice to take risks with defense rather than with finances"?[3] Did a
large U.S. military presence in Germany, Japan, or other rich countries
encourage freeloading? Or did it bind them in an international system
that discouraged foreign policy adventurism? Should greater energy security in North America free us from having to care, one way or another,
about who does what to whom in the Middle East? Or are vital U.S.

interests other than energy at stake in that region? If an administration could use the IRS to abuse its partisan opponents, how could *any* president be trusted with potentially more dangerous powers—like real-time secret monitoring of citizens' digital habits?

"Vigor of government is essential to the security of liberty," Alexander Hamilton wrote in *The Federalist*, a view to which most conservatives would subscribe. But how much vigor is "essential," and at what point does it become excessive? "That government is best which governs least," said Henry David Thoreau in what would become a conservative maxim. But just how little is "least"?

These are serious questions, and they could have used some serious treatment. It hasn't happened yet.

Tea Party Leftism

The Tea Party—in reality, a movement within a party—is routinely tarred by its critics as a collection of twenty-first-century Archie Bunkers: undereducated, lower middle class, and racially bigoted. Not quite. As *The New York Times* reported with evident surprise, Tea Party backers were "wealthier and more educated" than the general public.[4] A study by Yale professor Dan Kahan found that Tea Partiers were also scientifically more literate than the rest of the country. "I've got to confess, I found this result surprising," Kahan admitted to *Politico*. "As I pushed the button to run the analysis on my computer, I fully expected I'd be shown a modest negative correlation between identifying with the Tea Party and science comprehension. But then again, I don't know a single person who identifies with the Tea Party."[5]

The Tea Party is also no monolith, including when it comes to foreign policy. Marco Rubio, who rode a Tea Party wave in Florida to a Senate seat, holds sophisticated foreign policy views that could be labeled neoconservative. Ted Cruz, who did the same in Texas, is for the most part a foreign policy hawk, despite his populist opposition to military intervention in Syria.

Still, there's no way to discuss the Tea Party without noting that many of its more vocal spokespeople are case studies in what the late Richard Hofstadter famously called "the paranoid style in American politics." This is the style that proposes that Barack Obama is Kenyan by birth, Marxist by persuasion, Muslim by affinity, anti-American by intention. For much of the Tea Party, it isn't sufficient to indict Obama's presidency for bungled execution of policy, bad economic ideas, broken promises, timid foreign policy, self-infatuation, or bullying political ways. It's not enough to say Obama is a bad *president*. He is a bad *man*—an ingenious conniver who is successfully carrying out his goal to destroy America from within.

"It is time," Tea Party notable Larry Klayman wrote in September 2013, "that we, as Christians, Jews, people of faith and all true patriots say enough is enough and ourselves, in a very real way, 'Occupy Washington' to cleanse the nation of the half-Muslim, anti-white, socialist fraud in the White House before the nation goes under for the final count."[6] Following Assad's sarin gas attack on rebels in Damascus, the TeaParty.org Web site ran heavy with speculation that the attack had been orchestrated by Al Qaeda to goad the United States into intervening against Assad.[7] One "expert" witness cited by TeaParty.org was serial conspiracy theorist Jerome Corsi, best known for his book *Where's the Birth Certificate?* Rand Paul was also a skeptic: "Pat Buchanan had an article the other day and he asked the Latin phrase: *Cui bono?* To whose benefit is this? All of this redounds back to the benefit of the rebels . . . not the Syrian army."[8]

The conspiracy mind-set is hardly the sole preserve of the right: recall the way in which George W. Bush was accused of stealing the 2000 election and then of having lied America into a war with Iraq for the benefit of Dick Cheney's old firm Halliburton. But Tea Party paranoia is different from left-wing paranoia, which tends to travel from left to far-left. Without quite seeming to notice it themselves, the Tea Partiers have, on one issue after another, moved from right to left in an astonishingly short time.

Consider: In May 2013 Obama called for rescinding the September 2001 AUMF, Congress's declaration of war against Al Qaeda. Two months later, thirty House Republicans, including Tea Party favorite

Michele Bachmann, voted to do the same. After Edward Snowden fled to Russia that summer, Justin Amash, the libertarian-leaning Republican congressman from Michigan, insisted on calling him a "whistleblower." Paul went one better, praising Snowden as a "civil disobedient" in the mold of Martin Luther King, Jr. "I would say that Mr. Snowden hasn't lied to anyone," the Kentucky Republican told CNN. "He did break his oath of office, but part of his oath of office is to the Constitution." Klayman personally sued Obama in federal court to end the NSA's telephony metadata collection efforts. He won in the first round: "I have significant doubts about the efficacy of the metadata collection program as a means of conducting time-sensitive investigations in cases involving imminent threats of terrorism,"[9] Judge Richard Leon, a George W. Bush appointee, opined in his ruling.*

Then there was the spectacle of congressional Republicans demanding a vote for air strikes in Syria. Republicans had spent forty years opposing the War Powers Resolution—imposed by a Democratic Congress in 1973 on a politically crippled Richard Nixon—as an unconstitutional infringement on the president's powers as commander in chief. But now the Tea Partiers were borrowing a page straight from the anti–Vietnam War left. They were doing so, moreover, with the object of sparing an anti-American, pro-Iranian, terrorism-sponsoring dictator from U.S. military reprisal.

All these views would sit well with the editors of *The Nation*, the donor base of the American Civil Liberties Union, or the antiwar groups that used to rally against the war in Iraq. The dissonance might have seemed more apparent if those views weren't also gaining traction with

---

* Judge Leon was promptly overruled by Judge William H. Pauley III of the Southern District of New York. "The collection of breathtaking amounts of information unprotected by the Fourth Amendment does not transform that sweep into a Fourth Amendment search," Judge Pauley, a Clinton appointee, ruled. He also observed that if the NSA metadata program had been in place before 9/11, the plot might have been stopped. "Telephony metadata would have furnished the missing information and might have permitted the N.S.A. to notify the Federal Bureau of Investigation of the fact that [9/11 hijacker Khalid] al-Mihdhar was calling the Yemeni safe house from inside the United States."

the core of the GOP. "Male and Republican demographics showed the highest increase in concerns about security overreach and away from their traditional support of government counter-terrorism efforts," *The Wall Street Journal* reported in July 2013. As recently as 2010, a Quinnipiac poll had found, 72 percent of Republicans said counterterrorism efforts "did not go far enough." By 2013 the figure was down to 46 percent.[10] A Pew survey from that summer also found that Republicans were *less* likely than Democrats to support the NSA's intelligence collection efforts by a remarkable 44 percent to 57 percent margin.

Would such views have taken hold had Mitt Romney won the presidency in 2012? Probably not: political paranoia is often nothing more than the vapors of boiling partisanship. Over time, however, people stake out positions from which they cannot easily walk away. Whether these views congeal into a neoisolationist conservative consensus will depend on who next wins the White House.

REPUBLICAN "REALISM"

Another conservative foreign policy approach goes by the name of "Realism." It comes in two distinct varieties: faux Realists and real Realists.

Real Realists offer a coherent vision for conservative foreign policy. None of them is averse to using force in any number of circumstances, for wars large or small. None of them is embarrassed by the term "the American interest." Much less do they feel any need to put the interests of the "international community" ahead of America's. These Realists believe that power, not law, legitimacy, morality, or economics, is the ultimate coin of the realm in international relations. Unlike most neoconservatives, they do not consider the internal character of regimes to be a bar to a diplomatic relationship or a strategic opening: Kissinger's task in China, when he paid his secret visit to Mao in 1971, was to test the waters of a mutually fruitful alliance against the Soviet Union, not to denounce the dictator for the evil of his ways. The serious Realist will do whatever he must in the service of the national interest. But he will not be moved at all, except perhaps privately, to rescue others from their own often self-inflicted dilemmas or tragedies.

There is much to be said, conceptually, for this version of realism. But it belongs to an aging breed of Republican statesmen: Henry Kissinger, Brent Scowcroft, and James Baker. It belongs, too, to a past century, when democratic publics were more willing to accept *raison d'état* as sufficient justification for international action. In the 1980s French security services sank a Greenpeace ship in harbor in New Zealand in order to prevent it from trying to interfere with French nuclear tests in the Pacific. One photographer was accidentally killed. The incident was a scandal in its day, but French president François Mitterrand shrugged it off. It's almost impossible to imagine any Western leader today, including an American president, authorizing a similar operation against a similar target and not ending up disgraced, impeached, and possibly arrested. Realism, in its purest sense, has become politically unrealistic.

Then there is faux Realism. "I am a realist, not a neoconservative nor an isolationist," Rand Paul insisted in a 2013 speech to the Heritage Foundation. In another speech that year he cited Dwight Eisenhower as his role model. "We must be more prudent in our foreign policy. Eisenhower was right to observe that little wars can often lead to big wars."

It's hard to know what's more astonishing: Paul's ignorance of the meaning of the term "realist," or his unfamiliarity with Eisenhower's foreign policy record. Realism is an academic approach to the study of international relations, pioneered by the political scientist Hans Morgenthau, which holds among its core premises that "the state has no right to let its moral disapprobation of the infringement of liberty get in the way of a successful political action."[11] If that means, for example, firing a missile from a drone to kill a U.S. citizen while he is sipping a latte in a Detroit café because he stands in the way of "a successful political action," Morgenthau's Realism would not automatically forbid it. This is precisely the opposite of the "Fourth Amendment Conservatism" that Paul has sought to champion as a senator. Fourth Amendment conservatism may be principled or naïve, depending on your view. But whatever else it is, it isn't Realism.

As for Eisenhower, the thirty-fourth president engineered the 1953 coup that toppled the Mossadegh government in Iran and the 1954 coup that overthrew the Árbenz government in Guatemala, and sent fourteen thousand troops to Lebanon in 1958 to rescue a pro-Western government, among other interventions. The policy that came to be known as the "Eisenhower Doctrine" specifically extended U.S. security guarantees to friendly governments throughout the Middle East. He began the process of nation building in South Vietnam, spending $1 billion on the effort before Kennedy came to office. Much of the "military-industrial complex" Eisenhower is now remembered for cautioning against in his Farewell Address was his own creation. The United States had roughly two thousand nuclear weapons in its arsenal when he took office in 1953. It had more than eighteen thousand when he left it in 1961. Most of the Pentagon's major weapons systems date to his administration: the first nuclear submarine, the first nuclear "super-carrier," the B-52 bomber, the U-2, the first ICBM. Military spending during the Eisenhower years never fell below 50 percent of the federal budget and 10 percent of GDP. By contrast, military spending under Ronald Reagan never rose *above* 30 percent of government outlays and 8 percent of GDP.

It is true that Eisenhower interceded in 1956 against Britain, France, and Israel to stop the Suez campaign against Egyptian demagogue Gamal Abdel Nasser. Habitual critics of Israel like to cite the episode as an illustration of an American president willing to impose his will on a stiff-necked ally. But this again misses the historical record: after leaving office, Eisenhower would come to see his handling of Suez as the "biggest foreign policy blunder of his administration."[12]

Faux Realism is an attempt to appropriate a good-sounding word (who *doesn't* consider himself a realist?) with an academic gloss in order to justify nearly any set of personal foreign policy preferences. John Mearsheimer of the University of Chicago considers himself a "Realist." Yet he is the coauthor of a book, *The Israel Lobby and U.S. Foreign Policy*, that attempts to show what all Realist theory denies: namely, that states act for any reason—including the influence of a domestic lobby—other than their national interest. As for Paul, he espouses a form of Realism that amounts to a prescription for downsizing U.S. commitments abroad as part of a broader package of downsizing Big Government at home. As he told a roomful of college students when he was gearing up to run for the Senate in 2009, "you have to decide if we have an expansionist foreign policy that believes that we have to have 750 military bases and troops in 130 countries, or whether our foreign policy should be a little more directed toward what the founding fathers talked about and that is more defense of our country and less offensive type of foreign policy."[13]

From Faux Realism to Real Isolationism

Paul's foreign policy is often viewed as an effort to water down and make palatable the moonshine that is the worldview of his father, former Texas congressman Ron Paul, the libertarian who thinks America had it coming on 9/11 because we were "occupying" Muslim territories. Perhaps. Then again, the foreign policy of George Bush, Sr., didn't prove to be especially predictive when it came to his son's presidency. And Rand Paul remains a political work in progress.

Still, it's worth noting that there is a Republican precedent for a foreign policy that in many ways resembles Paul's. It eschews foreign meddling, stresses the importance of domestic civil liberties, is happy to gut the military for the sake of budgetary health, and thinks the rest of the world should sort out its own problems and leave us to ours.

That was the substance of the Republican presidencies of Warren Harding, Calvin Coolidge, and Herbert Hoover. The short-lived Harding administration's principal foreign policy accomplishment was the 1922 Washington Naval Treaty, the first in a long series of ultimately self-defeating postwar disarmament efforts. Coolidge, notes biographer Amity Shlaes, "spent much time plotting to fend off military spending demands, whether an army request for airplanes to defend the Panama Canal or a navy demand for battleships."[14] His other foreign policy achievement was the Kellogg-Briand Pact, which, he hoped, would further reduce arms expenditures by the expedient of outlawing the very thing for which the arms were made: war. As for Hoover, he ended the U.S. occupations of

Haiti and Nicaragua while his secretary of state, Henry Stimson, famously abolished the code-breaking Cipher Bureau—precursor to the NSA—on the grounds that "gentlemen do not read each other's mail." (Stimson would later revisit that very Edwardian judgment when he returned to government in 1940 as Franklin Roosevelt's secretary of war.)

Looking back, the wonder of the 1920s is how a treaty like Kellogg-Briand could have been taken seriously by anyone, much less adopted by the United States Senate 85–1. But this was the era of Prohibition, another well-meant and ill-fated attempt to conquer evil by renouncing reality. And as with Prohibition, it did not quite achieve its intended effect. War, like drink, cannot be abolished.

In 1931, Japan invaded Manchuria. In 1935, Italy invaded Ethiopia. In 1938, Germany invaded Czechoslovakia, with the acquiescence of the major powers. Each of these countries, the invader as well as the invaded, had signed on to the Kellogg-Briand Pact. The tragedies of the 1930s are well known. What's forgotten is how they flowed from the illusions of the 1920s, the same illusions that conservative advocates of the Retreat Doctrine harbor today.

WHAT IS CONSERVATIVE FOREIGN POLICY?

The serious conservative charts a course between two permanent American temptations. The first is the urge to save the world. The second is the yearning to retreat from it.

Over the past decade the preference of conservatives has swung from the first to the second like a pendulum that cannot come to rest in midcourse. A decade ago Republicans were on a mission to spread the blessings of democracy from Kabul to Cairo and from Ramadi to Ramallah. But burned by Iraq, exhausted by Afghanistan, and disheartened by the Arab Spring, conservatives are done with the freedom agenda, done with the Middle East, and, increasingly, done with idea that the United States has any particular responsibility to maintain global order.

Nor do a growing number of conservatives see the principal threat to the United States emerging from abroad. Ask a traditional foreign policy hawk what the number one threat to the United States is today, and he is likely to name known or potential adversaries: Iran, North Korea, China, or a resurgent Al Qaeda. But for the new breed of libertarian-minded conservatives, the real threat is "Europe." It's shorthand for the risk that the United States will follow European states down the road to social democracy, and from there to overregulation, overtaxation, overunioniza- tion, a declining work ethic, a ruinous appetite for cradle-to-grave entitle- ments, and ever increasing levels of national debt.

These fears should not be flatly dismissed. Spending by the federal government grew by more than $1 trillion between 2007 and 2012, *de- spite* Obama's withdrawal from Iraq. The number of Americans on food stamps rose steadily from 32 million when Obama took office to 47 mil- lion in 2013, even while the recession officially ended in June 2009. The labor-participation rate, below 63 percent in May 2014, is at its lowest level since 1978, as discouraged job seekers simply withdraw from the job market (creating the illusion of lower unemployment). Federal spending on entitlements now consumes 62 percent of the budget. Spending on Social Security rose 35 percent between 2002 and 2012; 46 percent for Medicaid; 70 percent for Medicare.[15]

And so on. Libertarian conservatives cite a cascade of such statistics to make the case that the most pressing threats to America's standing in the world come from within, and that unless Americans turn their attention to dealing with them we will put our status as a superpower at fundamental risk. The next chapter aims to put some of these fears in perspective.

But whatever your view of our domestic travails, the need to fix your house does not mean you won't also suffer if your neighborhood goes to seed. In the 1920s, Britain and France still counted as serious military powers, at least notionally interested in upholding a decent world order. Today, in the absence of Pax Americana, there is no Pax Europae or Pax UN or some other kind of benign and self-generating *Pax*. There is only a Pax Sinica, a Pax Rossiya, a Pax Tehranica. This is not an appealing vision for a New World Order. Nor is it one that will leave the United States alone while it repairs its roads and reduces its deficits.

The United States does not gain a respite from power politics by trying to beat a retreat from the world. On the contrary, American retreat fosters an international environment—unpredictable and volatile—that ultimately requires a return to the very thing small-government conservatives hate most: the expensive, intrusive, security-conscious state. It's also no accident that democratic countries that do the most to slash their military budgets and global commitments also have comparatively bigger welfare states: giving up on the notion that government has martial responsibilities is an invitation to give in to the temptations of ever-greater entitlements. Conservatives will not save money by shrinking the military. They will merely ensure that the money that's supposedly saved will promptly be spent on Obamacare bailouts.

What, then, should be the tenets of a conservative foreign policy?

It cannot be the freedom agenda—not, at least, in the ambitious terms George W. Bush laid out in his second inaugural. No president should have a foreign policy the aims of which are inherently unachievable. Nor should any president design a foreign policy that is destined from the outset to be hypocritical. There will always be occasions when the United States will have to work with despots to achieve immediate national aims; with China, Washington does so on a daily basis. Foreign policy offers many opportunities to do good. But foreign policy is not—or is not merely—an exercise in ethics, at least so long as the United States intends to remain a great power.

It cannot be a retreat from the world in the name of small government. We no longer are (and never really were) a Jeffersonian republic of virtuous yeomen, guarding our patch and minding our business. And smaller government is no guarantee of greater freedom—not if small means weak and defenseless. The United States has had globe-spanning interests for as long as it has been an independent state, and it has gone far abroad to war to defend those interests for over two centuries. The purpose of government is to *secure* freedom. That doesn't happen in a world of chronic insecurity and unchecked predator states.

It cannot be the pursuit of interests understood in the narrowest "American" terms. Critics of Pax Americana often allege that its demands put the interests of our allies ahead of our own. Yet it is also a core

American interest to have a reputation for reliability and seriousness—to be known, as a famous Florentine writer once put it, as a "staunch friend and a thorough foe." Critics of Pax Americana also complain that states such as Saudi Arabia and Japan are freeloaders, taking advantage of U.S. security guarantees so they do not have to field serious military forces of their own. But America is better served by a world of supposed freeloaders than by a world of foreign policy freelancers, constantly taking unpredictable chances with their own security at the risk of everyone else's, including ours.

It cannot be a foreign policy divorced from the realities of democratic politics. The problem with the wars in Iraq and Afghanistan was not that they were inherently unwinnable. Counterinsurgency operations, with their ten-year time frames, don't fail because of unsound tactics or breakdowns in military discipline. They fail because of breakdowns in public support. Then again, conservative foreign policy cannot be indifferent to the reality that democratic publics *also* want a measure of moral purpose in their foreign policies; they will not stand for would-be Richelieus in government pursuing manifestly cynical and self-seeking aims in the name of realpolitik. U.S. foreign policy will always have a large moral component that demands scrupulous conduct and decent, defensible aims.

What a conservative foreign policy *can* do is maintain global order in a way favorable to the security and prosperity of our friends, watchful of the ambitions of our adversaries, and mindful of the need to keep the countries caught in between—states such as Kuwait, Ukraine, and Vietnam—tilting toward us. Conservative foreign policy is in the business of shaping habits of behavior, not winning hearts and minds. It announces red lines sparingly but enforces them unsparingly. It is willing to act decisively, or preventively, to punish or prevent blatant transgressions of order—not as a matter of justice but in the interests of deterrence. But it knows it cannot possibly punish or prevent every transgression. It champions its values consistently and confidently, but it doesn't conflate its values and its interests. It wants to let citizens go about their business as freely and easily as possible. But it knows that security is a *prerequisite* for civil liberty, not a threat to it. Where it can use a finger, or a hand, to tilt the political scales of society toward liberal democracy, it will do so. But it won't attempt to tilt the scales in places where the tilting demands *all* of its weight and strength and endurance. It does not waste its energy or time chasing diplomatic symbols: its ambitions do not revolve around a Nobel Peace Prize. It prefers liberal autocracy to illiberal democracy, because the former is likelier to evolve into democracy than the latter is to evolve into liberalism. It knows the value of hope, and knows also that economic growth based on enterprise and the freest possible movement of goods, services, capital, *and* labor is the best way of achieving it. And it is mindful of the claims of conscience, which is strengthened by faith.

But it has no messianic ambitions of its own. It prefers predictability to transformation. The change it seeks and promotes is evolutionary.

WINTER 2013:
ECLIPSE IN AMERICA

★ ★ ★ ★

In February 2013 the port of New York received an unusual visitor. Christened *Eclipse* by its owner, Russian billionaire Roman Abramovich, the ship is 533 feet long, displaces 13,000 tons, and was built at a cost rumored to be around $1 billion. It is said to have two swimming pools, two helicopter pads, a crew of 70, bulletproof windows, armor plating around Abramovich's master suite, a missile-defense system, and—what else?—a mini-submarine, capable of diving to 160 feet. On the day it docked at Manhattan's Pier 90, *Eclipse* was the largest private yacht in the world.[1]

Like many New Yorkers whose commute takes them along the Hudson, I spotted *Eclipse* on the Monday after its arrival and was instantly curious to know more about it. The ship, it turned out, was only the most recent addition to Abramovich's collection of super-yachts—he owns four others, not including the 377-foot *Pelorus* he gave his ex-wife Irina as part of their 2007 divorce settlement. But what was *Eclipse* doing tied up to a pier in New York in the middle of winter instead of plying warmer waters in the Caribbean, the Mediterranean, or the South Pacific? And what was it doing there week after dreary week, for what turned out to be a three-month stay?

The answer arrived in early April, when Darya "Dasha" Zhukova, Abramovich's statuesque thirty-two-year-old girlfriend, gave birth to a girl named Leah. It was the couple's second child (his seventh), and—more notably—the second to be born in the United States. "I feel rootless but also rooted everywhere," the Moscow-born Zhukova told the *Financial Times* in 2009. "I feel very comfortable in L.A., New

York, London, Moscow, Paris." Yet when it came to their un-
born child, the cosmopolitan couple were careful to ensure
that she would have the sturdiest root of all in life: American
birth, and American citizenship.[2] When they'd secured it,
Eclipse set sail from New York in mid-May. The price of the
stay has been estimated at $500,000 a week.

Around the time Zhukova was giving birth New Yorkers were entertained by another story, this one about a
Chinese woman who bought a $6.5 million condominium in
the ultraluxurious One57 skyscraper, with towering views
of Central Park.

"We're running around the city looking up things, and I
finally said, 'Well, why exactly are you buying?'" Sotheby's
real-estate broker Kevin Brown asked the purchaser, according to an account in the *New York Post*. "And she said
that it had to do with her daughter either going to Columbia
or NYU, maybe Harvard, and so she needed to be in the
center of the city.... I said, 'Oh well, how old is your
daughter?' And she said, 'Well, she's two.'"[3]

Live in New York, L.A., South Florida, or the Bay Area,
and you'll come across stories like these all the time—
wealthy foreigners, socially and politically secure in their
own countries, doing whatever they can to gain a foothold
for themselves and their children in the United States.[4]

Nor are the stories simply anecdotal. "China's richest
are increasingly investing abroad to get a foreign passport,
to make international business and travel easier but also to
give them a way out of China," reports the Associated
Press.[5] "The United States is the most popular destination
for Chinese emigrants, with rich Chinese praising its education and health-care systems." The number of EB5 "investment immigration" visas—immediate green cards to any
foreigner willing to invest $1 million and create ten jobs in

the United States—nearly quadrupled between 2009 and 2011, with 78 percent of the applications coming from China.[6]

"While the [Communist] party touts the economic success of the 'Chinese model,' many of its poster children are heading for the exits," *The Wall Street Journal*'s Jeremy Page reported in 2012. "They are in search of things money can't buy in China: Cleaner air, safer food, better education for their children. Some also express concern about government corruption and the safety of their assets."

O nce it was the huddled masses yearning to breathe free that arrived by the millions on America's shores. They did so seeking freedom and opportunity and a better life for their children, and millions of them still come. But why is Abramovich—the fifth-richest man in Russia, owner of the Chelsea football club in England, a confidant of Vladimir Putin's—so keen to have his children born in the United States? Why did Chinese president Xi Jinping enroll his daughter at Harvard?

What is it, in short, that the world's rich, savvy, and powerful know about the United States—about the value of an American passport, the security of American property, the prospects of American enterprise, the benefits of American education—that Americans are either too oblivious or self-critical to notice? Why are the very people who are supposed to be the chief beneficiaries of what Fareed Zakaria calls the "Post-American World"—those sybaritic Russian oligarchs and self-made (or corrupt) Chinese millionaires—racing to take advantage of a country that, according to the oft-heard lament, suffers from decrepit infrastructure, a decadent culture, a lousy educational system, sclerotic bureaucracy, dysfunctional politics, an entitlement mentality, and declining economic prospects? If the twenty-first century belongs to China, why do China's best and brightest want their children to be anywhere but China for its duration?

If America is in eclipse, what was *Eclipse* doing in America?

CHAPTER 6

* * *

"Decline" and Retreat

In 1993, Jagdish Bhagwati, the distinguished Columbia University economist, wrote an astute essay in *Foreign Affairs* with the title "The Diminished Giant Syndrome: How Declinism Drives Trade Policy."[1] Though his focus was economic policy, he understood that declinism was more than just predictive. It was also, indeed mainly, *prescriptive:*

> The perception, far exceeding the reality, of American decline is having subtly harmful consequences for U.S. international economic policy. The curse of declinism . . . was indulged to excess by Bill Clinton's campaign. Its political success in ending Republican presidential reign adds a lethal edge to the prospect that U.S. leadership will be sacrificed to the myopic and self-indulgent pursuit of "what's in it for us" economic policies in the world arena.

Bhagwati's immediate fear was that the United States would respond to Japan's perceived economic ascendancy (Japan was already three years into a twenty-five-year period of economic stagnation, but nobody knew it at the time) by resorting to "get tough" protectionist policies that could only damage the open international trading system that had served America and the world extraordinarily well.

The deeper insight was that, like a clinical misdiagnosis, fundamentally groundless fears can nevertheless have devastating consequences if treated with the wrong medicine. Bhagwati's fears that the United States would turn toward protectionism in the 1990s didn't materialize because Bill Clinton turned out to be a committed free trader. But the current bipartisan conviction that the United States has overextended itself abroad is leading to its own bad medicine. A misplaced belief in decline is translating into a disastrous recommendation of retreat.

THE USES OF DECLINISM

Every decade or so, observes Josef Joffe in his astute book *The Myth of America's Decline*, America experiences an attack of declinism. It's a psychological disorder that's been with the United States from the beginning.

"We shall soon see this country rushing into the extremes of confusion and violence," wrote Mercy Otis Warren, the Massachusetts playwright and historian—in 1788. Paul Samuelson, who would go on to win a Nobel Prize in economics, predicted in the 1960s that, on then-current trends, the Soviet economy would surpass America's by 1984. In the early 1970s, two American scholars predicted that Japan's economy would match America's by 1990 at the latest. "The year 2000," they wrote, "will begin 'the Japanese century.'"[2] In the late 1980s, Yale historian Paul Kennedy, adapting a line from George Bernard Shaw, warned that "Rome fell; Babylon fell; Scarsdale's turn will come."[3] Like empires of the past, he wrote in *The Rise and Fall of the Great Powers*, America's economy would be bankrupted by its military spending, while Japan and Europe zoomed ahead. In 1990, as the Soviet Union was in the process of disintegration, *New York Times* columnist Anthony Lewis wrote: "Europeans and Asians are already finding confirmation of their suspicion that the United States is in decline."[4] The 1990s were saturated by conservative fears that Americans were, in Robert Bork's phrase, "Slouching Towards Gomorrah," even as the United States began registering historic declines in the murder rate (down 40 percent in the nineties), abortion (down 20 percent), and teen pregnancy (down 19 percent).[5]

And then Americans developed their current obsession with China, the new next big thing.

All these predictions—repeated so often they became the clichés of their day—weren't just wrong. They were *spectacularly* wrong. They mistook trends for truth. They assumed that the high growth rates of emerging economies would continue at their brisk pace for decades to come. They indulged in a nostalgia in which the past always compared favorably with the present, and in which change was equated with decline.

Looking abroad, especially at closed societies, they saw what those societies chose to show—military parades, powerhouse athletes, showcase factories and airports, official statistics, wise- and benevolent-seeming leaders—and missed or downplayed their weaknesses: repression and social discontent, inefficient allocation of capital, political corruption and crony capitalism, overmilitarization. They relied on data points of little predictive significance: the size of a trade surplus or deficit, for instance, or the amount of U.S. debt held by foreigners, or test scores at the grade-school level. They made a fetish of supposed autocratic efficiencies and downplayed America's capacity for social and economic renewal—a capacity that emerges from a system characterized by openness, pluralism, political and market choices, a willingness to experiment, a tolerance for failure, and the hope of a second chance.

Given this history, why does declinism persist in the mind-set of the American intelligentsia? Partly it's the fact that declinism, to adapt Clausewitz's formulation about war, is the continuation of partisanship by other means—a handy way for those who are out of power to accuse those in it not only of bungling the job, but of putting the country on the road to ruin. Partly, too, declinism tends to be a disguised criticism of democracy itself: of its inevitable partisanship, compromise, inefficiencies, and accommodations to changes in morals and culture. Declinism is also, often, a yearning for a more autocratic (or technocratic) form of governance that, if nothing else, can get things done. Not for nothing was Mussolini once admired in the West for making the trains run on time.

And yet, as Joffe notes, there's a deeper psychology at work. Why, he wonders, should predictions of imminent doom have such a magnetic pull for so many people? "The message has worked wonders," he notes, "because doom, in biblical as well as political prophecy, always comes with a shiny flip side, which is redemption. Darkness is the prelude to dawn."[6]

Put another way, decline is a very handy diagnosis when one is looking to prescribe a radical cure. How radical? How about being "China for a day," as Tom Friedman once fantasized in a column? "One-party autocracy certainly has its drawbacks," he wrote in 2009. "But when it is led by a reasonably enlightened group of people, as China is today, it can have great advantages. That one party can just impose the politically difficult but critically important policies needed to move a society forward into the 21st century."[7] Friedman apparently wishes that the United States could have a brief spell of autocratic government so that, like the masters of Beijing, it could get some big things done without the usual hassles of democratic government and bureaucratic red tape.

DECLINE: AN ALIBI FOR RETREAT

At least Friedman was offering the idea in the service of American *renewal*. By contrast, the thrust of current declinism is offered in the name of *retreat*. The declinist-retreatist school is now becoming a broad and popular church in the foreign policy community.

One particularly bald expression of this view came in 2010 from Tom Engelhardt of The Nation Institute. "Here's a simple reality: the U.S. is an imperial power in decline," he began, before proceeding to explain that it would be no gentle British dip into the second rank of nations but a fast fall ending in the sharp thud of massive unemployment and other dire things. And yet this is just what he thinks the country needs. "So here's the good news," he continued:

It's actually going to feel better to be just another nation, one more country, even if a large and powerful one, on this over-crowded planet, rather than *the* nation. It's going to feel better to only arm ourselves to defend our actual borders, rather than constantly fighting distant wars or skirmishes and endlessly preparing for more of the same.[8]

Engelhardt's thesis isn't so different from that of Michael Mandelbaum, a sober-minded professor at the School of Advanced International Studies:

Scarcity may . . . bring with it some benefits. It will make the foreign policy of the United States less prone to serious errors. . . . The enormous post–Cold War American margin of superiority in usable power over all other countries bred a certain carelessness that led to two major errors: the ill-advised eastward expansion of the Western military alliance in Europe, the North Atlantic Treaty Organization (NATO), and the disastrously incompetent occupation of Iraq.[9]

And then there is Richard Haass, president of the Council on Foreign Relations, who is not a declinist but who made a similar case in his book *Foreign Policy Begins at Home.*

Many of the foundations of this country's power are eroding. . . . Isolationism would be folly. At the same time, the United States must become significantly more discriminating in choosing what it does in the world and how it does it. Hard choices need to be made. . . . For the last two decades, American foreign policy . . . has quite simply overreached.[10]

Such passages are worth quoting just to show how common this thinking has become. The premise that America is in decline—if not terminally, then at least for many years to come—leads to the conclusion that America needs to dramatically downsize its reach, its ambitions, and

its responsibilities. What's more remarkable, however, is how many declinists seem to believe that, on balance, decline isn't such a bad thing. If
the United States is a country that chronically abuses its power in ill-
conceived or immoral foreign ventures, then a decline in that power
should mean a reduction in the damage America can wreak.

This is the not-so-well-kept secret to declinism: Not only is it a prediction and a prescription. It is also a wish.

DECLINISM REALITY CHECK

Let's have a closer look at the decline diagnosis: Is it true?

For the word "decline" to mean anything, it can't just signify a recession, or an incompetent administration, or a nostalgic sense, in Tennyson's
words, that "We are not now that strength which in old days/Moved earth
and heaven." National decline has to be measured against your *past*, your
peers, and your *prospects*. But that raises more questions: Compared with
which point in your past? Against which peers? Regarding which prospects?

First, the past: Is the point of historical comparison 1945, when the
United States accounted for half of the world's GDP and Europe, Japan,
China, and Russia lay in various degrees of ruin? Or is it 1991, when the
Soviet Union collapsed and the United States romped to victory in the
first Gulf War? This is another high point in American history, compared
with which most subsequent years are bound to seem worse. "With the
rapid rise of other countries, the 'unipolar moment' is over," observed the
2012 "Global Trends 2030" report from the U.S. National Intelligence
Council. But using the end of the Cold War as the point of comparison
creates a false impression of decline. Is the United States really less dominant today than it was forty years ago, when the Soviet Union was nearing military parity and encroaching in the Third World while the United
States was mired in political crisis, urban decay, and economic stagflation?

Recently a more startling point of historical reference has become
popular with the declinists: the Carter years. "Starting in the late '70s," said
President Obama in his December 2013 speech on income inequality, the
"social compact began to unravel." It's a theme developed by *New Yorker*

writer George Packer in his book *The Unwinding.* Starting "in or around 1978," he writes, "the institutions that had been the foundation of middle-class democracy, from public schools and secure jobs to flourishing newspapers and functioning legislatures, were set on the course of a long decline."[11] But is the United States really worse off now than it was in the years of the Carter "malaise"? Were the corporate titans of the late seventies—General Motors, Eastman Kodak, Bethlehem Steel—as dynamic and creative as an Apple, a Berkshire Hathaway, or a Costco? Were city streets safe in 1979, when there were 9.7 homicides per 100,000 people, compared with 2012, when there were 4.7? Who were the Sheryl Sandbergs or Oprah Winfreys of the 1970s to serve as role models to women in business? Did society feel like it was coming together when the Bronx was burning?

PEER REVIEW

Quaint as it now seems, it wasn't long ago that serious people were arguing that the United States would soon be eclipsed by Europe. One earnest title from 2004: *The European Dream: How Europe's Vision of the Future Is Quietly Eclipsing the American Dream.* Another, from 2007: *The Next Superpower? The Rise of Europe and Its Challenge to the United States.* In January 2010, Paul Krugman wrote, "The real lesson from Europe is the opposite of what conservatives claim: Europe is an economic success, and that success shows that social democracy works."[12] In March of that year, Krugman's Princeton colleague Andrew Moravcsik opined that "Europe is clearly the second superpower in a bipolar world."[13]

Barely a month after Moravcsik's article appeared in an academic journal, Europe's sovereign-debt crisis exploded. "From 1995 until 2013," notes the Trading Economics Web site, "Euro Area GDP growth rate averaged 0.4 percent reaching an all-time high of 1.3 percent in June of 1997."[14] In 2013 total unemployment stood at 12.2 percent. In Spain, Europe's fourth-largest economy, the rate peaked in 2013 at 27.2 percent.[15] As for the future, a report from the European Commission forecasts that, based on demographic trends alone, long-term economic growth in the EU will average 1.5 percent all the way out till 2060. Even under Obama, the United States has registered an average growth rate of 2.1 percent in the five years since it came out of recession in mid-2009.

What about supposedly "emerging" economies such as India, Russia, Brazil, and Turkey? Their generally high growth rates in the first decade of the twenty-first century inspired Fareed Zakaria's thought-provoking contention, in *The Post-American World*, that the defining geopolitical fact of the future will be the "rise of the rest." As evidence, he noted a 2003 study by Goldman Sachs predicting that by 2040 the top five emerging markets would have a higher GDP than the (Western) countries of the G7. "Twenty years ago," he noted by way of specific example,

> Brazil and Turkey would have been considered typical "developing" countries, with sluggish growth, rampant inflation, spiraling debt, an anemic private sector, and a fragile political system. Today, both are well managed and boast historically low inflation, vigorous growth rates, falling debt levels, a thriving private sector, and increasingly stable democratic institutions.[16]

Zakaria is no declinist; he understands and celebrates America's formidable inherent strengths. But he sees America's *relative* preeminence dimming in the presence of the new giants. Yet a funny thing happened to the emergence of a Post-American World: it failed to emerge. For all the hype about Brazil, its economy never really budged above 2 percent economic growth in the last decade. In the "Ease of Doing Business" rankings published annually by the World Bank, Brazil came in at number 116, behind Belarus, Pakistan, and Ukraine.[17] Labor productivity per Brazilian worker is half that of Mexicans and less than a third that of South Koreans.[18] The homicide rate in 2011 was 21.8 per 100,000 people, which is four times the rate in neighboring Argentina.[19] In the summer of 2013, the biggest protests in more than two decades erupted throughout the country, fueled by public anger over high taxes, low growth, inflation in the price of consumer goods, collapsing infrastructure, and corruption in major public works projects.

"Brazil is the country of the future—and always will be" goes the old saw about the South American giant. It remains true today.

Then there is Turkey, that other post-American showcase. Protests in Istanbul in the summer of 2013 that began as an effort to save a small park from redevelopment exploded into open violence between peaceful demonstrators and abusive police. A few months later, an internecine battle between once-allied factions of Prime Minister Recep Tayyip Erdoğan's Islamist coalition burst into view as police charged senior members of Erdoğan's cabinet, as well as his son, with corruption. Unlike Brazil, Turkey really has enjoyed an economic boom in the last decade, with real incomes rising close to 50 percent since 2003 (though the Turkish economy seemed to be on the verge of major economic trouble as this book was going to print, with a plummeting currency, rising inflation, and the specter of a collapsing real-estate sector). But also unlike Brazil, Turkey under Erdoğan has become the world's leading jailer of journalists, a place where social media Web sites are banned and political opponents of the government are routinely charged with tales of conspiracy to rival the most lurid moments of Stalin's show trials in the 1930s.

As for India, the 2003 Goldman Sachs study forecast that New Delhi's economy would be the world's third largest by 2040. That's ambitious, even if the new government of Narendra Modi succeeds in enacting an ambitious reform agenda. In 2014, India had a GDP of $1.84 trillion, not even one third of the current number three, Japan, with nearly $6 trillion. The IMF projects 5.1 percent growth for India in 2014, compared with 1.2 percent for Japan. On the (unlikely) assumption that these respective growth rates hold, India would have a $6.5 trillion economy by 2040—while Japan's would reach nearly $8.2 trillion. In the meantime, the United States, with $16.2 trillion in GDP and a projected 2014 growth rate of 2.6 percent, will have a GDP of $30.8 trillion.[20]

But the reality is that the supposed Indian economic miracle that was being widely celebrated just a few years ago has been running out of steam—victim of the country's populist (and fractious) politics, the timid reform instincts of its leaders, and the remnants of the infamous License

Raj. As Indian entrepreneur Sandeep Kohli noted in *The Wall Street Journal*, just opening a restaurant in New Delhi is every businessman's nightmare:

> First, you get a "No Objection" certificate from the Fire Department, which is followed by a Health license from the Municipal Corporation of Delhi. Then you need three different police clearances—one from the police station in the area where the restaurant is located, the next from the police station in the area where the restaurant manager lives, and then another one from the police licensing department.
>
> Next, you apply for Tourism & Excise licenses. The Excise license is issued only after approval from the Tourism department and it's all governed by the Punjab Excise Act of 1913. Inspectors check out the premises and paste a notice at the restaurant inviting objections from the neighborhood regarding the sale of alcohol in that area. This is accompanied by the beating of drums—literally. The restaurant also can't get a liquor license if it is near a place of worship or a school. Oh, and the process can only start once the restaurant is ready to open, potentially landing you with more serious delays.[21]

"For a country that seeks to be a global power, encourage entrepreneurship and investment, there is still a huge amount of red tape," Mr. Kohli delicately notes.

What about Russia?

Considering the outsized geopolitical role Vladimir Putin has played in recent years, and the skill and relish with which the Russian strongman has played it, it's worth considering Russia's objective economic situation. Russia's $2 trillion GDP is roughly the same as Italy's, a country with half Russia's population, one fifty-fifth its landmass, and almost none of its natural resources. Moscow may be home to the world's highest concentration of billionaires (eighty-four in 2013, as compared with sixty-two in New York, forty-three in London, and another forty-three in

Hong Kong).[22] But the average monthly wage in Russia is $804, or about a third of Italy's.[23] Fifty years ago Russia was considered a scientific and technological powerhouse. Yet since the end of the Cold War, only seven Russians have won a Nobel Prize—three of whom made their professional careers in the West. In that same period, the United States has produced 149 laureates, Britain 26, Germany 15, France 13, Japan 12, and Israel 8. Even Russia's dominance of chess competitions is no longer what it used to be, and its lost dominance in the game also tells the sad story of modern Russia. "Mr. Putin can do nothing to put the genie back in the chess bottle that was the Soviet empire," notes U.S. chess champion Yasser Seirawan. "When that empire collapsed in 1989, the intelligentsia of Russia and its satellites began to disperse to Western Europe, Israel and the U.S."[24] The chess prodigies, it is safe to say, are not going to be lured back to the Motherland by its neo-Soviet ruler.

And this is Russia after a decade of sky-high energy prices. That era is coming to a close as the United States again becomes the world's leading oil and gas producer, a crown it seized from Russia in 2013.[25] Corruption, underinvestment, high taxes, and thuggish behavior toward foreign investors and neighboring states alike are now beginning to take their toll. Russia's central bank believes there was $51 billion in capital flight in the first quarter of 2014 alone. The energy sector accounts for 65 percent of Russia's exports, an apparent source of strength that is also an Achilles' heel. "Russia is undergoing a catastrophic post-Soviet societal decline due to abysmal health standards, runaway drug addiction, and an AIDS crisis that officials have termed 'epidemic,'" writes Ilan Berman in his book *Implosion: The End of Russia and What It Means for America.*[26] A combination of a sub-replacement-level birth rate, short lifespans, and emigration means the population of Russia could fall to 52 million by 2080. One report noted that Russia would close more than seven hundred schools for lack of students; Russia's unemployment figures are low not because jobs are abundant but because labor is scarce.[27]

Former West German chancellor Helmut Schmidt once said about the Soviet Union that it was "Upper Volta with nuclear weapons." Not a lot has changed except the names of both countries.

THE CHINA CRUSH

Which brings us to the People's Republic.

For there to be declinism, there must also be, for lack of a better term, *risism*—the belief that somebody else is eating our lunch, cleaning our clock (and maybe even mixing our metaphors). For the present that country is China. News that students in Shanghai far outperform their peers in the United States on standardized international tests sounds loud alarms on American op-ed pages. The datum that China holds $1.28 trillion in U.S. debt is a source of persistent awe and anxiety—never mind that it's only a fraction of the nearly $6 trillion of total U.S. government debt held by foreigners. Meanwhile, experts debate when precisely China will overtake the United States as the world's leading economy: Will it be 2030, as predicted by the National Intelligence Council? Will it be 2020, as forecast by the chief economist at the Standard Chartered Bank? Will it be as early as 2016, as noted by both the International Monetary Fund and the Organization for Economic Cooperation and Development?

For an example of the slack-jawed awe that China inspires among today's risists, it's hard to beat *That Used to Be Us*, cowritten in 2011 by Thomas Friedman and Michael Mandelbaum. "This is a book about America that begins in China," they write. The book opens with Friedman describing his experience of boarding a high-speed train at Beijing's South Railway Station, "an ultramodern flying saucer of a building with glass walls and an oval roof covered with 2,246 solar panels." From there Friedman rides aboard a "world-class high-speed train" that reaches his destination in Tianjin, seventy-two miles away, in just twenty-nine minutes. He then contrasts that experience with his local metro line in Bethesda, Maryland, where repairs have been under way for months without getting anywhere.

The conclusion to be drawn from this comparison: "China is getting the most out of its authoritarianism. By contrast, we Americans are getting only 50 percent of the potential benefits from our first-rate democratic system."[28] It's vintage Friedman: mistaking anecdote for data, making an apples-to-oranges comparison, and reaching a morally dubious conclusion.

It's also factually wrong.

In February 2011, a few months after Friedman's brief ride, the Chinese Communist Party fired Liu Zhijun, the head of the railway ministry and the mastermind of China's high-speed rail ambitions. The official reason, reported *The New York Times*, was "severe violations of discipline," Communist Party code for personal corruption. But the problems went much deeper. Thousands of miles of high-speed track had been laid in record time at the price of shoddy construction. "A person with ties to the ministry," the *Times* reported that year, "said that the concrete bases for the system's tracks were so cheaply made, with inadequate use of chemical hardening agents, that trains would be unable to maintain their current speeds of about 217 miles per hour for more than a few years."[29] In July 2011 one bullet train collided with another, resulting in forty deaths and some two hundred injuries. Meanwhile, companies like Japan's Kawasaki are complaining bitterly that Beijing invited them into the Chinese market simply so they could steal their train designs. "Claiming most of the recently developed bullet trains as China's own may be good for national pride," says one Kawasaki executive, "but it's nothing but deceitful propaganda."[30]

The bullet train story is just one of many examples of the Chinese infrastructure mirage. China is not yet capable of producing a commercially viable single-aisle jetliner, despite spending $7 billion in an effort to do so. "Planes currently in development are not likely to be competitive when finally realized," noted a 2014 report from the Rand Corporation.[31] Or take this 2012 story from *Bloomberg News*: "Since 2007 China has experienced at least 18 bridge collapses. . . . These are not mere footbridges: They are major, expensive spans connecting key corridors."[32]

Then there is the tragedy of the "tofu-dregs," the term former Chinese prime minister Zhu Rongji gave to shoddily constructed government buildings. In May 2008 a devastating earthquake hit the province of Sichuan, instantly destroying hundreds of schoolhouses and killing at least five thousand students—the result of schools built on the cheap. It's a problem that affects China's skyscrapers, too: Chinese builders frequently use untreated sea sand (instead of river sand) in their concrete. The cheap concrete saves money, but the chlorine and salt in the sand corrode the steel that supports the building.[33]

The most glaring examples of tofu-dregs, however, are the economic statistics on which China makes its claims to being the world's new superpower. Since the time of Mao, village collectives and state-run companies have reported exaggerated production figures to local municipalities, which in turn report exaggerated productivity to their counties, right up the chain of economic dishonesty. The result is that China annually reports an estimated $1 trillion in make-believe growth. Li Keqiang, an economist and China's current premier, privately described his country's economic statistics as "man-made": China watchers now talk about the "Keqiang index"—measures of electricity consumption, railway cargo volume, and loan disbursements that the premier says he relies on—to generate a more reliable estimate of economic growth. To the extent that China has been able to bridge the gap between the Keqiang index and actual growth, it has been through large stimulus injections that exact their own long-term economic damages in capital misallocation and debt. "China's leaders may believe they need high growth to ensure that the recent credit binge does not lead to a wave of bankruptcies," notes Morgan Stanley's Ruchir Sharma. "But a new wave of low-quality loans only puts millions more borrowers at risk."[34]

These examples are also revealing for what they tell us about China's current rulers. To them, as to their Maoist forebears, economic development remains an act of *propaganda*. Hence the massive investments in showcase projects like high-speed trains with scant regard for how they might look, or work, a few years hence. Not only that, but those investments also illustrate the risks of government-led investment schemes' leading to the kind of crony capitalism that dominates the Chinese economy today. *Bloomberg News* has estimated that the aggregate net worth of the seventy richest delegates to China's National People's Congress was $89.8 billion in 2011, up $11.5 billion from the year before, and dwarfing the $7.5 billion aggregate net worth of "all 660 top officials in the three branches of the U.S. government."[35]

When Friedman and Mandelbaum write that China is getting the most out of its authoritarianism, they have it exactly backward: *it's the authoritarians who are getting the most out of China.* China's wealthiest 1 percent own 70 percent of the nation's private wealth. Five of the ten richest people in the country, and a third of the richest fifty, hold official government positions.

Yet China's problems go deeper than shoddy construction, endemic corruption, and misspent capital. A developing economy requires ever-increasing quantities of information, delivered at an ever-faster rate: more information makes possible the efficient identification of opportunities, risks, and prices. But a regime that imposes controls on the free flow of information—whether it concerns the state of a company's balance sheets or the country's GDP—will inevitably suffer mounting inefficiencies and potentially catastrophic failure whenever the gap between available and necessary information becomes too wide.

Then, too, the more sophisticated an economy, the more important it becomes to develop modern managerial techniques, with respect to both transparency with shareholders and investors, and independence from political control. But the essence of the Chinese "socialist market economy" is the domination of key industries—either directly or by proxy—by political hacks.

The most significant defect is this: A modern economy needs to create space for gadflies—for the misfit intellects and born contrarians who may often be nothing more than social nuisances but are also often the innovators and change agents. Political and economic systems that nurture gadflies—by providing meaningful legal guarantees of freedom of speech, conscience, and association; and by nurturing a culture that admires iconoclasm, rewards entrepreneurship, and offers second chances to those who fail on the first try—will be the systems that maintain an edge on their competitors.

Does modern China encourage gadflies? Or does it squash them?

STILL THE ONE

So far we've discussed American decline in terms of our past and our peers. What about our prospects?

Consider this bit of cheer from conservative commentator Mark Steyn: "A lot of the debate about America's date with destiny has an airy-fairy beyond the blue-horizon mid-century quality, all to do with long-term trends and other remote indicators," he writes in his book *After America*.

In fact, we'll be lucky to make it through the short-term in suffi-cient shape to get finished off by the long-term. According to CBO projections, by 2055 interest payments on the debt will ex-ceed federal revenues. But I don't think we'll need to worry about a "Government of the United States" at that stage. By 1788, Louis XVI's government in France was spending a mere 60 percent of revenues on debt service, and we know how that worked out for the House of Bourbon shortly thereafter.[36]

The ticking debt clock performs roughly the same function for many conservatives as the old Doomsday Clock of the *Bulletin of the Atomic Scientists*—always set just a few portentous minutes to midnight—once performed for liberals. This is somewhat odd, if not amusing, given that the debt was once an obsession of the left. Recall the liberal harrumphing that greeted Dick Cheney's reported observation that "Reagan proved that deficits don't matter."[37]

Debts and deficits do matter. But they're not the only things that matter. And they matter to different countries in different ways at differ-ent times. The United States emerged from the Second World War with a debt-to-GDP ratio of more than 100 percent. Yet winning the war was an excellent investment of national resources. The ratio also went up during the Reagan years, partly on account of sharply higher military spending. But persuading Mikhail Gorbachev that the Soviet Union was not about to beat the United States in an arms race was another good national in-vestment that helped end the Cold War. By contrast, the ratio was low (under 30 percent) during the stagflation years of the 1970s. And as the Congressional Research Service has noted in connection with Europe's economic crises, "Iceland, Ireland, and Spain all had extremely low government debt levels (much lower than the United States) and were running budget surpluses before the crisis."[38]

More important for predicting long-term economic health are GDP growth, ease of doing business, a stable and predictable legal and regulatory environment, attractiveness to foreign investment and immigration, a positive demographic outlook, an innovative culture, and a politics that is capable of adopting pro-growth measures, including entitlement reform. All this has taken a drubbing on Obama's watch, not least through his attempt to reengineer 18 percent of the U.S. economy with the Rube Goldberg device known as the Affordable Care Act.

But then, no administration is forever. And the main surprise of the U.S. economy since the financial crisis of 2008 has not been its vulnerability to financial and political shocks. It has been its resilience in the face of them. When the Standard & Poor's ratings agency downgraded America's long-held AAA bond rating in August 2011, it was treated in some quarters as the moment when the *Titanic* hit the iceberg. Yet a year later yields on ten-year Treasury bonds were down by a full percentage point, the price of gold was falling, and the Dow was up 14 percent. Since then, discretionary spending has fallen 10 percent from its 2011 peak, while the government's share of GDP has fallen from its 2009 postwar high of 25.2 percent to a more ordinary 21.5 percent.[39] In February 2014 data from the U.S. Treasury showed the deficit had fallen to 3 percent of GDP from 10 percent in 2010. "The rapidity of the deficit decline," noted economist Michael Darda, "is something not seen since the Korean War mobilization."[40]

There may be a lot of ruin in a nation, as Adam Smith said, and ruin is often apparent to the naked eye. To understand a nation's longer-term prospects, the important thing is to take stock of its (often hidden) capacity for renewal.

Take demography, where America continues to have a decisive population edge over its supposed rivals. By 2050, 27 percent of America will be over the age of sixty, up from 19 percent in 2012, according to UN data. That may be something to worry about, but compare that with the 34 percent of Chinese who will be sixty or older by 2050, up from just 13 percent now. Europe too will consist of 34 percent seniors by 2050, while in Japan it will be a staggering 41 percent, putting it on a path toward being the world's first democratic gerontocracy.[41] Then, too, the United States is expected to enjoy population growth of more than 28 percent, hitting the 400 million mark by mid-century. Yet Europe and Japan will see population declines of 1.5 percent and 14.9 percent, respectively. Put simply, the United States will remain a nation of comparative youth, growth, and vigor while the competition shrivels up.[42]

Now take education. A standard declinist cliché is that America's mediocre K–12 schools are failing to produce students with the necessary skills to compete in the twenty-first century. The state of public schools in America is indeed lamentable, and a tragedy for underserved minority students. But the United States at least partly compensates for the deficiencies of its K–12 education on the other end. Some 31 percent of Americans have had at least some amount of college education (not including vocational schools or community colleges), more than any other country in the OECD. By contrast, just 18 percent of French and 15 percent of Germans have spent time in college.[43] American universities took fifteen of the top twenty spots, and forty-four of the top one hundred, in global rankings compiled by the *Times Higher Education* survey.[44] The United States, notes Josef Joffe, produces 17 percent of the world's science and engineering Ph.D.s, more than any other country. And seven of ten foreign-born Ph.D.s wind up staying in the United States.[45] Meanwhile, no living person from Singapore, Finland, or South Korea (those K–12 powerhouses) has ever won a science Nobel.

Next consider competitiveness and innovation. A 2013 study by Ernst and Young ranks the United States as the global leader in what it calls "entrepreneurship culture."[46] There is about ten times as much venture capital per capita in the United States as there is in Europe.[47] In 2006, the World Bank placed America third, right after Singapore and Hong Kong, on its "Ease of Doing Business" report. In 2014 it had fallen to fourth place. Otherwise it remains far ahead of major economies like Australia (number 11), Canada (19), Germany (21), and Japan (27), to say nothing of China (96) and India (134). As of December 2013 nine of the world's ten (and forty-six of the top one hundred) largest publicly traded companies by market capitalization were American.[48]

And then there is the matter of culture. Why were all of the Big New Things of the past decade—from social media to iPhones and tablets to the shale oil and fracking revolution—Born in the U.S.A.? Why didn't they happen in Europe or China? "Entrepreneurship, which has been the engine of growth in the United States, has not been cultivated in an effective or systematic way in Europe," lamented a 2013 "Startup Manifesto" from young European entrepreneurs. "To create more businesses and more startups requires more than a change in policy," the manifesto continued. "It requires a change in mentality."[49]

It's not easy to quantify mentality. No doubt there are all kinds of metrics. Maybe there's an explanation for why Americans seem congenitally disposed to ask "Why not?" rather than "Why?" Whatever the case, consider this: the 1970s, another era in which there was a pervasive belief that America was in decline, were also the years in which Steve Jobs and Steve Wozniak founded Apple, Bill Gates and Paul Allen founded Microsoft, Larry Ellison started Oracle, and Bernie Marcus cofounded The Home Depot. As of December 31, 2013, the combined total market value of these four companies alone came to $1.16 trillion. The GDP of South Korea, the world's fifteenth-largest economy, is about $1.13 trillion.

To claim the United States is in decline today ignores this history. Right now, in a dorm room or a garage or an office cubicle, the next Marcus or Gates or Ellison is dreaming up the next Home Depot or Microsoft or Oracle. It's happening; you just can't see it. Declinists will always be able to point to *visible* evidence of everything that's going wrong with the United States as evidence that our best days are behind us. But America's future lies, as it always has, in things unseen and persons unknown.

JULY 1911:
A DISTANT ECHO

★　★　★　★

From the distance of the warship anchored in the bay the man on the beach made no immediate impression. He was waving his arms, shouting indistinctly, running back and forth under the unbearably hot African sun—probably a local merchant, trying to entice the sailors to his fishing village to peddle his wares. The orders from Berlin had been strict: no men were to be landed on this desolate stretch of the Atlantic shore. Only in the late afternoon, as the man stood motionless with his hands on his hips, did it seem to an officer aboard the SMS *Panther* that a native would never carry himself like that. Could he be European? A surfboat was sent ashore to find out.[1]

Thus did a man known to history as Herr Wilburg, a geologist with a Hamburg-based firm with interests in North Africa, come to enjoy the protection of Kaiser Wilhelm II's Imperial Navy in the broad bay of Agadir in southern Morocco on July 5, 1911.

Hurrah! A deed!" roared one article in the jingoistic German press. "Action at last, a liberating deed.... Again it is seen that the foreign policy of a great nation, a powerful state, cannot exhaust itself in patient inaction." The entire country seemed to be in a state of exaltation, convinced of its moral case and proud of its geopolitical skill. They called it the *Panthersprung*, the Panther's Leap, and delighted in all it seemed to connote: power, sleekness, inscrutability. "We are seizing this region once and for all," Arthur Zimmermann, later to become Germany's foreign secretary, told the Pan-German League. "An outlet for our population is necessary."

Yet what, exactly, had Germany accomplished? The *Panther*'s official mission was to protect "endangered Germans" in southern Morocco against allegedly restive natives. But there were no Germans in southern Morocco, literally none—except for Herr Wilburg, who had arrived, after a punishing overland journey, three days after the ship reached the bay. The *Panther* herself wasn't much of a warship: lightly armed, lightly armored; the kind of vessel, as one historian put it, used mainly for "impressing natives or bombarding mud villages."[2] Nor was southern Morocco the colonial prize Herr Zimmermann imagined it to be. There were rumors of rich iron-ore deposits, but there had never been a proper geological survey. Thousands of Germans would not soon be migrating to an unforgiving land to scratch out a subsistence living far from the Fatherland.

It didn't matter. Germany's bullying foreign secretary, Alfred von Kiderlen-Wächter, was sure he had pulled off a diplomatic coup. For years, Berlin had felt cheated in the race for overseas colonies. And it had felt especially cheated by France over the question of Morocco. In 1904, France and Britain had put aside their historic enmity with the Entente Cordiale, in which London had ceded Morocco to a French sphere of influence in exchange for Paris's ceding Egypt to a British one. The cozy arrangement had never sat well with Berlin. Sending a ship to Agadir, von Kiderlen-Wächter had reasoned, would put Paris on notice that Berlin would have to be placated.

That was Germany's calculation. But a Panther's Leap looks better from the perspective of the predator than it does from that of the prey. What does the beast want? On whom, or what, will it pounce next? In his history of the First World War, Winston Churchill wrote that with the *Panther*'s arrival in Agadir "all the alarm bells throughout Europe began immediately to quiver." France demanded to know whether Berlin wanted a piece of Morocco or only meant to bargain for other territories in Africa. The British wondered whether Agadir could serve as a German naval base on the North Atlantic, another ratcheting up of a naval arms race that threatened Britannia's maritime supremacy.

Yet Germany would not declare her intentions. British and French diplomats made urgent inquiries; they were met with Sphinx-like replies. For von Kiderlen-Wächter, this was a diplomatic gambit to improve his negotiating position. For David Lloyd George, Britain's chancellor of the exchequer and hitherto his country's foremost pacifist, it smacked of unbearable Teutonic arrogance. On July 22 he delivered his historic warning to Germany:

> If a situation were to be forced upon us in which peace could only be preserved by the surrender of the great and beneficent position Britain has won by centuries of heroism and achievement, by allowing Britain to be treated where her interests were vitally affected as if she were of no account in the Cabinet of nations, then I say emphatically that peace at that price would be a humiliation intolerable for a great country like ours to endure.

Only weeks before, in May, Kaiser Wilhelm had paid a visit to England to see King George V. "We will never make war over Morocco," the Anglophile kaiser—oldest grand-child to Queen Victoria—had assured his first cousin. Yet now the Royal Navy was on high alert. Churchill, as home secretary, ordered the Metropolitan Police to safeguard the navy's stockpiles of gunpowder as a precaution against would-be German saboteurs.

Were Europe's statesmen serious? Did they mean to go

to war over a place that, only weeks before, hardly anyone had even heard of? Could a dispute so contrived, in a place so peripheral, over stakes so trivial, plunge a civilized and prosperous Continent into an orgy of bloodletting? It seemed absurd, like a man dying on account of an infected mosquito bite. But such things have been known to happen.

In 1911, Europe would pull itself back from the brink. Britain sounded a conciliatory note. France gained Morocco as a protectorate in exchange for granting Germany territorial concessions in equatorial Africa. Germany took the deal after concluding that Morocco wasn't worth a war. By the fall, La Belle Époque resumed with all its former appearances of civilized amity. Marie Curie won the Nobel Prize (her second) in chemistry, the Chevrolet car company was founded, cable entertainment (via telephone) was introduced in the United States, and Roald Amundsen became the first man to reach the South Pole. It was a world of progress, prosperity, and discovery.

What would come next? Nobody knew.[3] "Were we after all to achieve world security and universal peace by a marvelous system of combinations in equipoise and of armaments in equation, of checks and counter-checks on violent action ever more complex and more delicate?" wondered Churchill.

> *Would Europe thus marshaled, thus grouped, thus related, unite into one universal glorious organism capable of receiving and enjoying in undreamed-of abundance the bounty which nature and science stood hand in hand to give? The old world in its sunset was fair to see.*
>
> *But there was a strange temper in the air. Unsatisfied by material prosperity the nations turned*

restlessly towards strife internal and external. National passions, unduly exalted in the decline of religion, burned beneath the surface of nearly every land with fierce if shrouded fires. Almost one might think the world wished to suffer.[4]

CHAPTER 7

* * *

The Coming Global Disorder
(Theory and History)

Since Barack Obama took office in 2009, the political order of the Arab world has nearly unraveled. The economic order of the European world is under strain. The countries of the Pacific Rim are threatened by a China that is by turns assertive, reckless, and insecure. Despite its fundamental weaknesses, Russia seeks to dominate its "near-abroad" through a combination of local proxies, dirty tricks, and outright conquest. Another international order—the nuclear one—is being fundamentally challenged by the acquisition of nuclear capabilities by two uniquely dangerous states, Iran and North Korea, which in turn invites their nearest neighbors to consider their own nuclear options. Al Qaeda may be diminished in some corners of the Middle East, but it is metastasizing in others. The United States is more reluctant than it has been for decades to intervene abroad, judging that there is better security in inaction than action. Traditional allies of the United States, uncertain of its purposes, are beginning to explore their options in what they suspect is becoming a post–Pax Americana world, encouraging freelancing instincts which Washington has a diminishing ability to restrain.

Is all of this merely the ordinary turbulence of international life—events that seem epochal and portentous when they happen but fade in significance over time? Or are we witnessing the crumbling of global order as most of us have known it?

Don't Worry, Be Happy?

Implicit in the argument made for American retreat is that the international environment today is basically unthreatening, certainly when compared with previous decades. "The world is not in great disorder," writes Fareed Zakaria. "It is mostly at peace with one zone of instability, the greater Middle East, an area that has been unstable for four decades at least."[1]

In this analysis, the United States has no rival like the Soviet Union or the Axis Powers of World War II, threatening us with conquest or annihilation. The worst of the shocks of the financial crisis in the United States and the euro crisis are now behind us; the risk that loose monetary policy would cause an inflationary spiral didn't materialize; the world economy, though weaker than it was in the 1990s, can hardly be described as a 1930s-style catastrophe.

Al Qaeda did its worst to us on 9/11 and is unlikely to manage the same feat twice; it will now be reduced to small-scale atrocities that require a focused response, not an open-ended one. The disorders of the Middle East are beyond the reach of our attempted cures. They will matter less to us in the years ahead as North America fracks its way toward energy superabundance. The Chinese bark is worse than its bite; Chinese leaders will not seriously risk their country's "peaceful rise" for the sake of some spits of rock and reef in the South and East China Seas. North Korea is a sinister regime and a regional threat, but it is no serious threat to the United States. Iran's atomic ambitions are less frightening the closer one looks at them: even if the Islamic Republic does acquire nuclear weapons, it is in no position to use them against anyone, particularly Israel; going nuclear, moreover, invites the Saudis to nuclearize and thus create an automatic balance of power.

In short, say the votaries of retrenchment and retreat, the idea that we live in an especially dangerous world just isn't justified by the facts. Instead, the main problems we face are right here at home. There is persistent income inequality and diminishing economic mobility that's killing the American dream. There is a National Security Agency that is just a few keystrokes away from becoming a Stasi for the digital age. There's an immigration system that liberals and conservatives agree, for fundamentally different reasons, is utterly broken. Advocates of the Retreat Doctrine do not counsel that America turn itself into a Hermit Kingdom. But they do believe that the world will usually sort itself out without the need for Washington to take action, or even a view, on every distant crisis and quarrel. In the meantime, we continue to live in a world of material progress and technological marvels, of trade and human mobility, of digital interconnectedness and global tourism and next-day delivery via Amazon Prime.

What, then, would preserve global order in the absence of Pax Americana? Broadly speaking there are three alternatives: a liberal peace, the balance of power, or collective security.

The concept of liberal peace dates back at least to the eighteenth century, when Montesquieu argued that "peace is the natural effect of trade," and Kant insisted that "the *spirit of trade* cannot coexist with war, and sooner or later that spirit dominates every people."[2] In the early twentieth century the British pacifist Norman Angell argued that the interconnectedness of the global economy had rendered military power passé—"that it is impossible for one nation to seize by force the wealth or trade of another."[3] In 1910, Nicholas Murray Butler, president of Columbia University and a future winner of the Nobel Peace Prize, dismissed the possibility of a brutal European war as totally absurd:

To suppose that men and women into whose intellectual and moral instruction and upbuilding have gone the glories of the world's philosophy and art and poetry and religion, into whose lives have been poured for two thousand years the precepts and inspiration of the Christian religion . . . are to fly at each other's throats to burn, to ravage, to kill . . . is to suppose the universe to be stood upon its apex.[4]

Nine decades later Tom Friedman offered his own recipe for permanent peace, the "Golden Arches Theory of Conflict Prevention." It postulated that "no two countries that both have McDonald's have ever fought a war against each other."[5] The theory fell apart when NATO landed bombs on Serbia, a country with several McDonald's restaurants, during the 1999 Kosovo war.

At a more sophisticated level of analysis there is a view that, as countries reach a certain level of economic development, the likelihood that they become and remain democratic grows. Political scientist Adam Przeworski even ventured some highly precise numbers for the relationship between per capita income and democratic durability. Wherever per capita income fell below $1,000, he predicted that a democracy could expect to last about twelve years. At $3,000 the lifespan rose to twenty-seven years. As income rose to $6,055, democracy could expect sixty years. "And what happens above $6,055 we already know," he wrote. "Democracy lasts forever."[6]

This is an important consideration if true, since no two mature democracies have ever gone to war with each other. And it fits nicely with the current belief that the world is, indeed, gradually becoming a better place. "By 2035," predict Bill and Melinda Gates, "there will be almost no poor countries left in the world"; more than 70 percent of the world's countries, they say, will have per capita incomes higher than China's in 2013.[7] Since China's per capita GDP is already north of $6,100, that should mean a world of permanent democracy, and perpetual peace, coming our way in just a couple of decades.

The second alternative to Pax Americana is a return to a more old-fashioned balance of power. Many have argued that such a return is inevitable as well as desirable—inevitable, because the United States cannot seriously hope to remain the preponderant global military and economic power indefinitely; desirable, because the costs of being the sole super-power are too exorbitant, the temptation to misuse the power too great, and the resentments of a world unwilling to permanently submit to Pax Americana too powerful.

Expectations of a return to a multipolar world aren't new. "When we see the world in which we are about to move, the United States no longer is in the position of complete pre-eminence or predominance [and] that is not a bad thing," Richard Nixon told a conference of executives in Kansas City in 1971. "As a matter of fact, it can be a constructive thing. . . . We now have a situation where four potential economic powers have the ca-pacity [to] challenge [the U.S.] on every front." The columnist Walter Lippmann, sounding much like the declinists of our own day, approved of Nixon's attitude: "His role has been that of a man who had to liquidate, defuse, deflate the exaggerations of the romantic period of American imperialism and American inflation. Inflation of promises, inflation of hopes, the Great Society, American supremacy—all that had to be de-flated because it was all beyond our power."[8] (The more things change, the more columnists say the same.)

In fact, the inflation-adjusted U.S. share of global GDP, 26 percent in 2013, isn't too far below the 27.7 percent it was when Nixon spoke in Kansas City. China's share has risen dramatically, from less than 1 per-cent to 8.7 percent, although that depends on crediting their statistics. As for the rest of the world, Japan's share of GDP has fallen slightly, from 9.9 percent to 8.6 percent; and the old EU-15 has fallen dramatically, from 35 percent to 24 percent. The old Soviet Union no longer exists, and modern Russia accounts for just 2.4 percent of the world economy.[9] So the multipolar moment isn't here yet in economic terms. Much less so in military terms: even as defense cuts were kicking in, the United States accounted for 42.6 percent of global military spending—as compared with 5.2 percent for China, 3.0 percent for Britain, and 2.2 percent for India.[10]

Such disparities raise the question of how a balance-of-power geopol-itics can be practiced in the absence of a genuine balance of power. One possible answer is to seek ways to reduce America's footprint while encouraging other states (or groups of states) to increase theirs. That seems to have been part of the Obama administration's calculus in encouraging NATO's European partners to take the lead in the 2011 Libya campaign, along with the deference it has shown to the Arab League in attempting to orchestrate a settlement in Syria. The administration has also welcomed Russian mediation with Bashar al-Assad over the Syrian dictator's chemical weapons stockpile, and conducted its nuclear diplomacy with Iran in concert with the five permanent members of the Security Council and Germany. It has made clear that it has little interest in acting unilaterally unless the contemplated action has broad international support—a kind of quasi-democratic balancing that throws the weight of world public opinion on the scale as a potential counterweight to the use of American power. Balance of power thus provides an overarching frame in which to explain and justify American retreat.

The third alternative to Pax Americana is collective security. Why should America shoulder the main burden of policing the world, so the argument goes, when there's a seventy-year-old institution known as the United Nations the purpose of which is to do exactly that? Advocates of the UN—there are many—say its successes have largely gone unheralded and its failures have been grossly exaggerated. What the organization most needs, they add, is greater responsibility and greater authority, which in turn require more investment in its capabilities, more participation in its decision-making processes, and more deference to its decisions, above all from the United States. In this reading, the many failures of the UN are not seen as the fault of the institution itself, but of the unwillingness of individual states to put their particular interests aside for the sake of a greater good.

Faith in the necessity, if not yet the competence, of the UN has also grown as more people have become convinced that the chief threats facing mankind are uniquely transnational. Few people take seriously the idea that North Korea might invade the south, or that the United States and Russia could find themselves embroiled in a war over Ukraine. But there is no shortage of anxiety about the risks of climate change or viral pandemics or nuclear proliferation or the effects of state failure on regional stability. "We face a new generation of threats, unlike any in history, which spill across borders and have global reach," insists UN secretary-general Ban Ki-moon. "No single country or group, however powerful, can deal with them alone."[11] More than a few Americans would be inclined to agree with that view.

BEEN THERE, DONE THAT

Each of these alternatives to the Pax Americana—the libertarian, balance-of-power, or idealist approach—offers serious ideas for serious consideration. But not one of them is new, and each has been discredited before.

Begin with the notion of liberal peace. Few decades in history were filled with greater reason for unlimited hope in human possibility than the decades preceding 1914. Per capita GDP in the quarter century before World War I (1888–1913) rose by an estimated 28 percent in Britain, 54 percent in Italy and France, 55 percent in Germany, and 61 percent in the United States.[12] Trade and tourism flourished; Germany and Britain were major trading partners. A vibrant peace movement produced the Hague Conventions of 1899 and 1907, the first of which declared illegal "the launching of projectiles and explosives from balloons, or by other new methods of a similar nature." In many ways, life just before the summer of 1914 was remarkably similar to the lives we lead now.

"What an extraordinary episode in the economic progress of man that age was which came to an end in August 1914!" John Maynard Keynes would recall just after the war:

> The inhabitant of London could order by telephone, sipping his morning tea in bed, the various products of the whole earth, in such quantity as he might see fit, and reasonably expect their early delivery upon his doorstep; he could at the same moment and by the same means adventure his wealth in the natural resources and new enterprises of any quarter of the world, and share, without exertion or even trouble, in their prospective fruits

and advantages; or he could decide to couple the security of his fortunes with the good faith of the townspeople of any substantial municipality in any continent that fancy or information might recommend. He could secure forthwith, if he wished it, cheap and comfortable means of transit to any country or climate without passport or other formality, could despatch his servant to the neighboring office of a bank for such supply of the precious metals as might seem convenient, and could then proceed abroad to foreign quarters, without knowledge of their religion, language, or customs, bearing coined wealth upon his person, and would consider himself greatly aggrieved and much surprised at the least interference. But, most important of all, he regarded this state of affairs as normal, certain, and permanent, except in the direction of further improvement, and any deviation from it as aberrant, scandalous, and avoidable. The projects and politics of militarism and imperialism, of racial and cultural rivalries, of monopolies, restrictions, and exclusion, which were to play the serpent to this paradise, were little more than the amusements of his daily newspaper, and appeared to exercise almost no influence at all on the ordinary course of social and economic life, the internationalization of which was nearly complete in practice.[13]

But the happy picture did nothing to prevent the well-heeled and urbane sons of London, Paris, Moscow, Vienna, and Berlin from marching eagerly to war in the high summer of 1914. The precise causes of the Great War are still debated by historians a century after its beginning. But what can't be disputed is that a prior century of economic interdependence, steadily increasing political freedoms and social mobility, and material and scientific progress did nothing to prevent a four-year European Armageddon. Perhaps a century of progress had exactly the opposite of a softening influence: the advent of war, wrote the historian Jacques Barzun, "spelled liberation from the humdrum of existence, with its petty cunning for selfish ends." When Sigmund Freud learned that war had been declared, he pledged to give "all my libido . . . to Austria-Hungary."

Nor was it only the concept of liberal peace that was debunked by the advent of the Great War. The balance of power defined European politics before World War I for the plain reason that a balance of power really did exist between Britain, France, Germany, Austria-Hungary, and Russia. None alone was strong enough to subdue any given combination of the others. And since ideology still played a secondary role in international politics (and none at all in serious diplomacy), there was little to prevent alliances from shifting rapidly to ensure that the balance of power be maintained as circumstances required. For all their intrigues and rivalries, the statesmen of Europe knew they belonged to a common civilization that operated according to commonly accepted notions of etiquette, equity, and fair play. That balance was in turn sustained by assiduous diplomacy and personal contact that gave precise expression to the ways, circumstances, and period in which a given balance would be maintained.

And yet the balance fell apart. Partly it was due to the ever-increasing complexity of the diplomatic and military dance. "In the end," notes Henry Kissinger, "the requirements of *Realpolitik* became too intricate to sustain."[14] But mainly it was because "balance" is an abstract concept that doesn't account for the changing condition of nations. In 1871, when Germany became a unified state, it had a population of just under 40 million, roughly at parity with France's 37 million. By 1914 the number of Germans had jumped to 66 million while France's population had barely budged. The demographic changes were reflected in economic power: In 1871, German and French GDP were evenly matched, at $71.6 billion (in 1990 dollars). By 1913 (the last full year of peace), German GDP stood at $237 billion, far surpassing France's $144 billion.[15] Such fundamental imbalances could not forever be contained by a balance-of-power system that did not reflect the shifting distribution of actual power. Nor could the balance of power satisfy a Germany that came to believe, not without justification, that the system was rigged to its disadvantage. A *balance* of power may seem plausible in theory. But the nature of *power* is that it seeks preeminence, not balance.

Finally there is the promise of collective security and its first cousin, arms control. Collective security rests on four remarkable propositions:

First, that law and morality can substitute for interest and opportunity when it comes to the behavior of nations. Second, that a nation will willingly go to war in defense of another to maintain an abstract principle—namely, the impermissibility of military aggression—even when its own security or interests are not immediately at stake. Third, that "public opinion" can be enlisted to dissuade and shame aggressors into civilized behavior. And, finally, that an organization that includes all nations, friends or foes, can nonetheless serve as an effective instrument for mediating disputes and preventing war.

As for arms control, it rests on the similarly hopeful belief that countries can find greater security with weaker defenses. "If all Nations will agree wholly to eliminate from possession and use the weapons which make possible a successful attack," Franklin Roosevelt cabled the sixty-nation Geneva Disarmament Conference in May 1933, "defenses automatically will become impregnable, and the frontiers and independence of every Nation will become secure."

For all of the inherent and obvious conceptual flaws in collective security, the world has been trying to make it work for close to a century—proving, if nothing else, that in the contest between idealism (however disappointed) and experience (however hard-won), idealism usually wins out. When asked what would be done if the League of Nations did not work, Woodrow Wilson replied: "If it won't work, it must be made to work."[16] The failure of the League is sometimes ascribed to the fact that the United States refused membership in it in 1920. But U.S. membership would have done nothing to change the core flaws of the collective security concept. Nor would it have made a political difference, given the broader American political refusal to involve itself in foreign quarrels. After Italy's 1935 invasion of Ethiopia, the United States imposed an arms embargo on *both* sides of the conflict.

The United States made another attempt to place collective security at the core of its strategic vision with the formation of the United Nations in 1945. Hope quickly ran afoul of reality—in this case, the reality that the Soviet Union would happily use the UN as an instrument of its propaganda but would not submit to it as a check on its power. If peace was going to be maintained for the long run after the Second World War, it would require something more than the consensus of the decent, the restraint of the wicked, the weight of global public opinion, and what Dean Acheson (mockingly) called "the nineteenth-century faith in the perfectibility of man and the advent of universal peace and law."[17]

What it would require is Pax Americana. We live under it not because it is easy or costless, but because the alternatives have all proved wanting or illusory. The alternative to Pax Americana—the *only* alternative—is global disorder.

WHAT IS GLOBAL DISORDER?

Let's be clear about what disorder is not: Disorder is not disaster—although it is frequently conducive to disaster. Disorder needn't mean decline: the sixteenth and seventeenth centuries were a period of brutal religious strife in Europe. But they were also the years in which Europe came to dominate much of the world. Nor, finally, is disorder always a bad thing: some "orders," such as the one Moscow brusquely imposed on its subjects from Riga to Prague to Tbilisi, richly deserved their downfalls.

Still, if disorder is not a shipwreck, it is a storm. Shipwrecks are events with abrupt causes and predictable outcomes. Storms can often be seen from a ways off, but their precise origins are obscure and their ultimate effects are unknowable. Shipwrecks are inevitably ruinous; storms, only potentially so. The victims of shipwrecks usually vanish without a trace. Storms can transform forever the lives of those who survive them. "When you come out of the storm, you won't be the same person who walked in," wrote the Japanese novelist Haruki Murakami in *Kafka on the Shore*. "That's what this storm is all about."

What disorder *is* is a high degree of unpredictability in global affairs. Aren't global affairs always unpredictable? They are, but it's important to distinguish between two different types of unpredictability: subsystemic and suprasystemic. To know the difference is to understand what disorder really means.

Subsystemic unpredictability is the sort we live with every day. Will a politician lose an election or die in office? Will a natural disaster in a poor country create a humanitarian crisis? Will an asset bubble burst? The answer to all three is yes, given enough time: the only question is the identity of the leader, the country, or the asset. Since we know these things are all destined to happen one way or another, we have in place various systems to make our responses as routine as possible. For the unseated leader there are laws of political succession. For the disaster-stricken country there are agencies of relief. For the asset bubble there is a kit of monetary and fiscal tools.

To speak of "global order" is to describe a world in which unpredictable events are almost always of the subsystemic kind. It's the world most readers of this book will have known all of their lives: a world in which change tends to be cumulative and evolutionary; in which small wars may be relatively common but revolutions are rare and major-power wars are unheard of; in which the patterns of life—personal, social, economic, political, international—proceed according to a long-established set of rules, routines, and expectations. It is also a world with a certain kind of moral order, typically observed even in the breach. One of the reasons the attacks of 9/11 were such a shock to the system was that the perpetrators rejected more than just the foreign policies and political systems of the West. They also rejected the West's moral categories, its distinctions between combatant and civilian, the guilty and the innocent—9/11 was not a subsystemic event.

Suprasystemic unpredictability, by contrast, is unpredictability that overwhelms our systems and damages the reference points by which we usually take stock of the world. This is the type of unpredictability that is both the cause and the major characteristic of the coming global disorder.

Anyone who has lived in a country experiencing a very high rate of inflation or abrupt currency devaluations has a sense of what this unpredictability is like. Money no longer adequately performs its core function as a store of value and unit of account. Savings are destroyed and the thrifty are made to feel like suckers. Black markets spring up like mushrooms, especially if the government imposes an official exchange rate. What happened yesterday becomes an uncertain guide to what's likely to happen tomorrow. Not for nothing was it Vladimir Lenin who is reported to have said that the best way to undermine the capitalist system was to debauch the currency.

Rapid social change is another potent source of suprasystemic unpredictability, especially when there is a wide gap between public expectations for change and the delivery of those changes by government. "The primary problem of politics," wrote Samuel Huntington in 1968, "is the lag in the development of political institutions behind social and economic change."[18] In 1968, Czechoslovakia had its Prague Spring, France its May protests, and Chicago its tumultuous Democratic National Convention. Western political institutions adapted themselves to the social movements of the 1960s; the Communist world violently repressed them. But the "order" the Brezhnev Doctrine produced simply drove the disorders deeper underground, where they would ferment for the next twenty-one years.

Then there is geopolitics. In the ordinary course of events, political parties alternate in power, social ideas come in and go out of fashion, nations jostle for influence, wars begin and burn out. All this is mainly subsystemic. We're used to it and, generally speaking, we handle it. But what happens when the state itself collapses? Or when military alliances or political unions fall apart? Or when an emerging great power seeks a fundamental revision of the global status quo in a way that better suits its interests and ambitions?

Ideas can also have suprasystemic consequences. Sometimes that comes with the *rise* of an idea. A first-century Roman aristocrat, for instance, could scarcely have imagined the effect that an obscure Judean cult propagating the (to him) preposterous notion that the meek shall inherit the earth would have on the destiny of his empire. Luther's doctrine that salvation was to be found *sola fide*—"by faith alone"—had similar effects on the religious and political foundations of Europe, as did ideas about the Rights of Man on the monarchies of the seventeenth and eighteenth centuries, as did Marxism on much of the world in the twentieth century.

Alternatively, suprasystemic unpredictability can emerge from the *decay* of an idea. *And what rough beast, its hour come round at last,/Slouches towards Bethlehem to be born?* In the early twentieth century, the sense that Christian civilization was nearing the end of its days caused many to fear, and many to seek, the coming of new orders, based on new dogmas, bringing into being new types and races of men. Tens of millions of people would perish violently in the name of these utopias.

Today, no such utopias are on the horizon—at least in the West, at least not yet. Yet Western political and economic models are under ideological assault. Globalization has run aground on the opposition of national leaders who want the material benefits of globalization without paying the political price in terms of transparency, accountability, and surrender of economic control. The frequent result is something called "state capitalism." In the Middle East, religious parties have ridden a democratic wave with the aim of delinking democracy (majority rule) from its usual twin, liberalism (individual rights). In South America, the late Hugo Chávez's "Bolivarian Revolution" has spawned misery in Venezuela—and imitators in Ecuador, Nicaragua, and Bolivia. In Europe, Islamists have learned how to turn liberalism against itself: demanding tolerance for their own intolerance; exercising legal rights they would deny others if given the chance; claiming a person's right to dress as she pleases in order to institute a dress code that applies to women only. And in the United States, the sense that our political system is broken has spawned doubts about the viability of the American constitutional system, if not of democracy itself.

Here is a second metaphor to sum up the difference between subsystemic and suprasystemic unpredictability. The former is anything that can happen within the walls of a house, whether it's quiet and productive or riotous and squalid. The latter is what happens *to* the house: the plumbing explodes, the floorboards collapse, the roof rots, the windows get blown out.

SUMMER 2013:
PRESIDENT "WHAT, ME WORRY?"

★ ★ ★ ★

*WASHINGTON—In polo shirt, shorts and sandals,
President Obama headed to the golf course Friday
morning with a couple of old friends, then flew to
Camp David for a long weekend. Secretary of State
John Kerry was relaxing at his vacation home in
Nantucket.*

*Aides said both men were updated as increas-
ingly bloody clashes left dozens dead in Egypt, but
from outward appearances they gave little sense
that the Obama administration viewed the broader
crisis in Cairo with great alarm.*

Thus did *The New York Times* report in July 2013 about
the administration's response to the violent power struggle
then unfolding in Egypt between the military and the Muslim
Brotherhood. Egypt is home to fully a quarter of the world's
Arabs. It has been the recipient of billions in American
military assistance and economic largesse. It controls the
Suez Canal. For four decades, since Anwar Sadat expelled
Soviet advisers and began tilting his country toward the
West, it has been a pillar of American influence in the Mid-
dle East.

Now the country was in the grip of the most profound
crisis in its modern history. Would it revert to the military
dictatorship it had been until just a year earlier, with which
successive U.S. presidents—including Obama himself—had
done business? Or would the Brotherhood—democratically
elected but illiberal, anti-Semitic, and anti-American—be
able to reclaim power?

Large things were at stake here, and not just for Egypt. Obama had said as much in his once-famous Cairo speech of 2009. "I have come here," the president told an adoring audience that June, "to seek a new beginning between the United States and Muslims around the world; one based upon mutual interest and mutual respect; one based upon the truth that America and Islam are not exclusive, and need not be in competition." Eighteen months later, as protesters descended on Cairo's Tahrir Square, he took the side of the crowd and demanded publicly that Hosni Mubarak, America's ally of thirty years, leave office. Not long after that, at the State Department, he said that it would be a "top priority" of his administration to "support transitions to democracy" throughout the Middle East.[1]

Then, after this flurry of presidential attention, things in Egypt became muddled and ambiguous, and the president's attitude became ambivalent and distant. This was no longer a morality play of right against wrong, truth against power, people against injustice—subjects dear to Obama. It was no longer ripe for a foreign policy sermon. It was the stuff of foreign policy itself: stating a position as opposed to having an attitude, and taking sides as opposed to standing aloof.

"A Prince," Niccolò Machiavelli advised, "is likewise esteemed who is a staunch friend and a thorough foe, that is to say, who without reserve openly declares for one against another, this being always a more advantageous course than to stand neutral."

Wise counsel. But not Obama's style. In September 2012, after protesters threatened to overrun the U.S. embassy in Cairo, Obama said of Egypt: "I don't think we would consider them an ally, but we don't consider them an enemy." Nine months later, when the army deposed Mohamed Morsi, again with the support of huge crowds in the street, the president was similarly noncommittal, refusing to call the overthrow a "coup," which it plainly was, but punishing Egypt's new rulers with cuts to U.S. military and economic aid.

Four years after his Cairo speech, just 16 percent of Egyptians had a favorable view of the United States, down from 30 percent in 2006, at the height of George W. Bush's global unpopularity.[2] The administration has performed the extraordinary feat of enraging every corner of Egyptian society, from the Muslim Brotherhood, who feel he sold out cheap on their democracy, to secularists, who believe his administration was too cozy with the Brotherhood, to the military, who know he sold out cheap on their historical alliance. After the United States refused to sell Egypt F-16 fighters, Cairo opened talks with Moscow, its military patron in the days of Nasserist glory.

Countries have options. An American president who does not honor the basic bargain of Pax Americana—military protection in exchange for diplomatic pliancy—will sooner or later squander the benefits of Pax Americana.

So it has been for Egypt, and so it is becoming throughout the world. Israelis don't trust Obama to honor his nuclear red lines for Iran after he ignored his chemical red lines for Syria. Neither do the Saudis. Poland and the Czech Republic felt betrayed by a reset with Russia that left them out in the cold. Rebels of the Free Syrian Army—fighting a two-front war against both the Syrian government and Sunni extremists in their own camp—feel betrayed by explicit U.S. promises of aid that never materialized. The Japanese have begun thinking out loud about their foreign policy options in the event the United States ceases to be a power in Asia. Steep cuts in the Pentagon's budget are being noted from the Baltic to Bahrain.

"The U.S. has to have a foreign policy," the billionaire Saudi prince Alwaleed bin Talal told *The Wall Street Journal* in November 2013. "Well defined, well structured. You don't have it right now, unfortunately. It's just complete chaos."

CHAPTER 8
★ ★ ★
The Coming Global Disorder
(Practice and Present)

W hat would happen," wondered Samuel Huntington in the early 1990s, "if the American model no longer embodied strength and success, no longer seemed to be the winning model?"

> People around the world would come to see the United States as a declining power, characterized by political stagnation, economic inefficiency, and social chaos. If this happened, the perceived failures of the United States would inevitably be seen as failures of democracy.[1]

In many ways this appears to be precisely what is happening to America's standing in the world. An America mired in long wars, deepening debt, and political paralysis does not necessarily seem like the role model of choice for other countries. In 2006 then–Iranian president Mahmoud

Ahmadinejad penned a letter to George W. Bush: "Those with insight can already hear the sounds of the shattering and fall of the ideology and thoughts of the liberal-democratic system," he wrote. "We increasingly see that people around the world are flocking toward a main focal point—that is the Almighty God." At the height of the financial crisis in 2008, a former KGB agent named Igor Panarin got the world's attention by predicting that the United States would break apart into six separate countries by 2010: "It would be reasonable for Russia to lay claim to Alaska," he modestly suggested.[2] During the government shutdown in September 2013, an editorial in Chinese state media caused a sensation by suggesting "it is perhaps a good time for the befuddled world to start considering building a de-Americanized world."

RISE OF THE REVISIONISTS

Such assertions may seem preposterous to American ears. But their significance lies in the conviction with which they are offered, and in the challenge they pose to American claims about both the goodness *and* the success of the liberal-democratic model. None of these ideas are held by all, or even most, Iranians, Russians, or Chinese. And they are by no means exclusive, or even original, to the three countries. But they are the centerpiece of the philosophical critique of pure Americanism coming from each country.

The Iranian challenge concerns questions of virtue and justice. The Islamic Republic sees the American model as spiritually bankrupt, an incubator of sexual promiscuity, homosexuality, pornography, consumerism, and materialism. And it sees it as a force for global injustice, or "Arrogance," by which it means imperialism, support for Israel, and corrupt bargains with secular Muslim rulers such as Egypt's Hosni Mubarak and the late Shah of Iran.

The Russian challenge is less about ideology than it is about revanchism and resentment, although Kremlin propagandists are also fond of making claims about Russia's role as a bulwark of Christian values and civilization. Putin seeks to reconstitute the Russian homeland not by making Russia a welcoming place to which Russians outside the country can return but by expanding Russia's borders to include Russians living in the so-called near abroad. And he wants to do so at the expense of the United States, a country he has always viewed as Russia's political, military, and strategic enemy. As for Panarin and his prediction of an impending American crack-up, what's frightening isn't the prediction itself, or that someone could make such a silly forecast and be taken seriously for it. It's that Panarin is the dean of the Russian foreign ministry's diplomatic academy.

The Chinese challenge is that liberal democracy is a recipe for bankruptcy and laziness: democracy allows people to vote themselves financial benefits via entitlements, special interest carve-outs, and other forms of welfarism that undermine incentives to work and save. Chinese policy makers also believe that liberal democracy lacks a sense of purpose, organization, and direction. The American way offends the mandarin ethic; the guiding wisdom comes from below, not above; from collective sensibility, not elite intelligence. There are no longer many grand, state-organized projects in the United States today, as there were with the Apollo program or the Tennessee Valley Authority. The United States, by this reckoning, is a nation adrift, still number one by virtue of its victory in World War II (another triumph of purposeful collective state action). But it lacks an anchor and will eventually run aground.

As long as a critical mass of Iranian, Russian, and Chinese leaders hold these views they will challenge the United States not simply because they seek to wrest power from it but also because they believe that it deserves to fall. In other words, their anti-Americanism is fundamental to their worldview, which is what makes it potent and dangerous.

This is also the story of the 1920s and '30s. "The Western Powers had hoped that their victory would usher in an era modeled in their own image," writes the historian Norman Davies. In 1914, he notes, Europe was a continent of nineteen monarchies and three republics. By 1919 it had fourteen monarchies and sixteen republics. But democracy didn't stick. "Hardly a year passed when one country or another did not see its democratic constitution violated by one or other brand of dictator. It cannot be attributed to a simple cause, save the inability of the Western powers to defend the regimes which they had inspired."[3]

Similarly today, Freedom House reports that political and civil liberties declined for an eighth year in a row. "While freedom suffered from coups and civil wars," notes the report, "an equally significant phenomenon was the reliance on more subtle, but ultimately more effective, techniques by those who practice what is known as modern authoritarianism. Such leaders devote full-time attention to the challenge of crippling the opposition without annihilating it, and flouting the rule of law while maintaining a plausible veneer of order, legitimacy, and prosperity." The description applies to Russia's Vladimir Putin, Iran's Hassan Rouhani, and China's Xi Jinping, as well as Turkey's Recep Tayyip Erdoğan, Venezuela's Nicolás Maduro, Ecuador's Rafael Correa, and—in the heart of Europe—Hungary's Viktor Orbán.

Can modern authoritarianism really succeed in getting the better of liberal democracy? Freedom House notes how today's dictators "have studied how other dictatorships were destroyed and are bent on preventing a similar fate for themselves." They also know how to help one another:

> At one level, a loose-knit club of authoritarians works to protect mutual interests at the United Nations and other international forums, subverting global human rights standards and blocking precedent-setting actions against fellow despots. More disturbingly, they collaborate to prop up some of the world's most reprehensible regimes. This is most visible at present in Syria, where Russia, China, Iran and Venezuela have offered diplomatic support, loans, fuel, or direct military aid to the Assad regime.[4]

That may not be enough to save them, in the long term, from the consequences of their own inevitable mistakes. But the key question isn't the ultimate verdict of history: it's whether "the long term" lasts five years, a decade, or five decades. The answer lies in the willingness of liberal democracies to challenge modern authoritarianism, in part by competing with it ideologically, as the United States did with the Soviet Union in the Cold War, and also by challenging it geopolitically. The Retreat Doctrine may pretend to do the former through "nation building at home." But it neglects to do the latter. It is an invitation to modern authoritarians to press their strategic advantage while they can.

So it has been with Russia. In 2005 Vladimir Putin said that the collapse of the Soviet Union was "the greatest geopolitical catastrophe" of the twentieth century. His foreign policy has been a methodical effort to reconstitute, if not the Union itself, then at least its old sphere of influence: through a full-scale invasion of Georgia (in the midst of the Beijing Olympics); the seizure of Ukraine's Crimean peninsula (just after the Sochi Olympics); election tampering, disinformation campaigns, covert military support to ethnic Russian separatists, and special forces operations in eastern Ukraine; political bribery in Kyrgyzstan; midwinter pipeline shutoffs in several former Soviet republics; assassinations in London; cyberwarfare in Estonia. In the meantime, Putin has brought back much of the spirit of the old USSR: the sham democracy, the transformation of news into propaganda, show trials for political opponents, the use of state power for ordinary criminal ends, and the reconstitution of the old elite *nomenklatura*. Russia is on course toward becoming a Soviet state, albeit one with regional rather than global ambitions, and without the economic encumbrances imposed by the abolition of private property.

So it has been with Iran. Tehran makes no secret of its intention to dominate Iraq and western Afghanistan as U.S. troops make for the exits. Nor has the regime been shy about fighting for its client in Damascus, or arming Hezbollah in Lebanon and Hamas in Gaza, or renewing its historic claims to majority-Shiite Bahrain. Some of this stems from traditional Persian nationalism, but more of it from Islamic revivalism.

And so it is with China. In 1984, Deng Xiaoping vowed that Beijing would respect Hong Kong's freedoms for fifty years, and that if reunification with Taiwan "cannot be accomplished in 100 years, it will be in 1,000 years." But Deng's doctrine of strategic patience died with him in 1997. In late 2011, Deng's successor Hu Jintao told a gathering of military officials that the navy should "accelerate its transformation and modernization in a sturdy way, and make extended preparations for warfare."[5] Against whom? Everyone, it seemed: within a year of Hu's remarks Beijing had deployed its first aircraft carrier and was picking maritime fights with Hanoi, Manila, Jakarta, and Tokyo. In September 2012 the Obama administration acknowledged that an attack on the Senkaku Islands, which the Japanese hold and the Chinese claim, would require the United States to come to Japan's defense under the terms of their 1960 mutual defense treaty. In December 2013 a Chinese naval ship crossed the bow of the USS *Cowpens*, nearly causing a collision with the $1 billion Aegis cruiser. In the meantime, Beijing has developed a global strategy of cultivating pliable, resource-rich countries in Africa, Latin America, and Southeast Asia through promises of easy cash and development aid. Since 2008, Venezuela alone has received $36 billion from Beijing, effectively underwriting a government that would otherwise have bankrupted itself long ago.[6]

Should the rise of the revisionists especially alarm the rest of the world? Iran, Russia, and China have been truculent powers for a long time without quite blowing up the world. But there are differences today. One is that each of them is more powerful now than it was a decade ago: Tehran has stared down domestic challenges to the regime and international challenges to its nuclear ambitions and is seeing its strategic gamble in Syria pay off. The Russian economy today is eight times the size it was when Putin came to power in 2000, growing from $250 billion to $2 trillion; military spending has also risen nearly threefold, to $90 billion. China has also seen massive growth in its economy over the same period, and its (published) military budget grew from $14.6 billion to more than $110 billion. These are astonishing increases, even if they rest on inherently weak foundations. (See chapter 6.)

A second difference is that each has noted that the United States is much more reluctant to exercise its own power, and each treats Washington with increasingly undisguised contempt. China made a point of abetting Edward Snowden's flight from Hong Kong to Moscow, just weeks after Obama had hosted Chinese leader Xi Jinping in Palm Springs. "In #Geneva agreement world powers surrendered to Iranian nation's will,"

Hassan Rouhani tweeted—and tweaked—in January 2014. In September 2013, right after the administration's Syria capitulation, Putin took to the op-ed pages of *The New York Times* to scold Obama: "I would rather disagree with a case he [Obama] made on American exceptionalism, stating that the United States' policy is 'what makes America different. It's what makes us exceptional,'" Putin opined. "It is extremely dangerous to encourage people to see themselves as exceptional, whatever the motivation."[7] However powerful the United States may be in any objective tally of its inherent and relative strengths, *it will be treated as a declining nation if it regards itself as one—and is seen by others to so regard itself.* "I fear that policy is advocated in the knowledge that there is not a will to carry it out, but people don't have the courage of their convictions to say 'we are just going to talk and not use force,'" notes James Jeffrey, a distinguished U.S. diplomat who served as Obama's ambassador in both Turkey and Iraq.[8] In the knowledge that U.S. policy makers do not have the will to use force except in the face of direct attack, Iranian, Russian, and Chinese policy makers are growing bolder.

Finally, it isn't clear whether the confidence with which the revisionist powers operate today leads to wiser decision making on their part. It may be the opposite: confidence often leads to rashness. When Putin secured the Winter Olympics for Sochi in July 2007, Russia was riding a wave of rising oil prices and rising geopolitical confidence. Yet the Olympics wound up being an advertisement for the regime's grandiosity, incompetence, corruption, and domestic insecurity. Iran's brinksmanship over its nuclear program has, at this writing, paid off. That could change if Israel carries off a successful strike, or if the tide of war changes again in Syria decisively against Assad, or if a war between Israel and Hezbollah ends with the terrorist group routed in the field.

As for China, a cliché about its foreign policy today is that they have been "playing chess while we've been playing checkers." Yet the truth of Chinese policy in Asia over the past decade has been (to use a better metaphor from Abraham Lincoln) a gallon of gall without a drop of honey, which has succeeded mainly in antagonizing its neighbors and driving them into closer alliances with one another and with the United States.

Observing Chinese behavior today reminds many observers of Germany in the run-up to the First World War: bullying but insecure; grasping but aimless; animated by no larger idea than nationalist paranoia and historical resentment. "What the Kaiser wanted most was international recognition of Germany's importance and, above all, of its power," observes Henry Kissinger. Yet "beyond the slogans lay an intellectual vacuum: truculent language masked an inner hollowness; vast slogans obscured timidity and the lack of any sense of direction."[9]

At what point does their boldness violate a red line from which an American president cannot retreat? How do revisionist states learn to respect boundaries of international acceptability that seem constantly to recede? How does the United States enforce global order through persuasion and moral example alone? When does reluctance to use force become an invitation to aggression?

And, perhaps most important, when does America's diffidence begin to reshape the calculations of our allies?

RISE OF THE FREELANCERS

For several years there has been intense speculation about whether Israel will strike Iran's nuclear facilities. At least as of the late spring of 2014 (when this book was delivered to the publisher), it has not done so, in large part because it has been under intense U.S. pressure not to act, and because it has public and private assurances from the administration that the United States will strike in the event Tehran sprints to acquire a bomb. Yet ever since America's very public climb-down on Syria after Assad had crossed Obama's chemical red line, Israeli decision makers have come to doubt that the United States would really make good on its assurances. As a result, the chances that Israel will attempt a strike—even as the dangers of doing so have risen over time—have increased.

This is not a prospect the United States should relish. If Iran's nuclear infrastructure is going to be attacked, it should be attacked *comprehensively*, and only America has the military assets to deliver a knockout blow. By contrast, an Israeli strike would pose profound regional hazards, as Iran will feel more confident launching a retaliatory blow against the Jewish state than it would against the United States. A drawn-out Iran-Israel war has unpredictable and possibly uncontainable effects that have the potential to draw the United States in on non-U.S. terms.

It is precisely because such foreign policy freelancing by Israel would be dangerous to American interests that the United States has promised Israel to do the job itself if diplomacy fails. The core purpose of Pax Americana isn't merely to deter our adversaries; it is to make sure that our allies are not tempted to take matters into their own hands when they feel their security is at stake. Thus the United States offers nuclear guarantees to countries such as Germany, Japan, and South Korea because we do not want them acquiring nuclear capabilities of their own. Thus, too, the United States until recently maintained forces sufficient to fight two major wars at the same time, not least to reassure a country such as Japan that American military involvement in the Middle East would not put their security in jeopardy. For the cost of underwriting these commitments—and the risk of being required to honor them—the United States gains immense influence over the strategic choices of our allies.

That influence came in handy for the administration of George H. W. Bush during the Gulf War in 1991, when it kept Israel from retaliating directly against Iraq for Saddam's Scud missile attacks. Doing so required redirecting U.S. warplanes and deploying commando units to hunt for Iraq's mobile missile launchers, putting American lives in harm's way. But it did convince then–prime minister Yitzhak Shamir that the United States was serious about defending Israel, serving America's larger interest in maintaining unity in its coalition. Today Obama is asking Israel to show similar restraint toward Iran on the basis of a promise that increasingly rings hollow among Israeli leaders. And this tempts Israel to act.

Thus the central contradiction of the administration's Iran policy: It wants a nuclear deal that takes account only of American needs, strategic and political, irrespective of the security considerations of U.S. allies. But the administration also wants those allies to toe the line and accept America's security parameters as their own. In the long run the contradiction cannot be finessed. If the United States wants to prevent an outbreak of foreign policy freelancing it has to make certain that it is taking serious account of the core strategic requirements of its allies. If, on the other hand, the United States prefers to define its security interests in narrowly American terms, it will have to accept the consequences of increased foreign policy freelancing.

Influence, like power, abhors a vacuum.

Already those consequences are becoming visible. In March 2011, without consulting the United States, Saudi Arabia abruptly moved two thousand troops into Bahrain—home to the U.S. Fifth Fleet—to shore up the local monarchy, largely in reaction to the administration's decision to cashier Hosni Mubarak in Egypt. "They've taken it personally because they question what we'd do if they are next," *The New York Times* quoted one American official describing the Saudi view.[10] In October 2013 the administration opted to withhold hundreds of millions of dollars in military aid to Egypt—including fighter jets, attack helicopters, and M-1 tanks—in protest over the military overthrow of Mohamed Morsi, the elected president from the Muslim Brotherhood. Within a month Russia was offering a multibillion-dollar package of fighter jets and attack helicopters. Also in October 2013 *The Wall Street Journal* reported that Saudi Arabia was reassessing its alliance with the United States after Obama had reneged on his promises to arm Syrian rebels and bomb Syrian chemical weapons sites. "In the run-up to the expected U.S. strikes, Saudi leaders asked for detailed U.S. plans for posting Navy ships to guard the Saudi oil center, the Eastern Province, during any strike on Syria," the *Journal*'s Ellen Knickmeyer reported from Riyadh. "The Saudis were surprised when the Americans told them U.S. ships wouldn't be able to fully protect the oil region, the official said."[11] The infuriated Saudis responded by threatening to stop buying arms from the United States—no small matter, given that Riyadh purchased $33.4 billion worth of weapons from the United States in 2011 alone.

Nor are the consequences restricted to the Middle East. In December 2013 Vice President Joe Biden spent an hour on the phone with Shinzō

Abe, fruitlessly attempting to persuade the Japanese prime minister not to visit the Yasukuni Shrine, the Shinto memorial that commemorates Japan's 2.5 million war dead, including a number of World War II war criminals. The prime minister's rebuff was partly a function of his brand of nationalism, but it also came in response to Biden's less-than-unequivocal rejection that month of China's assertion of an air defense identification zone over Japan's uninhabited Senkaku Islands. "Behind the scenes, though, another concern is growing: that the United States may one day be unable or unwilling to defend Japan," Reuters reports. "The worries are adding momentum to Abe's drive to beef up Japan's air and naval forces while loosening constitutional limits on action its military can take abroad."[12] Takashi Kawakami, an international relations expert at a Tokyo university, has warned that "this is one of the most dangerous moments in U.S.-Japanese relations," adding that "Japan is feeling isolated, and some Japanese people are starting to think that Japan must stand up for itself, including toward the United States."[13]

What else might happen as freelancing becomes more widespread? Almost certainly more nations will seek, if not a nuclear weapon itself, then a nuclear option. Will the world be a safer place when the Middle East has four or five nuclear powers—not just Israel and Pakistan, but also Iran, Saudi Arabia, Turkey, perhaps Egypt, potentially Algeria—each at daggers drawn with the others in ever-shifting configurations and tacit or formal alliances? If it is acceptable for Iran to enrich uranium independently, why not any other country that wants to keep its options open? In 2013 Japan and Turkey signed a nuclear cooperation agreement, including "a provision allowing Turkey to enrich uranium and extract plutonium, a potential material for nuclear weapons," according to a report in the *Asahi Shimbun*.[14] In 2014 Saudi Arabia, which plans to build sixteen nuclear reactors over the next twenty years, signed a nuclear cooperation deal with Jordan.[15] Then there is South Korea: Seoul has been pressing the United States to acquire uranium enrichment capabilities of its own, and a 2013 poll found that two thirds of South Koreans favored developing nuclear weapons as a counterweight to the North.[16] Even

Japan is keeping its options open: in October 2014 it plans to open the Rokkasho Nuclear Fuel Reprocessing plant, a $21 billion facility "capable of producing nine tons of weapons-usable plutonium annually . . . enough to build as many as 2,000 bombs," according to *The Wall Street Journal*.[17] Japan isn't (yet) seeking a nuclear arsenal, and in March 2014 it even agreed to relinquish a fraction of its stockpile in a symbolic bow to non-proliferation. But, as in Hollywood, it wants to option the rights.

There is a theoretical argument that nuclear proliferation has a stabilizing effect on global security, as nuclear weapons instill responsibility and discourage aggression—at least against other nuclear powers. Whether such a sunny view could survive the collapse of, say, the Pakistani government and its replacement by the Taliban is an open question.

But there's no need to forecast the apocalypse to fear the rise of freelancers. When it's every nation for itself, the bidding for influence can become dangerous. That was the lesson of Ukraine as the government of former president Viktor Yanukovych abandoned its bid to sign an association agreement with the European Union and instead moved to a customs union with Russia—a move sweetened by the offer of billions in soft loans and cheap energy from Moscow. The result was mass protests, then mass repression, a revolution, then the seizure of Crimea. Moscow's effort to return Kiev to its orbit and ultimately its control is essential to Vladimir Putin's quest to resurrect the Russian Empire. And it raises fundamental questions about the long-term independence of other post-Soviet states: Belarus, Kazakhstan, Kyrgyzstan, the Baltics. All of them are now in play.

How would the United States react to this world of freelancers? If history is a guide, it would turn away in disgust. "From Woodrow Wilson through George Bush," observes Henry Kissinger, "American presidents have invoked their country's unselfishness as the crucial attribute of its leadership."[18] When foreign policy ceases to be about the pursuit of a higher morality and instead becomes a mere contest of influence, the United States typically turns away in disgust. The flip side of America's native idealism is its susceptibility to disillusionment. That was the dominant motif of U.S. foreign policy after the First World War, and so it is again.

FREE RADICALS

The rise of freelancing and revisionist states is not the only harbinger of global disorder. There is also what one might call the "free radical" problem. In chemistry, a free radical is "an especially reactive atom or group of atoms that has one or more unpaired electrons . . . and that can damage cells, proteins, and DNA by altering their chemical structure." Free radicals were first identified at the University of Michigan in 1900—around the same time another collection of free radicals, widely known as anarchists, were making themselves known with a string of assassinations that included an emperor of Russia, an empress of Austria, a president in France, and a president of the United States. Today, Islamic jihadists march under the same banner of radical and violent opposition to the established order of states and the international system itself. But the free radical problem extends well beyond the matter of Islamic extremism and some of its more charismatic leaders.

Take nuclear proliferation. In January 2014, the Defense Science Board, an advisory group to the secretary of defense, released a report on the challenges of assessing nuclear monitoring and verification technologies. "The actual or threatened acquisition of nuclear weapons by more actors, for a range of reasons, is emerging in numbers not seen since the first two decades of the Cold War."

> The pathways to proliferation are expanding. Networks of cooperation among countries that would otherwise have little reason to do so, such as the A. Q. Khan network or the Syria–North Korea and Iran–North Korea collaborations, cannot be considered as isolated events. Moreover, the growth in nuclear power worldwide offers more opportunity for "leakage" and/or hiding small programs, especially since current resources to support safeguards are already strained and will be increasingly challenged by cases of noncompliance.[19]

The story of A. Q. Khan—who helped father Pakistan's bomb and then shared enrichment technologies and atomic bomb blueprints with

North Korea, Iran, and Libya—is one of the more lurid tales of the dark side of globalization. The frightening fact, however, isn't that it happened, past tense. It's how likely it is to happen again in more dangerous and surreptitious ways. At least the Bush administration had enough leverage over former Pakistani strongman Pervez Musharraf to put Khan out of business and shut his network down. And at least Khan was selling his nuclear wares to governments, not terrorist organizations.

But what do we know about the nuclear trade today? In 2007, Israel bombed a nuclear reactor in Syria that had been built by North Korea under the terms of a "science and technology agreement" signed a few years earlier by the two countries and likely financed by Iran. In September 2012, Pyongyang signed the same kind of agreement with Tehran, pledging to "cooperate in research, student exchanges, and joint laboratories."[20] In 2013 North Korea conducted a nuclear test, hinting that this time it had detonated a uranium-based device; some observers wondered whether the test had been conducted on Iran's behalf. Nor is Pyongyang's arms trade limited to other states. "North Korea supports various non-state actors that engage in terrorism," says North Korea expert Bruce Bechtol. "Hezbollah is probably one of the most profitable for them. . . . Now we see over the past couple of years they've been supplying al-Shabab, which is an al Qaeda–affiliated non-state actor terrorist organization in Somalia."[21] Pyongyang's arms trade is managed through an organization known as Office 99, which engages "a network of front companies in Asia, Europe and the Middle East [that] have partnered with Southeast Asian, Japanese and Taiwanese criminal syndicates to move cash and contraband," according to a 2010 report in *The Wall Street Journal.*[22]

Then there is the mysterious trade between Tehran and the regime in Venezuela. In December 2008 Turkish officials seized twenty-two containers destined for Venezuela from Iran labeled "tractor parts." Instead, they contained "enough to set up an explosives lab," according to a Turkish official quoted by the Associated Press.[23] In 2009, Manhattan district attorney Robert Morgenthau wrote that "over the past three years a number of Iranian-owned and controlled factories have sprung up in remote and undeveloped parts of Venezuela—ideal locations for the illicit production of weapons."[24] Another suspicious detail: "the Iran-Venezuela Joint Bank, based in Tehran, was opened in April 2009 with an initial capital base of $200 million," according to a report from the Carnegie Endowment for International Peace. "That money is managed by the Export Development Bank of Iran, which the U.S. Treasury Department has designated as 'proliferator' for providing or attempting to provide financial services to entities that advance Iran's nuclear program."[25]

But the free radical problem isn't only about what moves in the dark. It's also about what is being pushed from the realm of secrecy into broad daylight, thanks to the efforts of people such as Julian Assange and Edward Snowden.

Both men are examples of what's been called the "superempowered individual" using limited financial means and technical tools to wreak massive human and institutional damage. Judged by volume alone, Snowden's theft of secrets may rank as the single largest security breach in U.S. history. Nor were the data disclosures harmless, whatever one thinks of the "public interest" being served. "Most of the documents stolen by Edward Snowden have nothing to do with the privacy rights and civil liberties of American citizens or even the NSA surveillance programs," said Maine senator Susan Collins after a secret intelligence briefing to assess the Snowden damage. James Clapper, the director of national intelligence, insists the damage "includes putting the lives of members or assets of the intelligence community at risk as well as our armed forces, diplomats, and citizens." Clapper compromised his credibility last year by lying about the NSA metadata collection program, so his allegation must be treated with due caution. But what's not in dispute is that Snowden also disclosed the methods by which the NSA intercepted and tracked the communications of senior Al Qaeda leaders in the Pakistan hinterlands and gave away the real size of the CIA budget, until then one of the most closely held secrets in Washington. "Snowden has compromised more capability than any spy in U.S. history," Mike McConnell, a former NSA director, told *The Wall Street Journal*. "And this will have an impact on our ability to do our mission for the next 20 to 30 years."[26]

As for Assange, he did not simply expose the ordinary cable traffic of the U.S. State Department; he also put lives at risk by disclosing the identities of non-Americans who had worked in some fashion with American soldiers and diplomats. In Zimbabwe, opposition leader Morgan Tsvangirai was threatened with indictment on a capital offense for privately urging the United States to sanction the regime of Robert Mugabe. Assange was also remarkably cavalier about jeopardizing the lives of Afghan civilians who had provided information about the Taliban to Coalition forces. Declan Walsh, formerly a reporter for *The Guardian* newspaper, which published many of the original WikiLeaks cables, tells this story:

> I told [fellow *Guardian* reporter] David Leigh I was worried about the repercussions of publishing these names [of Afghan civilians], who could easily be killed by the Taliban or other militant groups if identified. . . . David broached the problem again with Julian [Assange]. The response floored me. "Well, they're informants," he said. "So, if they get killed, they've got it coming to them. They deserve it."[27]

Assange has since taken asylum at the Ecuador embassy in London in order to avoid extradition to Sweden, where he faces rape charges. In 2012 he hosted an interview show on Russia Today, the English-language mouthpiece of the Putin regime. Reporters Without Borders ranks Ecuador at number 114 in its 2013 index of press freedom, and Russia is at number 148.[28] Transparency International also puts both countries at the bottom of its tables.

So it is that the two most celebrated champions of government transparency in our time have taken refuge with some of the least transparent countries in our time. Is it a coincidence? Or is it the inherent logic of progressive people who so often seem to wind up making common cause with repressive regimes?

Whatever the case, the "free radical" problem arises from the ease with which a single individual can take advantage of the open architecture of the modern world to attack the foundations of the free world. It's a world in which a would-be jihadist can move with relative ease from Europe to the Middle East and back again. Where suppliers and financiers of nuclear materials can operate globally and anonymously. Where a quarter million sensitive diplomatic cables, downloaded by a U.S. Army private in Iraq experiencing a sexual identity crisis, can be provided to a shadowy Internet organization run out of a repurposed atomic bunker in Sweden by an expatriated Australian of no fixed address, and then published by news organizations in New York, London, Hamburg, Madrid, and Paris. Where a twenty-nine-year-old high school dropout, working in tandem with an American columnist living in Brazil and writing for a British paper, can pilfer closely held U.S. secrets using off-the-shelf software while evading detection by the very National Security Agency tasked with spotting someone like him.

Where in this crazy-quilt universe do sovereign jurisdictions apply? Where do they end? At what point does enforcement become pointless? Can democratic governments keep a diplomatic confidence or an intelligence secret without resurrecting Cold War security strictures? Are there any secrets even worth keeping? Is there even a point to attempting to prevent Iran from completing an indigenous nuclear capability when it can simply offshore those capabilities—as perhaps it already does in North Korea?

These questions are not unanswerable. But they are difficult, especially in free societies that naturally incline toward greater openness, greater access, greater transparency, and greater mobility. At some undetermined point every society recognizes that even good things can have their limit. The danger lies in the fact that societies typically only notice the limit when they crash into it.

FLYING ON ONE ENGINE

Let's recap: Americans hope that a smaller U.S. footprint in the world will refocus our resources and attention on things that need doing at home. They hope also that the world will find a way to take care of itself. Yet as the American retreat becomes increasingly noticeable, adversaries sense a strategic opening to revise regional, and global, order in a way that's more to their liking. And our allies are forced to consider their security options in ways they haven't for many years, comfortable as they were under the U.S. security umbrella. This creates a geopolitical environment that is less predictable, less manageable, and potentially more violent. To compound the problem, nonstate actors are increasingly capable of using limited means to profoundly alter the international security landscape. And the very concept of "state" is in many places collapsing.

Now add another factor: violent turbulence for a global economy whose traditional engines of growth are all sputtering. The global trade agenda is semi-moribund and globalization itself is in retreat: after peaking in 2007, there has been a 60 percent decline in cross-border capital flows. "For three decades," the McKinsey Global Institute reports, "capital markets and banking systems rapidly expanded and diversified, but now that process—called financial deepening—has largely ground to a halt."[29]

Start with Japan, which remains the world's third-largest economy with nearly $6 trillion in GDP even after twenty-five years of stagnation. Today the Land of the Rising Sun must confront the facts that it has the world's oldest population (median age 44.6 years compared with 36.9 for the United States), one of the lowest fertility rates (1.21 children per woman next to 2.06 for the United States), and the world's highest public debt-to-GDP ratio (214 percent against Greece's 161 percent). Since 1990 it has had sixteen prime ministers. Since 2000 it has averaged a growth rate of under 0.3 percent. It has the second-highest combined corporate tax rate in the developed world (after the United States), and a top income tax rate of 50 percent, more than twice the average Asian rate. Successive Japanese governments have spent more than twenty years pulling all the levers of fiscal and monetary stimulus—"Abenomics" mainly rehearses a failed formula on a grander scale. After a year of hope and hype, the vaunted Japanese recovery began showing sign of giving out, as the Abe government mostly shies away from taking on the pillars of the postwar economic system: the entrenched bureaucracy; the industrial conglomerates; the Post Bank behemoth; labor and consumer-protection rules that protect this or that industry group. To take just one instructive example, Sony, which in 1991 hired 1,000 college graduates, hired only 160 in 2013, partly because labor laws make firing a near impossibility. The result, *The New York Times* reported in 2013, was the Japanese equivalent of a New York City public school "rubber room" for delinquent teachers who just can't be fired: "Shusaku Tani is employed at the Sony plant here, but he doesn't really work. For more than two years, he has come to a small room, taken a seat and then passed the time reading newspapers, browsing the Web and poring over engineering textbooks from his college days. He files a report on his activities at the end of each day."[30]

Now turn to China. Chapter 6 described some of the ways in which China's rise had been overhyped in the West. But Beijing's problems are more immediate than chronic corruption, shoddy construction, and a demographic time bomb courtesy of the one-child policy. Beijing bulldozed its way through the 2009 financial crisis with the largest stimulus package in history, and now it sits on the world's biggest debt bomb. According to China scholar Minxin Pei, Chinese banks issued $5.4 trillion in new loans, or 73 percent of China's 2011 GDP, between the beginning of 2009 and the summer of 2012.[31] Another astute China watcher, former Fitch analyst Charlene Chu, puts the figure at somewhere around $15 trillion. Northwestern professor Victor Shih has described a system in which "local officials race against each other to borrow even more to finance grand projects before they rotate to new positions next year, while banks, which depend on new loans to illiquid borrowers to prevent old loans from becoming nonperforming, continue to pour credit into LGFV [local government financing vehicles] borrowers." Shih estimates the local government debt alone may be as high as 50 percent of China's 2010 GDP.[32] Even now Beijing hasn't applied the brakes: in 2013, lending actually grew by 20 percent. Total private and government debt, according to the Chinese Academy of Social Science, stands at 215 percent of GDP.[33] Making matters worse is that the system is opaque on multiple levels: Chinese leaders don't trust their own published statistics. Chinese borrowers are increasingly turning to a shadow banking system, which is connected to the formal banking system in a variety of murky ways, and which has issued an estimated $6 trillion in loans. What percentage of those loans are bad? The Chinese government insists it's no more than 1 percent. More skeptical watchers fear it might be in the neighborhood of 20 percent, if not higher.

What about the other so-called emerging markets? The largest of these is Brazil, followed by Russia, India, Mexico, Indonesia, and Turkey. Collectively, these six economies account for almost $9 trillion in GDP. And, to adapt Tolstoy's aphorism about families, each of them is unhappy in its own way. In Brazil, the inflation rate—nearly 6 percent in 2013—ran at more than twice the growth rate. Russia has discovered the downside of a commodity-based economy in an era of increasing resource (especially energy) abundance. India's annual growth rate, which hit a 10 percent stride in the middle of the last decade, is now under 5 percent, not good enough for a country that has added more than 200 million people since the turn of the century. Mexico has done better, with a political system that showed itself capable of jumping over the political third rail of state ownership of the energy sector. But the country remains mired in a drug war that has claimed as many as 80,000 lives and corrupted every stratum of society and government. Indonesia is becoming increasingly hostile to foreign investment. And Turkey is racked by the combination of the bursting of a real-estate bubble and political risk associated with the increasingly autocratic and capricious rule of Recep Tayyip Erdoğan.

"The trifecta of emerging-market miseries goes like this," notes portfolio strategy consultant Jay Pelosky.

The mismanaged: Venezuela and Argentina have devalued. The overly indebted: China and many of its Asian neighbors face very tough conditions created by the consumer-debt bubble. China is just beginning to try to stabilize a credit system that is opaque in the extreme. One example should suffice: The over $1 trillion "local trust" lending market, which itself has more than $600 billion coming due this year. The unbalanced: Various large nations, including Indonesia, Brazil, Turkey and South Africa, have large current-account deficits and thus depend on external financing. For most of these unbalanced countries, 2014 is also an election year, which sharply limits policy flexibility.[34]

Next there is Europe, a $17 trillion slice of the global economy. Though EU leaders believe they have survived the worst of the euro crisis, a 2012 report from the European Commission offers grim warnings on where the EU is headed.[35] Youth unemployment is 21 percent; among twenty- to twenty-four-year-olds, 15 percent are neither working nor in school, "and risk being permanently excluded from the labor market and dependent on benefits." The ratio of pensioners to workers, already high, will double by 2050. Europe's Muslim population will "easily double" by 2020; by 2050, one in five Europeans "will probably be a Muslim." Europe is experiencing a brain drain of its best and brightest. Some 370,000 Spaniards emigrated in 2011, many to Latin America.[36] Portuguese are leaving in large numbers to former colonies such as Brazil and Angola. The migration comes from "mostly the skilled part of the population," according to one European Union researcher.[37] "In one of my finance seminars, every single French student intends to go abroad," Sorbonne economics professor Jacques Régniez told *The Daily Telegraph*, adding that he estimates that one in four French students want to emigrate, "and this rises to 80 percent or 90 percent in the case of marketable degrees."[38]

A country's destiny can be measured in many ways, but perhaps the most decisive factor is whether it is capable of cultivating, attracting, and retaining its human capital. By this metric, Europe's future looks even bleaker. The European Commission report's description of Europe's long-term historical trajectory is sobering: In 1900, Europe accounted for 40 percent of global GDP. In 2000, it was 25 percent. By 2050, it could fall to as low as 15 percent. "Europe's share of global product may be lower than it was before the onset of globalization."

THE LAST ENGINE

So where is there relative strength? Many American readers may be surprised to learn it is in the United States, despite years of lackluster growth and employment figures, diminished productivity gains, ever higher levels of public debt, the uncertainty of what might happen after (or if) the Federal Reserve concludes its "taper" and returns to a normal interest rate policy, incompetent and abrasive bureaucracy, and an entitlement state that, with the Affordable Care Act, has grown larger even as its financial liabilities have come more sharply into view. In February 2014 the Congressional Budget Office warned that unemployment would not drop below 6 percent for the rest of Obama's term. Nor did it see things getting much better thereafter. "Beyond 2017," the CBO warned, "economic growth will diminish to a pace that is well below the average seen over the past decades," mainly on account of the aging population.[39] For the United States to grow at its historical growth rate of about 3 percent a year means the U.S. economy would grow more than tenfold by the end of the century. By contrast, at a European-level growth rate of 1.5 percent it would take an additional sixty years to reach the same benchmark.

That's a tough forecast. But economic predictions, particularly of the "limits to growth" variety that became fashionable in the 1970s, should be treated with skepticism. The United States, as noted in chapter 6, also retains unprecedented economic strengths, including an immensely disciplined and efficient corporate sector, near-total information transparency, the world's best universities, healthy demographic trends, receptivity to technological innovation and social change, and an intellectually vibrant political culture capable of generating fresh policy ideas. America, more than any large country in the world, has a capacity for adaptation and self-renewal. "Overall, many structural features continue to make the U.S. economy extremely productive," notes the World Economic Forum's Global Competitiveness Survey. "U.S. companies are highly sophisticated and innovative, supported by an excellent university system that collaborates admirably with the business sector and R&D. Combined with flexible labor markets and the scale of opportunities afforded by the sheer size of its domestic market—the largest in the world by far—these qualities continue to make the United States very competitive."[40]

Few personal stories better illustrate the point than that of Jan Koum, a thirty-eight-year-old immigrant to the United States who in 2014 sold his company, WhatsApp—a messaging subscription service for smart-phones that allows people to send texts anywhere in the world free of charge—to Facebook for a cool $19 billion in shares and cash. Koum and his mother had left their native Ukraine when he was sixteen, fleeing rising anti-Semitism, and moved to Mountain View, California, where they lived off food stamps. His mother took jobs as a nanny while he worked in a grocery store and moonlighted as a hacker. He enrolled at San Jose State University, dropped out, worked at Yahoo! for a few years, and then applied for—and failed to get—a job at Facebook. "Then in January 2009, he bought an iPhone and realized the seven-month-old App Store was about to spawn a whole new industry of apps," reports Parmy Olson in *Forbes*. Talking things over with friends in the Russian community of San Jose, Koum came up with the idea for WhatsApp and incorporated the company before the code for the application had even been written. Things began badly. The software was riddled with glitches, and hardly anybody seemed to use it. "After a game of ultimate frisbee with [WhatsApp cofounder Brian] Acton, Koum grudgingly admitted he should probably fold up and start looking for a job," Olson reports. "Acton balked. 'You'd be an idiot to quit now,' he said. 'Give it a few more months.'"[41]

Every detail in this true story rings an "Only in America" bell. The impoverished immigrant, fleeing persecution. The indifference to formal schooling. The freewheeling immigrant culture of Silicon Valley, with its American business ethos and global sensibilities. The speed with which Koum incorporated his business. The early frustrations and temptations to quit. The accidental way in which Koum, who started WhatsApp as a way of notifying a network of friends about what a user was doing at some particular moment, realized that its real value lay as a new instant-messaging service, and that its customer base was mainly abroad. The speculative, perhaps foolhardy way Facebook snapped up a company of fifty-odd employees for such a gargantuan sum on the basis of an estimate of its potential value.

With the exception of Israel, it is hard to imagine a WhatsApp emerging in any other advanced economy, where regulations, credentialing, and deeply ingrained habits of risk aversion are incompatible with the qualities of experimentation, serendipity, and a why-not mentality that made Koum an overnight billionaire.

Herein lies the core difference between the United States and its major economic competitors—the United States hasn't fallen into their traps. Emerging markets typically fall prey to the middle-income trap, in which countries that achieve a certain level of growth by opening their markets to foreign investment and exploiting cheap labor begin to stumble as rising wages lead to declining cost competitiveness. Europe has fallen into a welfare-state trap, in which increasing numbers of voters become reliant on state benefits that first slow economic growth and ultimately bankrupt themselves. Autocracies such as China and Russia, champions of so-called state capitalism, are being hobbled by a corruption trap, as they allocate capital to politically favored projects, which in turn are prone to inefficiency and corruption, while sharply limiting the free flow of information. Japan is a victim of what can be described as a culture trap: cultural traits that were strengths at one point of its economic development but have since become vices. Loyalty, civic-mindedness, and a sense of national solidarity—all commonly associated with the Japanese— may have much to recommend them, but they are no help to a country that desperately requires more immigration, a greater willingness to break with established norms, more transparent corporate governance, and a revival of economic animal spirits. Just consider: Japan, which in the second half of the twentieth century gave the world everything from bullet trains to the Walkman, now ranks twenty-second in innovation, right between Belgium and Austria, according to the 2013 Global Innovation Index.

Put simply, U.S. economic problems are mostly a consequence of bad—but fixable—policies. The problems faced by much of the rest of the world run much deeper. For reform to happen, something has to break. Incumbents who benefit from existing systems will resist the breaks fiercely. That means that when the breaks do happen they will be profoundly disruptive, potentially violent, and inherently unpredictable. All these breaks may also happen within a relatively short space of time, creating a cascade of trouble.

None of this is good news for Americans, even if it makes the United States appear stronger in comparison with other states. The strength of the American economy cannot in the long term derive from the economic weakness of its trading partners. There is, ultimately, only one economy, and it is the world economy. We are all passengers on the same plane, which needs all of its engines to function in order to fly. What happens as they begin to sputter and then flame out? How do they adapt their foreign policies to periods of economic stagnation or depression?

Historically, the pattern is this: Democracies become more risk-averse. Dictatorships become more risk-prone.

ASSASSIN'S MACE

In 1999, Qiao Liang and Wang Xiangsui, two colonels in the People's Liberation Army, published a remarkable book called *Unrestricted Warfare*. Reacting to the overwhelming U.S. victory in the conventional battle against Saddam Hussein in the 1991 Gulf War, and then to America's subsequent inability to win smaller fights like the one in Mogadishu, Somalia, in 1993, the officers predicted a sea change in the nature of warfare itself. How to adapt? The important thing, they argued, was to know the difference between "fighting the fight that fits one's weapons" and "making the weapons to fit the fight."

"Customizing weapons systems to tactics which are still being explored and studied is like preparing food for a great banquet without knowing who is coming, where the slightest error can lead one far astray," they wrote:

> the most modern military force does not have the ability to control public clamor, and cannot deal with an opponent who does things in an unconventional manner. On the battlefields of the future, the digitized forces may very possibly be like a great cook who is good at cooking lobsters sprinkled with butter[;] when faced with guerrillas who resolutely gnaw corncobs, they can only sigh in despair.[42]

It was an astute observation that would be borne out by U.S. experience in Iraq and Afghanistan. It was also a blueprint for the development of Chinese military strategy. For years, China has focused its military efforts on developing what it calls *sha shou jian*—critical battlefield weapons, also sometimes referred to as the "assassin's mace"—that could deprive the United States of its core battlefield capabilities. One such weapon was a missile that could kill a U.S. spy or communications satellite, which China successfully tested in early 2007. In 2013 the Chinese began fielding an antiship "carrier-killer" ballistic missile, the DF-21D, that could destroy a U.S. carrier as far as 1,700 miles from China's shores—more than enough to stop the United States from coming to Taiwan's defense in the event of war. In 2009, *The Wall Street Journal* reported massive cyberspying on the U.S. electricity grid. "Authorities investigating the intrusions," wrote reporter Siobhan Gorman, "have found software tools left behind that could be used to destroy infrastructure components."[43]

How effective are the new Chinese systems? It's difficult to say until they are tested in battle: as with the Soviet Union, it's important not to buy into Chinese propaganda or overrate their technological capabilities. But then it's also important not to discount them. U.S. Navy admirals have described Chinese ballistic missile capabilities as more sophisticated than America's. In 2006, Hezbollah was able to punch a hole in an Israeli ship using a Chinese-made antiship missile. As for the antisatellite missile test, Richard Fisher, Jr., of the Alexandria, Virginia–based International Assessment and Strategy Center explained it to me this way:

> There are a lot of parts to an anti-satellite kill. You have to track your target precisely. Lofting a kill vehicle and making it arrive at a very specific location at a very high rate of speed is also a tremendous technological problem. This is an ASAT capability that considerably exceeds our own.[44]

But even assuming that the U.S. armed forces retain a wide qualitative edge over the Chinese, it's also worth bearing in mind the military aphorism that "quantity has a quality all its own." In sheer numbers, the

Chinese have always had quantitative advantages: China has nearly one million more men under arms than the United States. In 2002, China's official military budget was $20 billion (though the real figure, according to U.S. estimates, was about $65 billion). By 2014, the official number had risen to $132 billion, the estimated one to $240 billion. The numbers— and the contrast with the United States—are even more impressive considering that China's military budget is not overburdened by personnel costs as that of the United States is.

Indeed, the closer one looks at trends in U.S. military spending, the more worrisome they appear. Even before Defense Secretary Chuck Hagel announced sharp reductions in military spending, the Pentagon was getting ever less of the proverbial bang-for-buck. On September 11, 2001, the U.S. Navy had a fleet of 316 ships. After a decade in which annual spending on the Navy jumped from about $130 billion to over $180 billion, it had just 285 ships.[45] In 2001 the average age of a plane in the U.S. Air Force was twenty-two years. A decade later, it was twenty-six years— about as old as many of the pilots who fly them—mainly because the Pentagon has been unable to field new aircraft in sufficient numbers to replace the older ones. The F-16, arguably the best single-engine jet fighter of all time, first flew in 1974 and was in service with the Air Force by 1978. The single-engine F-35 first flew in 2006 and won't be in service until 2015 at the earliest: it now takes the United States longer to field the next evolution in one-seater jets than it did to put a man on the moon. With the instructive exception of low-cost Predator drones, nearly every major acquisitions program undertaken by the Pentagon over the past decade has been an epic fiasco, from the F-35 to the KC-X aerial refueling tanker to the Littoral Combat Ship. The reasons range from the ever-increasing technical requirements of fielding best-in-class hardware to the ever more burdensome political and bureaucratic demands made on defense contractors. But the effects are worrisome: the United States gets less bang from its buck than ever before, while the cost to our adversaries to field technologies or use techniques that can defeat us is cheaper than ever. Or as Kipling put it in his famous poem about Afghanistan, "Arithmetic on the Frontier":

A scrimmage in a Border Station—
A canter down some dark defile—
Two thousand pounds of education
Drops to a ten-rupee jezail*—

How best to address this problem? Adm. Jonathan Greenert, the chief of naval operations, has suggested that the military needs to invest more in "trucks"—reliable, adaptable, long-lived platforms such as a nuclear aircraft carrier, ballistic missile submarine, or B-52 bomber that can be fitted with new payloads as missions and technologies evolve—than in "luxury sedans," built for a single mission on the basis of existing state-of-the-art technology. One such luxury sedan, the admiral notes, is stealth planes, whose ability to evade detection will diminish as increases in computer power make it easier for an adversary to generate an identifiable, and targetable, radar signature. By contrast, an older plane such as an F-18, with a proven airframe, has shown itself capable of being adapted for use as a fighter, a bomber, an electronic warfare platform, and even an aerial tanker.

Greenert's call for "payloads over platforms"[46] may well become the way the military thinks about its acquisitions for the future as budgets decline and the Pentagon makes a virtue of necessity. But that's over the long term. For the nearer term, terrorists, insurgents, pirates, hackers, "whistleblowers," arms smugglers, and second-rate powers armed with weapons of mass destruction and ballistic missiles will be able to hold the United States inexpensively at risk. This will further whet the American appetite for retreat while encouraging adversaries to test American limits—a classic vicious cycle unlikely to end well.

How will the testing happen? Another precept from *Unrestricted Warfare* suggests an answer. "The new principles of warfare," the authors argue, "are no longer 'using armed force to compel the enemy to submit

---

*   A *jezail* was a handmade musket, typically long-barreled and famously accurate, used by Afghan fighters against the British in the Anglo-Afghan wars of the nineteenth century.

to one's will.'" Instead they define modern warfare as "using *all* means, including armed force *or* non-armed force, military and non-military, and lethal and non-lethal means to compel the enemy to accept one's interest."

Note that the argument turns Clausewitz's famous dictum on its head: To Qiao and Wang, war is not the continuation of politics by other means. Instead, it is *politics*—along with diplomacy, espionage, sabotage, propaganda, economic pressure, and every other instrument of national power—that is the continuation of war by other means. So it has been in China's attempts to assert control over the South China Sea. Its historic claim is based on a (Nationalist) map from 1947 with nine dotted lines supposedly demarcating Chinese sovereignty. It insists that its two-hundred-mile "exclusive economic zone," an artifact of the UN's Law of the Sea, also gives it exclusive military rights—a deliberate misreading of the law that the UN is in no political position to refute. It has used its clout in ASEAN, including political bribes to client states such as Cambodia, to block regional efforts to establish a common set of rules governing the sea. It sends fishing vessels and coast guard ships, many of them secretly armed, to harass foreign naval ships or intrude on foreign waters. It plays games of chicken against foreign militaries; one such game in 2001 resulted in a midair collision between a Chinese fighter and an American P-3 Orion spy plane, resulting in a major international incident. It seizes atolls and semisubmerged barrier reefs and builds permanently manned outposts on them.

The use of ambiguous-aggressive means to achieve territorial ends has so far not resulted in the firing of a single shot—a good example, it would seem, of Sun Tzu's dictum that "to fight and conquer in your battles is not supreme excellence; supreme excellence consists in breaking the enemy's resistance without fighting." Except that the enemy's resistance hasn't been broken.

"At what point do you say 'Enough is enough'?" Benigno Aquino III, the president of the Philippines, wondered aloud in February 2014, on the subject of China's encroachment in the South China Sea. "Well, the world has to say it—remember that the Sudetenland was given in an attempt to appease Hitler to prevent World War II."

Usually it's the Israelis who sound grim warnings that it's 1938 all over again. But in the wake of America's retreat, the Munich analogy is gaining traction in unexpected places. We are on the cusp of global disorder.

JULY 2012:
A SPECK IN THE WATER

★ ★ ★ ★

Woody Island is a speck of land in the middle of the South China Sea, not quite a square mile in size. Over the past eighty years it has been occupied by France, Japan, the Republic of China, the People's Republic of China, South Vietnam, and, after a brief war in 1974, the People's Republic again. Now known as Yongxing to the Chinese (or Phu Lam to the Vietnamese, who still claim it), the island has an airstrip, a harbor, and a few hundred Chinese residents, none native-born, many of whom make their living as fishermen.

Why should anyone care about an obscure tropical island that you can only find on a map with a magnifying glass? Because China cares. On July 23, 2012, Beijing decreed that henceforth the little village of Sansha on Woody Island would be considered a "prefecture-level city" on a par with Chinese megacities such as Harbin and Guangzhou, complete with a mayor, a people's congress, a military garrison—and claims to administer the 720,000 square miles of surrounding waters, an area larger than the Gulf of Mexico. Beijing's coup was protested loudly by Vietnam and more quietly by the U.S. State Department, which fretted that the move ran "counter to collaborative diplomatic efforts to resolve differences" in the South China Sea. In response, Beijing called a U.S. embassy official to the carpet and demanded that the United States "shut up."

China's leaders are fond of advertising their country's "peaceful rise," and the pro-China chorus in the West has sought to engage Beijing as a "responsible stakeholder" in global affairs. Yet in recent years Beijing has provoked tense quasi-military confrontations over disputed waters with Japan, Vietnam, Indonesia, the Philippines, and even the United States, all the while insisting that it has "indisputable sovereignty" over nearly the whole of the sea.

"China is a big country and other countries are small countries," explained Chinese foreign minister Yang Jiechi at a regional summit in 2010. "And that is just a fact."

What is also a fact is that the South China Sea sits on estimated oil reserves of 213 billion barrels and equally massive reserves of natural gas. Fully one third of the world's overall volume of trade passes across the sea every year. Each of the sea's other claimants has reasons to accommodate Beijing even as they resent its bullying habits. China, it is sometimes noted, sees the sea not just as an economic resource and an extension of its sovereign domain, but as the natural basin for a twenty-first-century version of a Greater East Asia Co-Prosperity Sphere, this time under Beijing's sway.

The United States also has core national interests at stake in the South China Sea. America has long stood for freedom of the seas and flatly rejects China's maritime claims. A 1951 mutual defense treaty binds the United States to Manila, a 1960 treaty commits the United States to the defense of Japan and all of its territories, the 1979 Taiwan Relations Act binds the United States to Taipei, and a 2005 Strategic Framework Agreement formalizes a defense relationship with Singapore. U.S. military ties to Hanoi have strengthened dramatically in recent years. Thousands of U.S. service members are permanently based in nearby Okinawa and Guam. As part of the Obama administration's "pivot" to Asia, the United States plans to deploy more than 60 percent of its naval power to the Pacific by the end of the decade.

This would suggest that there is a limit to what the People's Republic can hope to achieve in the South China Sea. In what seems like a textbook illustration of the balance of power, Beijing's aggressiveness has alerted its neighbors to the common threat and drawn them closer to Washington. Perhaps all that would be required to head off future Chinese encroachments is an unequivocal message from Washington that the United States will not tolerate them.

But is the United States seriously prepared to come to the aid of its allies if the stakes involve little islands here or there? Is the theoretical risk of honor lost worth a flesh-and-bones price in lives lost? Should the United States be guaranteeing the security of prosperous countries, thousands of miles off, that probably spend too little on their own defense? "How horrible, fantastic, incredible it is that we should be digging trenches and trying on gas-masks here because of a quarrel in a far-away country between people of whom we know nothing." Such was the rationale of Neville Chamberlain as he confronted a similar set of dilemmas in the early fall of 1938.

And what about China: What does it want? Can its regional and global ambitions be satisfied by foreign concessions, or would those concessions only whet China's geopolitical appetites? A century ago, the world looked at Germany and saw a rising economic and military power in search of some higher national purpose. Failing to find one, it sought the deference and submissiveness it believed was its due. What it got instead was suspicion and resistance, fueling a cycle of resentment that fed on itself and could be whipped into frenzy over peripheral controversies and the smallest perceived slight.

Is that the history the world will be forced once again to reprise?

CHAPTER 9

* * *

A Scenario for Global Disorder

Predicting the future is a lucrative business with a lousy track record. Whether the forecast calls for demographic doom, economic boom, national decline, moral decay, or the rise of a new superpower, there's always a prophecy waiting to be published and marketed. Some of these predictions hold up for a few years; few can stand the test of a decade or two. The literature of "the future" is mostly a compendium of mistakes reflecting the fads of the past.

This isn't to say that there's no point to making predictions. "Plans are useless," Dwight Eisenhower once said, "but planning is indispensable." Just so with predictions: it isn't the forecast itself that has value; it's the *exercise* of forecasting. And the best forecasting is done when you seek the mundane in the seemingly exotic, rather than the exotic in the seemingly mundane.

With that in mind, let's paint a picture of the geopolitics of the near future, as Pax Americana begins to crumble under the weight of isolationist sentiment, nervous allies, and ambitious challengers.

HILLARY INHERITS

It's Christmas Day 2019. Hillary Clinton is president. She's mulling whether to run for a second term. The decision is by no means an easy one. After a blowout victory in the 2016 elections over Kentucky senator Rand Paul, she had been confronted with an endless parade of policy crises, domestic and foreign. Most of these she inherited. As president, she marveled at how powerless she felt to do very much about them.

The root of the problem, paradoxically, lay in the gathering strengths of the U.S. economy. In 2015 the U.S. Federal Reserve, which was already winding down the so-called quantitative easing programs of buying billions in U.S. Treasuries and mortgage-backed securities, began seeing signs of inflation. Though Janet Yellen was inclined to pursue an accommodative monetary policy, she could not ignore the political reality that higher prices were raising the cost of living for ordinary Americans while Wall Street continued to benefit from seemingly endless liquidity. Liberal newspaper columnists, who for years had urged the easiest money possible and mocked inflationary warnings, began instead to declaim against the moral outrage of a Federal Reserve that was taking sides with Wall Street against ordinary wage earners. Interest rates rose slowly at first and then, as the Consumer Price Index continued to rise, sharply.

Most observers assumed the result would be a severe recession in the United States, similar to the one that hit thirty-five years earlier when Paul Volcker was wrestling inflation to the ground. In fact, the immediate effects of higher rates on the U.S. economy were relatively mild, thanks to a corporate sector that had grown lean and disciplined since the Great Recession of 2008.

But the Fed's new direction had an immediate and devastating impact in much of the rest of the world. Higher interest rates meant a stronger dollar; a stronger dollar meant a drop in oil prices, which are globally denominated in dollars. The trend to lower prices was only compounded by the increase in North American supply thanks to the fracking revolution. The Russian economy, already hit by massive capital flight, was forced to start burning through its foreign reserves. The Saudis were hit, too, and fearful: In 2011 they had averted the "contagion" of the Arab Spring with a $130 billion stimulus package on jobs and housing. Now they wondered whether they could do it again as oil revenues ebbed and as the United States became the world's dominant energy producer.

Things were still worse for the Chinese economy. Though Beijing welcomed lower energy prices, the country's monetary policy was linked to the Fed's through the yuan's so-called crawling peg. As the cost of borrowing went up, the cost of servicing debt went up, too. A tide of bankruptcies swept over China's overleveraged companies and local governments. Capital began to flee the country, shrinking the deposit base of banks while leaving them with trillions of dollars in nonperforming loans. China's formidable foreign reserves were of no great help, since they were either invested in China's (suddenly illiquid) banks or otherwise held in U.S. Treasuries, which Beijing didn't want to sell down for fear of giving up the best assets in its balance sheet and throwing good money after bad.

How was the United States to respond to the great global markets meltdown of 2016? During the first Clinton administration the United States had responded swiftly to a variety of emerging-market crises. But in an election year there was no repeating that history. "America is not going to bankrupt itself bailing out reckless, hostile foreign governments while Americans are struggling at home," insisted Clinton as she cruised toward her 2016 nomination—a rare point of agreement with Senator Paul.

If anything, the troubles of other countries, China's most of all, lifted American spirits. Years of declinist talk finally came to an end. Foreign capital poured into the United States, buoying the Dow Jones Industrial Average and shoring up the high-end real-estate market. The U.S. Treasury had no trouble with bond auctions despite the usual dire warnings about long-term entitlement liabilities. America's share of global GDP rose as China's shrank, helped in part by sharp downward revisions of Chinese official growth figures going back twenty years.

America's apparent prosperity, however, was strictly relative. The unemployment rate hovered at a modest 6 percent, but that was mainly because so many Americans had dropped permanently out of the workforce.

Less employment also meant a smaller tax base just as baby boomers were retiring and the costs of their entitlements were booming. The debt-to-GDP ratio, just over 70 percent when Obama took office, reached a historically unprecedented 120 percent as he entered his last year as president.

That statistic alone had an effect on America's foreign policy outlook. What had begun as a tendency in the first years of the Obama presidency to eschew foreign entanglements and avoid even limited military strikes had, by 2016, hardened into a new national consensus. Why, Americans wondered, did the United States continue to spend nearly $8 billion a year annually to station close to fifty thousand troops in Germany, Europe's richest and largest nation, or an equivalent sum for our troops in Japan? In February 2016 Japan's prime minister paid his yearly visit to the Yasukuni Shrine to Japan's war dead. Ordinarily such visits had caused outrage in Asia while prompting muted protests from Washington. Not so this time: "Japan cannot continue to ask for America's protection while it honors war criminals and gratuitously provokes its neighbors," warned Joe Biden on *Meet the Press*. The Japanese government bristled at the warning, with one former senior adviser of the prime minister penning a defiant op-ed in the *Asahi Shimbun*: "Why should France, with no real enemies, have a 'right' to nuclear weapons while we in Japan, faced with an ever more hostile China and a Russia that continues to occupy Japanese territory, enjoy no such right?"

Ordinarily, episodes such as this one would have been followed by efforts to cool tensions. Not now. One well-known American foreign affairs pundit derided Japan as a nation of "old people, old corporations and old ideas, politically hidebound and fundamentally racist, doomed by debt and demography, seeking international relevance and national renewal through a policy of moral provocation and resurgent militarism." Why, the pundit asked, should the United States feel obligated by a decades-old security commitment to a moribund nation? It was a logic that applied to Taiwan, too. The island had long been building closer economic ties to the mainland while spending a pittance on its own defense. Why defend those who won't defend themselves?

As these points were being widely discussed in the United States,

Beijing made a sudden move: it seized Kinmen Island, a Taiwanese enclave just a few miles off the coast of Fujian Province. Better known to Americans as Quemoy, it had been one of the great flash points of the early Cold War when Mao bombarded the Nationalist enclave with artillery and Eisenhower sent the U.S. Seventh Fleet to help in its relief. But Taipei had chosen to demilitarize the island in the 1990s, and it had become a popular day-trip destination for Chinese from the mainland. Few people gave it a thought, until three battalions of Chinese marines seized it bloodlessly in February 2017, just weeks after Clinton's inauguration.

By seizing Kinmen, Beijing had sought to tip the psychological balance of power in its favor, without quite provoking a genuine military crisis. It also hoped to deflect rising public discontent with the country's sharply deteriorating economy and suffocating controls on the flow of information and exchange of ideas. It succeeded only too well. Taking Kinmen sparked a tidal wave of patriotic enthusiasm that Beijing found difficult to contain. "Patriotic Associations," often with ties to senior Chinese military officers but also populated by university professors and liberal-minded intellectuals, demanded immediate reunification of the Motherland: by getting to the right of the Politburo, the associations also became a vehicle for venting public dissatisfaction with the "pusillanimous men of Zhongnanhai," referring to the leadership compound in Beijing. For historians, it recalled the politics of Wilhelmine Germany, in which the kaiser, at once impetuous and insecure, found himself pushed toward increasingly aggressive maneuvers by a public opinion he found hard to ignore.

Beijing also miscalculated the effects of its Kinmen conquest on its Asian rivals. China's leaders had expected a weak U.S. response, which would unnerve and confuse America's allies. What they got was an American nonresponse: no U.S. carriers being sailed through the Taiwan Strait; no arms sales to Taipei; not even a formal protest at the Security Council. The administration's seeming indifference to Taiwan led leaders in Tokyo, Seoul, Manila, and Hanoi to conclude that the United States could not be counted on to ride to anybody's rescue. Within weeks of Kinmen's conquest the Vietnamese defense minister was in Moscow to arrange the purchase of submarines, missile boats, and top-of-the-line fighters. Japan's prime minister paid a visit to Seoul, dramatically falling to his knees in apology for Japanese wartime abuses in Korea. In exchange the two capitals agreed to a series of joint military exercises.

Then Japan made an even more unexpected move: under cover of darkness, the Japanese navy landed troops on the Senkaku Islands. The move was meant to forestall a Kinmen-style takeover of the contested islands by China. Instead, it led to a wave of rioting and violence against Japanese targets—tourists, diplomatic facilities, schools—throughout China. A mob set fire to the Japanese School of Dalian, leaving more than thirty children dead. The State Department issued a statement calling on "both sides" to "show restraint."

A MIDEAST ARMS RACE

Meanwhile, an election was held in Iran. Actually, two elections.

In June 2017, Hassan Rouhani won a second term as president of Iran. Few Iranians could have been dissatisfied with his performance. Thanks to a nuclear agreement with the West, in which Iran formally pledged never to build nuclear weapons or enrich uranium above a 20 percent level in exchange for a complete lifting of sanctions, Iran had achieved near normalization in its diplomatic relations with the world, including a U.S. diplomatic mission in Tehran. Billions in foreign direct investment, much of it going to the modernization of Iran's decrepit energy infrastructure, flowed into the country. Core nuclear capabilities were preserved, under UN monitoring, and the risk of an Israeli strike was averted. Bashar al-Assad remained in control of most of Syria. The withdrawal of U.S. forces from Afghanistan was followed by a Kabul-Tehran pact that gave Iran broad sway in Afghan politics. Iran continued to enjoy decisive influence in Iraqi politics, and dominated much of Lebanon through its proxy Hezbollah. It was a diplomatic tour de force worthy of a Bismarck or a Palmerston.

Two weeks after Rouhani's reelection came news of a more consequential sort: Ali Khamenei, for twenty-eight years the Supreme Leader of Iran, succumbed to prostate cancer just weeks shy of his seventy-eighth birthday. It would be the first transition of real power in Iran since the Ayatollah Khomeini's death in 1989. Hopes ran high in the West that the regime would leave the post vacant or revise the constitution to make it ceremonial, thereby giving Rouhani more effective power and turning the Islamic Republic into something approaching a genuine democracy.

However, not all Iranians were prepared to oblige Western wishes. Rouhani had always been viewed with suspicion by members of the ultra-conservative religious establishment and their allies in the powerful Revolutionary Guard Corps (IRGC). They were not about to abandon the concept of *Velayat-e faqih*, the Guardianship of the Islamic Jurist, that was at the heart of the Imam Khomeini's teachings. The Assembly of Experts, tasked with appointing the Supreme Leader, moved swiftly to install Khamenei's forty-eight-year-old son, Mojtaba, as the new Guardian Jurist.

The appointment did not go down well. Although trained as a cleric, Mojtaba did not have serious scholarly credentials, much less the rank of an ayatollah. The brazenly dynastic nature of the succession reminded many Iranians of politics in Saudi Arabia. Mojtaba was also widely believed to be one of the richest—and thus most corrupt—men in the country. And he was the man who had orchestrated the theft of the 2009 Iranian presidential election that brutally reinstalled Mahmoud Ahmadinejad for a second term.

What sort of figure would Mojtaba prove to be on the international stage? Many Western analysts painted him as a "pragmatic conservative" in the mold of his father's chief rival, Hashemi Rafsanjani. But that ignored the troubled psychology of a weak son trying to fill a powerful father's shoes. Mojtaba knew that he was viewed as an intellectual pretender by the religious establishment. What he did have was the support of the Revolutionary Guards, which was contingent on his promotion of an aggressive foreign policy, a repressive domestic policy, and continued financial favors, both institutional and personal. In September of that year, inspectors from the International Atomic Energy Agency reported that Iran had exceeded stipulated levels of uranium enrichment, although it was unclear whether this was by design or miscalculation. A month later, an Iranian opposition group alleged that Iran was building a secret plutonium plant, duplicating a similar facility in the city of Arak that had been mothballed in 2015 as part of a comprehensive "agreed framework" deal with the UN Security Council. The IAEA demanded access to the site; Iran refused. The stage was set for a confrontation.

It was just at this moment that the prime minister of Bahrain was assassinated. The assassin was a Shiite woman whose father had been tortured to death by the regime following the abortive 2011 uprising against the ruling Sunni family. The murder led to a wave of arrests, which in turn brought tens of thousands of protesters into the streets. At three in the morning on August 31, 2017, the Saudi ambassador to the United States placed a call to Secretary of State Samantha Power, informing her that Saudi troops would occupy the little kingdom, connected to Saudi Arabia by a sixteen-mile causeway. "You're either with us or you are against us," the ambassador curtly informed Power. The State Department immediately issued a statement calling on all sides to show restraint.

What followed was a massacre of Shiite demonstrators. The Clinton administration was unequivocal in its verbal condemnation. The Bahraini-Saudi government was equally unequivocal in its response: the U.S. Fifth Fleet would no longer be welcome in Bahrain. U.S. ships and aircraft were given seventy-two hours to leave Bahraini territory. U.S. servicemen living in Bahrain were given a week to pack up. The U.S. naval base was to be vacated in a month.

The Saudi seizure of Bahrain wasn't altogether unexpected: they had done as much six years earlier, and there was no question of their losing the island to a Shiite uprising when Iran continued to make claims on the place itself.

Then came the real shocker. On September 18, Riyadh announced that it had detonated a nuclear weapon at a previously secret test site in the remote Asir Mountains, near Yemen. For years, Riyadh had been dropping loud hints that they owned a share of Pakistan's nuclear arsenal and would respond forcefully to Iran's nuclearization, which they now took as an all-but-accomplished fact, despite Iran's diplomatic pledge. Yet, as with India's nuclear test in 1998, the Saudi test caught the CIA by surprise. Now U.S. policy makers were forced to reckon with the thought that America's nuclear diplomacy had failed not with its enemy but with its longtime ally.

Among the American public the reaction was a mixture of disgust and helplessness. Scenes of Saudi soldiers gunning down civilians during the Massacre of Manama were impossible to ignore. So, too, were the implications of Riyadh's abrupt nuclearization. Then again, commentators were quick to note that the United States, which had surpassed Saudi Arabia as the world's top oil producer two years earlier, was less dependent on Mideast oil than ever. What, then, was the point of an alliance with a country that was becoming ever more unpalatable morally even as it became ever more irrelevant strategically?

Such was the conventional wisdom in the late fall of 2017, and it bore on U.S. reaction to news that Iran continued to violate its obligations under the Agreed Framework. Why should the United States put itself at risk to enforce the agreement? Why wasn't Iran within its rights to seek a nuclear balance with its Sunni rival across the Gulf? Wouldn't a Saudi-Iranian nuclear standoff lead to a stable balance of power?

The Saudis saw it differently. Their crackdown in Bahrain was not merely a matter of preventing a small neighbor from falling into Tehran's orbit; it also was meant as a demonstration to the kingdom's own restive Shiite population that Riyadh would tolerate no protest. But the kingdom's hand was weakened by the decline in the price of oil; it could no longer afford the kind of expensive job schemes and public bribes that had kept the Arab Spring at bay in 2011. Going forward, the survival of the House of Saud would have to depend on the stick, not the carrot.

Saudi Arabia's declining revenues also spelled trouble for Egypt. The military regime of Abdel Fattah el-Sisi had never fully consolidated its grip on the country: mob violence against Coptic Christians led to an accelerating exodus of the population, further gutting what remained of the country's merchant middle class. Attacks on foreigners had an equally devastating effect on tourism, once the country's most reliable source of

foreign revenue. The Sinai was a no-man's-land for extremists and smugglers, fearfully policed by Egyptian military units and occasionally
intruded on by Israeli drones carrying out strikes with Cairo's tacit consent. The regime could ride out those storms, thanks to the subventions
of Riyadh and other friends in the Gulf. But now the financial flow was
turning into a trickle.

In January 2018 the Islamic Waqf in Jerusalem alleged that the Israeli
government intended to use a newly discovered ancient passage under
the Temple Mount to destroy the Al-Aqsa Mosque from below. A melee
between Muslim protesters and Israeli riot police led to the deaths of four
Palestinian boys. The Arab quarter of the Old City, and then Arab East
Jerusalem, exploded in riots. By nightfall, protests had spread not only to
Palestinian cities in Gaza and the West Bank, but also to the Israeli-Arab
towns in the Galilee. The long-anticipated third intifada had begun.

If the weapon of choice for the first intifada was the boy with the
stone, and of the second the bomber with the suicide vest, the third intifada was defined by the marcher with a key, symbolizing the Palestinian
demand for the "right of return" to pre-1967 Israel. Concluding that they
could never hope to prevail against Israel through violent means, Palestinian leaders sought instead to win through fierce moral pressure. Two
weeks after the Old City riot, an estimated sixty thousand residents of
East Jerusalem marched silently and peacefully in roughly one hundred
separate columns through the streets of West Jerusalem, doing nothing
more than holding up old keys. The influential Israeli commentator Anshel Pfeffer[1] got straight to the point: "If the Arab residents of Jerusalem
are truly an integral part of this 'united' city," he observed in his column,
"then why did the throats of Jewish Jerusalemites constrict in terror as
their near neighbors walked quietly, peacefully and lawfully down our
(supposedly) shared streets?" At a stroke, the march made the case for a
redivided city more effectively than twenty-five years' worth of fruitless
negotiations. A month later, another 100,000 Palestinians, also holding keys, marched toward the Qalandia checkpoint separating Ramallah
from Jerusalem. This time they sought to force their way through the

checkpoint. Israelis responded first with tear gas, then with rubber bullets. More than a dozen Palestinians suffocated or were crushed to death in the chaos; the scene was captured by hundreds of camera phones and instantly posted to YouTube. Within a week, student governments at more than a dozen U.S. college campuses approved boycott and divestment motions by wide margins. Within weeks, similar marches, in similar numbers and with similar results, were started in Bethlehem, Nablus, Tulkarm, and Jenin. The Palestinians had at last figured out how to apply maximum pressure on Israel's Achilles' heel: its susceptibility to moral reproach.

Coming so soon after Saudi Arabia's nuclear breakout and the unresolved Iranian nuclear crisis, the third intifada stirred panic in the Israeli public. Its worst nightmares were coming to pass in rapid-fire succession. Then came another nightmare: President Clinton, along with all her European counterparts and most media commentators, saw the intifada as an opportunity to demand Israeli acceptance of a Palestinian state within the 1967 borders and with East Jerusalem as its capital. Secretary Power was dispatched to Israel to deliver the message to Prime Minister Moshe Ya'alon that Israel had a fundamental choice to make: accept a Palestinian state within the 1967 borders or risk a profound diplomatic rupture with the United States. The Palestinian Authority immediately announced that it was prepared to accept any agreement that left it in possession of East Jerusalem and the West Bank with "mutually agreed swaps," and furthermore that it would also accept a narrow Israeli troop deployment along the Jordan River for five years. It also agreed to recognize Israel as "the nation-state of the Jews." In the meantime, the massive Palestinian marches and protests continued.

In early April 2018, a series of seismic events, each at precisely one o'clock in the afternoon on four successive days, were detected in the desert of southern Iran. The Islamic Republic announced that it had tested four nuclear devices, and that it would not hesitate to share them with Hezbollah. The scale of the test suggested that Iran's total arsenal was several times larger, and that it had fielded it over the space of several years even as it pretended to abide by the terms of the nuclear agreement.

The Crumbling Continent

In the spring of 2017 presidential elections were held in France. Conservative leader Nicolas Sarkozy handily defeated incumbent François Hollande in the first round of balloting. The real shock was the second-place finisher, Marine Le Pen of the Front National, who went on to take 34 percent of the vote in the second round. When her father, Jean-Marie Le Pen, made it to the second round against Jacques Chirac in 2002, he had scored just 18 percent to Chirac's 82 percent.

The resurgence of neofascism in Europe had long been predicted; now there was no doubting its arrival. In Spain, where youth unemployment had hovered around 50 percent for nearly a decade, there was a powerful revival of the cult of Francisco Franco, mostly among those too young to remember his dictatorship. In Antwerp, the xenophobic Vlaams Belang party dominated the politics of Flanders and pressed for the dissolution of Belgium. In Greece, the neo-Nazi Golden Dawn party, which took 0.3 percent of the vote in 2009, captured 17 percent in 2017.

Fascism wasn't the only resurging radicalism. In Portugal, which had lost more than a tenth of its population to emigration in just five years, the Communist Party overtook the Socialists as the main party of the left. Muslim neighborhoods throughout the continent—Neukölln in Berlin, Seine-Saint-Denis near Paris, Tower Hamlets in London—were fast turning into vast self-governing enclaves, complete with neighborhood vigilante groups that enforced strict dress codes on women and frequently assaulted outsiders who stumbled accidentally onto their streets.

Still, the core problem of European politics in 2017 didn't lie at the extreme ends of the political spectrum, but with the collapsing center. For years, European leaders had misdiagnosed the nature of the European disease and therefore failed to cure it. Europe did not, fundamentally, have a "debt" crisis. Nor did it have a euro problem, either: the common currency had proved far more resilient than the skeptics had ever thought possible. What Europe had was a growth crisis. Years had been wasted on the wrong cures: liquidity injections into insolvent economies; higher taxes on businesses and individuals already groaning under the weight of existing tax regimes; pan-European fiscal "coordination" mechanisms that were never seriously enforced. Europe needed regulatory regimes favorable to business (and job) creation and tax regimes that encouraged work and investment over idleness and evasion. But these straightforward expedients had only timid political support and faced ferocious ideological resistance from trade unions, public intellectuals, and the beneficiaries of the existing system of job protections, subsidies, handouts, set-asides. From the European Commission, the constant refrain was that Europe needed "More Europe," though the commission could never quite define what "more" meant beyond greater centralization of authority in Brussels.

"Europe seems to have embraced the wrong model of evolution," noted one astute German commentator in a 2017 op-ed. "Nothing in the current Europeanist mind-set ever seems to change until it is struck by some sudden calamity, as if it were an asteroid hitting us from outer space. We do not grow, we do not learn, we do not bend, we do not adapt. We merely alternate between stagnation and catastrophe."

The author would not have to wait long for the crisis to arrive. Germany, supposedly the paymaster of Europe and the engine of the continent's economy, had for years managed only tepid growth. Its economy slipped into recession in the second quarter of 2017; conditions became more acute with each passing quarter. In September 2018, one of Germany's state-owned *Landesbanken*, with a quarter trillion euros in assets, collapsed.

For years there had been whispered worries about the quality of supervision and management in Germany's *Landesbanken*, the publicly owned regional development banks that traditionally lent to Germany's state governments and local businesses, often for politically favored projects. In 2008 the banks had to be bailed out, but problems persisted. The *Landesbanken* would not merge. Larger private banks muscled into their core business. Like all European banks, they had been bruised by the collapse of emerging markets. Their management, more like a civil service, did not draw on the best and the brightest in the financial world. And their balance sheets—accounting for 15 percent of Germany's total banking assets—were stuffed with bad loans. Though the bank had survived various regulatory "stress tests," the markets quickly realized they were dealing with a zombie bank.

By itself, the failure of one bank would not have spelled serious trouble for Germany. But if one *Landesbank* was a zombie, the others had to be zombies too, or so the markets assumed. How was the German government, in a weakened economy, going to engineer a bailout of close to a trillion euros? It couldn't. Like Credit-Anstalt, the Austrian bank whose 1931 failure created a worldwide financial panic, the *Landesbanken* were both too big to fail and too big to be rescued.

For years, Germany had been the one functioning motor of the Eurozone's economy. No longer. Consumed by their own economic distress, Germans were in no mood to shoulder the burden of being Europe's paymaster. Talk of European "solidarity" suddenly seemed cheap: henceforward it would be every country for itself.

And every region. In June 2018 the people of Flanders voted in a referendum to declare their independence. The Belgian government would almost surely have opposed the move, but the country had not had a prime minister in two years. The new Flemish government's first order of business was to pass a law deporting noncitizen immigrants with criminal records. A month later, Catalonia followed Flanders into independence. In Italy, the secessionist Northern League won decisive victories in regional elections in Lombardy, Emilia-Romagna, and the Veneto. Commentators mused, as they had for years, about the "Europe of regions," but most of the victors in these elections were openly hostile to the European Union itself. For them, Europe was neither a political entity nor even a common civilization; it was, as Bismarck once put it, merely a "geographic expression."

RUSSIA REVANCHIST

However grave Europe's economic crisis, it was as nothing compared with the situation in Russia. The fall in energy prices had devastated the country's finances. And Russia's belated success in improving its energy infrastructure, slowing the depletion rates at its largest fields and opening new fields, only contributed to the problem: the combination of higher U.S. interest rates, global economies in recession, and a supply glut only sent prices lower. Opponents of the regime had long assumed that an economic crisis would inevitably weaken and perhaps cripple Putin's grip on power. Putin's answer was to crack down harder, stoke the fires of Russian nationalism and Soviet nostalgia, and look for opportunities to expand his influence in his near abroad. Europe's disarray and America's inward turn convinced him that he would face little opposition for doing so.

Where to strike next? One potential target was north Kazakhstan: ethnic Russians made up a plurality of the population in a territory about the size of Tennessee, and Putin had taken care to cultivate ties with local Russian nationalists. But would the game be worth the candle? There was little of strategic value there, and a population of about half a million people. More tempting were the Baltics, particularly Latvia and Estonia, whose governments had been hostile to him personally and where ethnic Russians made up more than a quarter of the overall population. Both countries were members of the European Union, and of NATO, and any attack on them would legally compel the Atlantic Alliance, including the United States, to come to their defense. But would the United States do so? The Russian army could, if it wished, seize both states in the space of a weekend; nothing the United States could do short of nuclear war or a massive conventional counterattack could stop it. Would Washington, in its isolationist mood, really risk a major military confrontation for the sake of little Riga and Tallinn? The notion was preposterous. The real prize for taking either state would be to showcase NATO's powerlessness, divide Europe from the United States, and further divide Eastern from Western Europe.

As Putin mulled his options, an event took place in the capital of Belarus. A small protest in Minsk's Independence Square against the long rule of Alexander Lukashenko was violently broken up by interior ministry police. Six weeks later, an anonymous Manifesto was sent as a text message and an e-mail to every Belarusian with a mobile phone or an e-mail address, as well as to several hundred Western reporters. Signed "Kościuszko," the name of the Belarusian-born eighteenth-century freedom fighter, the Manifesto made its sympathies plain:

PEOPLE OF BELARUS!

ENOUGH TO DICTATORSHIP! ENOUGH TO DECADES OF THIS THIEVING, CRIMINAL REGIME! ENOUGH TO POVERTY AND BACKWARDNESS! OUR FUTURE BELONGS TO THE WEST!

The Manifesto outlined a ten-point plan aimed at Lukashenko's overthrow, including nationwide work stoppages and strikes, spontaneous protests, road blockades, and "bloodless sabotage by those with the access and the means."

At first, the Manifesto was treated as a curiosity, even though the scale and technical sophistication required to disseminate it were impressive. But the texts and e-mails continued day after day, despite the best efforts of the interior ministry's experts to block them and track the source. And there was more. What began as "Kościuszko's" bold-faced sloganeering quickly turned into a kind of Belarusian WikiLeaks, with detailed personal information about the regime's top people, ranging from hidden assets and offshore bank account numbers to e-mail exchanges with mistresses. One revelation regarding a senior interior ministry official's secret gay life led the man to commit suicide. Another revelation, about an affair between a general and a colonel's wife, led the latter to shoot his commander. It was revolution by pasquinade: whoever he was, Kościuszko seemed to be taking a page from Gabriel García Márquez's novel *In Evil Hour*, in which a little South American town is transformed after gossipy posters, revealing scandalous personal secrets, are pasted all over town, provoking the mayor to impose martial law.

As each disclosure found its way to the inboxes of the people of Belarus the protests began to swell. By mid-July, Minsk's Victory Square was occupied by tens of thousands of people demanding Lukashenko's downfall. Riot police were ordered to attack the crowds. They refused.

Hundreds of them decided instead to join the protesters, publicly pledging to defend the crowd. A brigade of regular army troops stationed near Minsk was ordered by its commander to remain in its barracks.

It was at this point that a desperate Lukashenko issued a declaration of martial law—to save Belarus from "digital anarchists" and "Western saboteurs"—and called on Putin to intervene. The Kremlin had been preparing for weeks. On August 7 the first column of Russian tanks rolled across the border near Smolensk, while Russian paratroopers seized the international airport at Minsk. Protest leaders in Victory Square called on demonstrators to march on the presidential palace; as they did, helicopter gunships flew in low and menacingly overhead, but the demonstrators continued their march. Approaching the palace, they were fired upon. Within minutes, scores of corpses littered the road. The scenes were broadcast globally. A spokesman for the Kremlin went before cameras to announce that Russia was intervening to preserve the sovereignty of Belarus against "neofascist bandits."

The invasion of Belarus elicited only muted reaction in the West. Washington and European capitals denounced the violence as a matter of course. But unlike in Ukraine in 2014, there was no embattled democracy to defend against territorial aggression. "What has happened in Belarus is tragic, and I deplore it," said one Republican senator. "But it does not enlarge Moscow's sphere of influence, it does not change the balance of power in Europe, and it does not engage vital American interests." The United States imposed travel bans on Russian officials and several dozen Kremlin-connected oligarchs while urging NATO states to do likewise; the British government, fearing the effects of such a ban on their economy, declined to follow. Secretary Power was sent on a tour of Warsaw and the Baltic states as a show of American support. Asked by Polish prime minister Radek Sikorski just what, concretely, the United States would do in the event that Russia next attacked one of the Baltic states, she insisted that Putin knew his own limits and wouldn't dare attack a NATO state.

In January 2019, obscene anti-Russian graffiti defaced an Orthodox church in Tallinn. Then an Orthodox cemetery in the Russian-speaking Estonian town of Narva, right on the Russian border, was desecrated.

Several days later, an Estonian diplomat in Moscow was charged with rap-
ing and murdering a Russian prostitute. Each of these stories, coming in
rapid succession, led the news on Russian TV and in all the major papers.

IRAN IMPLODES

In March 2019, a violent public protest erupted in the city of Sanandaj,
the capital of the province of Iranian Kurdistan, following the torture
and execution in Tehran of several Kurdish political activists, including a
Sunni cleric accused of collaborating with PJAK, an anti-Iranian Kurdish
guerrilla group operating out of Iraq. Iran's systematic repression of its
Kurdish minority was an old story, but the brutality with which the regime suppressed the protests in Sanandaj was nevertheless notable: several
of the protest leaders were tied to military vehicles and dragged, half naked and initially alive, through the streets of the town.

This time, however, the shock tactics didn't work: far from quelling
the protests, the violence provoked Iranian Kurds to respond by seizing
army outposts and ransacking the local headquarters of the interior ministry. Within weeks the entire province was in a state of open revolt.

Tehran had always had to deal with its many restive minorities who,
collectively, accounted for about half of Iran's population. Typically, however, it dealt with one minority at a time. But the Kurdish revolt seemed
to have an electrifying effect on other minorities. In Tabriz, the capital of
Iran's Azeri provinces, more than one thousand demonstrators held a solidarity rally in the city's main park, only to be violently dispersed by Basij
militiamen. In Zahedan, the ethnic Balochi city on the opposite end of
the country, a Sunni mob set fire to a half dozen Shiite mosques. The regime's response was to bulldoze more than twenty Sunni mosques in the
neighborhoods from which the mobs had gathered.

Nobody doubted that it was the new Supreme Leader who ordered
and oversaw the regime's reprisals. But middle-class Iranians were stunned
when Rouhani delivered equally aggressive remarks in parliament, warning that every demonstrator would be branded *mohareb*—an enemy of
God—a designation that all but guaranteed a death sentence. The threat

struck a raw nerve. Rouhani was the regime's creature after all: when it came to domestic repression, the difference between "moderate" and "hardline" was a distinction without a difference. Within a week, hundreds of Iranians known for their politically liberal leanings were arrested and taken to the city's Evin prison. Tehranis, who ordinarily would have little sympathy for rebellious provincials, poured into the streets in protest. By nightfall, tens of thousands of demonstrators had occupied Azadi Square, waving large green banners. Basijis who ventured into the square were seized from their motorbikes and beaten up by the crowds. Uniformed policemen joined the demonstrators, helping fend off Basiji attacks. Reports surfaced of regular army units refusing orders to suppress the protests and of a senior Revolutionary Guard officer being shot dead as he sought to take charge of a mutinous army barracks.

Washington viewed these events with a sense of satisfaction—and hope for an opening. "We will not remain silent in our support for the people of Iran," Clinton said in a White House statement, an implicit rebuke to her predecessor's reluctance to speak up during the "Green Revolution" of 2009. "The United States stands squarely with the brave people of Iran, from Tabriz to Tehran, demanding their freedom." The White House also began examining its options for providing Iranians in revolt with genuine assistance. A swift and successful revolt against the Islamic Republic would, Clinton judged, neutralize the threat Iran posed to global security and provide the United States with a desperately needed geopolitical victory in the world. As Revolutionary Guards forces were called up to gain control of the streets of Tehran, the regular army was routed in Sanandaj and other towns in Iranian Kurdistan. The liberation struggle had begun. Demonstrators took heart at the news that victory over the regime was possible. The protests intensified. Violence by the Basij was met with violence in return.

The regime, however, had powerful resources. The Revolutionary Guards were well disciplined, well equipped, well funded, and convinced of their cause. Many of the ordinary Iranians who had been sympathetic to the Green Revolution in 2009 feared Iran's becoming another Syria— endless war leading to bottomless misery—and were not eager to join in an uprising even as they disliked the regime. The religious establishment in Qom, though privately offended by Mojtaba's elevation, nonetheless viewed the rebellion as a Sunni-led plot and publicly lent their support to the regime. And the regime had control of a nuclear arsenal, though how it might wield it, and against whom, was anyone's guess.

The fighting intensified. Scores of regular army units not controlled by the IRGC defected en masse to an umbrella opposition group, the Iranian Freedom Front, or IFF. Tehran, like Damascus several years earlier, became a patchwork of neighborhoods separated according to their opposition or support for the regime. In Shiraz, a suicide bombing in the historic Nasir al-Mulk Mosque was blamed, improbably, on a cell of Iranian Jews; it led to a pogrom in the old Jewish quarter in the city, in which more than one hundred mainly elderly Jews were murdered. Another twenty-five Jews were publicly hanged as the alleged ringleaders of the plot.

The Shiraz pogrom received considerable international attention. But it was only one in a long succession of atrocities: artillery attacks and bombing runs on rebel-held neighborhoods; Revolutionary Guards taken prisoner and beheaded; women raped; children shot. Refugees began spilling over Iran's borders; more than thirty thousand into Turkey in a single day. Each passing wave of refugees brought stories of a steep descent into anarchy. In April, President Clinton, fearing a repetition of her predecessor's error in Syria, ordered the CIA to begin covertly reaching out to the IFF and providing them with nonlethal, but militarily useful, aid: body armor, night-vision goggles, secure communications equipment. By May, the president reached the decision to begin providing lethal aid as well, including high-powered sniper rifles and shoulder-fired antitank missiles.

News of the covert aid quickly leaked. The Iranian government warned that it would hold Washington directly accountable for supporting the insurgents. In early June, more than a dozen American tourists visiting the ancient city of Ephesus, in western Turkey, died after a bomb attached to their tour bus was detonated. Fragments of the bomb had markings in Farsi. Clinton called for a resolution condemning Iran in the

UN Security Council but was blocked by Russia and China. The administration reacted by increasing the supply of arms to the IFF, hoping for a swift resolution. In an interview on background, one senior administration official saw only an upside for the United States: "A swift victory would be good for our interests, but an interminable civil war could be even better."

In fact, the American aid proved highly effective. The insurgents made good use of night-vision goggles and sniper rifles to ambush the Guards and target their commanders. A significant victory for the insurgents came in July, when the foreign minister was assassinated at long range in the Tehran airport as he returned from a trip to Moscow to coordinate Russian military aid. Barely a week later, a sniper's bullet took out Iran's defense minister.

More disturbing was an attack by an unidentified insurgent group on the Iranian nuclear reactor at the port of Bushehr, which failed to do significant damage to the reactor itself but raised the alarming possibility of a terrorist-induced Chernobyl. Western media began to speculate about the possibility of Western military intervention to seize Iran's nuclear stockpile. The speculation registered at the highest levels of the Iranian regime, and rose to paranoia when Israel's housing minister was quoted at a dinner party suggesting that Israel needed to consider a "nuclear 1967," a reference to Israel's preemptive strikes on the Egyptian and Syrian air forces in the Six-Day War. The minister was reprimanded for the remark by Prime Minister Ya'alon, but the Israeli government was clearly alarmed about the fate of Iran's nuclear weapons and appeared to have contingency plans to seize or destroy them in air strikes or commando raids. As with so many Israeli "secrets," the outlines of these plans quickly came into the public domain. Nor was Washington quiet about its own contingency planning: "We have specific and sophisticated methods to ensure that Iran will never succeed in using its weapons against any adversary," Clinton said at a press conference. The remarks echoed loudly with Mojtaba Khamenei and the senior ranks of the IRGC, who were now beginning to confront the possibility of a use-or-lose scenario for the arsenal they had struggled for decades to acquire.

In October, the Ayatollah Movahhedi-Kermani addressed the subject while leading Friday prayers in Tehran. "The Global Arrogance will learn soon enough that we are not fools; we have anticipated their designs. They shake their stick into a hornet's nest." The statement, which earlier would have been dismissed as mere propaganda, no longer seemed entirely rhetorical. The idea that the regime could lose the civil war was increasingly plausible. If they did lose, would they simply go quietly? Or would they exit in a blaze of fanatical glory, a kind of Islamist Götterdämmerung? It was one thing to argue that the Islamic Republic would never risk its survival by using its nuclear weapons. But would it use them when it knew its destruction was assured? It was a sharply unsettling possibility that had rarely been discussed as Americans had lulled themselves into thinking they could live with a nuclear Iran.

Within a month of the ayatollah's sermon, rebels had taken complete control of Tabriz, Shiraz, and Isfahan, and were close to controlling Mashhad, Iran's second city. Much of Tehran was outside of regime control. The balance of forces began to tip decisively toward the side of the insurgency. In early November, President Rouhani called for talks with the opposition. He was assassinated the next day. In his place, Mojtaba appointed Ahmad Vahidi, who had served as Mahmoud Ahmadinejad's defense minister and was widely suspected of coordinating the regime's underground ties to Al Qaeda, as interim president. Vahidi vowed that the regime would continue to fight: "We will triumph, whether it is in this life or the next."

In early December the Israeli government notified the Clinton administration that it would not wait on events and was prepared to undertake a preemptive strike using all weapons at its disposal on Iran's suspected nuclear sites, industrial as well as military. Clinton pleaded for time to consider.

What had possessed her, she wondered that Christmas, to run for president in the first place?

NOVEMBER 2009:
"PEAK OIL"

★　　★　　★　　★

It was the fall of 2009, and the end of the fossil-fuel era was at hand—or so said the experts.

"The world is much closer to running out of oil than official estimates admit," reported *The Guardian* newspaper, citing the testimony of a whistleblower at the International Energy Agency. "The senior official claims the U.S. has played an influential role in encouraging the watchdog to underplay the rate of decline from existing oil fields while overplaying the chances of finding new reserves."[1]

This was hardly the only warning of doom. Testifying to the Senate in July 2003, then–Federal Reserve chairman Alan Greenspan warned that "today's tight natural gas markets have been a long time in coming, and distant futures prices suggest that we are not apt to return to periods of relative abundance and low prices anytime soon."[2] In 2005, an energy consultant named Matthew Simmons became an international celebrity following the publication of his book *Twilight in the Desert*, which claimed that Saudi oil reserves were badly overstated and that, as a result, the world was headed for a massive energy shock. And it wasn't just Saudi Arabia. Experts pronounced that production in thirty-three out of forty-eight oil-producing nations had peaked and would quickly be depleted. "By 2012," warned the U.S. Defense Department in 2008, "surplus oil production capacity could entirely disappear."[3]

Paul Krugman weighed in, too: "We're living in a finite world, in which the rapid growth of emerging economies is placing pressure on limited supplies of raw materials, pushing up their prices. And America is, for the most part, just a bystander in this story."[4] So went the conventional wisdom, helping fuel the craze for alternative sources of energy such as wind and solar power, which the Obama administration was only too happy to help along.

As the people who thought they knew what they were talking about declared the end of an era, a handful of wildcatters, entrepreneurs, and visionaries were using a combination of two technologies—horizontal drilling and hydraulic fracturing, or "fracking"—to start a revolution in shale energy that was about to turn the United States into the world's largest oil and gas producer. And that wasn't all. More domestic energy made the notion of North American energy security, once thought of as a pipe dream, a rapidly approaching reality. It held the promise of reviving cost-competitive American manufacturing, as lower energy and transportation costs more than made up for the higher-priced labor. Fracking started a new American gold rush in places few people have ever heard of: Gonzalez County, Texas; Lycoming County, Pennsylvania; McKenzie County, North Dakota (2013 unemployment rate: 1.1 percent). It brought down the trade deficit and may create two million jobs by 2020. It gave U.S. foreign policy options it wouldn't have had before: oil sanctions on Iran, for example, subtracted more than a million barrels a day from the global energy supply but never showed up as a price at the pump.

Who started this revolution? Even today, names such as George Mitchell and Harold Hamm remain unknown to most Americans. These were men born to poverty: Mitchell was the son of a Greek goat herder who came to the United States to lay railway tracks; Hamm was the thirteenth child of sharecroppers who started out pumping gas and changing tires in Enid, Oklahoma. They were accustomed to hardship, excited by risk, and driven by a self-belief shared by almost nobody until their unlikely gambles spectacularly paid off. They spent millions of their own money on a hunch about shale oil that major oil firms were too skeptical to pursue for themselves. They were hardworking and largely self-taught. Hamm took "the dirtiest, nastiest jobs that no one else would touch, sometimes getting up in the middle of the night to clean tank bottoms or haul water to drilling sites," writes *The Wall Street Journal*'s Gregory Zuckerman in his book *The Frackers*. "Friendly, upbeat and eager to learn, Hamm continued to pick the brains of industry veterans to divine the secrets of the business, hoping to one day search for oil and gas.... [He] had a few hours during the day that were still free, so he built a library in his home and borrowed books about geology and geophysics."[5]

Mitchell's and Hamm's life stories are in the Horatio Alger mold. Yet the fracking story isn't merely about can-do spirit in an industry that prizes mavericks (or likes to think that it does). It's about technological innovation and, more important, commercial serendipity: the marriage of two technically distinct techniques through a process of trial and error. It's about federalism: fracking is happening because at least some state governments knew well enough to get out of the way of the frackers (one reason western Pennsylvania is mounting an economic recovery while its neighbors in upstate New York are not). It's about property rights: the United States is nearly alone in the world in giving property owners ownership rights to the minerals that lie below their land. "When private parties own the mineral rights (often surface land owners), they capture any expected benefits from new discoveries and associated production," notes economist Gary Libecap of the Hoover Institution. "Where governments own the mineral rights ... groups that do not directly benefit from fracking, or bear few costs from opposing it, can mobilize to slow or block use of the technology."[6]

What would have happened if George Mitchell had tried to start the fracking revolution in France or Germany? We know the answer, since both countries have effectively banned the practice. What if it had happened in China? We know the likely answer there, too, since the Chinese government would have demanded state ownership of both the resources and the production, thereby crushing future incentives for exploration and innovation. Russia? Corporations and oligarchs close to Vladimir Putin would have made Mitchell the proverbial offer that couldn't be refused.

All of which is to say that Krugman wasn't merely wrong about the relative availability of commodities. He was specifically wrong about the role America will play in the future of global energy markets. Other countries, including Britain, France, and China, sit on vast reserves of shale oil and gas, too—America's leadership in the fracking revolution is not some happy accident of geology. The difference is that the United States uniquely had the technological capability, financial markets, legal architecture, and capitalist culture to develop its hidden resource.

There is a broader lesson. Neither Mitchell nor Hamm invented anything; they were not the Thomas Edisons of their field. They simply made adaptive and innovative uses of technologies and methods already known. Yet in doing so they fundamentally renewed the possibilities of American energy. Could America's place in the world also be renewed, and Pax Americana restored, by applying lessons we've learned in other situations and disciplines to our foreign policy?

CHAPTER 10

* * *

A Way Forward

The simple fact is that if we do not lead, no one else will follow." So said Warren Christopher in 1995, and he, of all people, would have been the man to know.

Two years earlier, as Bill Clinton's secretary of state, he had paid visits to the capitals of Europe for consultations on what to do about the wars then consuming the Balkans. Clinton had campaigned for office lambasting George H. W. Bush's apparent indifference to the ethnic cleansing being committed by the allies of Serbian dictator Slobodan Milošević: "If the horror of the Holocaust taught us anything," the future president had said in August 1992, "it is the high cost of remaining silent and paralyzed in the face of genocide." Christopher's mission the following year was to develop a joint Western plan of action for the former Yugoslavia.

Instead, he was brusquely told to mind his own business. In the post–Cold War world, Europe, said the Europeans, would take charge of a European problem.

Christopher committed the disastrous error of taking the Europeans at their word and letting them try to sort out an international crisis on their own. Clinton compounded the mistake by persuading himself that the rivalries and hatreds of the region were simply too ancient, too deep-seated, to do much about. And so the siege of Sarajevo continued. And so the massacre of thousands of Muslim men and boys at Srebrenica happened. And so UN peacekeepers were held hostage and European diplomats were humiliated and American foreign policy was paralyzed and hundreds of thousands of people were killed or put into concentration camps or sent into exile by a minor Serbian potentate and his rat-faced lieutenants.

Amnesia tends to be the default state of mind of the American public when it comes to foreign policy: it is what we read in (or watch on) the news, and rarely the substance of our everyday lives. We typically approach foreign policy as spectators, not participants; as critics of the drama who can change the channel at any time, not as players on the stage with roles to perform. For all the toll of 9/11 and the wars in Iraq and Afghanistan, the number of Americans directly affected by them is a minuscule fraction of the overall population. Twenty years from now, memories of Iraq will become exceedingly faint: who was Tariq Aziz, or Muqtada al-Sadr, or Jalal Talabani? Just so with Balkan wars: how well do most Americans, even those who were paying attention at the time, remember the names of Ratko Mladić, Radovan Karadžić, or Franjo Tudjman?

Still, the travails of the Balkans are a useful and relatively recent reminder of how quickly chaos spreads when the United States retreats, and how soon order can return when it asserts its power. The fighting in the Balkans didn't just sort, or burn, itself out. It did not prove amenable to a succession of diplomatic initiatives (does anyone remember the Vance-Owen peace plan?). It was not resolved by the UN Security Council, or by the European Council, or the Council of Europe. It ended only when the United States intervened: first to help Croatia defeat Serbia in the largest European land battle since World War II, then to use airpower to end the four-year siege of Sarajevo, later to stop ethnic cleansing in Kosovo with a seventy-eight-day bombing campaign. Thousands of lives were almost certainly saved. The chaos of the Balkans did not overspill its borders as it has today in Syria. A dictator was deposed and sent to jail, where he died. The West demonstrated a capacity to act, not merely for the sake of humanitarian goals but also as an act of geopolitical hygiene. Serbia itself was rescued from dictatorship and transformed into a democracy that wants to join the European Union. And the cost was so light— not a single American killed in combat—that we easily forget how much was achieved.

Not all wars are fought so easily, or come to such decisive conclusions. It's a lesson learned painfully in Iraq. Then again, at least in the case of Iraq, it's worth recalling that the war there did not really begin in March 2003. Instead, as former Democratic senator Bob Kerrey pointed out at the time, the war was really an extension of the conflict that began when Saddam invaded Kuwait in 1990 and that had never really been concluded, despite the partial victory of the Gulf War. Not least among the mistakes of the war in Iraq was that it didn't end with the timely destruction of Saddam's regime in 1991.

But whatever view readers—or history—ultimately takes of that war, the United States cannot conduct foreign policy permanently in Iraq's shadow, no more than it could have done so in the wake of the war in Vietnam. Ultimately, we need a foreign policy that takes account not just of what we want in the here and now, but of who we are, what we have made of ourselves, and the way the world is.

Broken Windows

As the United States belatedly brought order to the chaos of the Balkans, Americans were bringing order to another place widely assumed to be beyond the reach of redemption: our streets.

The year 1991 was the annus horribilis for crime in the United States. More than 1.6 million cars were stolen that year. There were 3.1 million burglaries, 687,000 robberies, nearly 1.1 million aggravated assaults, 106,590 forcible rapes. And 24,700 murders.[1] In every category, crime was up from the year and decade earlier. A movie from the early 1980s, *Escape from New York*, imagined that by the 1990s Manhattan would become so ungovernable that it would be walled off and turned into a giant prison colony. The premise seemed fanciful at the time but not totally preposterous. As late as 1995, when the crime rate was beginning to come down, criminologists were predicting that a new wave of criminal "super-predators" would descend upon American neighborhoods. "If current trends continue, the number of arrests of juveniles for violent crimes will double by the year 2010," reported Fox Butterfield in *The New York Times*, citing a Justice Department report. "The report based its projection on a finding that arrest rates among juveniles ages 10 to 17 for violent crimes jumped 100 percent between 1983 and 1992."[2]

"Current trends," fortunately, did not continue.

In 1990, New York City registered a homicide rate of 30.7 murders for every 100,000 people. By 2001 it had come down to 8.1, a decline of 73.6 percent. (By 2012 it had fallen even further, to a rate of 5.0.) It was a similar, if slightly less dramatic, story in every other major U.S. city—a 55.8 percent drop in Boston, a 35.6 percent drop in Philadelphia. Crime fell in every big city and every relevant category.[3] It was social deliverance that happened despite the fact that many of the factors often cited to explain crime—bad schools, broken homes, poverty, the prevalence of guns, unemployment—remained largely the same from one decade to the next. Even a better economy doesn't explain it: crime fell in the prosperous years of 1992–2007, and continued falling despite the Great Recession and the higher unemployment that followed.

What happened? Even now the answers are a matter of intense debate. The crack epidemic crested in the early 1990s. The police began developing new management techniques, such as CompStat, to track and control patterns of criminal activity. University of Chicago economist Steve Levitt has famously posited that the Supreme Court's 1973 *Roe v. Wade* decision was a key factor, on the view that unwanted children are likelier to be criminals, and legalized abortion kept these unwanted children from being born in the first place.[4] Also, between 1992 and 2008, the number of law enforcement personnel rose by 141,000, a 25 percent increase,[5] while the adult incarceration rate nearly doubled between 1990 and 2000.[6] More cops on the streets; more bad guys behind bars. It's bound to have an effect.

Each of these factors doubtless played a role. But there was something else at work, too. In 1982, George Kelling, a criminologist at Rutgers, and James Q. Wilson, a political scientist at Harvard, penned an essay in *The Atlantic Monthly* that in time would become one of the most influential articles ever published. Titled "Broken Windows,"[7] it was an attempt to understand the nature of communal order, the way it is maintained, and the ways in which order turns into disorder. Their core insight turned on a social science experiment conducted in 1969 by Philip Zimbardo, a psychologist at Stanford. First, Zimbardo parked a car on a street in the Bronx, with the hood up and without license plates. Within ten minutes vandals begin to pick the car clean of its valuables: battery, radiator, tires. By the next day people began destroying the car, ripping up pieces of upholstery and smashing windows. Then, Zimbardo conducted the same experiment in tony Palo Alto, near the Stanford campus. This time, the car—also with the hood up and the license plates removed—sat untouched for several days. So Zimbardo smashed a window with a sledgehammer. "Soon, passersby were joining in," wrote Kelling and Wilson. "Within a few hours, the car had been turned upside down and utterly destroyed." The vandals, they added, "appeared to be primarily respectable whites." What to conclude?

> Disorder and crime are usually inextricably linked, in a kind of developmental sequence. Social psychologists and police officers tend to agree that if a window in a building is broken and is left unrepaired, all the rest of the windows will soon be broken. This is as true in nice neighborhoods as in rundown ones. Window-breaking does not necessarily occur on a large scale because some areas are inhabited by determined window-breakers whereas others are populated by window-lovers; rather, one unrepaired broken window is a signal that no one cares, and so breaking more windows costs nothing. (It has always been fun.)

The idea that the mere *appearance* of disorder encourages a deeper form of disorder cuts against the conventional wisdom about crime being a function of "root causes." And yet municipalities that adopted policing techniques based on the broken-windows theory—techniques that emphasized foot-patrol policing and the strict enforcement of laws against petty crimes and "social incivilities" such as graffiti spraying, turnstile jumping, and panhandling—tended to register sharp drops in crime and improvements in the overall quality of life. New York, which adopted the broken-windows techniques most enthusiastically, registered the sharpest declines in crime of any major city. In 2005, two researchers conducted a year-long study with the police department of Lowell, Massachusetts, to compare standard policing methods with the application of a broken-windows strategy: the results, wrote the study's authors, "lend considerable credibility to Wilson and Kelling's (1982) perspective that policing disorder can generate crime-prevention gains."[8] People with criminal proclivities tend to be social conformists—they will behave in ways that seem appropriate to the situation they see around them. If the situation appears orderly, it will influence their behavior accordingly. Even crooks know when "something just isn't done."

We are disposed to think that, as in thermodynamics, so too in human dynamics—entropy reigns; over time, order inevitably dissolves into disorder. Except that the drop in crime rates is a reminder that it remains possible to go the other way; to impose order on disorder; to fix supposedly intractable problems. Could it be that there's a "broken windows" cure not just for America's mean streets, but for our increasingly disorderly world at large?

RULES OF DISORDER

Barack Obama loves to talk about rules. When North Korea launched a ballistic missile in 2009, he warned that "rules must be binding. Violations must be punished. Words must mean something." When the regime of Bashar al-Assad used chemical weapons to murder more than one thousand people in Damascus in 2013, he insisted that "what happened to those people—to those children—is not only a violation of international law, it's also a danger to our country." After Russia seized Crimea in 2014, he denounced the Kremlin for "challenging truths that only a few weeks ago seemed self-evident, that in the 21st century, the borders of Europe cannot be redrawn with force, that international law matters, that people and nations can make their own decisions about their future."

The language is elegant; the words are true. Yet the warnings rarely amount to very much. North Korea followed its ballistic missile test with a nuclear test. In the same speech in which Obama warned Americans that they could not sit still for Assad's mass murders, he decided to sit still for them. His first response to the seizure of Crimea was to sanction a handful of Russians, send a few fighter jets to Poland and Lithuania, and refuse Ukrainian requests for military support.

This is how we arrive at a broken-windows world: Rules are invoked but not enforced. Principles are idealized but not defended. International law is treated not as a complement to traditional geopolitical leadership but as the superior alternative to it. "Moral leadership is more powerful than any weapon," said Obama in 2009, a remark that might have astonished the members of the generation—including the president's grandfather and great-uncle—who brought freedom to Western Europe through the turrets of their tanks. The moment the world begins to notice that rules will not be enforced, the rules will begin to be flouted. One window breaks, then all the others. The old expectations for order and the perpetuation of order no longer hold. If the American president lacks the moral will or the political stomach to enforce his chemical red line in Syria, what dissuades Tehran from marching across his nuclear red line? If the United States will do little more than wag its finger over Russia's seizure of Ukrainian territory—an act the Kremlin justifies with reference to historic and ethnic claims—what stops China from behaving likewise with Taiwan? If the United States won't honor the 1994 Budapest Memorandum by which Kiev gave up its nuclear weapons in exchange for a guarantee of its borders, why should Japan or Israel trust similar paper promises?

"Maybe this is what it means to live in the post-intervention era," wrote *The Guardian*'s Jonathan Freedland in a perceptive February 2014 column. "Few even call for action—in North Korea or Syria—because they know it's not going to happen. In the 1990s, those outraged by the Balkan war could believe that, if they only shouted loud enough, they would eventually get the international powers to act—which, eventually, they did. Now, after Iraq and Afghanistan, that belief has vanished."[9]

This is not a world readers of this book will want to inhabit, any more than they would want to live in a neighborhood of derelict buildings, garbage-strewn streets, and predatory gangs. Nor do we want to live in a world in which we act only in the event of what the Princeton philosopher Michael Walzer calls the "supreme emergency," when the barbaric enemy is at the proverbial gates. It does us no good to wait upon another Pearl Harbor or September 11 to feel we have sufficient moral or legal justification to act. We forget that World War II, "the good war," the war where there was no doubting the rightness of our cause, was also America's bloodiest in terms of battlefield fatalities, averaging nearly three hundred a day. The price of allowing order to collapse into disorder is steep.

RULES OF ORDER

The immediate goal of U.S. foreign policy should be to arrest the continued slide into a broken-windows world of international disorder. The broken-windows theory emphasizes the need to put cops on the street, the more the better, creating a sense of *presence*, enforcing community norms (even when infractions of them are not in direct violation of the law), punishing minor violations of the law, serving the interests of responsible local stakeholders, cleaning up the parks and streets, tearing down derelict buildings. Broken-windows policing emphasizes the need to deter crime, not react to it, to keep neighborhoods from becoming places that entice criminal behavior.

Is there a broken-windows formula for U.S. foreign policy?

There could be. It would require the United States to sharply increase military spending to upwards of 5 percent of GDP. But unlike in the past, it would lay greater emphasis on raw numbers—of ships, planes, and troops—than on high-cost technological wizardry. It would deploy more military assets for the protection of our allies. But unlike in the past, it would do so on condition that those allies invest significantly in their own defenses. It would sharply punish violations of geopolitical norms, such as the use of chemical weapons, by swiftly and precisely targeting the perpetrators of the attacks. But the emphasis would be on short, mission-specific, punitive police actions, not open-ended occupations for idealistic ends. It would be global in its approach: no more "pivots" from this region to that. But it would also know how to discriminate between core interests and allies and peripheral ones. It would seek to prevent local conflicts, such as the one in Syria, from spilling over their borders and becoming regional catastrophes. But it would do so by working vigorously through local proxies. It would place an emphasis on stability and predictability in international affairs. But it would put greater stock in behavioral norms than in international law.

A broken-windows approach to geopolitics would not try to run every bad guy out of town—a utopian ambition. But it would seek to keep their ambitions sharply in check and make the world a more congenial place for peaceful and ordinary states. Just as police feel a special duty to the elderly and more vulnerable residents of the neighborhood, the United States should take special care for the protection of little countries at risk from threatening neighbors. A current list of such countries would include the Baltic states, Ukraine and Georgia, Israel and Jordan, Taiwan and the Philippines.

Let's take each point in its turn:

Presence: It has become a cliché among progressives and libertarians alike that the U.S. military is overly committed abroad; that, as Rand Paul put it in 2009, we have troops in no fewer than 130 countries. That claim is preposterous, unless one counts the Marine detachments that provide minimal security at U.S. diplomatic facilities around the world. (That includes 44 Marines in Russia and 42 in China. Does Senator Paul count them, too?) In reality, U.S. forces have never been as *under*extended in recent history as they are today. In 1964 the U.S. Navy patrolled the seas with 859 ships. In 1984 there were 557 ships. That's down to 289 today.[10] Or compare U.S. force levels by country (including the U.S. homeland) in 1984 and 2012, ranked according to the size of deployments:[11]

1984	2012
1) USA: 1,623,550	1) USA: 1,214,099
2) Germany: 253,000	2) Afghanistan: 68,000
3) Japan: 45,761	3) Japan: 50,937
4) South Korea: 40,785	4) Germany: 47,761
5) United Kingdom: 30,078	5) South Korea: 28,500
6) Philippines: 15,319	6) Italy: 10,922
7) Italy:14,809	7) UK: 9,849
8) Spain:9,436	8) Spain: 1,727
9) Panama (Canal Zone): 9,354	9)Turkey: 1,505
10) Turkey: 5,449	10) Belgium: 1,174

Much of the difference between 1984 and 2014 is explained by the end of the Cold War. But we are no longer living in the halcyon years of the 1990s, either, even if the Obama administration is acting as if we are. On the contrary, we now live in a world that combines a diffuse global terror threat with renewed challenges from major powers. Worse, we live in this world with a global footprint that is as small as it has been since before the Second World War. American military power is becoming more of an over-the-horizon rumor than it is a visible and confident reality. For power to be believed *it has to be seen.* As with the broken-windows approach, it's not enough for the cop to be at the precinct station or even in his patrol car. He has to be walking his beat, a visible, reassuring, deterring presence.

For decades, the Pentagon has focused on the need to maintain its qualitative military edge to the exclusion of almost every other consideration—including cost, numbers, and even technological feasibility. The results have included the ultrasophisticated Seawolf submarine, of which the Navy intended to purchase 29 but wound up with 3; the F-22 fighter jet, of which the Air Force planned to buy 650 but wound up with 187; the space-age DDG-1000 Zumwalt, of which only 3 of the planned 32 will be built; and now the F-35 fighter, an all-eggs-in-one-basket project whose delays, cost overruns, and maintenance issues are already legendary. Altogether, the Pentagon spent $46 billion on canceled projects in the first decade of this century,[12] and many billions more on the R&D costs for programs that were ultimately fielded in numbers too small to justify the investment or make a decisive battlefield difference.

This is a typical case of making the best the enemy of the good: a cutting-edge Tiger-tank approach to war fighting as opposed to a mass-production T-34- or Sherman-tank approach. It is also inimical to the American interest in being able to field men and matériel in large numbers around the world fielding good-enough equipment. In 2012 I embarked on the USS *Bunker Hill*, an Aegis cruiser, serving as an escort to the aircraft carrier USS *Carl Vinson* in the Persian Gulf. Both are impressive ships, but what was most surprising to me was that they were the only two major U.S. surface combatants operating in the entire Gulf. Americans were not likely to notice the absence of U.S. forces in the region. But the Saudis and Bahrainis did notice—as did the Iranian spy ships that shadowed the *Bunker Hill* just a few thousand yards off our starboard side. It's the same story in Asia. "The Crimea makes us feel uneasy about whether the United States has not only the resolve but the strength to stop China," Japanese defense expert Satoru Nagao told *The New York Times*. "Between the Pentagon budget cuts, and the need to put more forces in Europe, can the United States still offer a credible deterrence?"[13]

Such doubts can only be put to rest if the United States can once again start deploying forces globally in large numbers. That will only happen when the White House understands that the world's policeman needs a global presence, and when the Pentagon (and Congress) rediscover the virtues of building affordably and plentifully. The goal is not to build a small number of unaffordable wonder weapons that maintain a generation-wide technological edge with a view toward fighting some hypothetical war. Rather, it is to build a large number of much cheaper weapons that are capable of being adapted and upgraded over time. Fewer F-35s, more upgraded F-15s and F-18s. The Pentagon needs to relearn the virtues of evolution, not revolution, in military affairs.

Reciprocity: Reversing the slide in America's military power and presence will be easier to accomplish, strategically and politically, if it is accompanied by commensurate military investments by our allies. There has to be community buy-in for broken-windows policing to work. The NATO Charter requires member states to spend at least 2 percent of their GDP on defense.

In 2014, only four NATO states—the United States, the United Kingdom, Greece, and Estonia—spent more than 2 percent of their GDP on defense, the baseline stipulated by NATO's charter. France spent 1.9 percent, Turkey 1.8 percent, Germany 1.3 percent, Poland 1.8 percent, Spain 0.9 percent. At the close of the Cold War, the German army had 360,000 men under arms and fielded 12 well-equipped divisions. Now a country with a GDP of $3.4 trillion fields 62,000 soldiers, 225 tanks, and about 40 attack helicopters. Lord Ismay's famous line about the purpose of NATO being to keep "the Americans in, the Russians out, and the Germans down" needs to be reformulated: Americans in, Russians out, Germans back. Nor can the argument credibly be made that Europe, in its economic distress, cannot afford to spend more on defense. In 1979, probably the worst year of Britain's postwar economic history, Westminster spent 4.9 percent of its GDP on defense. France that year spent 4 percent.[14] Even then the spending was not equal to the threat, but at least it was serious. It needs to become serious again.

Police actions, not occupations: "Broken windows" theory emphasizes the importance of the surface of things: the look of the neighborhood, the types of people walking the streets, their behavior. It is much less interested in all the things that go by the name of "root cause." The decision to try to democratize Iraq stemmed, in part, from the view that the root cause of the 9/11 attacks was a culture of autocracy in the Arab world that pushed political dissent into the mosques. It helps explain, as noted earlier, why the Bush administration embarked on ambitious projects in Iraq and Afghanistan to make them exemplary states (at least in the context of their region), rather than simply to make harsh examples of misbehaving rulers. The Pottery Barn rule is not a theory of international relations the United States should recognize.

Where the United States does have an obligation is to set and enforce basic global *norms*: that is, to establish and enforce a set of basic behavioral expectations. This is quite different from declaring or accepting international "laws" of dubious enforceability. And it is something the United States has routinely done: in Grenada in 1983 to reverse a Communist coup; invading Panama in 1989 to overthrow a narco-regime; going to war in the Gulf in 1991 to restore Kuwait's sovereignty; intervening in the Balkans in the 1990s to end the siege of Sarajevo, help Croatia defeat Serbia, and stop ethnic cleansing in Kosovo; deploying aircraft carriers near the Strait of Taiwan to dissuade Beijing from aggressive action against Taipei; overthrowing the Taliban after the 9/11 attacks; tipping the scales against Muammar Gaddafi in Libya in 2011. The incursion into Somalia would have succeeded (and long ago been forgotten) if the United States had limited its aims to relieving a famine instead of trying to stand up a failed state. And the war in Iraq might have succeeded also if its aim had merely been to depose Saddam after he had spent the previous decade flaunting his defiance of the United States, abusing his people, corrupting the Oil-for-Food program, supporting Palestinian terrorists, and generally misbehaving. Instead, the Bush administration pursued grander ambitions.

It's a depressing testimony to how warped the U.S. foreign policy debate has become that it is all but impossible to contemplate potential police actions in Syria—to punish the Assad regime for its use of chemical weapons—or in Iran—to destroy its nuclear programs—without thinking of them as "another Iraq." The cliché of the slippery slope incapacitates rational debate. Nobody wants another Iraq, and it is preposterous to suggest that a forty-eight-hour air campaign in Syria or a weeklong one in Iran (about the time required to achieve each objective) would devolve into a decade-long land war. At the same time, we do not want to live in a world in which a Milošević, a Saddam, or a Khamenei operates with impunity, safe in the knowledge that America is crippled by its fears of reprising Iraq.

Priorities, not pivots: The idea of the "pivot" was based on a conceit that the United States could choose where its future geopolitical challenges would lie. No more Middle East, because we would not be going to war there ever again, under almost any circumstances. No more Europe, because the Cold War was over and the United States and Russia had "reset" their relations. Latin America and Africa presented nothing more than nuisance challenges, like the Chavista regime in Venezuela, or humanitarian crises, like the unfolding tragedy in the Central African Republic. That left Asia.

But America's security challenge is global: the responsibility for policing global order does not come with the right to determine who will pose a significant threat to global order, and how, when, and where they will exercise the threat. At the same time, global responsibilities also require a sense of global priorities. Days before Russia invaded Ukraine—a move that could hardly have come as a surprise as the anti-Russian revolution in Kiev was reaching its climax—John Kerry was giving a speech on climate change in Jakarta. He was also devoting his attention to Israeli-Palestinian peace talks. The art of statesmanship, lost on the Obama administration, consists in knowing what matters, and when it matters most.

The alternative to the pivot, a one-directional and one-dimensional concept, is to think more carefully about the places that really matter to U.S. security. In a perceptive essay in *The American Interest*, Henry Nau lays out the case for pursuing America's "geo-ideological" interests: "Focus on freedom where it counts the most, namely on the borders of existing free societies." Those borders, Nau writes, divide the free countries of Asia from China and North Korea; the free countries of Europe from Russia; and Israel from its Arab neighbors. "When countries on these borders are threatened, America is threatened," Nau argues. "Why? Because as the specter of tyranny moves closer to the core of the democratic world, the world becomes a less hospitable place."[15]

One might add to Nau's list of borders Colombia's with Venezuela,

India's with Pakistan, and Iran's borders with almost all of its neighbors. Wherever the lines are drawn, the insight is a useful one: to know your core interests, find your front lines. The American interest is to be the defender of the world's responsible citizens—the geopolitical equivalents of the shopkeeper, the public librarian, the parish priest, the schoolkids, the elderly couples. They need to know that there's a policeman on the corner to ensure they aren't being harassed or hustled or menaced or mugged. And to do so not just in one neighborhood, as Obama's pivot effectively proposes to do, but in any place where their security might be at risk.

Put the fires out quickly: The pattern of international crisis management as it has developed over the past several decades is to take effective action only when it is nearly too late—when action is taken at all.

Consider the following sequence of events. A dictator represses an ethnic minority, or threatens a neighbor, or uses unusually brutish tactics to quell political dissent. In response, the Western media report the story and the State Department issues a travel advisory and a press release expressing concern and calling for restraint. The crisis escalates: a meeting of the Security Council is called, but the dictator's ally in Moscow or Beijing prevents the publication of even a mild statement. Instead, the Council agrees to keep itself updated on the unfolding situation. An atrocity occurs. The White House puts out a statement in the name of the president; pundits demand sanctions; the secretary of state calls in the dictator's ambassador in Washington for a stern talking-to. Events heat up some more and now there's a new chorus of pundits and policy makers, warning the United States to steer clear of someone else's civil war.

The debate in Washington isn't lost on the dictator, who denounces his domestic enemies as terrorists or foreign agents and perhaps invites a credulous celebrity or a marginal politician to pay him a visit. The United Nations imposes an arms embargo, which is supposed to starve the conflict of its weapons but inevitably favors the regime in power, with its ample supplies of guns and ammunition, over the rebel group or the endangered minority. As matters get worse, the nearest regional organization— the African Union or Arab League or ASEAN or EU—decides to appoint a high-level representative, preferably an ex–foreign minister of some relatively inoffensive country. After several weeks the representative puts forward a peace plan; the regime accepts the plan in principle but subverts it in practice; the opposition rejects it outright.

Matters go from bad to worse. Refugees begin pouring into a neighboring country, requiring international aid agencies to build tent cities. The State Department announces hundreds of millions of dollars in humanitarian aid; the Treasury Department imposes financial sanctions on the regime's leadership and its banks. The White House issues a statement, saying it is sending an "unmistakable signal" that brutality "doesn't pay." The Pentagon begins to draw up plans for targeted strikes. Matters typically only come to a head when there is some especially appalling atrocity. Only then does the United States consider doing something beyond issuing diplomatic demarches and calls for restraint.

The scenario I describe here is loosely based on events in Syria, but it could also describe the crisis in the Balkans or several African states in the 1990s. It's a pattern that repeats itself with numbing regularity. What's extraordinary, however, is that the West considers taking serious action against the aggressor only after thousands of people are dead. No police or fire department would wait until a house is consumed in flames before it started putting it out. Yet that's how the West has operated with international fires in a curious nod to notions of international law or legitimacy it knows it may, at some point, need to ignore. The result is history repeating itself as tragedy, over and over again. And it is history as precedent: the geopolitical arsonists know the world will not interfere so long as the fires being set don't choke the West with their smoke.

The United States cannot put out every geopolitical fire. Inevitably it has to choose which of those fires risks burning down the entire neighborhood, if not the international system itself. It also has to decide what level of capability it is willing to deploy, for how long, at what kind of risk, in the service of what sort of outcome. Conflicts rarely offer a purely binary choice between doing nothing, on the one hand, and a full-scale invasion on the other. A cruise missile strike against a single radio tower in Rwanda could have helped prevent the Hutus from broadcasting the plan of attack against the Tutsis during the 1994 genocide, potentially saving thousands of innocent civilians at no cost in lives, and little in treasure, to the United States. Covert U.S. aid to Croatia that same year decisively turned the tide of that war against Serbian dictator Slobodan Milošević, again at no serious cost to the United States. Meaningful aid to Syrian rebels early in the conflict, before jihadists had infiltrated the conflict, would almost certainly have had a similar effect, as would cruise missile strikes incapacitating the Syrian air force.

We need to rethink habits of crisis management that are never effective at the beginning of the crisis, and only sometimes effective toward the end of it, when thousands of people have already been sent to an early grave. Does such an approach lack for international or moral legitimacy? Perhaps it is time for a political leader to make the case that *preventing* tragedy should enjoy greater moral legitimacy than reacting to it.

An Ounce of Prevention

Broken-windows theory has always been intensely controversial. Its theoretical merits, moral justifications, and practical results remain debated by criminologists, civil liberties activists, and politicians to this day. There will be readers of this book who will accuse me of advocating what amounts to a global "stop-and-frisk" policy—the policing method, widely used in New York City under Police Commissioner Ray Kelly, that allowed police officers to detain and search people they suspected of carrying illegal firearms. I plead guilty to the accusation. New York City, where stop-and-frisk and other broken-windows methods of policing have been used most intensively, is the safest big city in America. The Son of Sam is no longer on the prowl; joggers aren't at risk of "wilding" attacks in Central Park; anti-Semitic riots are a thing of the past. By any measure, New York is immensely better off today, after twenty years of omnipresent, no-nonsense policing, than it was in the twenty years that went before.

Yet there's a paradox. In his famous 1993 essay, "Defining Deviancy Down," Daniel Patrick Moynihan observed how Americans had become inured to ever-higher rates of violent crime by treating as "normal" criminal activity that would have scandalized past generations of Americans. "We are getting used to a lot of behavior that is not good for us," the late senator from New York wrote.[16] Twenty years later, the opposite has happened. We have defined deviancy *up*. But having done so, we have tended to forget how much better things are now than they were before. In 2013 New York City elected a mayor in part on the basis of his fervent opposition to the very policing methods that made New York safe enough for him to get elected in the first place. Social disorder leads us to a psychology of increasing indifference; social order contributes to a mind-set of obliviousness.

Americans have lived in a relatively orderly world for so long that we have become broadly oblivious to how good that world has been for us. It also helps explain why, in recent years, we have blithely adopted a foreign policy that neglects to do the things that have underpinned that orderly world: global security commitments, military force adequate to those commitments, a willingness to intervene in regional crises to secure allies and confront or deter aggressive regimes.

But perhaps the thinking is beginning to change. The evidence of where the Obama administration's foreign policy has led is becoming difficult to ignore: Russia's invasion of Ukraine; China's aggressive maritime claims against Japan and the Philippines; Iran's confident march to nuclear capability; North Korea's nuclear tests; the unfolding chaos in Iraq; the calamity in Syria. Averting one's eyes, keeping our hands clean, staying out, remaining in a supine position, is not a foreign policy option for the United States. There is a growing sense that if America provides no leadership, authoritarian regimes will quickly fill the breach; that if our red lines are exposed as mere bluffs, more of them will be crossed; that if our commitments to our allies—both the ones we generally like and the ones we have no option but to accept—aren't serious, those friends might abandon us; that if our threats against our enemies are empty, our enemies will be emboldened, and we will have more of them. If history does not end—and it hasn't—then the United States does not get a holiday from it.

In other words, the internationalists, of both conservative and liberal stripe, have a political case to make—a case that will become stronger as the consequences of Obama's foreign policy become more evident. Not all Americans relish the prospect of being treated with naked contempt by a Bashar al-Assad or a Vladimir Putin. We are not indifferent to the fate of democratic states faced with aggressive neighbors: Israel, Ukraine, Taiwan, Estonia, Georgia. We are not utterly deaf to pleas for help by people who will die if we do nothing. We believe we have the greatest stake in a global order that bends toward our values and ideals.

And we believe there is something to be said for Benjamin Franklin's observation about the value of an ounce of prevention. It's worth recalling the full quote, which appeared in *The Pennsylvania Gazette*, on February 4, 1735:

> In the first Place, as an Ounce of Prevention is worth a Pound of Cure, I would advise 'em to take care how they suffer living Coals in a full Shovel, to be carried out of one Room into another, or up or down Stairs, unless in a Warmingpan shut; for Scraps of Fire may fall into Chinks and make no Appearance until Midnight; when your Stairs being in Flames, you may be forced, (as I once was) to leap out of your Windows, and hazard your Necks to avoid being oven-roasted.

The Philadelphians of the day got the point. Within a year of the article's appearance, the city had its first fire department. What's a good rule for urban policy is a good rule also for global politics.

INDISPENSABLE AND INESCAPABLE

This chapter began with a description of the Lazarus-like revival of the oil-and-gas business in America. The story, with its rags-to-riches, larger-than-life heroes and their against-the-grain way of thinking, is quintessentially American. It is also the story of America itself: written off by the experts, declared past its prime, suffused with almost crippling self-doubt—but steadied by a faith in its possibilities and its purpose. The United States surprised itself with the shale revolution. Then again, we surprised ourselves, too, by winning the Cold War in the 1980s, getting crime under control in the 1990s, and leading the digital revolution in the 2000s.

We can surprise ourselves again by once more proving worthy of the geopolitical moment. In fact it is nearly inevitable that we will. The question is how long it will take. Are we reprising the relatively brief post-Vietnam era of weakness and diffidence? Or are we back to the interwar years—a sustained inward turn that was only overcome when a global emergency was already upon us? Even then it took leadership of a very high order to shake the United States out of its isolationist slumber.

Whatever we do, we need to understand that American preeminence is not going anywhere. We are not Britain, on the eve of a slow fade from the global stage. Nor are we France, on the verge of some spectacular and sudden national collapse. Great powers are not felled by small wars. Major economies are not destroyed by sluggish recoveries. We will remain the world's leading power for decades to come. Every future president of the United States will be the leader of the free world. When any country in the free world is threatened, it will look first to Washington for an anchor or for a lifeline. We will remain the preferred target for any ambitious terrorist group. We will be the prime enemy for any ambitious revisionist power. Proof of innocent intent, demonstrations of good faith, nuclear disarmament pacts, and diplomatic resets will not spare us their enmity. Remaining aloof and on good terms with the whole world may be a policy option for New Zealand and Costa Rica, but not for the United States. One can only be alone when one is left alone. We will not be left alone, at least not while we remain preeminent. And we will remain preeminent for as long as we remain a country in which people like George Mitchell, Harold Hamm, and Jan Koum have a chance to thrive.

Their success—and yours, too—rests on the pillars that sustain our liberties. Among those pillars: American power with the reach and credibility to keep our enemies in check and far away; power that fosters global conditions of predictability, prosperity, decency, and freedom. *Do not make mock of uniforms that guard you while you sleep,* warned Kipling. Do not dismiss America from its job as the world's policeman, either. When the thugs and scofflaws show up in your neighborhood, as they sometimes do, you'll be grateful to know that cop is still walking his old beat, a reassuring presence in a still-dangerous world.

ACKNOWLEDGMENTS

In the beginning there was an idea: a book about the future of Israel. To help me think it through, Roger Hertog convened a panel of experts. They quickly helped me realize that what I had in mind would be the wrong book, at the wrong time, by the wrong guy. Right on all counts. I thank Elliott Abrams, Bill Kristol, Neal Kozodoy, Eric Cohen, Suzanne Garment, and Roger himself for steering me away from the shoals.

A few weeks later, in the summer of 2012, I wrote a long essay under the title "The Coming Global Disorder." I had the good fortune to have it published in *Commentary* and the great fun to be edited by John Podhoretz and Abe Greenwald. Along the way I was lucky to have Eric Cohen of the Tikvah Fund, Peter Briger of Fortress Capital, and Seth Klarman of the Baupost Group give me opportunities to develop my thesis in roundtables, speeches, and seminars. Following publication, Dan Senor championed the book in a half-dozen invaluable ways, without which it never would have reached as wide and as influential an audience as it has. I am profoundly grateful, too, to Fareed Zakaria, David Brooks, James Hoge, Charles Lipson, Dennis Prager, David Wolpe, and Meir Soloveichik—distinguished interlocutors and sparring partners who generously lent their time and energy to make my book events far more enlivening than they otherwise might have been.

Chris Calhoun is my agent. Chris is smart, fun, committed, ethical, independent, and exceptionally good at his job. And he led me to my superb publishers at Penguin/Sentinel. Adrian Zackheim got the idea, got me, and got the book. He also understood that global disorder was a subsidiary point to my real thesis, which is America's retreat from global responsibility. Changing the title meant rewriting much of the book, but I'm happy to have done it. He and his talented team—Kathy Daneman, Justin Hargett, Will Weisser, Brooke Carey, Jesse Maeshiro—have been as patient with me as they have been enthusiastic about the project. Special thanks also go to Margot Stamas, my exceptional publicist, who worked tirelessly to make sure the book reached the widest possible audience.

Niki Papadopoulos shaped and sharpened this manuscript in scores of ways. She's a world-class critic, stylist, motivational coach, taskmaster, midwife, and ego/neurosis/crisis manager. In other words, she's my editor.

I'm fortunate to work for the world's best newspaper. Paul Gigot, the editorial-page editor of *The Wall Street Journal*, looked on this project with an indulgent eye and cut me the slack I needed to get it done. I have profited from the insight and reporting of all of my editorial-page colleagues, and I'm grateful they rarely object when I steal their food. I'm especially indebted to Bari Weiss, who went over this manuscript with her gimlet eye and impeccable editorial judgment. No less important have been my two gifted research assistants, Alexander Kazam and Kate Havard, both of whom came my way thanks to the Tikvah Fund. I've sent Alex and Kate down more dead-end streets, intellectually speaking, than I care to think about. But I have them to thank for keeping this manuscript moving along the right road.

This book is dedicated to my late father, Charles J. Stephens, who instilled in me a love of history, philosophy, foreign policy, and writing that explains my entire career. He gave me the unconditional love without which I would never have amounted to a thing. My mother, Xenia Stephens, has given me all of that, too; to her, especially, I owe my moral compass. My siblings, Gabrielle and Mark, have showered their little brother with love, consideration, and forbearance even when he was obnoxious or thoughtless, which was often. And I'm blessed with an extended family, stretching from New Mexico to Hamburg, who have greatly enriched my life by accepting me so fully into theirs.

Above all there is my own family: my beloved wife, Corinna, my compass and rock and lodestar, who has sacrificed more evenings and weekends on the altar of this book than either of us cares to count. (Also, she never mixes metaphors.) And there are our wonderful children, Lara, Noah, and Katya, who have put up with their absentee dad for too long. They remind their parents every day of what it means to love. They give our lives its best purposes, its fondest hopes, and its deep abiding joys.

NOTES

May 2014: Last Convoy Out of Sangin

1. Interview with author, May 5, 2014.

CHAPTER 1: COME HOME, AMERICA

1. David E. Sanger, "Global Crises Put Obama's Strategy of Caution to the Test," *The New York Times,* March 16, 2014, accessed April 7, 2014. http:// www.nytimes.com/2014/03/17/world/obamas-policy-is-put-to-the -test-as-crises-challenge-caution.html?hp.

2. "US Ship Force Levels," Naval History and Heritage Command, accessed April 7, 2014. http://www.history.navy.mil/branches/org9-4.htm.

3. Hans M. Kristensen, "B61-12 Nuclear Bomb Design Features," *FAS Strategic Security Blog,* April 16, 2014, accessed April 17, 2014. http:// blogs.fas.org/security/author/hkristensen/.

4. Franklin Foer and Chris Hughes, "Barack Obama Is Not Pleased," *The New Republic*, February 11, 2013, accessed April 7, 2014. http://www .newrepublic.com/article/112190/obama-interview-2013-sit-down -president.

5. Eli Lake and Josh Rogin, "Exclusive: U.S. Intercepted Al Qaeda's 'Legion of Doom' Conference Call," *The Daily Beast,* July 8, 2013, accessed April 9, 2014.

6. Seth G. Jones, "The Accelerating Spread of Terrorism," *The Wall Street Journal,* June 3, 2014, accessed on June 13, 2014. http://online.wsj.com /articles/seth-jones-the-accelerating-spread-of-terrorism-1401837824.

7. John Vinocur, "Europe Loses Trust in Obama," *The Wall Street Journal*, November 11, 2013.

8. Henry Samuel, "Nicolas Sarkozy Sees Barack Obama as 'not a Leader but a Follower', Says Aide to Former French President," *The Telegraph*, September 6, 2013, accessed April 17, 2014. http://www.telegraph.co.uk /news/worldnews/middleeast/syria/10291053/Nicolas-Sarkozy-sees-Barack -Obama-as-not-a-leader-but-a-follower-says-aide-to-former-French- president.html.

9. Ellen Knickmeyer, "U.S. Moves on Syria, Iran Anger Saudi Arabia," *The Wall Street Journal*, September 29, 2013, accessed April 14, 2014. http:// online.wsj.com/news/articles/SB100014240527023036433045791049100000 0148876.

10. Jeffrey Heller and Alistair Lyon, "Israel's Defense Chief Says U.S. Projecting Weakness," Reuters, March 18, 2014, accessed April 22, 2014. http:// www.reuters.com/article/2014/03/18/us-israel-usa-idUSBREA2H0SV 20140318.

11. Marissa Newman, "Iranian General: Obama's Threats Are 'the Joke of the Year," *The Times of Israel*, March 4, 2014, accessed April 7, 2014. http:// www.timesofisrael.com/iranian-general-obamas-threats-are-the-joke-of -the-year/#ixzz2v1bF22DF.

12. "Turkish PM's Top Aide Says Erdoğan One of Only Two World Leaders," *Today's Zaman*, August 29, 2013, accessed April 07, 2014. http://www .todayszaman.com/news-324831-turkish-pms-top-aide-says-erdogan -one-of-only-two-world-leaders.html.

13. Stuart Grudgings, "As Obama's Asia 'Pivot' Falters, China Steps into the Gap," Reuters, October 6, 2013, accessed April 7, 2014. http://www .reuters.com/article/2013/10/06/us-asia-usa-china -idUSBRE99501O20131006.

14. Doug Cameron, "Pentagon Insists Pacific 'Pivot' Plan Intact," *The Wall Street Journal*, March 4, 2014, accessed April 7, 2014. http://online.wsj .com/news/articles/SB10001424052702303630904579419131885358504 ?KEYWORDS=Pivot&mg=reno64-wsj.

15. Jeremy Herb, "Is Obama Pivot to Asia on Hold?" *The Hill*, March 30, 2014, accessed April 17, 2014. http://thehill.com/blogs/defcon-hill/202092-is -obama-pivot-to-asia-on-hold.

16. Trefor Moss, "America's Pivot to Asia: A Report Card," *The Diplomat*, May 5, 2014, accessed April 7, 2014. http://thediplomat.com/2013/05/americas -pivot-to-asia-a-report-card/.

17. Aaron Blake, "Few Americans Want 'Firm Stand' Against Russia in Ukraine," *The Washington Post*, March 11, 2013, accessed April 7, 2014. http://www.washingtonpost.com/blogs/post-politics/wp/2014/03/11 /few-americans-want-firm-stand-against-russia-in-ukraine.

18. Vali Nasr, *The Dispensable Nation: American Foreign Policy in Retreat* (New York: Anchor, 2013).

19. Mark Mazzetti, Robert F. Worth, and Michael R. Gordon, "Obama's Uncertain Path Amid Syria Bloodshed," *The New York Times*, October 22, 2013, accessed April 7, 2014. http://mobile.nytimes.com/2013/10/23 /world/middleeast/obamas-uncertain-path-amid-syria-bloodshed .html.

20. "Former Obama Aide Now One of Fiercest Critics of Administration's Stance on Syria," transcript, *The Lead with Jake Tapper*, CNN, September 2, 2013. http://transcripts.cnn.com/TRANSCRIPTS/1309/02/cg.02 .html.

21. Ed Dolan, "Ten Years On, New Estimates of the Economic Cost of the Wars in Iraq and Afghanistan," Econ Blog, *EconoMonitor*, March 13, 2013, accessed April 7, 2014. http://www.economonitor.com/dolanecon /2013/03/18/ten-years-on-new-estimates-of-the-economic-cost-of-the-wars -in-iraq-and-afghanistan-2/.

22. Arthur Schlesinger, Jr., "Desperate Times," review of *Roosevelt and the Isolationists, 1932–45* by Wayne S. Cole, *The New York Review of Books*, November 24, 1983, accessed April 7, 2014. http://www.nybooks.com /articles/archives/1983/nov/24/desperate-times/.

23. Bill Keller, "Our New Isolationism," *The New York Times*, September 8, 2013, accessed April 7, 2014. http://www.nytimes.com/2013/09/09 /opinion/keller-our-new-isolationism.html.

24. Norman Davies, *Europe: A History* (Oxford: Oxford University Press, 1996), 938.

Winter 1947: The Birth of Pax Americana

1. Dean Acheson, *Present at the Creation: My Years at the State Department* (New York: W. W. Norton, 1969), 196–98.

2. Paul Johnson, *Modern Times: The World from the Twenties to the Eighties* (New York: Harper & Row, 1983), 439.

3. Quoted in Daniel Yergin, *Shattered Peace: The Origins of the Cold War* (Boston: Houghton Mifflin, 1978), 280–81.

4. Tony Judt, *Postwar: A History of Europe Since 1945* (New York: Penguin, 2006), 76.

CHAPTER 2: PAX AMERICANA AND ITS CRITICS

1. John C. Culver and John Hyde, *American Dreamer: A Life of Henry A. Wallace* (New York: W. W. Norton, 2000), 413.

2. Ibid., 445–46.

3. Quoted in Clarence E. Wunderlin, *Robert A. Taft: Ideas, Tradition and Party in U.S. Foreign Policy* (Oxford: Rowman & Littlefield, 2005), 78.

4. Quoted in Susan Dunn, *1940: FDR, Willkie, Lindbergh, Hitler—the Election amid the Storm* (New Haven, Conn.: Yale University Press, 2013), 74–75.

5. Robert A. Taft, *The Papers of Robert A. Taft, 1939–1944,* vol. 2, ed. Clarence E. Wunderlin Jr. (Kent, Ohio: Kent State University Press, 2001), 242–43, 245–46.

6. Dunn, *Election amid the Storm,* 57.

7. Wunderlin, *Taft,* 121.

8. Quoted in ibid., 125.

9. Robert A. Taft, *The Papers of Robert A. Taft, 1945–1948,* vol. 3, ed. Clarence E. Wunderlin, Jr. (Kent, Ohio: Kent State University Press, 2003), 198.

10. Ibid., 260.

11. The World Bank, "GDP (Current US$)," World Development Indicators, updated April 2014, accessed April 16, 2014. http://databank.worldbank.org/data/home.aspx.

Fall 2005: Pax Americana at the Edge

1. Bret Stephens, "Chinook Diplomacy," *The Wall Street Journal*, December 22, 2005. http://online.wsj.com/news/articles/SB113522072648729208?mg=reno64-wsj&url=http://online.wsj.com/article/SB113522072648729208.html.

2. "America's Global Image Remains More Positive Than China's," Pew Research Center, July 18, 2013. http://www.pewglobal.org/2013/07/18/chapter-1-attitudes-toward-the-united-states/.

CHAPTER 3: THE OVERDOSE OF IDEALS

1. Freedom House, "Freedom in the World 2013," accessed April 9, 2014. http://www.freedomhouse.org/sites/default/files/FIW%202013% 20Booklet_0.pdf.

2. Figures are in constant 2000 dollars, per World Bank data.

3. Piers Brendon, *The Dark Valley: A Panorama of the 1930s* (New York: Alfred A. Knopf, 2000), 616.

4. Bret Stephens, "The Other Susan Rice File," *The Wall Street Journal,* December 11, 2012.

5. Aaron David Miller, "The False Religion of Mideast Peace," *Foreign Policy,* April 19, 2010. http://www.foreignpolicy.com/articles/2010/04/19/the _false_religion_of_mideast_peace#sthash.4NqY11iQ.dpbs.

6. *The 9/11 Commission Report: Final Report of the National Commission on Terrorist Attacks upon the United States,* official government edition (Washington, D.C.: U.S. Government Printing Office, 2004), 196.

7. Ibid., 202.

8. Osama bin Laden, quoted in Dexter Filkins, "The Plot Against America," *The New York Times,* August 5, 2006, accessed April 9, 2014.

9. Robert L. Pollock, "The Voice of Iraq," *The Wall Street Journal,* June 24, 2006, accessed April 9, 2014. http://online.wsj.com/news/articles /SB115110398646189506.

10. It will be many years before Americans will be able to gain a sober perspective on the intelligence failures that preceded the Iraq war. When future historians look into the matter, however, they'll find that a good place to start is the July 2004 report from the Senate Select Intelligence Committee, "U.S. Intelligence Community's Prewar Intelligence Assessments on Iraq," endorsed on a fully bipartisan basis and based on the examination of thirty thousand pages of intelligence assessments and source reporting and interviews with more than two hundred people. Among its salient conclusions:

    Conclusion 83. The Committee did not find any evidence that Administration officials attempted to coerce, influence or pressure analysts to change their judgments related to Iraq's weapons of mass destruction capabilities.

    Conclusion 84. The Committee found no evidence that the Vice President's visits to the Central Intelligence Agency were attempts to pressure analysts, were perceived as intended to pressure by those who participated in the briefings on Iraq's weapons of mass destruction programs, or did pressure analysts to change their assessments.

Conclusion 95. The Central Intelligence Agency's assessment on safehaven—that al-Qaida or associated operatives were present in Baghdad and in northeastern Iraq in an area under Kurdish control—was reasonable.

Conclusion 102. The Committee found that none of the analysts or other people interviewed by the Committee said that they were pressured to change their conclusions related to Iraq's links to terrorism. After 9/11, however, analysts were under tremendous pressure to make correct assessments, to avoid missing a credible threat, and to avoid an intelligence failure on the scale of 9/11. As a result, the Intelligence Community's assessments were bold and assertive in pointing out potential terrorist links.

Similarly, the 2005 Robb-Silberman report, another bipartisan blue-ribbon investigation whose credibility is not disputed, noted, "While some of the poor analytical tradecraft in the pre-war assessments was influenced by this climate of impending war, we have found no evidence to dispute that it was, as the analysts assert, their own independent judgments—flawed though they were—that led them to conclude that Iraq had active WMD programs."

It's also worth recalling the conclusions of the so-called Duelfer Report of the Iraq Survey Group, which conducted the authoritative search for Iraq's WMD. "Iraq was within striking distance of a *de facto* end to the sanctions regime, both in terms of oil exports and trade embargo, by the end of 1999," the report noted.

Saddam wanted to re-create Iraq's WMD capability—which was essentially destroyed in 1991—after sanctions were removed and Iraq's economy stabilized, but probably with a different mix of capabilities to that which previously existed. Saddam aspired to develop a nuclear capability—in an incremental fashion, irrespective of international pressure and the resulting economic risks—but he intended to focus on ballistic missile and tactical chemical warfare (CW) capabilities. (Emphasis in the original.)

All this is important to stress not as a way of settling old (and, by now, tedious) scores, but to clear away the thicket of conspiracy theories, partisan "truths," and sundry ideological neuralgias that pass for much of our collective thinking about the Iraq war.

Fall 2009: Afghanistan Agonistes

1. "Afghanistan," *Polling Report*, July 18, 2009, accessed April 9, 2014. http://www.pollingreport.com/afghan.htm.

2. "Obama's Speech at Woodrow Wilson Center," The Council on Foreign Relations, August 1, 2007, accessed April 9, 2014. http://www.cfr.org /elections/obamas-speech-woodrow-wilson-center/p13974.

3. "The Good War, Still to Be Won," *The New York Times,* August 19, 2007, accessed April 9, 2014. http://www.nytimes.com/2007/08/20/opinion /20mon1.html.

4. Bob Woodward, *Obama's Wars* (New York: Simon and Schuster, 2010), 127.

5. Jennifer Agiesta and Jon Cohen, "Poll Shows Most Americans Oppose War in Afghanistan," *The Washington Post,* August 20, 2009, accessed April 9, 2014. http://www.washingtonpost.com/wp-dyn/content/article /2009/08/19/AR2009081903066.html?hpid=topnews.

6. "Time to Pack Up," *The New York Times,* October 13, 2012, accessed April 9, 2014. http://www.nytimes.com/2012/10/14/opinion/sunday /time-to-pack-up.html?pagewanted=all.

CHAPTER 4: THE RETREAT DOCTRINE

1. Woodward, *Obama's Wars*, 155.

2. "Documented Civilian Deaths from Violence," *Iraq Body Count,* accessed April 9, 2014. http://www.iraqbodycount.org/database/.

3. "ICasualties: Operation Iraqi Freedom and Operation Enduring Freedom Casualties," Iraq Coalition Casualty Count, 2009, accessed April 8, 2014. http://icasualties.org/.

4. Woodward, *Obama's Wars*, 227.

5. Ibid., 301.

6. Thomas L. Friedman, "Don't Build Up," *The New York Times,* October 27, 2009, accessed April 9, 2014. http://www.nytimes.com/2009/10/28 /opinion/28friedman.html.

7. U.S. Department of Defense, *Sustaining U.S. Global Leadership: Priorities for 21st Century Defense* (Washington, D.C.: U.S. Government Printing Office, 2012), 3.

8. David E. Sanger, *Confront and Conceal: Obama's Secret Wars and Surprising Use of American Power* (New York: Crown Publishers, 2012), 244.

9. Robert Burns, "Hagel Says US Military Must Shrink to Face New Era," *AP Online,* February 24, 2014, accessed April 9, 2014. http://bigstory.ap .org/article/hagel-propose-big-cuts-army-2015-budget.

10. Tony Capaccio and Gopal Ratnam, "Hagel's Budget Seeks Smallest U.S. Army Since Before 2001 Attack," Bloomberg.com, February 24, 2014, accessed April 9, 2014. http://www.bloomberg.com/news/2014-02-24 /hagel-said-to-propose-lowest-army-level-since-before-9-11.html.

11. Steven Losey, "Welsh: Up to 25,000 Airmen, 550 Planes Would Go if Sequester Continues," *Air Force Times*, September 23, 2013, accessed May 21, 2014. http://www.airforcetimes.com/article/20130923/NEWS/309230019 /Welsh-Up-25-000-airmen-550-planes-would-go-sequester-continues.

12. David Sanger, "Even with a 'Light Footprint,' It's Hard to Sidestep the Middle East," *The New York Times*, November 17, 2012, accessed April 14, 2014. http://www.nytimes.com/2012/11/18/world/middle-east-challenges -obamas-light-footprint.html?_r=0.

13. Marc Huger, Wolfgang Reuter, and Christoph Schennicke, "'I Take Responsibility': Obama's G-20 Confession," *Der Spiegel*, April 6, 2009, accessed April 17, 2014: http://www.spiegel.de/international/world /i-take-responsibility-obama-s-g-20-confession-a-617639.html.

14. Marcus Baram, "Obama Administration Cut Funding to Promote Democracy in Egypt, Disappointing Human Rights Activists," *The Huffington Post*, January 28, 2011, accessed April 9, 2014. http://www.huffingtonpost .com/2011/01/28/obama-cut-egypt-funding_n_815731.html.

15. Kirit Radia, "Secretary Clinton in 2009: 'I Really Consider President and Mrs. Mubarak to Be Friends of My Family,'" *ABC News,* January 31, 2011, accessed April 9, 2014. http://abcnews.go.com/blogs/politics/2011 /01/secretary-clinton-in-2009-i-really-consider-president-and-mrs -mubarak-to-be-friends-of-my-family/.

16. Farah Stockman, "US Funds Dry Up for Iran Rights Watchdog," *The Boston Globe,* October 6, 2009, accessed April 9, 2014. http://www .boston.com/news/world/asia/articles/2009/10/06/us_cutoff_of_funding _to_iran_human_rights_cause_signals_shift/.

17. William Lowther, "US to Cut VOA Broadcasts in Chinese," *Taipei Times,* February 16, 2011, accessed April 9, 2014. http://www.taipeitimes.com /News/front/archives/2011/02/16/2003495998.

18. Simon Shuster, "Russian Human Rights: Is the U.S. Backing Off?" *Time*, June 5, 2010, accessed April 9, 2014. http://content.time.com/time/world /article/0%2C8599%2C1994101%2C00.html.

19. Mike Shuster, "Iran Blames U.S., Others for Post Election Protests," NPR, June 30, 2009, accessed April 9, 2014. http://www.npr.org/templates/story /story.php?storyId=106083627.

20. Juan Cole, "Khamenei Blames Obama for Post-election Disturbances, Demands Non-intervention as Prerequisite to Improved Ties," *Informed Comment*, March 22, 2010, accessed April 12, 2014. http://www.juancole .com/2010/03/khamenei-blames-obama-for-post-election.html.

21. Congressional Budget Office, *The 2013 Long-Term Budget Outlook* (Washington, D.C.: U.S. Government Printing Office, 2013), accessed April 18, 2014. http://www.cbo.gov/sites/default/files/cbofiles/attachments /44521-LTBO2013_0.pdf.

22. Patterson Clark, "Spending on the Military, 1988–2012," *The Washington Post,* March 26, 2014, accessed April 22, 2014. http://apps.washington-post.com/g/page/world/military-spending-1988-2012/892/.

23. "Why France Can't Fight," *The Wall Street Journal*, January 29, 2013, accessed April 19, 2014. http://online.wsj.com/news/articles/SB100014241 27887324624404578257672194671036.

24. Griffe Witte, "Despite 'Wake-up Call' in Ukraine, Europe Reluctant to Bolster Its Militaries," *The Washington Post*, March 27, 2014, accessed April 18, 2014. http://www.washingtonpost.com/world/europe/despite-wake-up-call-in-ukraine-europe-reluctant-to-bolster-its-militaries/2014/03 /27/91e041d4-b4f6-11e3-b899-20667de76985_story.html.

Summer 2013: "Let Allah Sort It Out"

1. Patterson Clark, "Spending on the Military: 1988–2012."

2. John Harwood and Jonathan Weisman, "House Republicans Say Voters Oppose Intervention," *The New York Times,* September 6, 2013, accessed April 12, 2014. http://www.nytimes.com/2013/09/07/us/politics/house -republicans-say-constituents-are-strongly-opposed-to-a-syria-strike.html ?pagewanted=all.

3. Sarah Dutton, Jennifer De Pinto, Anthony Salvanto, and Fred Backus, "Poll: Obama Faces Skeptical Public on Syria," *CBS News*, September 10, 2013, accessed April 12, 2014. http://www.cbsnews.com/news/poll-obama -faces-skeptical-public-on-syria/.

CHAPTER 5: REPUBLICANS IN RETREAT

1. John Fund, "Who Is Barbara Lee?" *The Wall Street Journal,* September 17, 2001, accessed April 12, 2014. http://online.wsj.com/news/articles /SB122418640015141825.

2. Barbara Lee, "Why I Opposed the Resolution to Authorize Force," *San Francisco Chronicle*, September 23, 2001, accessed April 12, 2014.

http://www.sfgate.com/opinion/article/Why-I-opposed-the
-resolution-to-authorize-force-2876893.php.

3. Brendon, 612–13. The statesman in question was, of course, Neville
    Chamberlain.

4. Kate Zernike and Megan Thee-Brenan, "Poll Finds Tea Party Backers
    Wealthier and More Educated," *The New York Times,* April 14, 2010,
    accessed April 22, 2014. http://www.nytimes.com/2010/04/15/us/politics
    /15poll.html.

5. Tal Kopel, "Eureka! Tea Parties Know Science," *Politico,* October 17, 2013,
    accessed April 19, 2014. http://www.politico.com/story/2013/10/tea-party
    -science-98488.html.

6. Larry Klayman, "Obama, Come Out with Your Hands Up!" RenewAmerica
    .com, September 16, 2013, accessed April 19, 2014. http://www.renewamerica
    .com/columns/klayman/130916.

7. "Limbaugh Suspects Obama Conspired with Al-Qaeda to Frame Bashar
    Al-Assad—Tea Party," TeaParty.org, September 3, 2013, accessed April
    22, 2014. http://www.teaparty.org/rush-limbaugh-suspects-obama
    -conspired-with-al-qaeda-to-frame-bashar-al-assad-28084/.

8. Matt Wilstein, "Rand Paul Suspects Chemical Attacks 'Launched by
    Rebels, Not Syrian Army,'" *Mediaite,* August 28, 2013, accessed April 20,
    2014. http://www.mediaite.com/online/rand-paul-suspects-chemical
    -attacks-launched-by-rebels-not-syrian-army/.

9. Josh Gerstein, "Judge: NSA Phone Program Likely Unconstitutional,"
    Politico, December 16, 2013, accessed April 19, 2014. http://www.politico
    .com/story/2013/12/national-security-agency-phones-judge-101203.html.

10. Andrew Aylward, "Poll: Most See Snowden as Whistleblower Not Traitor,"
    The Wall Street Journal, July 10, 2013, accessed April 22, 2014. http://
    blogs.wsj.com/washwire/2013/07/10/poll-most-see-
    snowden-as-whistleblower-not-traitor/.

11. Hans J. Morgenthau, *Politics Among Nations: The Struggle for Power and
    Peace*, Fifth Edition, Revised (New York: Alfred A. Knopf, 1978), 12.

12. Peter W. Rodman, "Policy Brief: Don't Destabilize Algiers," *Middle East
    Quarterly*, December 1996, 17–20, accessed April 14, 2014. http://www
    .meforum.org/420/policy-brief-dont-destabilize-algiers.

13. http://www.washingtonpost.com/blogs/post-politics/wp/2014/04/07
    /rand-paul-in-09-cheney-pushed-iraq-war-to-benefit-halliburton/.

14. Amity Shlaes, *Coolidge* (New York: HarperCollins, 2013), 390–91.

15. Alison Acosta Foster, "Government Spending: Growth and Trend Charts of US Federal Spending by Year," *Special Report 121* (Washington, D.C.: Heritage Foundation, 2012), accessed April 13, 2014. http://www .heritage.org/research/reports/2012/10/federal-spending-by-the-numbers -2012.

Winter 2013: Eclipse *in America*

1. *Eclipse* has since been eclipsed, so to speak, by the 590-foot *Azzam*, built by Germany's Lürssen shipyard for the emir of Abu Dhabi. Robert Frank, "World's Largest Yacht," *USA Today*, April 13, 2013, accessed April 14, 2014. http://www.usatoday.com/story/money/business/2013/04/13 /lurssen-yacht-azzam/2067709/.

2. Zhukova's children would not automatically be entitled to U.S. citizenship had they been born outside the United States, even though Zhukova herself is a naturalized U.S. citizen. It isn't clear Zhukova could have met the test of continuous residence, or at least demonstrated it to the satisfaction of punctilious State Department bureaucrats. "The Immigration and Naturalization Law § 1409—Children Born Out of Wedlock," Cornell University Law School Legal Information Institute, accessed April 17, 2014. http://www.law.cornell.edu/uscode/text/8/1409.http://www.law .cornell.edu/uscode/text/8/1409.

3. Jennifer Gould Keil, "$6.5M Apt. for Toddler," *New York Post*, March 28, 2013, accessed April 14, 2014. http://nypost.com/2013/03/28/6-5m-apt -for-toddler/.

4. In southern California, so-called maternity tourism is a booming business for boardinghouse operators catering to expectant Chinese mothers. "A two- or three-month stay at one of the houses in the Los Angeles area can range from $12,000 to $50,000, which includes lodging, meals, transportation, prenatal and nursery care and assistance in documentation preparation after the child is born. A deluxe package—with around-the-clock, one-on-one nursery services for the newborn, a personal beauty and fitness consultant, and seasonal dishes prepared by star chefs—can cost as much as $80,000." June Chang, "Birth Tourists: Going for the 14th Amendment," *China Daily*, May 17, 2013, accessed April 13, 2014. http://usa.chinadaily.com.cn/epaper/2013-05/17/content_16506471 .htm.

5. Louise Watt, "Top of Chinese Wealthy Wish List? To Leave China," Associated Press, September 7, 2011, accessed April 13, 2014. http://news .yahoo.com/top-chinese-wealthys-wish-list-leave-china-065826880 .html.

6. Jeremy Page, "Plan B for China's Wealthy: Moving to the U.S., Europe," *The Wall Street Journal,* February 22, 2012, accessed April 14, 2014. http://online .wsj.com/news/articles/SB10001424052970203806504577181461401318988.

CHAPTER 6: "DECLINE" AND RETREAT

1. Jagdish Bhagwati, "The Diminished Giant Syndrome: How Declinism Drives Trade Policy," *Foreign Affairs,* Spring 1993, 22–26.

2. David P. Calleo and Benjamin W. Rowland, *America in the World Political Economy* (Bloomington: Indiana University Press, 1973), 197.

3. Paul Kennedy, *The Rise and Fall of the Great Powers* (New York: Vintage Books, 1989), 533.

4. Anthony Lewis, "When You Believe in Lies," *The New York Times,* October 7, 1990, accessed April 15, 2014. http://www.nytimes.com/1990 /10/08/opinion/abroad-at-home-when-you-believe-in-lies.html.

5. See Peter Wehner and Yuval Levin, "Crime, Drugs, Welfare—and Other Good News," Commentary, December 2007, accessed on June 17, 2014. http://www.commentarymagazine.com/article/crime-drugs-welfare-and -other-good-news/.

6. Josef Joffe, *The Myth of America's Decline: Politics, Economics, and a Half Century of False Prophecies* (New York: W. W. Norton, 2013), 47.

7. Thomas L. Friedman, "Our One-Party Democracy," *The New York Times,* September 8, 2009, accessed April 14, 2014. http://www.nytimes.com /2009/09/09/opinion/09friedman.html?_r=1.

8. Tom Engelhardt, "Why the Troops Are Coming Home," *Tom Dispatch,* September 21, 2010, accessed April 14, 2014. http://www.tomdispatch .com/post/175298/tomgram%253A_engelhardt%2C_why_the_troops _are_coming_home/.

9. Michael Mandelbaum, *The Frugal Superpower: America's Global Leadership in a Cash-Strapped Era* (New York: Public Affairs, 2010), 9.

10. Richard Haas, *Foreign Policy Begins at Home: The Case for Putting America's House in Order* (New York: Basic Books, 2013), 1–10.

11. George Packer, "Decline and Fall: How American Society Unravelled," *The Guardian,* June 19, 2013, accessed April 14, 2014. http://www.theguardian .com/world/2013/jun/19/decline-fall-american-society-unravelled.

12. Paul Krugman, "Learning from Europe," *The New York Times,* January 10, 2010, accessed April 15, 2014. http://www.nytimes.com/2010/01/11 /opinion/11krugman.html.

13. Andrew Moravcsik, "Bipolar Order: Europe, the Second Superpower," *Current History*, Spring 2010, 91, accessed April 14, 2014. http://www .princeton.edu/~amoravcs/library/current_history.pdf.

14. Joana Taborda, "Euro Area GDP Growth Rate," *Trading Economics*, February 4, 2014, accessed April 15, 2014. http://www.tradingeconomics .com/euro-area/gdp-growth.

15. Phillip Inman, "Eurozone Youth Unemployment Reaches Record High of 24.4%," *The Guardian*, November 30, 2013, accessed April 15, 2014. http://www.theguardian.com/business/2013/nov/29/eurozone-youth -unemployment-record-high-under-25s.

16. Fareed Zakaria, *The Post-American World* (New York: W. W. Norton, 2008), 26.

17. "Economy Rankings," The World Bank, *Doing Business: Measuring Business Regulations*, June 2013, accessed April 14, 2014. http://www .doingbusiness.org/rankings.

18. "The 50-Year Snooze," *The Economist*, April 19, 2014, accessed April 20, 2014. http://www.economist.com/news/americas/21600983-brazilian -workers-are-gloriously-unproductive-economy-grow-they-must-snap-out.

19. The United Nations, *Global Study on Homicide* (New York: United Nations Office on Drugs and Crime), accessed April 15, 2014. http://www .unodc.org/documents/data-and-analysis/statistics/Homicide/Globa _study_on_homicide_2011_web.pdf.

20. Rupa Duttagupta and Thomas Helbling, "Global Growth Patterns Shifting, Says IMF WEO," *IMF Survey*, October 8, 2013, accessed April 15, 2014. http://www.imf.org/external/pubs/ft/survey/so/2013/NEW100813A.htm.

21. Sandeep Kohli, "The License Raj Is Dead. Long Live the License Raj," *The Wall Street Journal*, February 13, 2009, accessed April 15, 2014. http:// online.wsj.com/news/articles/SB123451653488482115.

22. Ricardo Geromel, "Forbes Top 10 Billionaire Cities—Moscow Beats New York Again," *Forbes*, March 14, 2013, accessed April 15, 2014. http://www .forbes.com/sites/ricardogeromel/2013/03/14/forbes-top-10-billionaire -cities-moscow-beats-new-york-again/.

23. "Russia Average Monthly Wages," *Trading Economics*, accessed April 20, 2014. http://www.tradingeconomics.com/russia/wages.

24. Yasser Seirawan, "New Champions Check Russia's Hegemony in Chess," *The Wall Street Journal*, April 27, 2014, accessed April 28, 2014. http:// online.wsj.com/news/articles/SB10001424052702303532704579483940841797528?mg=reno64-wsj.

25. Russel Gold and Daniel Gilbert, "U.S. Is Overtaking Russia as Largest Oil-and-Gas Producer," *The Wall Street Journal*, October 2, 2013, accessed April 15, 2014. http://online.wsj.com/news/interactive/USBOOM1002?ref=SB10001424052702303492504579111360245276476.

26. Ilan Berman, *Implosion: The End of Russia and What It Means for America* (Washington, D.C.: Regnery, 2013), 10–11.

27. Sujata Rao, "Russia's People Problem," Reuters, December 13, 2013, accessed April 15, 2014. http://blogs.reuters.com/globalinvesting/2013/12/13/russias-people-problem/.

28. Thomas L. Friedman and Michael Mandelbaum, *That Used to Be Us: How America Fell Behind in the World It Invented and How We Can Come Back* (New York: Farrar, Straus and Giroux, 2011), p. 11.

29. Michael Wines and Keith Bradsher, "China Rail Chief's Firing Hints at Trouble with High-Speed Trains," *The New York Times*, February 17, 2011, accessed April 15, 2014. http://www.nytimes.com/2011/02/18/world/asia/18rail.html?pagewanted=all.

30. Norihiko Shirouzu, "Train Makers Rail Against China's High-Speed Designs," *The Wall Street Journal*, November 17, 2014, accessed April 15, 2014. http://online.wsj.com/news/articles/SB1000142405274870481420457550735322114616.

31. Keith Crane, Jill E. Luoto, Scott Warren Harold, et al., "The Effectiveness of China's Industrial Policies in Commercial Aviation Manufacturing," April 4, 2014, RAND Corporation research report, accessed on June 16, 2014. http://www.rand.org/pubs/research_reports/RR245.html.

32. Adam Minter, "China's Bridges Are Falling Down," *Bloomberg News*, August 29, 2012, accessed April 15, 2014. http://www.bloomberg.com/news/2012-08-29/china-s-bridges-are-falling-down.html.

33. Ian Steadman, "Poor-Quality Chinese Concrete Could Lead to Skyscraper Collapses," *Wired UK*, March 21, 2013, accessed April 29, 2014. http://www.wired.com/2013/03/poor-quality-chinese-concrete-could-lead-to-skyscraper-collapses/.

34. Ruchir Sharma, "Don't Believe China's Illusory Growth Numbers," *The Wall Street Journal*, October 30, 2013, accessed April 15, 2014. http://online.wsj.com/news/articles/SB10001424052702303448104579152181633939984.

35. "China's Billionaire People's Congress Makes Capitol Hill Look Like Pauper," *Bloomberg News*, February 27, 2012, accessed April 29, 2014. http://www.bloomberg.com/news/2012-02-26/china-s-billionaire-lawmakers-make-u-s-peers-look-like-paupers.html.

36. Mark Steyn, *After America: Get Ready for Armageddon* (Washington, D.C.: Regnery, 2011), 4–5.

37. Ron Suskind, *The Price of Loyalty: George W. Bush, the White House, and the Education of Paul O'Neill* (New York: Simon & Schuster, 2004), 291.

38. Congressional Research Service, "The Sustainability of the Federal Budget Deficit: Market Confidence and Economic Effects," by Marc Labonte (Washington: Government Printing Office, December 2012). http://www.fas.org/sgp/crs/misc/R40770.pdf.

39. Stephen Moore, "The Budget Sequester Is a Success," *The Wall Street Journal*, August 11, 2013, accessed April 15, 2014. http://online.wsj.com/news/articles/SB10001424127887323477604579000933006361834.

40. Michael Darda, *Macro Brief for Feb. 12, 2014*, MKM Partners. https://research.mkmpartners.com/.

41. The United Nations, "Population Ageing and Development 2012" (New York: United Nations, September 2012). http://social.un.org/ageing-working-group/documents/2012popageing.pdf.

42. OECD (2012), "OECD Environmental Outlook to 2050" (Paris: OECD Publishing, June 2012). http://www.keepeek.com/Digital-Asset-Management/oecd/environment/oecd-environmental-outlook-to-2050_9789264122246-en#page51.

43. Organization for Economic Cooperation and Development, "Education at a Glance 2013: OECD Indicators," September 2013, accessed June 15, 2014. http://www.oecd.org/edu/eag2013%20(eng)—post-BàT%2013%2009%202013%20(eBook)-XIX.pdf

44. "The Times Higher Education World University Rankings 2013–2014," Thomson Reuters, March 25, 2014, accessed April 15, 2014. http://www.timeshighereducation.co.uk/world-university-rankings/2013-14/world-ranking.

45. Joffe, *The Myth of America's Decline*, 203.

46. *The EY G20 Entrepreneurship Barometer 2013*, Report no. CY0559, Ernst & Young, 2013, accessed August 27, 2013. http://www.ey.com/GL/en/Services/Strategic-Growth-Markets/The-EY-G20-Entrepreneurship-Barometer-2013.

47. Ben Rooney, "How Entrepreneurial Is Europe?" *The Wall Street Journal*, November 11, 2013, accessed April 15, 2014. http://blogs.wsj.com/tech-europe/2013/11/11/how-entrepreneurial-is-europe/.

48. "Fortune 500 2013: Annual Ranking of America's Largest Corporations from Fortune Magazine," *Fortune/CNNMoney*, December 31, 2013, accessed April 14, 2014. http://money.cnn.com/magazines/fortune/fortune500/.

49. Startup Europe, "A Manifesto for Entrepreneurship & Innovation to Power Growth in the EU," January 2013, accessed April 15, 2014. http://startupmanifesto.eu.

July 1911: A Distant Echo

1. Robert K. Massie, *Dreadnought: Britain, Germany, and the Coming of the Great War* (New York: Ballantine Books, 1991), 727.

2. Ibid, 726.

3. One man who thought he knew was Oswald Spengler, a penniless intellectual with mystical tendencies who would later become famous for *The Decline of the West* (1918). The Agadir crisis persuaded Spengler that a general European war was inevitable and "crystallized his nascent vision of the future political transformations of the West," according to his biographer John Farrankopf. It was a vision in which the West was entering a winter "of materialism and skepticism, of socialism, parliamentarianism, and money." This would be followed by an "age of the coming Caesars," marked by a "new kind of primitivism." From that, a new cycle of civilization was supposed to follow. Like many famous would-be prophets, Spengler was mostly a crackpot—but also something of a seer.

4. Winston S. Churchill, *The World Crisis 1911–1918* (New York: Charles Scribner's Sons, 1931), 91–92.

CHAPTER 7: THE COMING GLOBAL DISORDER
(THEORY AND HISTORY)

1. Fareed Zakaria, "America Plays Its Role in a Changing World Right," *The Washington Post*, February 27, 2014, accessed April 22, 2014. http://www.washingtonpost.com/opinions/fareed-zakaria-america-plays-its-role-in-a-changing-world-right/2014/02/27/b1bb0c40-9fee-11e3-b8d8-94577ff66b28_story.html.

2. Immanuel Kant, *Perpetual Peace, and Other Essays on Politics, History, and Morals* (Indianapolis: Hackett Publishing, 1983), 125.

3. Norman Angell, *The Great Illusion; a Study of the Relation of Military Power in Nations to Their Economic and Social Advantage* (New York: G. P. Putnam's Sons, 1911), 10.

4. Nicholas M. Butler, *The International Mind* (New York: Charles Scribner's Sons, 1912), 49–50.

5. Thomas L. Friedman, "Foreign Affairs Big Mac I," *The New York Times,* December 8, 1996, accessed April 12, 2014. http://www.nytimes.com /1996/12/08/opinion/foreign-affairs-big-mac-i.html.

6. Adam Przeworski, "Democracy and Economic Development," in *The Evolution of Political Knowledge,* ed. Edward D. Mansfield and Richard Sisson (Columbus: Ohio State University Press, 2004), 9. http://politics .as.nyu.edu/docs/IO/2800/sisson.pdf.

7. Bill and Melinda Gates, "Three Myths on the World's Poor," *The Wall Street Journal,* January 17, 2014, accessed April 15, 2014.

8. Walter Lippmann, quoted in Tom Switzer, "The World Today, Foretold by Nixon," *The New York Times,* July 5, 2011, accessed April 15, 2014. http:// www.nytimes.com/2011/07/06/opinion/06iht-edswitzer06.html.

9. U.S. Department of Agriculture Economic Research Service, "GDP Shares by Country and Region Historical," December 19, 2013, accessed April 22, 2014. http://www.ers.usda.gov/data-products/international -macroeconomic-data-set.aspx#.UuAggmj0CqQ.

10. Joffe, *The Myth of America's Decline,* 93. From: International Institute for Strategic Studies, *The Military Balance 2012* (London: Arundel House, 2012).

11. Ban Ki-Moon, "Need for the UN Is Greater Than Ever," *The Sydney Morning Herald,* December 31, 2010, accessed April 15, 2014. http://www .smh.com.au/federal-politics/political-opinion/need-for-the-un-is-greater -than-ever-20101230-19b0g.html.

12. J. Bolt and J. L. van Zanden, *The First Update of the Maddison Project: Re-Estimating Growth Before 1820,* Maddison Project Working Paper 4 (2013), accessed April 15, 2014. http://www.ggdc.net/maddison/maddison -project/data.htm.

13. John Maynard Keynes, *The Economic Consequences of the Peace* (New York: Harcourt, Brace and Howe, 1920), 12.

14. Henry A. Kissinger, *Diplomacy* (New York: Simon & Schuster, 1994), 160.

15. Bolt and van Zanden, *The First Update of the Maddison Project.*

16. Woodrow Wilson, quoted in Dore Gold, *Tower of Babble: How the United Nations Has Fueled Global Chaos* (New York: Crown Forum, 2004), 221.

17. Dean Acheson, *Present at the Creation: My Years in the State Department* (New York: Norton, 1969), 111.

18. Samuel P. Huntington, *Political Order in Changing Societies* (New Haven, Conn.: Yale University Press, 1968), 5.

Summer 2013: President "What, Me Worry?"

1. The White House, Office of the Press Secretary, "Remarks by the President on the Middle East and North Africa," news release, May 19, 2011. http://www.whitehouse.gov/the-press-office/2011/05/19/remarks-president-middle-east-and-north-africa.

2. "Egypt: Opinion of the United States," Pew Research Center, Washington, D.C., July 2013, accessed April 17, 2014. http://www.pewglobal.org/database/indicator/1/country/64/.

CHAPTER 8: THE COMING GLOBAL DISORDER
(PRACTICE AND PRESENT)

1. Samuel P. Huntington, *The Third Wave: Democratization in the Late Twentieth Century* (Norman: University of Oklahoma Press, 1991), 287.

2. Andrew Osborn, "As If Things Weren't Bad Enough, Russian Professor Predicts End of U.S.," *The Wall Street Journal,* December 29, 2008, accessed April 17, 2014. http://online.wsj.com/news/articles/SB123051100709638419.

3. Davies, *Europe: A History,* 943.

4. Freedom House, "Freedom in the World 2014," accessed April 9, 2014. http://www.freedomhouse.org/report/freedom-world/freedom-world-2014#.U1B6XFdXZqQ.

5. "Hu Jintao Tells China Navy: Prepare for Warfare," *BBC News,* July 12, 2011, accessed April 17, 2014. http://www.bbc.co.uk/news/world-asia-china-16063607.

6. "Venezuela Says It Receives $5 Billion Promised by China," *The Wall Street Journal,* December 28, 2013, accessed April 17, 2014. http://online.wsj.com/news/articles/SB10001424052702304483804579287380476597494.

7. Vladimir V. Putin, "A Plea for Caution from Russia," *The New York Times,* September 11, 2013, accessed April 17, 2014. http://www.nytimes.com/2013/09/12/opinion/putin-plea-for-caution-from-russia-on-syria.html?hp&_r=0.

8. Gayle Tzemach Lemmon, "Military Force vs. Diplomacy: Can You Have One Without the Other?" *Defense One,* January 31, 2014, accessed April 17, 2014. http://www.defenseone.com/ideas/2014/01/military-force-vs-diplomacy-can-you-have-one-without-other/78014/.

9. Kissinger, *Diplomacy,* 171.

10. David E. Sanger and Eric Schmitt, "U.S.-Saudi Tensions Intensify with Mideast Turmoil," *The New York Times,* March 14, 2011.

11. Ellen Knickmeyer, "Spy Chief Distances Saudis from U.S.," *The Wall Street Journal*, October 21, 2013, accessed June 14, 2014: http://online.wsj .com/news/articles/SB10001424052702303902404579150011732240016.

12. Linda Sieg, "Insight: Japan Unease over U.S. Alliance Adds Fuel to Abe's Security Shift," *Reuters*, February 4, 2014, accessed June 16, 2014: http:// www.reuters.com/article/2014/02/04/us-japan-usa-alliance-insight -idUSBREA131L120140204.

13. Martin Fackler, "Nationalistic Remarks from Japan Lead to Warnings of Chill with U.S.," *The New York Times*, February 19, 2014, accessed June 16, 2014. http://www.nytimes.com/2014/02/20/world/asia/nationalistic-remarks -from-japan-lead-to-warnings-of-chill-with-us.html?hpw&rref=world.

14. "Japan's Energy Pact with Turkey Raises Nuclear Weapons Concerns," *Asahi Shimbun,* January 7, 2014, accessed June 16, 2014. http://ajw.asahi .com/article/behind_news/AJ201401070060.

15. "Saudi Arabia, Jordan Sign Nuclear Pact," *Utilities Middle East*, January 29, 2014, accessed June 16, 2014. http://www.utilities-me.com/article -2659-saudi-arabia-jordan-sign-nuclear-pact/.

16. K.J. Kwon, "Under Threat, South Koreans Mull Nuclear Weapons," *CNN*, March 18, 2013, accessed June 16, 2014. http://www.cnn.com/2013/03 /18/world/asia/south-korea-nuclear/.

17. Jay Solomon and Miho Inada, "Japan's Nuclear Plan Unsettles U.S." *The Wall Street Journal*, May 1, 2013, accessed June 16, 2014. http://online.wsj .com/news/articles/SB10001424127887324582004578456943867189804.

18. Kissinger, *Diplomacy*, 46.

19. U.S. Department of Defense, "Assessment of Nuclear Monitoring and Verification Technologies" (Washington, D.C.: U.S. Government Printing Office, 2014), 12. http://www.acq.osd.mil/dsb/reports/NuclearMonitoring AndVerificationTechnologies.pdf.

20. Donald Kirk, "Nuclear Deal? New North Korea and Iran Pact Raises International Concern," *The Christian Science Monitor,* September 20, 2012, accessed April 17, 2014. http://www.csmonitor.com/World /Asia-Pacific/2012/0920/Nuclear-deal-New-North-Korea-and-Iran-pact -raises-international-concern.

21. Changsop Pyon, "Interview: Syria, Iran Main Buyers of North Korean Chemical Weapons," *Radio Free Asia,* March 10, 2013, accessed April 17, 2014. http://www.rfa.org/english/news/korea/interview-10032013130040 .html.

22. Jay Solomon, "North Korean Pair Viewed as Key to Secret Arms Trade," *The Wall Street Journal*, August 31, 2010, accessed April 17, 2014. http://online .wsj.com/news/articles/SB10001424052748704741904575409940288714852.

23. "Turkey Holds Suspicious Iran-Venezuela Shipment," *Associated Press– YNet*, January 6, 2009, accessed April 17, 2014. http://www.ynetnews .com/articles/0%2C7340%2CL-3651706%2C00.html.

24. Robert M. Morgenthau, "The Emerging Axis of Iran and Venezuela," *The Wall Street Journal*, September 8, 2009, accessed April 17, 2014. http://online .wsj.com/news/articles/SB10001424052970203440104574400792835972018.

25. Nima Gerami, "Why We Should Be Concerned About Venezuela's Nuclear Ambitions," Carnegie Endowment for International Peace, September 24, 2009, accessed April 17, 2014. http://carnegieendowment .org/2009/09/24/why-we-should-be-concerned-about-venezuela-s-nuclear -ambitions/4yds?reloadFlag=1.

26. Rachel King, "Ex-NSA Chief Details Snowden's Hiring at Agency, Booz Allen," *The Wall Street Journal*, February 4, 2014, accessed April 17, 2014. http://online.wsj.com/news/articles/SB10001424052702304626804579363 651571199832.

27. David Leigh and Luke Harding, *WikiLeaks: Inside Julian Assange's War on Secrecy* (New York: Public Affairs, 2011).

28. Reporters Without Borders, "Press Freedom Index 2013—Reporters Without Borders," 2013, accessed April 17, 2014. http://en.rsf.org/press -freedom-index-2013%2C1054.html.

29. Susan Lund, Toos Daruvala, Richard Dobbs, Philipp Härle, Ju-Hon Kwek, and Ricardo Falcón, "Financial Globalization: Retreat or Reset?" McKinsey & Company, March 2013, accessed April 17, 2014. http://www.mckinsey .com/insights/global_capital_markets/financial_globalization.

30. Hiroko Tabuchi, "Layoffs Taboo, Japan Workers Are Sent to the Boredom Room," *The New York Times*, August 16, 2013, accessed April 17, 2014. http://www.nytimes.com/2013/08/17/business/global/layoffs-illegal-japan -workers-are-sent-to-the-boredom-room.html.

31. Minxin Pei, "Are Chinese Banks Hiding 'The Mother of All Debt Bombs'?" *The Diplomat*, September 10, 2012, accessed April 17, 2014. http://thediplomat.com/2012/09/are-chinese-banks-hiding-the -mother-of-all-debt-bombs/.

32. Victor Shih, "China Needs a Credit Crunch," *The Wall Street Journal*, June 29, 2011, accessed April 17, 2014. http://online.wsj.com/news/articles/SB10 001424052702304447804576413201123156890.

33. "China's Financial Squeeze," *The Wall Street Journal*, January 11, 2014, accessed April 17, 2014. http://online.wsj.com/news/articles/SB200014240 52702303848104579307923177519860.

34. Jay Pelosky, "Jay Pelosky: Ominous Signs for the Global Recovery," *The Wall Street Journal*, February 6, 2014, accessed April 17, 2014. http://online.wsj.com/news/articles/SB1000142405270230468090457936522140 5781630?KEYWORDS=Jay+Pelosky.

35. The European Commission, "Global Europe 2050" (Luxembourg: Publications Office of the European Union, 2012), accessed April 17, 2014. http://ec.europa.eu/research/social-sciences/pdf/global-europe-2050 -report_en.pdf.

36. Gabriel Stargardter and Paul Day, "Reversal of Fortunes Sends Spaniards to Latin America," Reuters, October 31, 2012, accessed April 17, 2014. http://www.reuters.com/article/2012/10/31/us-spain-emigration -idUSBRE89U1C820121031.

37. Liz Alderman, "Young and Educated in Europe, but Desperate for Jobs," *The New York Times*, November 15, 2013, accessed April 17, 2014. http://www.nytimes.com/2013/11/16/world/europe/youth-unemployment-in-europe.html?gwh=D3EB1BBFC62513D04E0E7E3B8925DAA5&gwt=pay.

38. Anne-Elisabeth Moutet, "Down and Out: The French Flee a Nation in Despair," *The Daily Telegraph*, October 20, 2013, accessed April 17, 2014. http://www.telegraph.co.uk/finance/10390571/france-hollande-taxes -socialist-farrage.html.

39. Congressional Budget Office, *The Budget and Economic Outlook: 2014 to 2024*, 1, accessed April 17, 2014. http://www.cbo.gov/publication /45010.

40. Klus Schwab, *Global Competitiveness Report 2013–2014*, World Economic Forum. http://www3.weforum.org/docs/WEF_GlobalCompetitiveness Report_2013-14.pdf.

41. Parmy Olson, "Exclusive: The Rags-to-Riches Tale of How Jan Koum Built WhatsApp into Facebook's New $19 Billion Baby," *Forbes*, February 19, 2014, accessed April 17, 2014. http://www.forbes.com/sites/parmyolson /2014/02/19/exclusive-inside-story-how-jan-koum-built-whatsapp-into -facebooks-new-19-billion-baby/.baby/?utm_source=twitter&utm _medium=partner&utm_campaign=quote+tweet.

42. Qiao Liang and Wang Xiangsui, *Unrestricted Warfare* (Beijing: PLA Literature and Arts Publishing House, 1999), accessed April 17, 2014. http://www.cryptome.org/cuw.htm.

43. Siobahn Gorman, "Electricity Grid in U.S. Penetrated by Spies," *The Wall Street Journal,* April 8, 2009, accessed April 17, 2014. http://online.wsj .com/news/articles/SB123914805204099085.

44. Bret Stephens, "China's Gift," *The Wall Street Journal,* January 23, 2007, accessed April 17, 2014. http://online.wsj.com/news/articles /SB116951840203184482.

45. The Department of the Navy, *FY 2013 Budget Estimates* (Washington, D.C.: U.S. Government Printing Office, May 2012), 15, accessed April 14, 2014. http://www.finance.hq.navy.mil/FMB/13pres/FY13_DataBook.pdf.

46. Admiral Jonathan W. Greenert, "Payloads over Platforms: Charting a New Course," *Proceedings Magazine,* July 2012, vol. 138/7/1, 313, accessed April 17, 2014. http://www.usni.org/magazines/proceedings/2012-07/payloads -over-platforms-charting-new-course.

CHAPTER 9: A SCENARIO FOR GLOBAL DISORDER

1. Cheers, Anshel!

November 2009: "Peak Oil"

1. Terry Macalister, "Key Oil Figures Were Distorted by US Pressure, Says Whistleblower," *The Guardian,* November 10, 2009, accessed April 17, 2014. http://www.theguardian.com/environment/2009/nov/09/peak-oil -international-energy-agency?guni=Data:in%20body%20link.

2. Alan Greenspan (Chairman of the Federal Reserve), "Testimony of Chairman Alan Greenspan, Natural Gas Supply, Before the Committee on Energy and Natural Resources, U.S. Senate," July 10, 2003, accessed April 22, 2014. http:// www.federalreserve.gov/boarddocs/testimony/2003/20030710/default.htm.

3. Terry Macalister, "US Military Warns Oil Output May Dip Causing Massive Shortages by 2015," *The Guardian,* April 12, 2010, accessed April 22, 2014. http://www.theguardian.com/business/2010/apr/11/peak-oil-production-supply.

4. Paul Krugman, "The Finite World," *The New York Times,* December 26, 2010, accessed April 17, 2014. http://www.nytimes.com/2010/12/27 /opinion/27krugman.html.

5. Gregory Zuckerman, *The Frackers: The Outrageous Inside Story of the New Billionaire Wildcatters* (New York: Portfolio/Penguin, 2013), 153.

6. Gary D. Libecap, "Three Cheers for Fracking," The Hoover Institution, March 5, 2014, accessed April 22, 2014. http://www.hoover.org/publica tions/defining-ideas/article/170026.

CHAPTER 10: A WAY FORWARD

1. "United States Crime Rates 1960–2012," The Disaster Center, accessed April 22, 2014. http://www.disastercenter.com/crime/uscrime.htm.

2. Fox Butterfield, "Grim Forecast Is Offered on Rising Juvenile Crime," *The New York Times,* September 8, 1995, accessed on July 23, 2014. http://www.nytimes.com/1995/09/08/us/grim-forecast-is offered-on-rising -juvenile-crime,html.

3. Brandy Zadrozny, *The Daily Beast,* January 1, 2014, accessed April 17, 2014. http://www.thedailybeast.com/articles/2014/01/01/the -year-in-murder-2013-marks-a-historic-low-for-many-cities.html.

4. Steven Levitt, "Understanding Why Crime Fell in the 1990s: Four Factors That Explain the Decline and Six That Do Not," *Journal of Economic Perspectives,* vol. 18-1 (Pittsburgh: AEA Publications, 2004), 168.

5. United States Department of Justice Bureau of Justice Statistics, *Hiring and Retention of State and Local Law Enforcement Officers, 2008,* by Brian A. Reaves (Washington, D.C.: U.S. Government Printing Office, October 2012), accessed April 22, 2014. http://www.bjs.gov/content/pub/pdf/hrslle o08st.pdf.

6. Levitt, "Understanding Why Crime Fell in the 1990s," 178.

7. James Q. Wilson and George L. Kelling, "Broken Windows," *The Atlantic Monthly,* March 1982, accessed May 21, 2014. http://www.theatlantic .com/past/docs/politics/crime/windows.htm.

8. Anthony A. Braga and Brenda J. Bond, "Policing Crime and Disorder Hot Spots: A Randomized and Controlled Trial," *Criminology* 46 (2008): 598.

9. Jonathan Freedland, "Why It's a Good Time to Be a Dictator Like Kim Jong-Un," *The Guardian*, February 19, 2014, accessed April 22, 2014. http://www.theguardian.com/commentisfree/2014/feb/18/north-korea -good-time-to-be-dictator.

10. U.S. Navy Naval History and Heritage Command, "U.S. Navy Active Ship Force Levels, 1886–Present," June 10, 2011, accessed April 22, 2014. http://www.history.navy.mil/branches/org9-4.htm.

11. "Historical Military Troop Data," VetFriends.com, accessed April 22, 2014. http://www.vetfriends.com/us-deployments-overseas/historical -military-troop-data.cfm.

12. John Reed, "$46 Billion Worth of Cancelled Programs," *Defense Tech*, July 19, 2011, accessed April 22, 2014. http://defensetech.org/2011/07/19 /46-billion-worth-of-cancelled-programs/.

13. Helene Cooper and Martin Fackler, "U.S. Response to Crimea Worries Japan's Leaders," *The Washington Post*, April 5, 2014, accessed April 22, 2014. http://www.nytimes.com/2014/04/06/world/asia/us-response-to-crimea-worries-japanese-leaders.html#.

14. http://www.nato.int/nato_static/assets/pdf/pdf_1979_12/20100830_1979-021.pdf.

15. Henry R. Nau, "Conservative Internationalism," *The American Interest*, May/June 2014, 63.

16. Daniel Patrick Moynihan, "Defining Deviancy Down," *The American Scholar*, Winter 1993. http://www.utexas.edu/law/journals/tlr/sources/Volume%2092/Issue%206/Koppelman/Koppelman.fn051.Moynihan.DefiningDeviancy.pdfp.30.

INDEX